Praise for *...*

'A well-timed warning about the dir[...]er health and sacrificing happiness fo[...] a fascinating journey, peppered with en[...]sto- ries. But his message is deeply seriou[...] is challenging. A "must-read" for anyone who cares abou[...]c. A book that could change the world.'

Dr Michael Dixon CVO, OBE, FRCP (hon), FRCGP
Chair of the College of Medicine

'A profoundly insightful and personal book with a powerful message: a new economics guided by care for people and planet is urgently needed. I applaud Tim Jackson and this manifesto for a healthy and sustainable world.'

Riane Eisler, author of *The Chalice and the Blade*
and *The Real Wealth of Nations*

'*The Care Economy* rocks. Enjoy the rhythms of this compelling take-down of the dismal science and dance to the beat of new economic principles, joyfully explained. This music will stick in your head.'

Nancy Folbre, author of *The Invisible Heart*

'The absence of "Care" as a primary purpose of economics limits the reach of policy. Tim Jackson shows not only what is missed by this, how policy must stretch to be inclusive, but also what gives us a better economics as a discipline and what might be a better economy.'

Michael D. Higgins, President of Ireland

'Why do we sacrifice health for wealth? Why are we so careless with care? From the staggering rise of chronic disease to the dark persistence of gender-based violence, Tim Jackson's sharp, uncompromising examination of capitalism's failings is also a passionate call to arms. A manifesto for *The Care Economy*.'

Stephanie Kelton, author of *The Deficit Myth*

'We are taken on a tour of everything that makes, breaks and takes care. Yes, care, this word that has been denuded so much in today's thoughtless culture by soppiness, shallowness and exploitation. Tim Jackson cuts through much of the cant about care to show why a care-full society is the good society and how that requires infrastructure. With many personal details and his wondrous but lightly worn erudition, he shows that unless we restructure the economy and how we live to deliver deep care, society will be taken by brutal forces into ever starker divisions. I'd like all politicians to read this brilliant book.'
Tim Lang, Emeritus Professor of Food Policy
City & St George's, University of London

'What is care, anyway? Care is Misery. Care is Cure. And therein lies the rub and our salvation. Because care is half of *homo sapiens*, half of us. The justice ethic, and the care ethic; the male rubic, and the female rubric. It's our burden and our legacy. Tim Jackson has plumbed the depths of economics, psychology, philosophy and spirituality to confront us with that which we can't ignore – we were born to care, and when we choose not to, we kill ourselves, our children and our planet.'
Robert Lustig MD, MSL, neuroendocrinologist
author of *The Hacking of the American Mind* and *Metabolical*

'If you want to understand why it's high time to reframe the whole concept of care (and you should), then start here. Drawing insights from literature, politics, psychology, philosophy, biology, feminism, pop culture and more, every chapter of *The Care Economy* surprises, provokes and illuminates. Profoundly radical and ultimately practical, it is also that rare thing for a book from an economist – a clear and gripping read.'
Sue Pritchard, Chief Executive,
Food, Farming and Countryside Commission

'If you ever doubted what truly matters in life, you need doubt no more. Prosperity, equity and harmony between people and planet are all about health, not wealth; about care, not growth. Tim Jackson takes us on a remarkable journey, exploring how to reshape the global economy, making his case with compassion, honesty and analytical force.'
Johan Rockström, Professor of Earth System Science, University of Potsdam
author of *Breaking Boundaries* (now a Netflix documentary)

'A forthright and original book. Jackson encourages his readers to think afresh about their own well-being – and that of humanity and the planet.'
Matthew Taylor, Chief Executive, NHS Confederation

'Is there such a thing as poetic economics? A postgrowth page-turner? Everyone who dreams of a better world should read this compelling account of how a care economy could replace our current capitalistic, growth-addicted system.'
Joan Tronto, author of *The Caring Democracy* and *Who Cares?*

'In this deeply personal book, Tim Jackson takes readers on a wonderful journey into the possibilities for an economy of care, offering a unique take on the potential for modern economic practices to be transformed into something more humane, universal and healthy for people and planet.'
Remco van de Pas, International Institute for Global Health, UN University

The Care Economy

The Care Economy

Tim Jackson

polity

Copyright © Tim Jackson 2025

The right of Tim Jackson to be identified as Author of this Work has been asserted in accordance with the UK Copyright, Designs and Patents Act 1988.

First published in 2025 by Polity Press

Polity Press
65 Bridge Street
Cambridge CB2 1UR, UK

Polity Press
111 River Street
Hoboken, NJ 07030, USA

All rights reserved. Except for the quotation of short passages for the purpose of criticism and review, no part of this publication may be reproduced, stored in a retrieval system or transmitted, in any form or by any means, electronic, mechanical, photocopying, recording or otherwise, without the prior permission of the publisher.

ISBN-13: 978-1-5095-5428-7
ISBN-13: 978-1-5095-5429-4 (pb)

A catalogue record for this book is available from the British Library.

Library of Congress Control Number: 2024942690

Typeset in 9.5 on 14 pt Fournier by
Cheshire Typesetting Ltd, Cuddington, Cheshire
Printed and bound in Great Britain by Ashford Colour Ltd

The publisher has used its best endeavours to ensure that the URLs for external websites referred to in this book are correct and active at the time of going to press. However, the publisher has no responsibility for the websites and can make no guarantee that a site will remain live or that the content is or will remain appropriate.

Every effort has been made to trace all copyright holders, but if any have been overlooked the publisher will be pleased to include any necessary credits in any subsequent reprint or edition.

For further information on Polity, visit our website:
politybooks.com

To the memory of
Valerie Marjory Sylvia Haywood
1931–2018

Contents

Prologue   xi

In which we first encounter the goddess Care, acquaint ourselves with her role in Roman (and Greek) cosmology – and learn to distrust the patriarchy.

The Road to Hell   1

In which we're introduced to two key propositions: that prosperity is primarily about health rather than wealth; and that, in consequence, the economy should be organized around care rather than growth. And in which it becomes clear that nothing is ever that simple.

Euphoria   13

In which we learn to distinguish between the maintenance of health, the avoidance of pain and the pursuit of pleasure. From the dubious remedies of the nineteenth century to the opioid crisis of the twenty-first, we discover how a restless desire for euphoria has been weaponized in the pursuit of profit.

Vital Signs   28

In which the joy of wild swimming introduces us to the wisdom of the body – the ability to regulate our own 'internal environment'; and in which we learn what happens when that ability is disturbed, either occasionally (as it is in nature) or systematically (as it is in capitalism).

The Myth of Care   43

In which we ponder the true nature of care, not as a moral injunction but rather as a restorative force: a central organizing principle so indispensable to organic life that it's deeply engrained in our instincts; and in which we start to explore why this principle is constantly overridden by economics.

No Good Deed   60

In which we pay a visit to the birthplace of a dream and learn how a vision of universal healthcare inspired the welfare state; and in which we discover what happened when that dream was exposed to the harsh light of the market and to the changing burden of global disease.

Passerelle   78

In which we begin to understand how the principle of care can help us define a viable alternative to the lure of eternal growth: an economy that is compatible with the limits of a finite planet, consistent with the principle of social justice and more conducive to human wellbeing.

Shoot the Messenger   97

In which the history and epidemiology of diabetes offer insights into a 'pandemic' of chronic diseases which now threatens to swamp healthcare and overwhelm the public purse; and in which we confront the battle between the protection of global health and the pursuit of economic growth.

The Lost Generation   114

In which the dawn light across the Paris skyline illustrates the sometimes conflicting demands of our physical and psychological wellbeing. Gertrude Stein's 'lost generation' and Florence Nightingale's career provide contrasting backdrops to the 'food wars' that now compromise our health.

Care in the Time of Cholera   129

In which we encounter the bacterium E. coli *in the protected waters of Chichester Harbour and trace the history of sewerage from the cholera outbreaks of the nineteenth century to the regulatory failures of today. Hygiene, gut health and social reform all support the curious idea that disease itself is a form of care.*

Pathogenesis   141

In which a territorial spat between two French chemists turns into a schism at the heart of medicine – a rift between two distinct views about how to combat disease; and in which we learn how capitalism itself became the arbiter in this dispute, ultimately favouring the side that generates more profit.

Death and the Maiden   159

In which we encounter the economist William Baumol on the road to Stonehenge and learn why computers get cheaper but healthcare doesn't. The philosopher Hannah Arendt and the ancient gods of healing help us unpack the structural forces within capitalism which undermine care.

Fuck the Patriarchy   182

In which the novels of Daphne du Maurier, the history of pre-modern witch hunts and the curious phenomenon of Barbenheimer help us to untangle the troubled relationship between gender, violence and care; and in which we finally confront the distorted logic of the patriarchy.

Land's End   209

In which the rugged Cornish coastline holds the clue to an abiding puzzle and we begin to see how our own existential anxiety creates the potential to destroy the world. The confrontation between care and violence is offered a partial resolution through the task of coming to terms with our own mortality.

Jenga   229

In which we draw together the main strands of the argument and synthesize the contours of the care economy – not as a subsector of business as usual or as a site of special pleading, but as a powerful vision with the potential to renew our sense of shared prosperity and deliver a state of wellbeing.

The Red Pill   246

In which we tackle the question 'What shall we do about it?', explore a long legacy of policy proposals and synthesize several incarnations of care: as a principle, as an investment, as an unpaid debt, as climate action, as freedom and as a new foundation for cultural meaning.

Acknowledgements	257
Notes	260
References	290
Index	305

Prologue

'What was I made for?'
Billie Eilish, 2023

In the beginning there was Chaos. The earth was without form and void. And darkness was upon the face of the deep.

After a while it got lonely there. So Chaos allowed Terra to form herself. Terra was the mother of Saturn and the grandmother of Jupiter. She was the mother of everything. In Roman mythology at least. And in Greek too, where she was called Gaia. But that's another story. Or the same story in a different language. As most things are.

At any rate, thanks to Terra, there was soon a whole family of gods and goddesses running around on Mount Olympus. Mostly they spent their time squabbling over power. As families invariably do. Which drove Terra crazy and quite frankly wore her out.

So whenever she could she took to hanging out with her friend the goddess Care. By the time of this story, as often as not, you'd find them chilling together down by the river. And while Terra was taking an afternoon nap, Care sat happily beside her, absent-mindedly playing around in the mud.

Many aeons later the psychologist Carl Jung did something similar. He swore it helped him think. Neuroscience now confirms it. Unfocused playful activity stimulates the parasympathetic nervous system, which encourages the body to rest and digest. And yes. It can aid the creative process too. So all in all it's a good thing.

Back then Care seemed to know all this instinctively. Probably because, at that point, there was less to remember. So fewer things had been forgotten. Since then we've largely forgotten almost everything. It's amazing how much it's possible to forget when you try to remember so much. But then again, without all that forgetting there wouldn't be much need for learning. Or books, come to think of it. So what would we all do then? Right?

Anyway. This is all backstory. Here's the frontstory.

One day, during her post-prandial creative downtime, Care finds that she's managed to sculpt something strange and unusual out of the mud: a small, lifeless figurine that looks a bit like her.

'Wow,' she thinks. 'Wouldn't it be cool if she could move and talk and write books and stuff?' But not having the power to breathe life into clay, she decides to ask Jupiter to do it for her.

Now the big man is a scary dude. Even though he's just a grandkid. Son of Saturn. Grandson of Terra. A third-generation god. Or fourth if you count Chaos. But he also happens to be in charge of the sky. And of thunder. Which gives him the right to be kickass bad. Apparently.

He's already put his old dad (Saturn) out to pasture and become the top god. Top dog. The CEO of deities. And in fact he's destined to stay that way until Christianity comes along and knocks him off his perch.

But strangely Jupiter has always had a soft spot for Care. So when she asks him to breathe life into the figurine he smiles fondly.

'Yes of course, my dear,' he says. And then pauses. 'Provided . . .'

(Beware the patriarchy. There's always a 'provided'.)

'Provided what?' says Care.

'Well, I'm the one that's breathing life into him,' says Jupiter.

'She's not a him,' says Care. 'She's a her.'

'So I get naming rights.'

'No way!' retorts Care.

'No breath then,' snaps Jupiter. And he turns to go.

'No, wait. Wait!' Care calls after him. 'Terra! Terra! Make him wait! Don't let him go!'

'What now?' sighs Terra, dragging herself out of sleep. Could they really never get along without her? Just for a moment? But she calls Jupiter back anyway. Because she too has a soft spot for Care. And when Care explains what's going on Terra says:

'Who gave you the mud?'

'Um. You did?'

'I did?'

'You said I could play with it.'

'Then she should have my name,' decides Terra.

'See!' says Care to Jupiter. 'I told you she's a she.'

'Give that thing to me,' snarls Jupiter, grabbing the figurine. 'I'll breathe some fire into it for you.' And he puffs violently into the figurine's clay mouth.

'Not fire,' cries Care. 'Life!'

'Done.' Jupiter laughs. 'Hello little me,' he says.

'It's not all about you!' says Care, snatching the drowsy figurine away from him.

'My breath. My name,' says Jupiter.

'Not gonna happen.'

And seeing they're not going to stop, Terra suggests they ask Saturn, who by a stroke of good fortune happens to be passing by.

Now Saturn is a cool dude. God of almost everything that matters, like agriculture and time and having parties. He's also a mature, well-balanced judge of people and situations. Just the sort of leader who gets rolled over in favour of a Machiavellian bully. But not for the first time, faced with something tricky to navigate, Saturn comes up trumps.

'Her body belongs to Terra because you're the one that donated the mud,' he tells his mum. 'You can have it back when she dies.'

'Her spirit belongs to Jupiter because you're the one that breathed life into her,' he tells his son. 'You can have it back when she dies.'

'And what about me?' cries Care, looking pretty dismayed at how this is all going.

'You, my dear, get to look after her as best you can for as long as you both shall live.'

'Really?!'

'To have and to hold.'

'To the end of time!'

'In sickness and in health.'

'I'm so happy!'

'Til Death shall tear you cruelly asunder.'

'Thank you, Saturn! Thank you!' says Care.

And with that they all go about their business. Which is to say that Terra settles down for a nap, Jupiter goes off to stir up a storm somewhere and Saturn plods on home to tend his vines. And that's when it occurs to Care.

'Hey wait. Wait!' she cries. 'We didn't give her a name!'

But they've left already. Or gone to sleep. Out of earshot. On to the next.

'Oh dear,' says Care. 'Oh well,' she says.

And then she turns to the little figurine, who is now blinking and looking at the world around her in wonder and astonishment. What am I doing here? What was I made for?

'What's your name, little thing?' Care asks her sweetly.

'Barbie,' says the figurine. 'My name is Barbie.'

The Myth of Care
(a long time) after Gaius Julius Hyginus

1

The Road to Hell

'The road to hell is paved with good intentions.'
Anon

My task was simple. Or so I thought. I sat down to write this book just as the world was emerging from the coronavirus pandemic, confident it wouldn't take long. I had a strong narrative and a clear backstory. The characters were already familiar to me. And, to be honest, the concept of the book is pretty simple to convey.

There are two central ideas. They are connected to each other in fairly obvious ways. The first is that human prosperity, properly considered, is primarily about health rather than wealth. The second is that, in consequence, the economy should concern itself first and foremost with care, in all its forms, rather than with relentless growth, as it does at the moment.

That's pretty much it.

My journey towards these two ideas began a long time ago. Possibly even in childhood. More recently, it came from thinking about the nature of human prosperity. And in particular from thinking about what prosperity can possibly mean when we're living on a lonely rock in the middle of nowhere, hurtling through the universe at a million miles per hour.

What can it mean for us to live well on a small blue (finite) planet?

Deceptively simple. It doesn't take long to see that it's actually a complex question. To answer it you probably need some psychology. Some sociology perhaps. And a little history wouldn't go amiss. You also need some economics, of course. As my title suggests. *The Care Economy* is in part at least a book about the economy.

That's not to say it's full of statistics or equations. For me, that's not what economics is. Sometimes, of course, you have to get your hands dirty with data. And every now and then a little conceptual analysis is definitely in order. But first and foremost, I see economics as a lens through which to understand how we organize society in pursuit of our common wellbeing. It's the study of answers to my 'deceptively simple' question.

That question also demands some attention to philosophy. In the old days that used to be taken for granted. Economics was part philosophy from the outset. Later, economists created a sophisticated discipline that not many people could understand. Quite often not even economists. And that, to my mind, is a recipe for disaster. Not knowing how to organize society or, worse still, appointing a small number of people to tell you (in a language you don't speak) how best to do it for you – that's a catastrophe waiting to happen. Something to be avoided. At all costs.

So *The Care Economy* is a book about the economy for people who aren't necessarily economists. It's for people who don't even like economics as much as for those who do. It's for people who hated economics at school, like I did, as well as those who loved it. It's a book for people who feel that economics has nothing to do with them as well as those who realize that it probably does and feel it might be a good idea to know a bit more about it.

In short you need no qualifications to read this book. Because you need no qualifications to care about the care economy. You just need to care. Which, of course, doesn't apply to everyone. But in all probability those people who don't didn't bother picking up this book in the first place. And if they did, I guess they can always change their mind.

It's also worth saying that you don't need to be an expert in care either. If we take prosperity as health seriously, I'm going to argue, our job is not just to delve into specific sectors of the economy which we happen to label with the word 'care'. The care economy isn't a standalone sector. It isn't some desirable cherry on the top of the economic cake. I'm saying something different here. I'm saying this. Because prosperity is primarily about health, the economy should always and everywhere be about care. In talking about the care economy, I'm talking about economy *as* care. That's my case.

The state of wellbeing

It stands to reason I'll need to define some terms. First up, I'll need to be clear what I mean by health and what I mean by care. But it's relatively easy to come up with some working definitions for both those concepts.

Fortunately, the World Health Organization (WHO) has done a pretty good job already. Back in 1948 when it was founded, it defined health as 'a state of complete physical, mental and social wellbeing and not merely the absence of disease or infirmity'. Maybe today we'd want to include planetary wellbeing in that list. It's difficult to imagine how we could achieve the rest of those things on a sick planet. But aside from that, it's a definition that's definitely stood the test of time. As a starting point, that's good enough for me.

When it comes to care, it's a little trickier. But I've always been drawn to a framing of care by the US writers Berenice Fisher and Joan Tronto. They define care as 'an activity that includes everything we do *to maintain, continue and repair* our "world" so that we can live in it as well as possible'. That seems broad enough to me to include all – or at least many – of the things we mean when we talk about care.

Care for the young. Care for the elderly. Care for the sick and the faint of heart. Care for our family. Care for our community. Care for our home. Care for the material conditions of life itself. And, of course, it would definitely include care for the planet that sustains us. Care for the climate. Care for the soil. Care for the oceans. Care for our 'world'.

When we get down to details, these initial definitions may need some adjustment. Particularly if we want to do justice to the specific dynamics of health or to the singular qualities of care. Dimensions that I'll have to unfold further if I want to bring you along with me. But for now they work. They're definitely good enough for me to give you a sense of what I'm aiming at.

In one sense they make my thesis self-evident. Perhaps even tautological. If care is about maintaining and continuing a state of wellbeing, then of course the economy should be all about care. What else would it be doing? On the other hand, it's clearly a long way from what the economy actually is doing. Most of the time at least. So there's definitely some scope for inquiry.

Aside from that my case is simple. Let's say straightforward. Nothing is ever entirely simple. It all seemed very manageable. The book was already in sight. I agreed a deadline with my editor. I negotiated a short retreat from my day job. And at the end of 2021 my partner Linda and I decided to rent a small cottage in rural Wales where I would catch up on reading and make a start on writing. Three things happened more or less simultaneously.

The invisible heart

The first and perhaps most predictable thing, obvious if I'd thought about it for a moment or two, was that I found myself marooned in a foreign country without a valid passport. I'm not talking about Wales. That's still a part of the British Isles. For the moment at least. This particular stranding was metaphorical.

The Care Economy was a good title. Short, simple and to the point. It seemed like a suitably inclusive label under which to pursue my project. But my reading immediately reinforced something blindingly obvious. It wasn't my label. It wasn't my country. The terrain had already been charted extensively by pioneers who came before me. And almost exclusively those pioneers were women.

It was women who'd highlighted the essential nature of care. Women who'd pointed out the poor treatment of carers. Women who'd developed an entire discipline of feminist economics premised on the importance of care to human life.

That's not remotely surprising. To this day most of what we refer to as care work is carried out by women. So inevitably it was women who'd largely concerned themselves with understanding care, with exploring its challenges and with exposing its fundamentally gendered nature.

I'm not saying we should take that division of labour for granted. I don't believe we should. But amongst economists I'd say the gender bias is even more pronounced. Male economists have concerned themselves endlessly with economic efficiency. With productivity. With technology. With investment. And in particular with economic growth. Reams and reams have been written about economic growth.

These male economists have also spent a lot of time praising Adam Smith's 'invisible hand'. That's the mythical force which claims to translate narrow selfish interest into the common good through the magic of market-based mechanisms. But they've left woefully unexplored what the US feminist economist Nancy Folbre has called the 'invisible heart' of society. Even today that heart is kept beating largely through the underpaid or unpaid labour of women. It would be totally meaningless to write anything about the care economy without recognizing this fundamental truth.

I'd known that all along. At an intellectual level. But I hadn't really understood what it might mean until I immersed myself in the landscape. What it meant for the project. Or for me personally, as a proponent of something I wanted to call the care economy. Or even, I suppose, as a man.

I hadn't even started writing. I could see the reviews. I could write them myself. 'White male economist mansplains care.' Terrific. Just what the doctor ordered. But I only had myself to blame. I'd wandered into the land of the invisible heart in my big male economist boots. With the very best of intentions, for sure. But without stopping to check my footwear.

On the other hand, I realized, I'd been steeped in this division from a very early age. To some extent we all are. There's no avoiding it. Maybe it's relevant to the perspective I take. But that doesn't invalidate the case. Let's acknowledge that at the outset. But prosperity as health still makes for a powerful proposition. Economy as care is the obvious corollary to that. If the care economy feels gendered, that's probably because it is. So why should being a man trip me up?

And if it does, then too bad. I've been flat on my face before. Not long ago actually. Quite literally.

Use the difficulty

Shortly before that trip to Wales, we assumed the care of a small black-and-white cat. Just for a few weeks, while his owner was away. At first he hid behind the sofa. Resolutely. Very slowly, he gathered enough courage to emerge into the light of day. Usually unannounced. And occasionally at breakneck speed.

It was on one of those occasions that I caught a brief flash of white from the corner of my eye and then saw the floor rising up to meet me. In an instinctive effort not to step on the kitten, I fell awkwardly and smashed my foot against a doorpost. The cat was fine. Long gone. The doorpost was fine as well. The foot definitely wasn't.

A broken toe is not the end of the world. I know. It's not even the beginning of the end of the world. Most fractures heal in six to eight weeks. Although sometimes the tissue injuries can linger on. Like this time. And their failure to heal can sometimes be a sign that something else isn't quite right. Like this time. Over the next year or so the pain in my toe became a pain in my foot and then a much more severe pain in my hip. At one point I had pain down the entire right-hand side of my body. Not obviously conducive to good writing.

The actor Michael Caine has a story for just this sort of circumstance. When he was young he was rehearsing a scene which involved him coming onstage through a doorway into the middle of an argument between a married couple. On one occasion the actor playing the husband had managed to knock over a chair which now blocked Caine's entrance. Poking his head round the door, the young actor asked the director what he was supposed to do.

'Use the difficulty,' came the reply.

'What do you mean?' said Caine.

'Use the difficulty,' said the director. 'If it's a comedy, fall over it. If it's a drama, pick it up and smash it.' And I guess if it's a book about the care economy, take a good hard look and see if you can figure out what it's doing there in the middle of your writing plans. This particular chair was there to remind me of some inconvenient truths about my own health. And some hard facts about the care economy. Amongst them, for sure, was a disconcerting lesson about the relationship between care and time.

Care disrupts time. It throws our plans out of the window. Challenges emerge without warning. Tasks change and evolve. Time stops making sense. Care belongs 'in the world of *kairos* time,' as the social innovator Hilary Cottam has pointed out. It belongs to a time that's measured by flow and connection. It's different from '*chronos* time', which is measured in minutes and deadlines. In the logic of care, writes the philosopher Annemarie Mol, 'time twists and turns'. In that sense it's a lot like writing. A place where the clocks move slower. Or faster. Or backwards. And sometimes not at all.

I've always found that insight fascinating. But I might not have dwelt on it if it weren't for the chair. The cat. The toe. What I'm saying is, the book definitely has a different shape to the one I imagined when I set out to write it. A bit like my toe, I guess, which has a pronounced kink in it even to this day.

Champagne problems, I hear you mutter. And you might be right. Worse things happen at sea. Much, much worse, as it turns out. Barely two months after my accident, everything changed again. For all of us. And for the entire context of this book.

Good intentions

In the winter of 2021, when we set off for Wales, the world was still living in the shadow of the pandemic. Omicron and Delta were less deadly than earlier variants. But even so they reminded us of the fragility of human health. Of the centrality of care to our lives. And of the value to society of our carers. We would change, after the pandemic, because we understood at last what really matters. Some of these lessons would surely find their way into government policy.

The US government signalled its intentions early. The Biden administration first introduced its ambitious 'Build Back Better' Bill in April 2021. It would spend a massive $3.5 trillion on the task of post-pandemic recovery. The money would be used to improve public infrastructure, to fight climate change and to extend the reach of vital care services to more and more people. It would be paid for in part by higher taxes on corporations and on the rich. Its vision was to create a better society for everyone when the storm of the coronavirus was finally over.

The Bill passed the House of Representatives in November 2021. But it was famously derailed in the Senate when a lone Democrat refused to support it. Senator Joe Manchin argued that it was too expensive. The country couldn't afford to pay for it, he said. It was useless to point out that they couldn't afford not to. Attempts to thrash out a compromise failed. And by the early months of 2022, negotiations had more or less stalled. That's the point at which world events took on a different and more sinister hue. Out of the Covid frying pan. Into the military-industrial complex.

Early on the morning of 24 February 2022, Russia invaded Ukraine, escalating a conflict that had been playing out on the edge of Europe – and on the edge of political attention – for most of the previous decade. By the time we were listening to the news, early on that Tuesday morning, Russian troops were within sight of the Ukrainian capital. Commentators were anticipating an early capitulation by Volodymyr Zelensky's government. Tanks would be rolling through the centre of Kyiv before sundown, they said.

Six million refugees and more than half a million casualties later, those early predictions looked naïve. Laughable even, if it weren't all so tragic. No one had taken account of the fierce resistance of a besieged nation. Nor had they anticipated the resolve of NATO to arm a country it considered an ally against a country it deemed a foe. This was not just about Ukraine, we were told. It was about democracy. It was about freedom. It was a battle for the soul of Europe. It was a struggle for the spirit of the West. NATO allies would do whatever it took to save the free world from autocracy. Even if it meant pushing Build Back Better into the long grass.

One thing it clearly took was money. In the first two years or so of the war the West committed over $400 billion to Ukraine in military and financial aid. That's more than the entire national income of the besieged country. They comforted (or convinced) themselves that this was worth the pain by pointing out that Russia had lost as much or more in military expenditure and the destruction of financial capital. Approaching $1 trillion in total. All for the want of diplomacy. And yet even these sums were dwarfed by the knock-on effects on the global economy.

Sanctions on Russia pushed the price of oil and gas to an all-time high. The cost of living began to go through the roof. Ordinary household budgets were caught in the crossfire. Governments were caught in the headlights. Their playbook had been drawn from a different economic era. A place where cheap money could solve big problems. That trick had definitely come in handy through the pandemic. But now things were different. With heavy debt, low growth, rising inflation and high interest rates, a sense of panic was setting in. 'Stagflation' was not what we needed. But suddenly we were staring down its barrel. A new reality had dawned.

Good intentions for the post-pandemic era were fading fast. Build Back Better was transformed into a much leaner, much meaner, much more keenly focused fiscal instrument. Worth only a third of the original Bill, the Inflation

Reduction Act was eventually signed into law in August 2022. Its revised focus was on curbing inflation, investing in domestic energy production and reducing the federal government deficit. These were the new priorities of the day. Care for people and planet would have to wait. We had stumbled, as Chris Rea says in his 1989 rock classic, on the road to hell.

The road to hell

Things change. Of course they change. But this wasn't just about change. It certainly wasn't just about new and more punishing economic conditions. Something else was going on. The very idea of care was at risk of seeming facile, facetious even, in the face of the brutality and insecurity unleashed by war. An irrelevant luxury at best. A fatal distraction at worst.

That sense was reinforced when Hamas militants crossed into Israel on 7 October 2023. At least a thousand people were killed and around two hundred and fifty people were taken hostage. But the carnage that day was quickly dwarfed by the scale and ferocity of the retaliation. Israeli forces bombed Gaza relentlessly, reducing much of the strip to rubble. More than a million people were displaced. Tens of thousands of civilians died. Almost half the initial casualties were children. At one point a child was dying in the Gaza strip every ten minutes, according to UN observers.

It should have been a moment for global leadership. For western politicians to support the calls for a ceasefire. To broker peace. To step back from the brink of instability. Instead they condoned and facilitated military aid to Israel just as they did in Ukraine. And instead of diplomacy they began to ramp up the rhetoric of war. Defence budgets had been declining since the end of the Cold War. But the hawks could sense their moment. The tragedy on the ground was brushed aside. The clamour for military spending was cacophonous.

And soon it was joined by calls to reintroduce some form of draft. Compulsory military service for young men and women. We're living in an increasingly unstable world, came the almost universal refrain. From the European Union. From the US. From the UK. From NATO. That this instability was one in which our own politicians were complicit seemed to pass them by. It felt like we were being primed, gas-lighted and emotionally blackmailed into a world where war and violence are inevitable.

It was all so patently the very opposite of care. Violence carries away all reason. Vengeance begets vengeance. Rage begets rage. In the space of a year the world had been dragged ruthlessly out of its long Covid daze. Lockdown was over. Solidarity was a delusion. Rose-tinted dreams of a better world would have to wait. It was time to get real. And reality had a distinctly violent face.

I felt as though we were living in a world where the sanctity of health and the ethos of care were vague shadows from another life. The last vestiges of a dream we once had, fading like the morning mist in the harsh light of day. And as for my project of positioning care as an organizing feature of the post-pandemic economy, it lay, temporarily at least, in ruins.

Care's nemesis

And then, at some point, I recalled a BBC Radio 4 show I'd listened to back in February 2022. It was the afternoon of the day Russia invaded Ukraine. A panel of experts was discussing how the West should deal with Putin now that the 'inevitable' had happened. Much of the discussion was predictable. Arm Ukraine. Counter force with force. Weaken Russia. Remove Putin from power. Do whatever it takes. Not much recognition of the patent failure of the West to exercise diplomacy for over thirty years. Or of NATO's broken promises to Russia not to expand eastwards.

But there was one contribution from Mary Kaldor, director of the Conflict Research Programme at the London School of Economics, which took me by surprise. She called out what was happening as a manifestation of 'toxic masculinity'. Not just as an isolated act of aggression by an autocratic Russian President. But as a phenomenon that had taken hold of society, exemplified in our leaders, even in the West, for decades. Perhaps longer. A phenomenon perpetuated through a male propensity for violence whose ultimate expression is always war.

I went back and listened to it again. I noticed how quickly Kaldor was shut down by the other (male) participants on the panel. They hated it. They couldn't countenance the idea that something systemic was going on. Some co-dependency between Putin and the West. Something inherently masculine. On this day we were all supposed to roundly condemn the enemy. Not question our own culpability. I hated it too. I hated the idea that my own gender is mired in toxicity. But the more I thought about her comment, the harder it became for me to ignore it.

It reminded me of something I had read in Kathleen Lynch's *Care and Capitalism* – one of many excellent and fierce feminist critiques of the marginalization of care in modern society. There was one particular point she'd made which struck home with me forcefully. If we want to reposition care in society, she argued, we have to understand its nemesis: war and violence. 'To ignore violence when speaking about love, care and solidarity,' she said, 'is to ignore what lives in their shadows.'

And in understanding violence, we can't avoid the realization that it's primarily enacted by men. And that it's most often enacted on women. Reports of systematic sexual violence have emerged from almost every war in history, including the conflicts in Ukraine and the Middle East. The casual sacrifice of women and girls in Gaza hospitals reached appalling levels in the first few months of the Israeli assault.

I started to feel that the eclipse of care by violence in the aftermath of the pandemic was not an accident. It wasn't just a question of bad timing. It wasn't a historical inconvenience. It was part of a pattern that repeated itself. Over and over again. It was like the swing of a pendulum. A tension that haunts civilization. A conflict with deep social and cultural roots. Played out continually. Throughout history. Across society. And perhaps even inside the human psyche.

There's obviously an aspect to that conflict which is gendered through and through. But there's also something which transcends the simplicity of gender binaries. Something that forces us to confront fundamental aspects of human nature and of social behaviour. Something which holds a spotlight up to the values we claim to hold dear. Something that calls into question the hopes and the visions that we cling to. And it started to change my understanding of the care economy. And of my task in writing about it.

As I began to find my bearings on the road to hell, it slowly dawned on me. There is still a need to articulate prosperity as health. Still a reason to articulate economy as care. But my assignment is not so much to point out the blindingly obvious as to ask why the blindingly obvious doesn't happen. Over and over again.

The book as a journey

Almost without me noticing it, *The Care Economy* had turned into something different. When I compare the book you're reading now against my original intentions, I'm filled with a sense of astonishment at the creative process. Your children are not your children, the poet Kahlil Gibran once said. They come through you but they are not of you. I suppose you can say the same about books. About this book certainly.

It starts in roughly the place I imagined I would. I explore our conceptions and misconceptions about what health is (Chapter 2). And what it's not. I tease out the differences between health, the pursuit of pleasure and the avoidance of pain. Those differences are vital in being able to convey what I mean when I talk about prosperity as health.

And then I begin to develop what will turn out to be two critical themes. One concerns health as a process of adaptation (Chapter 3). The other portrays care as a restorative force (Chapter 4). These are important elaborations on the definitions of health and of care with which we set out in this chapter. But they are both absolutely vital in understanding the care economy.

At this point I happened to visit the town of Tredegar, in Wales, the birthplace of Britain's National Health Service (Chapter 5). It wasn't foreseen originally. Which illustrates perfectly what I was saying about writing. But that visit was powerful. It gave me an insight into what happens when the principle of care meets the harsh light of the economy.

I expand on that theme in the next few chapters. By probing the relationship between care and my own previous work on post-growth economics (Chapter 6). By examining the pressures placed on healthcare by the changing global burden of disease (Chapter 7). And by exploring the forces which have given rise to those changes (Chapter 8).

So far so good. The book was maybe slightly off track. But not a lot. And then it decided to take on a life and direction of its own. I think that happened for a couple of reasons. The first was that I began to find myself caught up in it not only as an observer but also as a subject. Not just through gender. Not just through history. But also through the ramifications of that seemingly innocuous fall which tripped me up at the outset. The second was that I began to go down a rabbit hole. That's always a danger when you're deep in a writing project. And you always have the option to shake it off. Or wriggle your way back out again. Whatever the metaphor ought to be. Sometimes, though, you just can't get the scent of a mystery out of your nostrils. Particularly when, as in my case, the whole thing had become deeply personal.

So then there's nothing for it. Down you go. Tearing at the veils of history. Unravelling the threads of the past. Trying to figure out, in this case, what had happened to medicine itself that we find ourselves now so far from home with an overburdened healthcare system and an unpayable healthcare bill. Particularly when the insights that could have saved us from this fate were already well known, not just decades but centuries ago.

You might say that's all academic. You might ask what use it is to dwell on arguments that are lost in the mists of the past. But one of the things I learned in this section of the book (Chapters 9 and 10) is that they're not just lost in the past. Those insights are still not listened to. Worse. They've been expunged deliberately from the canon of knowledge. They are still demonized as quackery. Or relegated to the background in favour of principles and practices which owe most of their authority to commercial interests. And have little or nothing to do with health.

But history is obviously not the only thing we need if we're to understand the predicament we're in. And at this point in the book I made a renewed effort to take back control. I knew I must explore the economic structures which consistently lock out care (Chapter 11). And I was absolutely determined to come back and do justice to the question of gender and violence (Chapters 12 and 13) which I've already hinted at here.

By now I was feeling increasingly that the whole thing would benefit from some kind of overall synthesis. Something you could read as a stand-alone piece if you wanted to. Something that would pull the threads of my argument together (Chapter 14). And once I'd done that, I realized too that I couldn't get away without at least some kind of response to the resounding question: what on earth can we do about it? Chapter 15 responds to that daunting task.

I don't remember when it first occurred to me to ground the whole thing in the places I encountered along the way. The case I'm making in the book is a generic one. It travels intellectually over several millennia and across several continents. The arguments are clearly anchored to a western perspective but they draw on insights from cultures from east and west. They are as relevant to the economies of the South as they are to those of the North.

But you can't write convincingly from the abstract. Particularly when the intellectual territory shifts and swirls around you. So I began to allow the physical geography of my own journey to enter the writing process. At one level this book can almost be read as a travelogue. Place. Politics. Personal health. Literature. The history and sociology of ideas. All these things began to weave themselves into its narrative arc.

And I think it was their presence on the journey that finally made me realize something crucial. The deep currents of violence and the dark shadow of war may still be wreaking their tragedies on the world. And the leadership we so desperately need may be retreating further and further from the shores of any meaningful diplomacy. But this was not the wrong time to be writing about the care economy. It was precisely the right one.

2

Euphoria

> *'Life reveals itself in pain.'*
> Boris Groys, 2022

I'm sitting in the waiting room of the Minor Injuries Unit at the Llandrindod Wells Memorial Hospital. Not a soul in sight. It's cold outside. Snowing lightly as it has been for a few days now. But comfortingly warm inside. The old building creaks a little, the way old buildings do. Aside from that it's so damn quiet I'm not even sure I'm in the right place.

It reminds me of somewhere. But I can't place it. Perhaps the hospital where, as a kid, I took my first job, mopping blood off the floors of the operating theatre at the end of each working day. Or maybe the local cottage hospital where my mother once worked as a physio. Either way, it's something old school. Something from a bygone age. But it's January 2022. So what the heck? Maybe nobody gets minor injuries in mid-Wales anymore. Or perhaps it's a post-Covid thing, I think to myself. There were clear instructions online to phone ahead before attending. I'm glad I did.

Expecting to have to wait a while, I take out my notebook. I've been asked to write a programme note for the launch of an extraordinary film installation by the German artist and film-maker Julian Rosefeldt. His subject matter is the dystopian nature of capitalism. But he calls his film *Euphoria*.

If you happen to be Gen Z, that title will immediately remind you of Sam Levinson's controversial and critically acclaimed HBO series of the same name. No offence to the millennials, Gen X and the boomers. You may well have come across it too. If you have, your reaction was probably to be scared witless for the world your kids are living in. Like I was. But then I'm not exactly the target demographic.

Euphoria the series follows a group of American high-school students as they 'navigate love and friendships in a world of drugs, sex, trauma and social media'. The show's first season was a runaway success when it hit the screen in 2019. It made instant stars of its young stars, except of course Zendaya, who was already a star. But her role as Rue certainly cemented her status as 'a cultural icon in the making'. It also won her a couple of Emmys and a Golden Globe Award.

In stories and films, and even in real life, euphoria carries a sense of excitement. Something that lifts our lives and our loves above the everyday. Something light and almost transcendent. But quite often it also conveys dangerous overtones, as though being truly happy must always carry a price. Which of course it sometimes does.

That sense of seductive danger is probably why psychiatrists define euphoria not just as happiness or wellbeing, but as an 'exaggerated' sense of elation. One that is groundless, disproportionate to its cause or inappropriate to real events. None of which sounds particularly healthy.

But here's the thing I've just discovered. In its original meaning the word was derived from the Greek *eu-* (εὐ), which means well, and *phoros* (φορος), which just means bearing or carrying. Euphoria described a condition of 'bearing well' or very simply 'being healthy'. Not even something as nebulous as happiness then, but health pure and simple. It was used by doctors as early as the seventeenth century to refer to good outcomes from clinical treatments. To describe a situation where their patients were responding well to medical intervention. The opposite of dysphoria. When things were obviously going downhill.

So is euphoria really just another way of thinking about health? Is health what Rue is chasing? Or is euphoria an exaggerated form of health? What would that even mean? Surely you're either healthy or you're not. I'm trying to decide if any of this is remotely useful in defining prosperity as health when suddenly the door opens and a woman pokes her head round.

'Are you the man that fell over a cat?'

Very funny.

I give what I hope is a wry smile and limp after her to the X-ray room. The images confirm that, yes, the toe is broken and, no, there is nothing much to be done about it. By that time the news has gone viral. Or the equivalent of viral in a deserted old hospital in the middle of rural Wales.

I'm sitting there getting shown how to bind one toe to the next when the empty corridors suddenly discharge a whole stream of people I never realized were there. All keen to take the piss out of the Englishman who broke his toe tripping over a cat. Trying not to trip over a cat, I insist. Don't worry, they tell me. You're in good hands now. Llandrindod Wells is pretty famous as a health resort. Or at least it was. Back in the day.

Health as prosperity

As the name suggests, the main attraction of Llandrindod Wells is the local spring water – the wells. People had known about them from time immemorial. But in the middle of the eighteenth century they caught the attention of a German doctor named Diederich Wessel Linden, who was keen to try them out on himself. Evidently they did him some good. Because he decided to write about them. And his *Treatise on the Three Medicinal Mineral Waters at Llandrindod, in Radnorshire, South Wales*, published in 1756, put Llandod (as it's known to the locals) on the map.

Quite soon a small unassuming village evolved into a thriving spa town. The place to be. A resort where those seeking refuge from the rapid industrialization of Britain could hang out, socialize with others, cure their various ailments and go back home glowing with health. Half a century later Llandod was attracting visitors from all over Europe. And with them came unaccustomed wealth. Monetary wealth. Prosperity, if you will. In the conventional sense of the word.

It looks like a success story. A town that monetized health and profited massively from it. What's not to like? It's not a million miles from what Fidel Castro had in mind, for example, after the fall of the Soviet Union. Cuba's healthcare system became world famous. The country turned its home-grown doctors into a kind of cultural export. They travelled all over the world on loan from Cuba, with significant revenues flowing back to the Castro government in return.

Or perhaps the Cleveland Clinic is a better example? Founded a hundred years ago in Cleveland, Ohio, it now exports US-style high-tech healthcare all over the globe. It's an interesting venture for sure. Set up as a non-profit, but it definitely caters to the upper echelons. That means it can pay its doctors extremely well. Which is not always welcome. In London the clinic has been accused of sabotaging the National Health Service (NHS) by offering consultant salaries upwards of £300k for working just a couple of days a week, equivalent to around $1m a year. Not quite the salary of a top-flight soccer player – or even a mid-range executive in a FTSE 100 company. But five times the top-rate consultant's salary paid in the NHS. And a lot better than the $25k a year you can expect as a doctor in Cuba. So yes. A very different ballgame.

But what's clear is that health is something people value. And can sometimes afford to pay for. So if you're able to cash in on that, you can do very well for yourself. As Llandod did. At least for a while. Today the town is not the thriving metropolis it once was. Hence perhaps the uncanny silence of the waiting room in Minor Injuries. And the Memorial Hospital is not exactly the

Cleveland Clinic. Although. To be honest. I do now have a soft spot for it. And for all its unexpectedly kind and unnecessarily mischievous staff.

At any rate, it's definitely a useful place to start my journey. To illustrate my argument. To make my case. First, that health matters, that people value it. Second, that sometimes they're prepared to pay handsomely for it. And when they are, it's possible to make an easy buck from it. Third, and perhaps this is the most important point of all, that health and wealth are different beasts. Thinking about prosperity as health is not the same as plundering health for wealth.

Whatever prosperity may or may not be, it doesn't make sense to equate health with monetary wealth. In fact sometimes it's downright wrong to. It isn't true that you can always monetize health. And even when you can, that's not necessarily a good thing. Those insights go right to the heart of my arguments in the book. Health and wealth are not the same thing. Sometimes they're not even compatible with one another. As I want to argue here, casting prosperity as health is not about substituting certain kinds of economic activities with others as the source of economic success and financial wealth. It's a profoundly different way of thinking about things. And some of this is usefully illustrated by Llandod's water cure.

The water cure

There's a long scientific pedigree supporting the curative power of cold water. Perhaps that's not surprising. Rumour has it our distant relatives crawled out of the ocean half a billion years ago. So going back there is always cathartic, strangely comforting and sometimes even a bit inspirational. Certainly the most relief my toe had during that stay in Wales was walking barefoot through the waves at Aberdyfi, not far from where we were staying.

Apparently I'd have done even better if I'd been brave enough to dive right into it. But I hadn't yet got to that point in my journey. The sea temperature in Wales in mid-January rarely rises much above 10°C (50°F). So yes. At that point cold water swimming seemed like a downright crazy idea. Although nothing like as mad as the treatments in Linden's *Treatise* on the waters at Llandod.

Some of them were completely bonkers. Others were downright dangerous. The waters were supposed to cure everything from scurvy to leprosy and from insanity to 'disorders of the fair sex'. (Sexism isn't what it used to be.) Bathing, scrubbing and near drowning were combined with blood-letting while drinking the water (to make the blood run more briskly). And sometimes foul-smelling waters were administered in such huge quantities that patients would literally die from it.

To give him his due, the German doctor doesn't approve of everything he sees. He's mostly just describing what was happening there. And some of it may well have had some positive benefit. Linden himself certainly believed he'd been cured of his ailments. Though it's not entirely clear now how serious they were. Some of the craziness was clearly just the monetization of the desire for health, pure and simple. The unscrupulous exploitation of people desperate to get well. To feel better. To find some relief from pain. That wouldn't happen nowadays, right?

It's so easy to condemn the wisdom of the past. We all have a tendency to think we're cleverer than those around us. Psychologists call it a superiority bias. But when it comes to those who came before us, there's the added influence of a deeply rooted cultural assumption about progress. It stands to reason we're wiser today than people were yesterday. Because that's what progress is all about. So inevitably the wisdom of the past is seen as stupidity today.

There's an uncomfortable implication of this conviction which it's worth bearing in mind, though. If that's really the direction of progress, then some at least of today's wisdom is likely going to be seen as stupidity tomorrow. And quite possibly that means it's already stupid today. In fact it's not even remotely difficult to find examples where that's the case. Let me just give you one. It has to do with pain. Or, more precisely, with the relationship between pain, pain management and health.

The problem of pain

'Life reveals itself in pain,' writes Boris Groys in the epigraph with which I opened this chapter. In a fascinating exploration of the 'philosophy of care' he suggests that '[e]verybody lives in the anticipation of pain. And that means in anticipation of the loss of one's world.' Or to put it another way: pain sucks. So whatever takes it away is deemed to be good.

There are a few pain management remedies that have stood out from the crowd throughout the ages. One of them is opium. We've known about its miraculous effects since forever. And because of its distinctively narcotic properties, it's also been prone to a lot of abuse. That's one of the premises of Levinson's *Euphoria*. Getting rid of pain – psychological pain as well as physical pain – is just a short step away from the pursuit of euphoria, it seems.

The history of that pursuit is both fascinating and horrifying. The first reference to the opium poppy confirms its use among the Sumerians in

Mesopotamia more than five thousand years ago. The Sumerians called it *hul gil*, the joy plant. For pretty obvious reasons. As the narcotic effects of opium became more widely known, its use spread across Asia and into Europe. The Greek physician Hippocrates, the 'father of medicine', who lived around 400 BCE, had a relatively sanguine view of its benefits – and its risks. Opium is highly addictive.

But when the Swiss physician and alchemist Theophrastus von Hohenheim, better known as Paracelsus, introduced opium into western medicine in a solution of alcohol which he called laudanum, it swiftly became a cure-all. With some reason in some cases. But often just for the feel-good effect. At times it was even recommended for people who weren't actually sick, in order to 'optimize the internal equilibrium of the human body'. That would have been a cool idea. If only it had worked. More often the lure of laudanum led to dependency and addiction.

At any rate, pretty soon, the use of opium became important enough to warrant getting control over its production. The poppy grows best in high and arid places. Most opium is cultivated along the mountain ranges that run from Turkey to Myanmar. And it's usually grown by small farmers in isolated regions. Isolation so often hides sinister consequences. One is that the opium trade has proven virtually impossible for governments to close down. Even when they wanted to. Another is that it's constantly been vulnerable to exploitation. By anyone with the power to do so.

In the 1700s the British took control of an extensive poppy-growing region in India. With no intention at all of closing it down. Instead, they used the East India Company to smuggle its produce into China, along the Silk Road – a network of trade routes linking Europe to Asia. The profits were used to import Chinese luxury goods such as silk, tea and porcelain back into Europe. It was all going wonderfully well until, in the 1830s, alarmed by rising addiction rates, the Chinese government decided they did want to shut it down. Britain resisted. China insisted. And the two countries ended up engaging in two Opium Wars to resolve the issue.

Back then Britain's military power was superior enough for a bit of gunboat diplomacy to be pretty much all that was needed. Even if the cause was entirely questionable. During the first Opium War the young William Gladstone – later to become Prime Minister – famously declared to the British parliament: '[A] war more unjust in its origins, a war more calculated to cover this country with permanent disgrace, I do not know, and I have not read of.' Gladstone's sister almost died from an opium addiction. So it was clearly personal. And I'm pretty sure we've had a few more of those wars since he made that remark. But that's another story. Or a different part of the same story. One that will have to wait for now.

The point is that on this occasion Britain prevailed. The opium trade survived. And when, during the 1849 Gold Rush, Chinese men and women migrated in their thousands to the US, there were enough addicts among them to establish highly popular opium dens in almost every Chinatown across the country. By the 1870s, opium smoking was all the rage, particularly in the no longer quite so Wild West. Addiction was rising so fast that legislation had to follow. San Francisco was the first city to outlaw opium dens in 1875 and the recreational use of opium and its derivatives went underground. For a while. It might have stayed there, but for medicinal use. Which happened to be taking off around the same time.

The clinical use of opium relies almost entirely on a chemical component of the poppy known as morphine and a variety of its derivatives. Morphine itself was first isolated in the early 1800s by an inquisitive twenty-one-year-old pharmacist's assistant named Friedrich Sertürner. Messing about in his spare time, he managed to extract an organic alkaloid compound from the resinous gum secreted by the poppies. He named it *morphium* after the Greek god of dreams, Morpheus.

From around 1827 onwards it was marketed as a commercial drug. But its use was expanded massively with the arrival of the hypodermic syringe in the mid-1850s. And by the time the opium dens were outlawed, morphine had totally revolutionized clinical pain management. In particular it provided relief from acute pain in a way that had simply not been possible before. So it had a massive impact on palliative and post-operative care. I always associate it with a very faint, slightly sickly odour which I still recognize from my days mopping up blood in that operating theatre.

And as it happens, its effectiveness in managing pain is also something I can personally vouch for. Some years ago I injured myself playing tennis and began to suffer chronic pain in my lower back and pelvis. I laid off tennis. In fact I gave up anything strenuous. I tried some gentle stretching and some yoga. That helped a bit. They gave me some non-steroidal anti-inflammatory pain-killers. Those gave me stomach ache. I consulted doctors and physios and osteopaths. But nothing was really working.

Eventually a hospital X-ray picked up some degeneration in the cartilage of my left hip. Genetics come home to roost, I thought. And I wasn't entirely wrong about that. But not entirely right either. The consultant proposed an operation to 'resurface' my hip joint.

Resurfacing

In fact resurfacing is a bit of a euphemism. It's basically a form of hip replacement. But it's more conservative of the bone and offers swifter chances of recovery afterwards. In principle. That's one of the reasons it's often offered to people who want to get back to physical activity. Tennis players, for example.

The former world number one Andy Murray had the same op, aged 32, and was out competing again at the highest level within a year or so. I was almost two decades older when it happened to me and definitely no match as a tennis player. But I did hope to play again. So, like Andy, and even though it wasn't massively good timing, I decided to take the op.

I had this mad idea I could use the recovery time to make a start on a major book-writing project. Use the difficulty. I guess I subscribed to that notion even then. So I spent the days before the op pulling together all my background material. Papers from a series of workshops I'd hosted. Articles I'd found and not yet read. Notes I'd taken myself along the way. And plenty of blank paper in case I got inspired. I had it all in a big blue ring binder which I lugged with me to the hospital, one morning in May 2008.

It was over a bank holiday weekend. And when I got there it was all very quiet. Perhaps this was the hospital I was trying to remember in Llandod? Except that this time it was warm outside and this hospital was modern and bright. It didn't creak at all. I remember my hip being incredibly uncomfortable as they wheeled me down from the ward. But the early summer sunshine was coming through the windows. A pale light was dancing on the white sheets. It all seemed very dreamy. They must already have given me a pre-op sedative, I guess. And then I was counting backwards from one hundred while a thick fog of cool nothing rose up to meet me.

Next thing I knew I was back on the ward. Resurfacing. My brain was making strange connections. And it seemed to be moving very fast. All on its own. The sunshine was still dancing on the walls. But something was different. Where there had been pain there was now a strange and very sweet sensation. What was that? Ah yes. The absence of pain.

Was that it? Was I better now? When could I play tennis again?

Not yet, they said.

But later that day I was allowed to get out of bed and sit in a high-backed chair for my tea. That definitely felt like progress. Slow progress. But progress all the same. My brain was still strangely active. My thoughts turned to my writing. It felt too good an opportunity to miss. So, in the quiet of the evening, I took the big blue folder out of the cupboard by the bed and balanced it on my lap. After a couple of minutes or so of restless contemplation I picked up my pen and started to write. It was all flowing very easily.

A little bit later a nurse came by to check on me. Hello, she said. What's that you're doing? There was a note of amusement in her voice. Or was it alarm? An anxious smile played round her mouth. Oh it's just some work, I said.

You do know you're still on morphine, she said.

And at that point the smile became a full-on laugh. I laughed too. Which is easy. When you're on morphine. Later that night, when sleep was elusive, and the stuff was still buzzing round my brain, the funny side wore off. But at the time. And even now. If you think about it. It is mildly amusing. The writing project in question turned into the book *Prosperity without Growth*, which ended up being translated into some twenty or so languages. And definitely changed my life. It started its life on morphine.

The poppy's gift

I'm not recommending that as a strategy. Not even for writing books. To be honest, not much of that first evening's work survived. And I guess you could say that I was one of the lucky ones. I hated the side-effects of morphine more than I liked the euphoria it delivered me to. So I was never really tempted to over-indulge. But I can see very easily how that could happen. And I've known people to whom it has happened. Like Gladstone, when you witness that, you can't help wondering if it's really the right kind of thing to go fighting wars about. Or relying on too heavily for pain management.

Even in its clinical forms morphine is highly addictive. I suppose you could say that the absence of pain is pretty addictive. In and of itself. Anyone who's suffered from chronic pain would probably agree. You'll do whatever you can to avoid it, that's for sure. When the drug wears off, the pain is back. And, of course, you want rid of it again. You have the demand. They have the supply. That's the morphine economy.

But in case I haven't made this clear already the morphine economy is not the same thing as the care economy. It's not that they've nothing to do with each other. It's just that you can't substitute one for the other. And if you're tempted to, you'll fall into a dangerous pit. Because on top of the obvious desire to be rid of pain there's a couple of other forces at play. And together they create a recipe for disaster.

First off, the poppy's gift isn't just the absence of pain. It really is more like euphoria. One of the ways it functions is by triggering a flood of the feel-good chemical dopamine in what's known as the mesolimbic reward system – that part of the brain responsible for controlling your physiological and cognitive reward mechanisms. Opioids slap that response into overdrive. And if pain is the alternative, then euphoria is highly addictive.

There's another, more dangerous dynamic. The body adapts. When the drug wears off, you need a higher or more frequent dose to maintain the same euphoric response. Or even to retrieve the same absence of pain. That can happen even with everyday pleasure. The dopamine response is triggered by surprise. And to get that surprise you have to either leave sufficient time between triggers for expectations to reset. Or up the intensity of the trigger.

In the case of prescription opioids this dynamic turns out to be disastrous. If you wait for the reset, pain comes back with a vengeance. If you up the dose, then you're on a never-ending spiral. All of that makes kicking the habit as demanding as hell. Without help it's virtually impossible. And the pain you discover along the way can be worse than the pain you started with. So why would you bother to quit at all? Unless of course you wanted to live. And for some even that is not a strong enough incentive.

These characteristics are no secret. That's why for the longest time there were strict guidelines on clinical usage. Morphine was generally only prescribed for those suffering from acute or terminal conditions. Mainly for post-operative recovery, in the treatment of cancer or during palliative and hospice care. And a lot of effort was put in to finding safe and effective alternatives.

Believe it or not, that's where heroin came from. Bayer first marketed heroin in 1898 as a 'non-addictive' cough and pain relief medication. And in 1906 the American Medical Association recommended its use to addicts to wean themselves off morphine. As it turned out, that was a bad strategy. Heroin is twice as powerful as morphine and just as addictive. So by 1924 its use was criminalized. But ninety years later, at the peak of its power, heroin was still killing around fifteen thousand people a year.

At that point its use began to decline. And that might look like a victory for drug enforcement. But it wasn't. It had far more to do with the spectacular rise of other powerful and entirely legal opioids. Most notably oxy.

Dopesick

The painkiller oxycodone was first synthesized from an opium-based compound called thebaine in 1916. But it wasn't until the arrival of a powerful time-release prescription drug called oxycontin – or 'oxy', as it became known on the street – that things really started to go off the rails. And that might not have been the case either if it wasn't for a story that combined ignorance, greed and a complete failure in regulatory oversight.

Broad brushstrokes, it goes like this. In the mid-1990s, struggling with financial debts and declining demand, a drug company called Purdue Pharma owned by the Sackler family embarked on an aggressive marketing campaign to persuade doctors to prescribe oxy. Not just for acute pain, as had been the case for morphine. But for effective pain relief even in mild or moderate cases.

An accident at work A muscle spasm. Bursitis. Dislocation. Fractures. Neuralgia. Arthritis. The aftermath of a fall. You name it. Oxy would give you your life back. Suddenly a powerful opioid was widely available on prescription from your local GP. And that availability unleashed a demon on society. At one point doctors in America were writing two hundred and fifty-five thousand opioid prescriptions a year – enough to supply every adult in the US with a bottle of oxycontin.

How that happened is shocking. But if you want the details, they're easy enough to find. Hulu's *Dopesick* and Netflix's *PainKiller* are both compelling dramatizations of the story. Both of them are grounded in extensive research. The two accounts differ in their focus. *Dopesick*'s main lens is the perspective of the doctor. It follows the story of his initial resistance to prescribing the drug to his patients and his eventual addiction to it. *PainKiller* is seen primarily through the eyes of a junior attorney trying to bring the Sackler family to justice.

Both accounts tell of Purdue's aggressive marketing and sales campaign. Both of them reveal the misuse of science, the abuse of due process and the appalling oversight of the regulatory system itself. Both of them bring to life the suffering of those who lost their health, their livelihoods and sometimes their lives to oxy. Be warned. It's harrowing stuff.

Perhaps most shocking of all was Purdue's response as evidence began to mount of the damage wreaked by oxy on people's lives. Instead of owning the issue or rowing back on the sales drive, they engaged in a flagrant campaign of blaming the victim. The problem was not the drug itself or even the way it was prescribed. The problem was its abuse by a hardcore element of serial drug users who were illegally obtaining prescriptions. Oxy was not the problem. If it hadn't been oxy it would have been something else, Purdue insisted. Astonishingly this attitude still prevails. In places where it definitely shouldn't.

Even today, for example, the website of the US Drug Enforcement Administration (DEA) describes oxycodone as a 'popular drug of abuse among the narcotic-abusing population'. The description suggests a routine prescription painkiller, criminally misused by a small minority of persistent addicts. People who would destroy themselves any way they could, given half a chance.

Dopesick and *PainKiller* both reveal that that's a profoundly dangerous – and duplicitous – reading of the situation.

The reality is more shocking. Oxy singlehandedly kickstarted an opioid crisis propagated through legalized prescription pain relief. That crisis has now claimed the lives of more than half a million people in the US. Worldwide, the WHO estimates that around six hundred thousand people die from drug use every year. A quarter of them from opioid overdose.

Those numbers could easily get worse before they get better. The latest twist in the story involves an alarming rise in the abuse of an opioid fifty times more powerful than oxy. Fentanyl is finding its way onto the streets through fake prescriptions. Often pretending to be scripts for oxy. And sometimes containing fentanyl in lethal concentrations.

Hounded by lawsuits, Purdue Pharma eventually filed for bankruptcy in 2019. As part of the settlement, the Sackler family, who owned it, reached an agreement with the court which would involve them contributing $6 billion towards the treatment of opioid addiction. It would also give them immunity from prosecution and leave a significant proportion of the family wealth intact. The settlement was overturned by the Supreme Court in June 2024. And almost two decades after oxycontin was licensed as a prescription drug, those directly accountable for what followed have still not been brought to justice.

Dangerous liaisons

So here's my question. Are we really the clever ones? Which is more stupid? Allowing a few unscrupulous quacks to peddle dodgy remedies alongside the more established benefits of the water cure? Or legalizing the prescription of a powerful narcotic with known addictive properties and turning a blind eye for nearly two decades to its rampant and crooked commercialization? All because of the wealth that pharmaceutical sales accumulate?

And aside from the more obvious lack of scruples or common greed of those who profited from the supply chain of tragedy, where exactly does the stupidity lie? Who or what should ultimately be held accountable for the opioid crisis?

Common to both my stories in this chapter is the desire for health. And that desire is central to my thesis. The value of health is self-evident. In fact the origin of the word 'value' lies in the Latin *valere* – meaning to be well, to be strong, to be healthy. So of course we value health. Without health we have nothing. Without health it's difficult to make sense of prosperity. Without health the pursuit of wealth begins to look pale.

But surely it makes no sense to blame the opioid crisis on our desire for health? That would be like blaming those unlucky victims of the cures in Llandod for their own demise at the hands of devious charlatans.

It seems to me a part of the problem is we've mixed up health with pleasure. And pleasure with the absence of pain. I'm not saying that's entirely wrong. The two things clearly have something to do with each other. In the words of the Indian-American neuroscientist V.S. Ramachandran, '[P]ain is an *opinion* on the organism's state of health.' But it has no direct correlation with disease or injury. It's a 'protector' not a 'detector', insists the British doctor Monty Lyman.

And a part of the reason we've so thoroughly confused health with the absence of pain is that the latter has been so easy to monetize and such a ready source of profit. But the consequences of these false liaisons are exceptionally dangerous. We've precipitated an opioid crisis that has hurtled out of control and is ripping through the fabric of society in cities across the world. Accelerated by the illusory promise of euphoria.

Surprisingly that one word brings us round full circle. Medical science long ago muddled up health with euphoria. And the cause was opium. Or, to be more precise, it was laudanum. The historical coincidence is striking. The physician Thomas Sydenham popularized a form of Paracelsus's opium-based tincture in Britain in the 1660s. The first reference to the medical definition of euphoria as health was in 1665, just as that seductive cure-all was beginning to find widespread use.

It would not be a stretch to suppose that when doctors treating their patients with laudanum saw 'improvements' which they described as euphoria, some at least of what they were looking at was the impact of opium on the opioid receptors in the brain. Masking pain for sure. But simultaneously over-stimulating the dopamine response and triggering states of exaggerated elation inappropriate to real events. What they took for health was indeed euphoria.

Profit and loss

There's something else the stories in this chapter have in common. Aside from the desire for health. Aside from the confusion of health with euphoria. The dysfunctional consequences of the use of morphine, just like the dysfunctional varieties of water cure, are driven forwards, sometimes relentlessly, by the pursuit of profit. There are clearly circumstances – like the case of Purdue Pharma – where profiteering has bordered on greed. And where greed has been strategically mobilized in the pursuit of profit. And where both have capitalized on the desire of ordinary human beings to avoid pain and to find euphoria. But there's also something more systemic going on.

Profit is vital to the accumulation of wealth. It's the lifeblood of the monetary economy. The maximization of profit and the accumulation of wealth drive growth in the GDP. And that process is legitimized by the equation of wealth with prosperity and growth with progress. So, if we're looking for villains, we must look beyond misconception. We must look beyond wrongdoing and greed. We must look beyond the human susceptibility to misdirection driven by the desire for health – or even by the pursuit of euphoria. We can't entirely shift the blame onto human nature.

I believe it's more accurate to say that the dysfunctional dynamic rests at the very heart of our culture. Inside a society organized so specifically around the pursuit of profit. Inside our misguided conceptualization of prosperity. The accumulation of wealth is the foundation of the capitalist economy. Its legitimation lies in the assertion that more and more is always better and better. That same philosophy aligns increasing prosperity with economic growth. It allows us to overlook both greed and profiteering – even when it leads to such disastrous consequences as the opioid crisis or the drowning of invalids in the name of health – because we believe it points in the same direction as the arrow of social progress.

Perhaps that philosophy also borrows something from our relentless pursuit of euphoria. Wealth – and the pursuit of wealth – clearly has some of the characteristics associated with addictive unbalanced cycles of dependency common to the pursuit of euphoria. That's certainly the conclusion Julian Rosefeldt comes to in his own commentary on *Euphoria*. But the picture he paints there is deeply dystopian.

If this is true, then our search for culprits leads right back to the damaging assumptions buried at the heart of our cultural view of prosperity. That isn't to condone individual greed. Nor is it to excuse criminality. It doesn't even absolve us of responsibility. Either at the individual or at the cultural level. Of course, it's foolish to be duped into miracle cures peddled by hacks. Of course, it's negligent not to regulate and even to encourage unscrupulous companies profiteering from tragedy. Of course, there's a sense in which its insane for a sane society to allow any of these things to happen.

But the point is that all of it is driven and justified and legitimated by the cultural idea that the relentless pursuit of more is the engine of social progress. If we're searching for villains. For the origins of the dysphoria that haunts us. Perhaps we should re-examine the cultural myths on which our society is built.

It's an idea I shall come back to again. That our culture is itself pathogenic. The pursuit and accumulation of wealth create a dynamic within which human ambitions are distorted. Human nature is turned on itself. Human neurobiology becomes our own worst enemy. Pathological outcomes are inevitable. And this all happens for a very simple reason. The pursuit of prosperity conceived as wealth is profoundly at odds with the goal of prosperity construed as health. The former has a logic of accumulation and growth. The dynamic of health is dramatically different. It's time to look at that dynamic in more detail.

3
Vital Signs

*'All the vital mechanisms, however varied they may be,
always have one purpose, that of maintaining the integrity
of the conditions of life within the internal environment.'*
Claude Bernard, 1878

On a windswept day the sea embraces the Pembrokeshire coastline like a restless lover. Wave after wave hurls itself against the rocky peninsulas and rolls majestically into sandy coves. White crests mark the contours of a never-ending ecstasy.

To stand on the headland or to sit on one of those beaches is to bathe in powers so vast and ancient that human affairs seem tiny and insignificant. You may not know it but somehow you can sense it. The rocks beneath your feet belong to an era before the dawn of human time. The oldest of them come from the Precambrian period, more than half a billion years ago. At that point Wales was lying 60° below the equator in a continent known by geologists as Gondwana, close to the Antarctic circle.

It's come a long way since then. Dragged here and there by continental drift. Battered by climate change. Contoured and re-contoured by sea level rise and fall. Its journey to meet you here is almost unfathomable. And it clearly isn't over yet. Confident as it stands against the incessant waves, the coastline is no match for the power of its lover. Or for the tectonic shifts that are still in play beneath you. They will go on shifting for aeons. Long after you've moved on.

On this particular day there's a deceptive serenity to it all. Yesterday's storm has passed. And only the lightest wind now ripples the surface of the sea. The steel grey ocean is still moving. Still rolling. Its caress is still passionate. But here in the shelter of the bay on a low tide, it all has a post-climactic feel. Almost tender.

It's a year since I bathed my broken toe in the waves on the beach at Aberdyfi. And here we are in Wales again. A different beach. Another writing retreat. The toe has recovered. But my foot now aches obsessively whenever I'm on it for too long. And sometimes even when I'm not. On the advice of a podiatrist, I've invested in some insoles which lift the arch of my foot and provide a comforting support. But after an hour's walk along a rocky path, the ache can still become a sharp and insistent pain.

That's not really what's occupying me, though. I'm trying to make sense of the incessant rhythm of the waves. It seems sometimes like a constant conversation. It feels almost animal in its intensity. But I know it's just the constant play of physical forces seeking balance around a moving point of stillness that's never quite reached. Constantly surpassed. Almost retrieved. And then lost again. On a day like today, the movement is barely perceptible. But the dance goes on.

We're just contemplating whether it's worth removing our boots and bathing our feet at the water's edge when an elderly woman wrapped in a bath gown strides past us towards the sea. Barely breaking step, she casts the gown aside and marches into the waves. Gloves. Hat. Bathing suit. She's already fully immersed and swimming confidently out towards a fishing buoy some twenty metres or so from the shore. I shiver involuntarily. And then watch her progress with envy and admiration. Paddling in the shallows seems paltry all of a sudden.

Later we learn she belongs to a group of cold water swimmers called the Bluetits. For obvious reasons, she says, with an unselfconscious chuckle. Founded by a local woman named Sian Richardson in 2014, the group now has more than a hundred thousand members. It's one of many such groups all round the world. Throwing yourself into cold water whatever the season is a thing. Apparently. And not mad at all. As it happens. There's a whole science behind it.

When I get to look it up, I find that this science underlines something quite remarkable. Health too is a restless dance around the still point. Or, to be more accurate, around a host of still points. We are never in balance. But we are constantly striving for it. Just like the restless ocean. Perhaps that's a part of the lure of ocean swimming. Even though the biting cold appears to go directly against one of the most fundamental necessities of life.

98.6° Fahrenheit

As every first-time parent soon discovers, a healthy human body must maintain a core temperature of about 37°C (98.6°F). That's the body's thermal still point. One of its many still points. Around it lies a 'normal' range from about 36.5° to 37.5°C within which the core temperature varies throughout the day.

As we prepare for sleep, the blood vessels on the skin begin to dilate. That process draws heat away from our vital organs. Our core temperature falls very slightly. It stays that way through the early stages of sleep. Then later, sometime around dawn, it begins to rise again. The cooling down slows our metabolism and facilitates rest. The warming up prepares us for the activity of a new day.

Circadian rhythms aside, our central nervous system works continuously to regulate the core body temperature within that range. Whatever we happen to be doing. Whatever's going on around us. It demands a constant vigilance. And it involves a continuous process of thermoregulation. We shed heat when the core temperature rises. We generate extra heat when the core temperature falls. We sweat when it's hot outside. We shiver when it's cold. And just before we start to shiver, remarkably, we'll turn up the internal temperature through a process called thermogenesis which burns the calories stored in the brown adipose tissue (brown fat) that clusters round our vital organs. Warming us up from the inside.

The most extraordinary thing about all this is that we barely even notice it's happening. There's no need for us to notice it. We don't need to lift a finger. It's all part of the armoury of thermal regulation controlled by our central nervous system. It's a seamless part of an integral design and for the most part it's astonishingly successful. Which is just as well. Because outside that narrow range the safety margins are remarkably thin.

The tell-tale signs of fever are a parent's worst nightmare. But even fever, it turns out, is part of the plan. A higher core temperature is better for fighting infection. And the body itself seems to know when to stop and generally won't push the core temperature above 40°C. Internal malfunction or a set of extreme external conditions can upset that plan, of course. And the results are not good. Above 40° for too long and you're at risk of a seizure, brain damage or even death.

In the summer of 2023, the city of Phoenix, Arizona, suffered a record-breaking thirty-one days in a row with temperatures above 43.3°C (110°F). More than five hundred people died. A year later, pilgrims visiting Mecca were exposed to temperatures which exceeded 50°C (122°F) for several days. Thirteen hundred people died. And in the blazing heatwave of 2022, there were almost sixty-two thousand excess heat deaths in Europe. These tragic incidents are part of the reason accelerating climate change is not a good idea.

The ability of an organism to destroy the conditions on which its own survival depends seems paradoxical somehow. It's taken evolution millions of years to figure out the right temperature for the best possible functioning of our vital organs. It's taken us a couple of hundred years to shift the external conditions so far that the job becomes impossible. Of course, we wouldn't be the first species to foul our own nest. Cyanobacteria managed it two and a half billion years ago. And we wouldn't be here without their unwitting efforts. But we might be about to go one better in terms of own goals. We're doing it knowingly. And as Kim Stanley Robinson makes clear in the graphic opening of his *cli-fi* novel *The Ministry for the Future*, the consequences won't be pleasant.

Ice Mile

Aside from sleep, the body tends not to regulate its internal temperature downwards that much. So far as we know. And that does seem to be wise. It knows the dangers. We are warm-blooded creatures, after all. More than a couple of degrees lower than 36.5° and you're at risk of hypothermia. More than an hour or so below 32°C and you're in danger of cardiac arrest.

Which brings me back to the Bluetits. Given the body's overriding desire to maintain its core temperature as close as possible to 37°, why would anyone be tempted to plunge into waters which haven't even reached double digits?

There is even a thing called the Ice Mile which cold water swimmers aspire to. It involves swimming a mile in water that is 5°C or less. It's carried out under strict regulations set by the International Ice Swimming Association. Which makes sense. Given the limits of physical endurance, it seems like a good thing to regulate for safety. But why would there be anything to regulate in the first place? Why would anyone want to do that? Unless humans are by default mad.

I can understand the immersion in a watery environment. That's probably something to do with the womb. The ubiquitous origin story for all of us. (So far.) But then, it was warm in the womb. A snug and comfortable resting place. The perfect launch pad for our subsequent excursions in the world. Conveniently maintained at more or less the core temperature our young bodies needed. The one we were designed for. And that's a far cry from what greets you when you venture into the ocean in winter.

Maybe it really is primitive. Perhaps the desire comes from before the dawn of human time. When Wales was still down under. And before our earliest ancestors crawled warily out of the ocean. Perhaps they left some yearning for home in a quiet corner of our reptilian brain. There's some interesting behavioural evidence that this might indeed be the case. Vestiges of physical characteristics. Reflexes, if you will, that remain useful to us on occasions. And in particular if you're tempted to take that icy plunge.

There'll be a shock. Let me warn you. In fact, you only need to dip your feet in the sea at Aberdyfi to recognize that. But this will be something different. An order of magnitude more shocking. At least. As you venture into a cold sea beyond your ankles, the folly of your decision will assault you. Why am I doing this? Can I go back now? Is anyone watching? Make this stop!

By the time the water reaches your midriff, shock becomes an inadequate word for what's going on. At that point your inner core is beginning to feel the cold. So your body's thermal regulation mechanism is in overdrive. Your heart rate is rising rapidly. Brown fat is being fired up for central heating. Your pores are being closed to prevent more heat loss. Any surplus heat in your periphery is being drawn rapidly towards the core to try and protect your vital organs, leaving the outer layers of your skin a characteristic bluish colour.

But blue tits are the least of your worries. Cortisol and adrenaline are pumping through your veins to increase your metabolic rate. Your body thinks you've been assaulted by a dangerous enemy who is trying to kill you. So it's activated your sympathetic nervous system. That's the stress response which prepares you for fight or flight. It hasn't figured out that the enemy is you. Your own mad intentions.

As the water reaches your chest and the cold reaches your lungs, you'll gasp. Involuntarily. However much experience you have. And that involuntary gasp sets off a pattern of rapid breathing. Hyperventilation. Your body is drawing in as much oxygen as possible in case you have to stay under water for a long time. It's a distant echo from a time when that's exactly what our ancestors would have been doing at this point in their immersion.

But hey. Just as a reminder. You gave up their adaptive advantage back in the Silurian period, four hundred million years ago. Which means you should be careful floundering about in this watery environment. If you gasp at the wrong moment, the chances are you'll end up with a lungful of icy water. Which is not good. In case you're wondering.

That's another good reason for that thoughtful guidance from those who've done it before. Don't try this alone. Work out your exit before you get in. Have warm clothes ready. And this very helpful tip from the Ice Swimming Association. 'Instruct your recovery people' before you go in. 'You may not be able to communicate' when you need to! That's mainly for those aiming for the extreme conditions of the Ice Mile. But if it's your first time cold water swimming, it's definitely all still useful – essential – advice.

Inner morphine

At this point the whole adventure still seems mad. Why would anyone subject themselves to this? Aside from some form of bravado. Some foolish determination to challenge yourself. Or to challenge nature. Or to compete for attention.

Or to step outside the boundaries of the everyday. Or to explore the edges of your own perseverance.

But once you're in you're in. The shock subsides a notch. And there's suddenly something almost comforting about the buoyancy of the water. The way it holds you up. The way it moves against your skin. The way your body moves through it. This fluid environment is very different from the harsh gravity of the land. And the reptile in you missed that, right?

Quite likely too, you'll begin to notice your surroundings properly for the first time about now. And what you see, with the renewed vigilance of the reptile, is nature. Pure and simple. And it's cool. Not cool like the cold that's working its way to your core. But cool like amazing. It induces a sense of awe.

Awe is good. Awe generates endorphins. The chances are they're coursing through you now. It's not unlike the mechanism of the 'runner's high'. Endorphins are the body's natural opioids. The name 'endorphins' is a contraction of the word '*endo*' (meaning inner) and 'morphine'. They're also released through physical exercise. And they seem to be associated with the satisfaction of using your skills to meet some kind of challenge. Very soon they'll be flooding the opioid receptors in your mesolimbic reward centre, where they'll release the feel-good hormone dopamine.

Physiological and psychological reward systems are intertwined. In more ways than one, as it happens. When cold water hits your face, it stimulates the vagus nerve, which runs all the way from the brain to the large intestine with branches down either side of the neck. That nerve controls the body's parasympathetic nervous system. It's the one that slows you down when the danger is past. You move from fight or flight (sympathetic) to rest and digest (parasympathetic). And that's a whole lot pleasanter place to be. Blissful by comparison.

The exhilaration is even better once it's all over. Alongside a renewed acquaintance with the simple pleasure of physical warmth, you're going to be proud of your achievement. You've pushed the boundaries of our own experience. And you've survived. Your mad adventure has paid off. You definitely have a hint of euphoria. And without the nasty side-effects of morphine and its derivates. In fact, if you make a habit of it, your new recreational activity may even have long-term health benefits. If the emerging science of cold water swimming is to be believed.

The cathartic ocean

The roots of the idea that the ocean has beneficial properties for human beings lie way back in antiquity. Shortly before his death in 406 BCE, in his play *Iphigenia in Tauris*, the Greek playwright Euripides declared that 'the sea can wash away all evils'. Religious historian Kimberley Patton takes that quote as the starting point for a fascinating exploration of the ambivalent consequences of our belief in the sea's healing properties over the ensuing centuries.

Admittedly human fascination hasn't always served the ocean well at all. Our faith in its vastness has triggered massive overfishing. It's also led to the indiscriminate disposal into the sea of everything from toxic and radioactive wastes to human shit. Aspiring ocean swimmers take note. Particularly if you're taking your dip anywhere near a combined sewer overflow.

But it's not just the willingness of the ocean to absolve our material sins that Patton has in mind. The cathartic properties of water have long been recognized. We've come across it already. Cold water immersion was part of the cure in spa towns like Llandrindod Wells. Sea dipping became particularly popular in the UK around the same time. It reached its peak in the late eighteenth and early nineteenth century – even though at that time few people could swim. And after a bit of a decline, it's undergone a surprising renaissance in the last decade or so. As its popularity has risen, so too has our understanding of the potential health benefits.

A lot of the science relates to the benefits of sea swimming for chronic psychological conditions like anxiety and depression. A report in the *British Medical Journal* (*BMJ*) describes the case of a twenty-four-year old woman who'd suffered from depression for seven years. After mixed experiences with medication she embarked on a weekly programme of cold open water swimming. Over the course of the next few months she kicked the meds. And a year later she was still free of them.

This kind of outcome probably has something to do with the sheer thrill of throwing yourself into ice-cold water and coming out alive. Using your skill to meet a challenge. Proving yourself. It also illustrates the now well-established psychological advantage of just being in nature. Immersed in nature. Quite literally in this case. It's an example of the strategy of green social prescribing, pioneered by British doctor William Bird.

But the benefits of cold water swimming are physiological as well as psychological. They seem to emerge in part through a mechanism very similar to the one we looked at in the last chapter. The body's home-grown opioids and cannabinoids activate the reward circuits. Endorphins are part of nature's own answer to depression. They can also be the body's own answer to pain. Endorphins don't just act on the reward centre. They also block the body's pain receptors.

Not surprisingly then, there's evidence that cold water swimming can help to manage chronic pain. One article in the *BMJ* describes 'a case of unexpected, immediate, complete and sustained remission of postoperative intercostal neuralgia' after a patient took up cold water swimming. Intercostal neuralgia sounds nasty. And it is. It's the name for the pain associated with inflamed or irritated nerves in the chest. Endorphins might be expected to offer a temporary relief from that. But 'complete and sustained remission' seems to indicate something more effective than short-term pain blocking is in play.

No one is entirely sure how that works. But cold water is known to reduce inflammation. And we know that inflammation is key to many chronic conditions. So that could well be part of it. The anaesthetist Mark Harper cites similar cases in his book *Chill: The Cold Water Swim Cure*. The anecdotal evidence is strong, even if the pathways for long-term improvement are unclear. Part of the problem is there's no real commercial benefit in making them clear. So nobody's done the research.

Harper proposes that cold water immersion improves the body's resilience to stress. And that's one of the mechanisms for long-term pain reduction. That's a fascinating insight. It's supported from within both psychology and physiology. And from the way stress works in the body. Stress itself is a normal adaptive response. Acute stress generates a hormonal response which enables us to respond swiftly to all kinds of acute threats – real or perceived. But in the long run too much exposure to the hormones stress releases in us – cortisol mostly – is bad.

Pumping the blood full of cortisol, raising the heart rate and increasing our blood pressure tends to be functional for short periods. But if we're never allowed the space and time to relax and reset – or indeed if we're deliberately held away from that state of relaxation for all sorts of reasons – then stress can lead rapidly to chronic conditions. Hypertension (high blood pressure), inflammation, anxiety and depression are all known to be related to stress. And these in their turn are precursors to chronic 'non-communicable' diseases such as heart disease, strokes, arthritis and cancer.

The difference between good stress and bad stress rests on two key factors. The first is the frequency of our exposure. How often we're getting stressed out. In a hyperactive society, in which we're assaulted – sometimes deliberately – by a constant stream of physical, social and emotional stressors, good stress is much more likely to turn into bad stress. It's another example of something we've already seen. Sometimes pathogenesis lives at the cultural level. It's another of those places where culture itself is the culprit. Where social norms embedded within visions of the good life take a toll on our long-term health. Where health is at the mercy of wealth.

The second factor is how we view the stress we're experiencing. If we see it as an imminent threat to our physical survival, it's much more likely to lead to long-term damage than if we regard it as a challenge through which we have the opportunity to learn and grow. That's clearly harder to do when the stressors come hard and fast. And easier to do when we have time to reset, to recharge, to rejuvenate. Time in particular to enjoy the rewards of the parasympathetic nervous response to the mastery of stress. That difference in perspective really does seem to matter. Not just in psychological terms but in physiological terms as well.

So maybe Harper is right. Improving our resilience to stress could be a powerful therapeutic intervention. And here the lesson is very simple. If paradoxical. Stress can teach us to cope with stress. Even as chronic stress can be pathological, acute stress can help us thrive. Those insights are evident even outside cold water swimming. Martial arts, yoga and tai chi aim for something similar. Strength and resilience through stress. In fact, most forms of physical training proceed by stressing the body. Not too much. But enough to teach the muscles to be stronger, more flexible, more agile. To teach the body to be faster or leaner or more efficient. Or to teach the brain how to stay calm in the face of stress.

That first plunge into the ocean invokes the stress response. However often you've been there, it's still going to happen. But your body learns by exposing itself to stress. And that makes it more resilient to stress. What doesn't kill you makes you stronger. As the saying goes. Of course, the flip side is: stress can also kill you. Even acute stress. People have died from cold water immersion. Prolonged exposure to temperatures below 10° can have a drastic impact on core body temperature, even for the most well-insulated body.

Turns out the close operation of the sympathetic and the parasympathetic nervous responses can itself be dangerous. They're not typically superimposed on each other in quite the way that happens with a sudden cold water immersion. One of these responses tells your heart to speed up. The other one tells it to slow down. So you can see why it might get confused. Make your mind up, your body's yelling. What is it you want from me? The combination can potentially trigger cardiac arrhythmia – a temporarily irregular heartbeat. Not immediately lethal. Unless you happen to have some underlying heart condition.

So. In summary. Yes. Throwing yourself willingly into the icy sea could perhaps make you stronger. More resilient to stress. Better able to cope with all kinds of threats. It might allow us, as Harper suggests, to shift the stress response to a physiological level rather than pathological level. At the very least, the whole experience is going to take you out of your stressed-up world long enough to find some sense of relaxation and perhaps a little of the body's own euphoria. So it may well be worth it. As long as you follow some simple rules.

The truth is, our understanding of all this is still very much in its infancy. 'There is evidence of benefits,' says Mike Tipton, editor of the *Experimental Physiology* journal and probably the foremost expert in the science of cold water swimming. 'But we're in the realms of snake oil if you start telling people that it's a cure all that will solve all your problems.'

Which is just as well. Because that's not my intention. It isn't really the point of this story at all. This isn't a health journal. And it's certainly not a self-help guide. Swim if you want to. Find some other form of exercise if you prefer. Slouch on the couch if you must. Most of what we know suggests that some kind of activity is going to do you more good. Under most circumstances. But none of that is why I'm raising the matter here.

That chance encounter on a beach in Pembrokeshire. This brief exposure to the madness of cold water swimming. Our excursion into the curious workings of the sympathetic and parasympathetic nervous system. It all demonstrates something profound about the nature and logic of health. And in particular it illustrates that health has a nature and logic which is completely different from the nature and logic of the accumulation of wealth.

More than that. It's deeply at odds with it. In a very particular sense. Health is all about balance. Wealth is all about more. If you're constantly striving for more, it's going to be hard to find your balance. Hard even to see where that point of balance lies. And next to impossible to stop when you get there. It's one of the central findings of experimental physiology.

The wisdom of the body

The founder of the field of experimental physiology was a French physician named Claude Bernard who lived from 1813 to 1878. He's best known today for proposing what he called the constancy of the internal environment (*le milieu intérieur*). It didn't particularly take off at the time. But his work was the origin of the idea that our bodies maintain certain vital parameters within specific ranges through processes of internal feedback and regulation.

It was to be another half a century before the Harvard physician Walter Cannon expanded on this idea. His 1932 book *The Wisdom of the Body* argued that evolutionary pressures to improve energy efficiency in the ancestral environment led to the evolution of sophisticated systems of self-regulation. These systems allow the body to maintain its internal environment in the face of changing external conditions. He called the process homeostasis.

Core temperature is one of those internal conditions. Homeostasis provides the process through which a living organism regulates the temperature around its vital organs to try and keep them within a safe thermal environment. It doesn't always achieve it. Particularly when it's thrown into ice-cold sea water. But that process of trying to achieve it is constantly in play. And finding the balance matters. Because outside that narrow range lies death.

Around the time that Bernard was writing, a few physicians had begun to notice a connection between body temperature, pulse and breathing. In 1866 a couple of interns at New York Hospital called Edward Seguin and William Draper published a paper in the *Chicago Medical Journal* reporting on the progress of three cases of pneumonia. It seems to have been the first paper to have coined the term 'vital signs' to refer explicitly to those three variables: body temperature, heart rate and respiratory rate.

Back then it wasn't so easy to measure these things. Thermometers were commonly over a foot long and it could take up to twenty minutes to get a good reading. Accurate pocket watches emerged only with the need to monitor the timely arrival and departure of trains on the fast-expanding railroads in the 1860s and 1870s. But by the late 1800s, it was entirely possible for medical staff to take regular readings of all three of Seguin and Draper's vital signs.

The emergence of blood pressure as a fourth vital sign is more recent. The characteristic sounds of systolic and diastolic blood pressure were first identified by the Russian physician Nikolai Korotkov in 1905. But it wasn't until 1970, with the arrival of practical measurement equipment, that blood pressure was formally included in routine measurements. Given its clear relationship to heart disease and other chronic conditions, you can see why that's a good thing.

Clearly these four measurements are not all that matters to health. On the ward, for example, it's common to measure the level of oxygen saturation in the blood. Bernard proposed that blood glucose level was another factor the body attempts to regulate. Cannon identified numerous parameters (including blood fat, protein, calcium and blood alkalinity) which are also subject to homeostatic control. We'll see in what follows why some of these factors have a strong claim to be indicators of health.

And then in 1996 the American Pain Society (APS) spearheaded a campaign to have pain recognized as 'the fifth vital sign' of health. It was the same year that oxycontin was licensed as a legal prescription drug. So it was a massively convenient argument for the pharmaceutical industry who collectively funded the APS. If the avoidance of pain is a vital sign, then a doctor who fails to prescribe relief is as negligent as one who forgets to take their patient's pulse or fails to observe that their temperature has reached a fever pitch.

With Purdue's help the APS campaign successfully persuaded doctors routinely to score their patients for pain. By the turn of the millennium, a standardized smiley chart became a key diagnostic tool in doctors' surgeries across the US. And it legitimized the routine prescription of opioids even for the relief of mild or moderate pain. But as a report from the Homeland Security and Government Affairs Committee pointed out in 2018, APS had in the process systematically 'amplified and reinforced messages [favouring] increased opioid use'. And the campaign for a fifth vital sign was quietly dropped.

So for the moment the four vital signs remain the four vital signs. Their virtue lies in being able to define both a 'normal range' and the 'critically abnormal' values outside which there's a clear indication that something is going wrong. A normal adult at rest will have a heart rate between around sixty and a hundred beats per minute. They'll breathe in and out between twelve and eighteen times a minute. And they'll have a systolic blood pressure between 90 and 120 millimetres of mercury (mm Hg) and a diastolic pressure between 60 and 80 mm Hg. And of course their core body temperature will remain close to 37°C (98.6°F). Unless they stay too long in a cold ocean.

When values remain within those normal ranges, people tend to have better chances of remaining healthy. Outside those ranges things start going wrong. A longitudinal study involving more than a million observations revealed what happens for 'critically abnormal values' – meaning temperatures of below 35° and above 38.9°C, heart rates above 120 bpm, respiratory rates less than twelve and more than twenty-four breaths per minute, and systolic blood pressure below 85 mm Hg. There was a striking correlation between values in those abnormal ranges and adverse health outcomes. And the authors found that the 'simultaneous presence of three critically abnormal vital signs' was associated with 'very high mortality'. When your body fails to regulate its vital signs within the narrow ranges assigned to them, you may well die. That's health for you. Balance matters.

The limits of wisdom

Back on the beach the tide is coming in. The sea is insatiable. Her appetites rise and fall with the moon. With the seasons. With the wind. As her waves meet your shore, the surf is beginning to rise. The still point is once again lost in commotion.

My recent elderly acquaintance is back home now, I imagine. With a cup of hot tea. And I'm out here still watching the ebb and flow of the waves. Still listening to their incessant conversation. Still trying to interpret a language of which I know only the basics.

Marine science defines the tidal range at each location in relation to what it calls *chart datum*: the depth of water as measured at the lowest of low tides throughout the whole year. A fixed point in a world of constant change. For each day the tide tables report four heights above chart datum and the four times at which they occur – roughly six hours apart. Two are low tides and two high. Between low and high the mean sea level – the still point – charts a definable path. It's constantly moving. And yet it's in balance. It's in a predictable motion.

On top of all this predictable regularity, the wind and the waves impose their own chaotic motion. What we see on the beach is always the fusion of constancy and change. Which is why it's sometimes hard to see that it all remains precariously in balance.

Health too is a dance between stability and chaos. In a healthy organism the vital signs all live in definable ranges. Raising your heart rate, increasing your blood pressure, messing with the pattern of your breathing and drastically attacking your core body temperature – all of which happens during cold water swimming – is a decided assault on the balance of your internal environment. A threat to your physical survival. And yet most people do survive. So long as they get out of the water before hypothermia sets in.

The point of homeostasis is to bring us safely home again. To keep our internal environment in balance. Even as the world outside goes crazy. Even as the storms and hurricanes way out in the Atlantic forever threaten to disturb the picture. Health itself is not so much about the definition of values as it is about our ability constantly to return to the still point. Until, for some reason, we're no longer able to.

Homeostatic effectiveness diminishes with age. That's predictable, I suppose. The slow running down of the body has no ultimate cure. As yet. The accumulation of stresses and strains. The genetic lottery that determined the efficiency of the homeostatic mechanism in the first place. All of this and more determines how long that process takes. But none of it prevents the inevitable. The even keel is denied to us all in the long run.

But long before that point – before the inevitable expiry date – things can also go wrong. Despite the best intentions of the wisdom of the body. And sometimes because of it. This point has been made exquisitely by the neuroscientist Peter Sterling in his book *What Is Health?* There he follows the scientific arguments for the evolution of homeostasis from our ancient ancestors in the Precambrian to the hominids that still stalk the shoreline of Wales – and elsewhere, of course.

Several decades earlier, Sterling and his collaborator Joseph Eyer had coined the term *allostasis* to refer to the idea of stability through change. They used it to describe the possibility that the body's own physiology changes reflexively as it attempts to maintain internal coherence in the face of external conditions. And to reflect the possibility that such changes don't always result in a return to the still point. Or even to a specific normal range. The outcome of the body's best intentions may be that the still point itself ends up changing. Or that the range changes. Sometimes permanently and not always to the good.

There are some spectacular examples of this tendency. Healthy astronauts spending months at a time in the International Space Station experience substantial muscle loss. They sometimes lose as much as 50 per cent over the course of stint spent spinning round the globe. And their bone density declines on average by around 1–2 per cent per month. Their bodies are adapting of course to the new environment of microgravity. Homeostasis is still in play. But the external conditions have changed so radically that the 'normal' ranges no longer apply. Our bodies are adapted to planet Earth. Much like the tides are.

But outer space is not the only place where the wisdom of the body comes up against an environment for which it was not adapted. It also happens right here on earth. Inside capitalism. Inside consumerism. Inside the ideology which insists that prosperity is about wealth. Inside the relentless accumulation of more. It happens right at the place where more stops being better and becomes too much. The point which the ideology of more obscures so effectively from us.

Too many calories rather than too few. Too much sugar. Too many refined carbohydrates. Too much saturated fat. Too many painkillers. Too much euphoria. Too many stressors. Too much stress. All of it designed specifically to persuade us to buy more. To produce more. To consume more. Overconsumption in pursuit of profit. Profit in pursuit of the accumulation of wealth. Wealth justified as the foundation for prosperity. Health sacrificed on the altar of growth.

This burden of physiological and psychological impacts is called the allostatic load, which is defined as the 'long-term result of failed adaptation or allostasis, resulting in pathology and chronic illness'. And this allostatic load is rising in modern society specifically because we are poorly adapted to the conditions of capitalism. Or to be more precise. Because capitalism – the relentless pursuit of more – is poorly adapted to the dynamics of human health.

Make no mistake. This allostatic load is quantifiable in human misery. Exposed relentlessly to dietary sugar, we have no hope of reaching the still point for blood glucose. Addicted to drugs, our search for euphoria becomes the road to hell. Exposed to constant stress, cortisol rips through our body with no respite. Inflammation, hypertension and diabetes follow. The constancy of exposure interferes with our reward circuits. Suppressing the normal dopamine response. Delivering anxiety and depression. Or else gearing those reward circuits towards the search for ever greater stimuli. Leading to addiction, abuse, overdose and suicide. The pursuit of prosperity as wealth has come at a devastating cost.

Sterling is adamant. There's a direct clash between the wisdom of the body – designed over millennia under a very specific set of evolutionary conditions – and the culture in which we are trying desperately to navigate health. And this conflict is leading to what US economists Anne Case and Angus Deaton have called the 'deaths of despair' which now haunt the so-called advanced economies. Worldwide, each year, eight hundred thousand people commit suicide. Millions more die from stress-related disease.

Here we are once again. Not far from where we were at the end of the previous chapter. Face to face with a pathology rooted at the heart of our culture. But with a more detailed understanding of the dynamics underlying it. A better sense of the limits of the body in the face of its external stressors. And greater awareness of the allostatic load that emerges when those conditions are at odds with those for which we were adapted. A place where the dynamics of the accumulation of wealth are dramatically opposed to the dynamics of the preservation of health. A place where the need for balance is systematically overturned by the imperative of growth.

This is not a short dip in a cold sea. It's a long and relentless immersion in a pathological ocean. A place where the wisdom of the body can no longer bring us safely back to the shore.

4

The Myth of Care

'Never looked for, always there.
Cursed and flattered. I am Care.
Have I never crossed your path?'
Goethe, 1832

It's time to get back. The night is falling. Not long ago a crescent moon was racing the clouds. Every now and then she would emerge abruptly, cast her silver rays on the dark grey ocean and disappear again. But now the cloud has thickened. A weather front is approaching from the Atlantic. The wind has picked up considerably. And I wrap my jacket more tightly against its winter chill.

In the distance, briefly, I catch sight of the light from the lighthouse on Strumble Head. Appearing and disappearing. Its regularity offers a strange combination of security and insecurity. And then it too is lost in low cloud. Leaving no obvious aid to navigation for any vessel making its way through the Irish Sea. Thank goodness for GPS.

Suddenly I'm aware that I too am far from home. I've walked a long way on sore feet. And I've barely touched on the question of care. Of what it is. Of what it's not. Of how we define Fisher and Tronto's 'world'. The world we need to maintain, continue and repair. The care economy still feels like a grainy image, coalescing dreamily from an old-school developing tray under the red glow of the darkroom light.

I'm sure it will resolve in time. Isn't that just chemistry? Or alchemy perhaps. I'm just not sure which element will aid in the process of resolution. At this point it seems entirely possible we could end up adding some fatal ingredient to the alchemical solution and losing our way entirely.

And then. Right on cue. I'm on the point of leaving when one such ingredient presents itself. Through a sudden gap in the racing clouds the moon appears. Unannounced and brilliant. Startling in its clarity. Dappling the ocean. Illuminating the texture of the waves. Shedding the kindness of her light on an otherwise unrelenting darkness. No wonder the ancients worshipped her alongside the more obvious deity of the sun. And then, as suddenly as she appeared, she is gone. Leaving behind a gift. An ingredient. A question.

Does the moon care for us?

It's a strange ingredient. I have no idea where it came from. Perhaps a combination of this brief splendour and my inner conversation. Your ideas are not your ideas. To paraphrase the poet Kahlil Gibran, 'They come through you but they are not of you.' You can no more reject them than deny your feet the pleasure of walking home.

Which. Now that I think about it. Does Uber operate in Cwm-yr-Eglwys? I take out my phone. No bars. Hey ho.

Does the moon care? I know it appears that she does. But I'm not talking about appearances. That would just be anthropomorphism. A vastly underrated and hugely entertaining way of interacting with the 'demon-haunted world'. But it isn't exactly science. So that's not what I'm saying here. At least. I'm not admitting to it.

What I'm getting at is something different. And to find it means going back. Back to the cottage. Back to my pile of books. Back in time. Back to the beginning. And then perhaps back again. To before the beginning.

The birth of Rome

We are born into care. We arrive in the world naked and helpless. Our survival hangs precariously on the attention we receive from those around us. More often than not those faces will resolve into the likeness of people we'll remember for the rest of our lives. Our mum and dad. The woman whose womb, until recently, provided our entire life support system – and part of our love for the sea. The man without whose contribution, however brief, our existence would have been impossible. Parental care – and the maternal bond in particular – is the foundation for life.

Indisputably that foundation isn't always solid. And when it crumbles, as the Canadian-Hungarian physician Gabor Maté has pointed out, the implications are always keenly felt. For a long time. The absence of care in infancy invariably has damaging implications both on physical development and on psychological health in later life. But even in those cases, perhaps especially in those cases, no one truly escapes some dependency on care. Even those at the mercy of proxy parents are the inevitable recipients of care.

Mewling and puking in our nurse's arms, we arrive in the world knowing little of our origin and less about our destination. Unable to fend for ourselves, innately reliant on the kindness of strangers, we depend for our very survival on certain kinds of behaviours we call care that emerged at a very early stage in evolution.

The essential nature of care – of interdependency – is heightened by the evidence of similar behaviours in almost every other species under the sun. Maybe care is particularly important for humans. That seems to be partly because of our very slow development in early life. And that in turn is because we arrive only partly formed, as it were. In a more fully formed state, it turns out, we'd never get through the birth canal. So what passes for human intelligence – bigger brains, let's say – bears an intimate relationship to the evolution of care. Humanity has a special relationship with care.

But that doesn't mean care is uniquely human. It's certainly vital for mammals as a whole, because they rely on their mother's milk for survival. But even mammals aren't exactly a special case. Pretty much all vertebrates have one thing in common. Apart from a backbone. They exhibit behaviours that look a lot like care. The more you look the more you find. Care seems to have played at least as significant a role in the evolution of species as its much more famous behavioural cousin selfishness.

'If exploitation of others were all that matters,' writes the evolutionary biologist Frans de Waal in *The Age of Empathy*, 'evolution would never have gotten into the empathy business.' Something more than dog eat dog was needed to get the whole thing going, he and other evolutionary biologists are now convinced.

The force of care is so strong that it even makes sense to speak of an instinct to care. Which might explain why sometimes the object of care possesses only a passing genetic similarity to the carer. The love that people have for their pets, for instance, the care they lavish on them and the grief that attends their loss bear witness to this. But that instinct is by no means a one-way street.

The foundational myth of Rome revolves around twin brothers, Romulus and Remus, who are cast adrift at birth on the river Tiber. The basket they're in floats down the river and comes to rest by a sacred fig tree where the two brothers later build the city of Rome. But their ability to live long enough to achieve that feat depends on the care they receive as infants from a she-wolf and a woodpecker, emissaries of the god Mars, who as it happens turns out to be the boys' father. I guess that means there was a genetic motivation after all. So maybe it doesn't count.

Try this one. When a three-year-old boy slipped from his mother's arms and fell into the gorilla enclosure at the Brookfield Zoo outside Chicago in 1996, an eight-year-old female gorilla called Binti Jua picked him up, protected him from other gorillas and brought him safely back to the zookeeper, whence he was returned to his relieved mother. Binti Jua became famous. She was an early internet sensation. So much so that when she died there was a collective outpouring of (human) grief. We cared about her because she cared for one of us. Or because she personified the idea that care is vital. For all of us.

And if that doesn't convince you, there's a regular procession of similar stories haunting social media these days. Dogs rescuing kids. Dolphins rescuing dogs. Giraffes helping zebras. Ducks rescuing hedgehogs. You name it, it's out there. In the age of creeping artificial intelligence (AI), who knows if it's real or fake. But it clearly speaks to something that has deep roots in us.

Years later, in another zoo, a slightly less careful gorilla named Harambe had to be shot to rescue another small child who had fallen into another enclosure. So please don't try this at home. And for the sake of our rapidly declining gorilla population keep tight hold of your rugrats near the ape pit. Or better still. Campaign to protect gorillas in the wild.

But here's my question. Was Binti Jua's apparently selfless act an act of care or was it not? Did care cross species that day? Or is that also anthropomorphism? Was it instinct? Was it empathy? Was it care? What defines whether something is or isn't an act of care? Let me try another example. Another challenge.

'This is an act of care'

On the morning of 22 April 2021 nine women arrived early at HSBC bank's Canary Wharf headquarters in London. Before anyone could stop them they set about smashing the ground-floor windows of the building with hammers and chisels. They were all arrested and charged with causing half a million pounds' worth of criminal damage to the building.

The women were all members of the climate protest group Extinction Rebellion (XR) and the action was a protest against HSBC's financial support for fossil fuels. The bank had signed a pledge as part of the 2015 Paris Agreement to try and keep the global temperature rise from climate change to less than 1.5°C above the pre-industrial average. Since that time, they'd invested more than $80 billion in fossil fuels. The same fossil fuels that cause the same climate change that pushes the temperature above 1.5° leading to the same extreme weather events that are already killing people.

The science is crystal clear. The impacts are going to be profound. Heat deaths. Crop failures. The melting of the Arctic and Antarctic ice sheets. Sea level rise. Storms, droughts, floods and wildfires. The collapse of coral reefs and fish populations. The stalling or weakening of the ocean's 'thermohaline' circulation system, which regulates global weather patterns. All of this lies in the dystopian future imagined (with alarming verisimilitude) in Kim Stanley Robinson's *The Ministry for the Future*.

But it isn't just about the future. The damage is already happening. And so is the pain. Playing out in Phoenix or in Mecca. Writ large in the droughts in Africa and Southeast Asia. In the increasing frequency of heat waves in Europe. In the wildfires in California and Australasia. With the damage inflicted first and foremost on the poor and the most vulnerable. On women. And on children. That was the XR women's point.

The UN's International Children's Emergency Fund (UNICEF) has estimated that more than forty-three million children were displaced from their homes by climate change during a six-year period during the last decade. That's around twenty thousand children each day, having to pack up whatever they could take and leave home. Not knowing when or if they might ever come back.

'I've spent my life caring for the people around me,' said one of the XR protestors, Sue Reid, a retired community worker. 'I refused to stand by while HSBC poured money into the very thing we know is causing unimaginable harm.'

During the protest the women wore cloth patches sewn in green and purple and bearing the words 'better broken windows than broken promises'. It was a reference to the colours and slogan of the Suffragettes, who had taken to the streets of London in March 1912 to protest for women's right to vote. A hundred and twenty-six women went to trial for their part in that particular protest just a century or so ago. And of those hundred and twenty-six, seventy-six were sentenced to hard labour. Hard labour. For daring to ask for the vote? Eventually their cause was won. But it took flair, courage and the willingness of women to endure immense physical deprivation to get to that point.

The HSBC nine wouldn't be treated so harshly. Much to the disappointment of the hardliners. But they were still facing custodial sentences. And they knew it. Particularly as their case came to court just after new legislation was passed which clamped down massively on the right to protest. But in the end it took the jury less than four hours to agree on a verdict. All nine walked free. It was an extraordinary turnaround. One in the eye for totalitarianism. The right to civil disobedience has always been one of the most fundamental rights of liberal democracy.

But here is the point of the story. During the action the women had decorated their hammers and their chisels with signs and slogans. Clare Farrell, one of the founders of XR, had painted her chisel with the words 'we act with love'. Love had always been a key plank in XR's armoury. True, the police and the courts and the politicians who had systematically criminalized them in the five years since the group was founded had always given that argument short shrift. But Sue Reid went even further to connect the dots for them.

On the day of the protest she told reporters: 'We're in a planetary emergency and people are dying right now. Just because it's not on our doorstep doesn't mean it's not already happening. . . . What we're doing today is an act of care.'

An act of care. Hang on a minute. So the systematic destruction of reinforced glass in the middle of London can sometimes be an act of care? The women thought so. The jury thought so. And at a stretch we could situate that particular protest quite easily in Fisher and Tronto's definition of care. Things we do to maintain, continue and repair our 'world'. Particularly if in this case the 'world' means the physical climate and the ice caps and the fertility of the agricultural soils on which humanity's breadbasket depends. Though not so easily of course if it includes the plate glass windows of powerful financial institutions.

The point is this. When does something start being an act of care? And where does it stop? Characterizing the smashing of windows as an act of care does seem to rather complicate things. Doesn't it? Maybe I'm wrong. But I feel we need a little more granularity here.

Symbolic health

The trouble with a word like *care* is that it's used so widely we tend not to question whether we know what it means. Whether its meaning differs according to who its subjects are. What its objects are. Whether care constitutes the same thing or something different in any specific instance.

We care for our kids. We care for our family. We care for the sick and the disabled. We care for the dying. We care for our homes. We care for our complexion. We care for our community. We care for our country. We care for our football team. We care for the planet. We care for the future.

Self-evidently these objects of care differ widely. Almost inevitably the acts of care implicit in them differ widely too. Not to mention that in most of those sentences you could replace the word *for* with the word *about* and they would all still make sense. But they'd have slightly different meanings again.

It's worth making a couple of obvious points here. The first is that we don't only care for human beings. Or even just for living organisms. Inanimate matter can also be an object of care. In fact caring for material things turns out to be a key strategy in caring for the planet. And that in its turn has profound implications in terms of caring for our own future. All of those tasks are legitimately the concern of the care economy.

The second point is that we are social as well as physical beings. We have psychological as well as material needs. And so it makes sense to speak of what the philosopher Boris Groys calls care for our 'symbolic bodies' as well as care for our physical bodies. We care for our reputation, for example. We care for our identity. We care for our place in society. We pursue what I'm going to call here 'symbolic health' as well as physical health.

I suppose the WHO definition of health already hints at the same conclusion. Health is not just the absence of disease or infirmity. It's a state of physical, psychological and social wellbeing. And it's particularly useful to bear this in mind in a world where almost one in eight people suffer from some kind of mental health problem.

Strangely those numbers are even more shocking in the so-called advanced economies. More than one in five adults in the US are experiencing mental illness. Almost one in three have been treated for depression at some point in their lives. And those numbers are getting worse not better. Depression and anxiety now cost the global economy $1 trillion annually. And the costs are not merely financial. The decline in mental health is contributing to the alarming rise in 'deaths of despair' that we encountered at the end of the last chapter.

There can be little doubt then that symbolic health matters. It too must be a part of our consideration for the care economy. As individuals – and as a society – we must continually divide our time and attention between physical health and symbolic health as we navigate this duality within us. That doesn't mean that the allocation of care between the physical and the symbolic body is always a zero-sum game. Physical and symbolic health can clearly coexist.

In fact, for the lucky few, they can even be mutually supportive. The more successful we are in the symbolic game the better our chances in the physical game. Those with good symbolic health – higher status, stronger reputation, more celebrity – stay healthier and live longer. And generally speaking it's the poor, the deprived and those with lower social standing who suffer poorer health and die young.

Conversely, of course, the ability to secure good physical health tends to afford greater opportunities for symbolic health. Many of those whose names lived on in history had enormous resources at their disposal while they were alive. History is written by the victors. Few of our enduring heroes emerged out of abject penury and physical deprivation. Though, of course, when they do, we tend to celebrate them even more because of it.

Rags to riches is an attractive meme. Christianity itself emerged from such a story. In Andrew Niccol's science fiction film *Gattaca* the genetically 'inferior' Vincent (played by Ethan Hawke) overcomes the disadvantages of his birth by borrowing the identity of the genetically perfect Jerome (Jude Law) and fulfils his impossible dream of going into space. The moral of the story hangs on the irony that Jerome fails to succeed despite being given every advantage while Vincent transcends his genetic imperfections through force of will and spirit. And, of course, he 'gets the girl' (Uma Thurman) in the process.

Hollywood fantasy aside, physical health and symbolic health are clearly not the same thing. In fact Groys elevates this tension between them to the role of a central theme in philosophy. His *Philosophy of Care* is an intriguing and lucid exploration of the constant conversation between care of the physical and care of the symbolic body. Within individuals. Across society. Over time. And also, as he makes particularly clear, within the history of philosophy.

What becomes obvious is that physical health and symbolic health represent quite distinct objects of care. They involve very different acts of care. And it turns out that the question of how we allocate our time and resources between them becomes absolutely central to our understanding of care. In fact this tension is going to haunt our deliberations throughout the book. It will even threaten at one point to overturn the core distinction I want to make between the care economy and the growth economy. I'll get to all that later.

In the meantime there's something else that's bothering me about this now widened definition of care. It isn't only that the word *care* is in common usage and carries multiple meanings. It's that generally almost all of these meanings convey a kind of unquestioned virtue. They are loaded with moral rectitude. They consistently imply positive, complimentary connotations. And by associating ourselves with care, we ourselves aim to borrow those connotations.

My concern is this. Rather than being helpful, these moral claims tend to obscure something vital about the function of care – and its intimate relationship with health. Let me try and explain what I mean.

Moralities of care

Care is good. Care is so central to life that it takes the form of something instinctive. Care is something powerful enough to cross between species. And by demonstrating care we aim to become good by association. To prove we care is to lay claim to a moral position that goes broadly unquestioned. To admit to not caring is to forgo our moral worth.

To reinforce this indivisible goodness, care is frequently associated with things which in themselves are also considered to be unequivocally good. If you ask people what qualities they associate with care, they'll likely say things like love (Clare Farrell's XR hammer). Compassion. Empathy. Sympathy.

Tenderness. Gentleness. Healing. Attention. Affection. Concern. They won't necessarily even question the origins of these associations. It will seem obvious.

But when a word achieves the status of an unassailable good, it becomes virtually useless as an analytic tool. It ends up being just another claim to the moral high ground. Or else just true by design. Its supposedly self-evident nature becomes deeply problematic. There are too many people in too many ways laying claim to this moral worth. In some cases with good reason. But in some cases just to prove themselves to be standing on the right side of some imagined history. Moral grandstanding. Virtue signalling. Humble bragging. Call it what you will.

Taken at face value, this moral unassailability of care makes the job of defining the care economy massively more difficult. It presents the care economy either as tautological or as moralistic. A case of special pleading. And yet throwing away the moral component of care doesn't help us much either. Why would we want to define a care economy at all if there weren't something good about it? Something worth having?

It helps to remember that no word has an intrinsic right to moral authority. Any moral claim is contingent at best. And thoroughly misleading at worst. And it's somewhat liberating to remember this. We won't always realize it. And even more rarely admit it. But language is typically, inherently, perhaps even inevitably, blind to its own cultural origins. So we won't even necessarily be aware when our moral meanings are culturally contingent. We'll always tend to read them as absolute because they arrive fully formed from the culture of which we are part. 'Obviously care is good. How could you possibly think otherwise?'

But it's useful to point out that all language, all use of language and in particular each moral claim that implicitly captures the meanings of our words has its roots in specific places and times. Some of them quite recent.

Prior to the early 1980s, according to the bioethicist Warren Reich, the word *care* 'had never emerged as a major concept in the history of mainstream Western ethics'. In a fascinating essay on the history of care, he dates the arrival of those moral connotations of care quite precisely to the publication of a book written by the philosopher Carol Gilligan.

In a Different Voice, published in 1982, establishes what Gilligan calls an 'ethic of care'. She elicited this idea by listening (for the first time apparently) to what women and girls said about making moral decisions. Her argument was that this care ethic is a specifically female approach to moral judgement, distinct from the 'ethic of justice' which seems to characterize men's moral compass.

Before Gilligan's 'care ethic', says Reich, care made no particular moral claim and was not particularly prominent in the study of ethics. Its meaning was broadly descriptive rather than normative. Care referred to activities that in some way or another formed part of the ordinary lexicon of everyday life – for everyone. On the one hand these activities included the worries and anxieties that arise from insecurity or concern, the burdens that can sometimes drag us down. The 'cares of the world', if you like. And on the other hand it denoted the activities of attending to or providing for the welfare of others.

It's interesting to note in passing that these two different meanings of the word *care* are associated with two distinct routes through which the word itself passed into the modern English language. *Care as suffering* comes through a Germanic root, via the old Saxon word *cara*, which means lament, and the old High German *kara*, which means grief. That sense is still present in modern German in *Karwoche* (Passion week) and *Karfreitag* (Good Friday). *Care as attention to needs* comes from the Latin *cura* – which translates both as cure and as care. Strangely etymologists insist that there's no linguistic connection between these two separate meanings. Even though evidently they are connected in meaning.

But Reich's point here is that before Gilligan's ethic of care, common usage offered no particular moral division of labour between men and women. When it comes to the cares of the world, we're all subject to them. That's neither moral nor immoral. Nor is it particularly gendered. And as for the second meaning of care, the activities of provision can (and do) include all kinds of tasks. Some carried out by women. Others carried out by men. None of them carrying any particular moral claim over the other.

There's clearly a great deal more I'm going to have to say on all this. And in particular on the relationship between gender and care. That much has been obvious from the start of my journey. The question of who cares – and in what capacity – leads us straight to the land of the invisible heart. Not quite in the way I first thought perhaps. But Carol Gilligan is going to turn out to be a useful guide for us when I eventually return to that task.

For now, I'm still puzzling over the question of the moon. So I want to take us further back. Before HSBC. Before XR. Before feminism. Before the birth of Rome. Not just for the hell of it. But rather so that we can try and identify whether and when breaking windows is an act of care. And whether the moon cares for us.

The myth of care

So let me go back to the beginning. Or nearly the beginning. To the Prologue. To the fanciful but not entirely frivolous casting of an old Roman myth with which I began the book.

The story has to do with a mythical creature, a goddess named Care. In Latin, of course, her name was Cura. Which means – as we now know – care. Not to be confused with *cara*. Which is either the feminine form of the Latin adjective meaning beloved or the old Saxon word for lamentation. Or with the word *caritas*, which means love. So. Yes. Perhaps it is a bit confusing. And that confusion may explain something of the linguistic games we play when we associate care with irreducible good.

At any rate the myth of care has some vital lessons for us. So let me just recap briefly the version I gave in the Prologue. The broad outlines go something like this.

> The goddess Care is playing on the banks of a river one day when she happens to fashion a small figurine out of mud and asks Jupiter to breathe life into it.
>
> Jupiter agrees but demands naming rights. Care is not happy at all about that. So they wake up Terra (the goddess of the Earth), who stakes her own claim to the creature on the grounds that the raw materials came from her.
>
> Since none of them can agree, they decide to consult Saturn, who has a reputation as a level-headed kind of guy. He quickly comes up with what seems, to this day, like an elegant solution.
>
> Since the mud came from Terra, says Saturn, she can have its body back when the thing dies. Since its spirit comes from Jupiter, he can have that back.
>
> In the meantime, Care gets to look after it for as long as it happens to live. Come rain or shine. Come hell or high water. In sickness and in health. Till death us do part.

The origins of the myth aren't clear. Its first appearance in the written record is associated with a certain Gaius Julius Hyginus who lived around the first century CE. His collection of fables was published sometime during the second century. We don't know where he got the story from originally. The myth of care doesn't seem to appear elsewhere, outside his collection. But obviously the incident itself happened much longer ago. In the mythical land of Mount

Olympus, the home of the Roman (and Greek) gods. According to Hyginus. Who of course might well have made the whole thing up.

And it's worth pointing out that my version of the myth, the one in the Prologue, differs in some respects from the Hyginus version. First off, I play a bit on the question of gender. But also the ending didn't quite happen as I describe it. I have my reasons for these departures, which I'll come back to in case they're not already obvious. But just for completeness, in the original myth, Saturn doesn't forget about naming rights. It's a bit unfair to suggest he does. And the figurine doesn't claim the name Barbie. Because at that time Ruth Handler (who invented Barbie) hadn't been born and the entertainment company Mattel (which commercialized her) didn't exist. Yet. More on that later though.

What really happens (in Hyginus) is that Saturn decides to name the figurine *homo* from the Latin word *humus*. Which means dirt or mud. Makes sense, right? Dust to dust. Ashes to ashes. *Homo sapiens*. Wise dirt. Clever mud. Better than stupid mud, I guess. Though sometimes you'd wonder. The point is. The myth makes clear that this little figurine represents us. Humanity. Human beings. And its message is that Care is our lifelong companion. Goddess. Guardian. Protector.

It's interesting that this origin myth focuses mainly on the second of the two distinct meanings of the word *care*. Obvious, I suppose, since it corresponds to the root drawn from the Latin. And as Reich points out, 'the primordial role of Care is to hold the human together in wholeness while cherishing it' throughout its entire life. A comforting, unquestioning and (in the context of the myth) divine solicitude.

The Hyginus myth pays less attention to the Germanic component. The cares of the world. In my take I've hinted at it. Care's delight at being given the task of providing for her figurine and the obvious love and attention she's going to lavish on her are both tempered, for the reader at least, by the inevitable reality of Barbie's eventual demise.

It's something we can never quite ignore. Whatever we care for will die. Sooner or later. 'Everything put together sooner or later falls apart,' as Paul Simon once put it. Maybe it sucks. But there's no point denying it. And perhaps, inexplicably, it's our latent knowledge of that inevitable suffering that leads us to pay attention to the objects of our care in the first place. Perhaps the two distinct roots of the word *care* are conjoined in ways which defy linguistic orthodoxy. One way or the other that Germanic strand from the etymology of care casts a strange shadow over the meaning and interpretation of care.

Once I've stumbled on that shadow, I begin to find it all over the place. One of its most profound incarnations comes in the final act of the second part of Goethe's *Faust*. At this point in the story, Faust has just discovered that in the course of his plans to grab as much land as he possibly can, his henchmen have managed to kill an old couple he was fond of. He's already not best pleased. And then four 'grey women' show up at his door. Want. Debt. Need. And Care. He manages to lock three of them out. But Care finds a way through the keyhole.

'Who are you?' asks Faust in agitation. 'I'm just here,' replies Care. 'Never looked for, always there. Cursed and flattered, I am Care.' She then proceeds to blind him. At which point Faust suddenly begins to see everything more clearly. 'In my inmost soul a bright light shines,' he declares. He doesn't know it yet, but this is the light that will eventually save his soul.

Goethe had taken his inspiration for the character of Care from a poem by his mentor Johann Gottfried Herder. The poem was a retelling of Hyginus' myth of care. And then in the very first ever issue of what was to become a famous German literary journal, a historian named Konrad Burdach writes a sixty-page essay about all this. Linking Care in *Faust* to the original myth. At that point, the philosopher Martin Heidegger reads the essay and picks up the story. It becomes the centrepiece for his 1927 *Sein und Zeit* (*Being and Time*), a book which 'permanently altered the course of philosophy in continental Europe'.

Heidegger uses the myth to illustrate his argument that care is fundamental to our humanity. Inseparable from our existence. To be human is to be in a state of care. And this intimate relationship with care lasts our entire life. From birth until death us do part. Just as the Hyginus story suggests. That relationship is established in part by the role that care plays as an intermediary between matter and spirit. It's the force, according to the myth, which maintains matter and spirit on the same plane of existence. Care is essential to life. And for Heidegger this gives the state of care in which we find ourselves an existential character. It's not just an arbitrary behaviour or an emotion that we choose to adopt or not to adopt. It isn't a moral choice. It's a condition in which we inevitably find ourselves. Without care we don't exist.

In some ways I rather like what's beginning to emerge from this. It hasn't entirely defined what the act of care consists of. What that force is that mediates between matter and spirit. But we're closing in on something. On the one hand by understanding its inevitability. And on the other by acknowledging its end result. Namely the lifelong process of keeping body and soul together. At least for a while.

This version also presents us with a view of care as its own authority. As its own justification, if you like. Because without care we are lost. That's clearly a part of what the myth is telling us. And it's part of what Heidegger is drawing attention to. This framing could still give a moral force (should we need one) to the actions or emotions we describe as care. But it also roots them in a reminder (lest we forget) that without those actions we are nothing.

Whether we care about care or not, its reality is vital to any meaningful concept of human existence. Acting without care is counter to our own being. It's a kind of nonsense. But how does that help us specifically when it comes to characterizing what is and what is not an act of care? How does it help me answer the question that's standing in the way of me getting back home?

Gravity

Is it far-fetched to imagine that the moon cares for us? At one level it seems to be. Obviously the objects of care can include inanimate objects. But don't the subjects of care need some form of consciousness? Care involves emotion. Care presumes motivation. And it demands attention.

The moon certainly attends us. In a certain sense. In a purely inanimate way. But so far as we know, it has no emotions. No motivations. Its attention appears fortuitous rather than directed. Its presence in our lives seems like an accident of cosmology.

On the other hand that accident is a pretty significant one. Without it we might not even exist. The moon propels the tidal streams which stabilize temperatures within a relatively habitable range. It controls the restless dance of the tidal range around the still point. And that dance provides living conditions for the myriad creatures who inhabit the boundaries between the ocean and the land. We're distantly related to some of them. Our ancestors depended on that environment. So the chances are we wouldn't even be here if it weren't for the moon.

Perhaps its most essential function is just being there. Its gravitational force is what holds the earth's axis at a steady 23.5 degrees away from the upright as we orbit round the sun. That tilt is what ensures the regularity of the seasons. Without the moon the axis would wander anywhere between 10 and 45 degrees, creating absolute havoc with climatic conditions. Anthropogenic climate change would look like a walk in the park. If there were anyone there to see it.

The moon's attention to task is as constant as the goddess Care in the Roman myth. Her gravity exerts a massive stabilizing influence on our external conditions. Without her, homeostasis wouldn't even have a shout. She maintains the possibility of health. Is it fanciful to call that care?

(Before you answer that, you should maybe know that the moon has been moving slowly away from us for millions of years. A couple of centimetres or so a year. As she moves, the days grow slightly longer and the tidal range diminishes infinitesimally. It'll be a while before her influence declines to a point where it's noticeable. But hey. Be nice to her. And maybe don't see her only as a source of mineral wealth. There's no doubt at all we'll miss her when she's gone. Some scientists believe that Jupiter might help to stabilize things if the moon weren't there. But we've already seen how fickle he can be.)

My own answer is that it may not be care. But the moon's constant attention illustrates something fundamental about what care is. The function of care is to maintain and restore the condition of health. It operates as a restorative force. A balancing force. Just as the moon does. Just as homeostasis does.

Motivation. Emotion. Conscious attention. All of these are relevant, of course. Mainly because they bring us humans into the zone of care. Into the space where we can contribute to the maintenance and restoration of health. They incline us towards care, if you will. And without them we'd be at the mercy of emotions and motivations that look compromising to health at best. And fatal at worst. But these drivers themselves are not the essence of care. Its most fundamental property and its core function is to aid the ability of the body to maintain its own health. To act as a restorative force.

So when we talk about ourselves as carers, we're not the first in line for the role. The sun. The moon. The planets. The earth's ecosystems. Gaia (the Greek name for the goddess Terra). These are our primary carers. And this primary care operates incessantly. Consistently. Unendingly. Like the goddess in the myth, its constancy is quintessential. A constant moderation of the external conditions within which the next level of care must function.

And that next level of care isn't what we'd normally call care either. Our secondary carer is the wisdom of the body. It's the constant regulation of the internal environment in the face of changing external conditions. It's the dance around the set of physiological still points that define organic equilibrium.

Again, you might want to object that this process isn't 'really' care. It doesn't seem to involve motivation or emotion. At least not in the sense that we'd normally assume. That's definitely a bit more of a grey area, though. It's not so clear cut as with the moon. Because quite clearly the wisdom of the body does make use of our neurophysiology and our psychology in its mode as carer. Emotion and motivation could be seen as part of that process.

In fact if care is what holds body and soul together, as the myth suggests, then perhaps employing both physiological and psychological functions to achieve the goal of restoring health is much more precisely care than our mixed up morally loaded notions of it.

At any rate, one thing is clear. The wisdom of the body embodies the most fundamental dynamic of care. Its aim is the maintenance and restoration of health. And it definitely pays attention. Our homeostatic sentinels are always on guard. Whether we're conscious of them or not. Something inside us is attentive as hell. And it seems to me that this constancy of attention – and the restorative force it exerts – is what's critical here. Not just in answering my enquiry about the moon. But in understanding care.

Careful whispers

I have a feeling it's time to leave. And it's not just the ache in my body. The cold in my bones. The hunger in my belly. My mind is also in need of respite. It's too full of contestation. Of claim and counter-claim. As I make my way back along the rugged coast path, I'm followed by a chorus of disapproval.

Care is something profoundly human. How can you dehumanize it in this way? Care is something sacred. Why are you trying to turn it into something profane? Care is a precious quality. What's the point of deconstructing it? Care belongs to us. To the people who care. Who are you to steal it away from us?

But I'm not trying to steal it away, I say. I'm trying to return some stolen goods. We do care a disservice when we allow it to be unconditionally associated with an unassailable good. We diminish care by employing it to exonerate actions which are completely and utterly opposed to the maintenance and restoration of health. Because then it can be used and abused for any purposes that its users and abusers happen to claim for it.

I care for my kids by letting them eat sweets all day. I care for those in pain by offering them an endless supply of opioids. I care for my political friends by sending them bombs to kill the children of their enemies. I care for my country's reputation by corrupting its politics with the proceeds from those arms. I could go on. But none of these things maintain health. None of them promote resilience or restore balance. None of it is care.

Defining care as a restorative force doesn't exclude the 'caring professions'. On the contrary. They all still matter. The doctors. The nurses. The midwives. The teachers. The childcare workers. Those who care for the sick and the disabled and the elderly. Those who care for and maintain our buildings, our houses, our soil, our climate, our homes. These tasks remain as important as they always were. As central to life and health as ever. On the other hand they must earn the right to be called care. It doesn't simply follow by association.

It's worth pointing out here too that care – in the sense I'm defining it – isn't simply about dampening external conditions. It's about supporting the wisdom of the body. And this wisdom evolves over time. At birth, the infant brain doesn't even regulate temperature properly. The ability develops over the first few years of childhood. In fact this characteristic of learning to regulate is adaptive. It conveys evolutionary advantages over arriving fully formed with all regulatory mechanisms intact. Learning is key to adaptation.

And that's why care sometimes involves stimulation. Through immersion in cold water, for instance. Through exercise. Through deliberately invoking stress to improve the body's own resilience. So long as the stimulus is acute rather than chronic. So long as it lies within the capability of the body to adapt. So long as it's enacted with attention. Stress itself can be an act of care.

Attention is obviously vital. The moon attends. The body attends. And we as tertiary carers in a complex web of care must also attend. Care must always listen and respond to the state of health. To the force and direction of external conditions. To the body's own vitality and its capacity for resilience. The fundamental quality of care is attention.

But its functional role is balance. Care is a restorative force. Its job is to improve the capacity of the body to return to balance. To facilitate the return to the still point. To aid and abet the dance.

5

No Good Deed

*'No society can legitimately call itself civilised if a sick
person is denied medical aid because of lack of means.'*
Aneurin (Nye) Bevan, 1948

A couple of days later we're sitting in the Tredegar Arms hotel contemplating the lunch menu. It's offering us a familiar pub fare. Probably decent enough. No guarantee it's going to be nutritious. But it's been a long morning already. And after an early start we're in need of sustenance. Comfort food, preferably.

Behind us now the coast, the moon and the myth of care. My writing retreat is over. We're heading home. But we've stopped off here in Tredegar for a reason. It's the birthplace of Britain's much loved and deeply abused NHS. And while we're (more or less) in the neighbourhood, I want to see it for myself.

I'm not really sure what I expect to find here. At first sight the town is a close facsimile of a thousand other post-industrial towns across the country. Once vital to the British Empire, they now lie broken, dormant, desperate for recovery. Of which, occasionally, there are some tell-tale signs.

Nestling on the outskirts of the town is Parc Bryn Bach (Bryn Bach Park). An award-winning nature reserve. Three hundred and forty acres of 'stunning grass and woodland' with a 36-acre lake at its heart. Two hundred years ago this was a scene of utter devastation. Now it's a vibrant tourist attraction, offering archery, bush craft, caving, a driving range, fishing, hill-walking and (of course) open water swimming. An alphabet of leisure pursuits, designed to prove that restoration is possible. And to attract tourism to the region.

The town itself is another matter. Walking down Morgan Street towards The Circle with its famous clock tower, we pass a parade of empty and shuttered windows. Scaffolding signals the intention to renovate. The occasional tattoo studio and nail bar give credence to the idea that, yes, this is the twenty-first century. But these all seem like the vestiges of late capitalism. It doesn't feel much like recovery.

'If you know what you want, it might be wise to order now,' says the woman behind the bar, pointing towards a group of young mums just arrived with their brand-new offspring. Their dress, their demeanour and their conversation are bright and full of hope. They certainly don't signal deprivation. Most of them sport fashionable tattoos. And their nails all look immaculate.

'Good idea,' I smile. 'What do you recommend?'

'The vegetarian lasagne's the best thing on the menu,' she tells me with an air of quiet confidentiality. Comfort food, I think to myself. Just what we need. And because I haven't quite understood the danger of comfort food at this point, I say:

'Sounds perfect.'

It's not perfect. Unfortunately. Nothing against the bartender. As lasagne goes, it was one of the best. And as I settle down to look over my notes with a pint of lime juice and soda in my hand, that's not perfect either. Because I'm a living, breathing example of a shift in population health against which care is fighting a losing battle. I just don't know it yet. I'm too busy absorbing the lessons from this short visit to the Welsh Valleys.

Anniversary

Back in January 1948, the town's MP was Aneurin (Nye) Bevan. Seventy-five years ago more or less to the day we're here, he announced the arrival of a new national health service. Immensely popular with his constituents and disliked in almost equal measure by his political opponents, Bevan was the health minister in Clement Attlee's postwar Labour government and a formidable advocate for the welfare state.

The new NHS would be free to everyone at the point of use, Bevan promised. And it would come into force, he vowed, on 5 July 1948. The precise date wasn't entirely arbitrary. It was the third-year anniversary of Attlee's resounding electoral victory following the Second World War. But choosing that date was still a massive gamble.

The NHS was a radical disruption to the brew of private surgeries, well-paid consultants and run-down charity hospitals that had presided over Britain's dilapidated healthcare system prior to that. The initial resistance of the British Medical Association was legendary. 'Six months before the Appointed Day,' wrote the historian Pauline Gregg, 'it looked as though the whole edifice might crash through lack of support from the medical profession.' But it happened. Just six months later. On time. As advertised.

Much of that was down to Nye Bevan. Some of it was down to Tredegar. Bevan being unavailable for comment, it's to Tredegar that I've turned. Looking for insights. Looking for answers. Answers to questions that are formulating themselves chaotically in my mind as I shift the focus of my inquiry from the dynamics of care to the structure of the economy.

Now that we have some sense of care, what can we say about the care economy? The question still seems too difficult at this point. But I can already glimpse some useful starting points. How does society navigate health? How does the economy negotiate care? What are the core design principles of care in the economy? Why aren't they working?

Tough questions still. I'm not looking for easy answers. But I'm hoping somehow that being here, at the birthplace of a dream, I might ingest some wisdom from the ghosts of the past. And find, if not answers, then at least some clues to follow.

The birthplace of a dream

Bevan was born in Tredegar in 1897. His father was a Welsh coal miner and his mother was the daughter of a colliery engineer. At fourteen years old, he was working in the pits himself. That was by no means unusual. In the Welsh Valleys the fate of men, women and children had been tied to mining for a century and a half by the time Bevan was born.

Thanks to its post-Cambrian walkabout, Wales had been blessed with extraordinary mineral wealth. That wealth lay tantalizingly close to the surface of the earth. In the early days, coal, iron ore and limestone could more or less be scratched out of the ground by hand. Or with picks and shovels at least. A process known at the time as patch-working or 'patching'.

That's where Bryn Bach dates from. The lake that now hosts kayaks and paddleboards was first excavated to provide water for the steam engines that served the mines and the foundries. Hungry for steel, industry expanded rapidly wherever coal and iron ore lived side by side. And that was definitely the case in the Welsh Valleys. Very soon the surface mining turned underground. The rich seams of coal became a source of enormous financial wealth for a new generation of capitalists and a sink of cheap labour from the working class.

The demand for men fit enough to spend twelve hours digging at the coalface rose so fast that the labour force soon spread to women and children. By the middle of the nineteenth century, the patches had become famous – and infamous – for a culture of hard graft, poor living conditions and bare-knuckle fist fights. If that sounds like aggression under duress, that's only part of the truth. It was the only form of entertainment on hand. And perhaps also a way of establishing the credentials of physical strength within a ready pool of manual labour from which capitalism could flourish.

When I first read about the fist fights, I couldn't help thinking about the curious incarnations of allostasis. That innate mechanism through which an organism attempts to find its equilibrium in the face of harsh external conditions. These visceral contests could sometimes go on for days. And they clearly borrow something from the gladiatorial ethos of the martial arts. Strength through combat. Fitness through adversity.

But what kind of external conditions make it functional to enhance physical health by slogging it out with another man in the mud. For the sake of a temporary pedestal from which tomorrow you will inevitably be toppled by another younger and fitter contender for the crown? At what point does a potentially functional evolutionary mechanism turn into a deeply dysfunctional social problem?

That question definitely haunted the Earl of Shaftesbury, Lord Anthony Ashley Cooper. In 1842 he lobbied the government to set up a Royal Commission to look into working conditions in the mines. It was the fate of women and children that bothered him most. In 1838 twenty-six children had been killed when a mine collapsed near Barnsley in Yorkshire. Eleven of them were girls. And the youngest, Sarah Newton, was just eight years old.

On the top of a monument that marks their graves is a verse from St Matthew's Gospel. 'Therefore, be ye ready.' Or in other words. You're gonna die. So follow the Lord and get your affairs in order. As though dying in the mines is somehow ok if you're a true believer. As though exploiting kids is forgivable as long as they've been to Sunday school. As though sacrificing them to the engine of capitalism is fine as long as they're 'ready'.

Shaftesbury's findings shocked the nation. Particularly unseemly to Victorian sensibilities were revelations that women were working half-naked alongside men at the coalface. The women 'lead a sort of half-savage life', the report concluded. 'Hardy, and exposed to all kinds of weather, they work as hard as the men, from whom they differ but little in dress, and quite equal in grossness.' Obviously it was the depraved mores of the working class that were at fault here. But still it had to be stopped.

The Mines and Collieries Act of 1842 made it illegal to employ women, or children under the age of ten, in an underground capacity. Difficult to enforce, it backfired on the families reliant on the income from mining to survive. It may even have contributed to greater child labour in the long run, as parents sent more of their precious offspring down the mines. By the early 1900s, when Bevan left school, two-thirds of the adult male population were still working in the mines. And kids as young as fourteen worked alongside them.

For Nye Bevan, though, the mine was a godsend. School had been a horror. Plagued by an intense stammer, he'd been bullied by an oppressive headmaster. Working in the pits was a walk in the park by comparison. The work was gruelling. The conditions were oppressive. And employment was always at the mercy of economic forces that lay way beyond the control of the workers. But there was also a kind of dignity. And a sense of community.

During the First World War, mining boomed and Tredegar flourished. But when the war ended, demand declined. The steelworks in the neighbouring town of Ebbw Vale closed down. And foreign competition began to put a downward pressure on the mines. Raising unemployment. Squeezing wages.

Between 1919 and 1921, Bevan spent a couple of years studying at the Central Labour College in London. Even as a kid he'd been an avid reader. At college he immersed himself in economics, philosophy and history, all from a broadly socialist perspective. The Labour College was an experiment. It was only to last a couple of decades. But at the point Bevan was there it was in its heyday. And it was teaching an orthodoxy very different from one taught in Oxford and Cambridge. Marx and Engels were a recognizable backdrop to the struggle of the miners and foundry workers in his own hometown.

By the time he returned to Tredegar, Bevan was beginning to understand something more about his own mission in life. He would spend hours discussing politics with his father, whose health at this point was deteriorating rapidly. There was something noble to be found in the mining communities of the Valleys. And it went way beyond bare-knuckle fist-fighting in the patches.

That view was shared by a young Scottish medic named A.J. Cronin who took up a position as a junior doctor in Tredegar. In a semi-autobiographical novel called *The Citadel*, he describes the day he first arrived in the Valleys in October 1924. On a small train pulled by a coal-fired steam engine along a single-track railway.

> The mountain tops were hidden in a grey waste of sky but their sides, scarred by ore workings, fell black and desolate, blemished by great heaps of slag on which a few dirty sheep wandered in vain hope of pasture. No bush, no blade of vegetation was visible. The trees, seen in the fading light, were gaunt and stunted spectres. At a bend of the line the red glare of a foundry flashed into sight, illuminating a score of workmen stripped to the waist, their torsos straining, arms upraised to strike. Though the scene was swiftly lost behind the huddled top gear of a mine, a sense of power persisted, tense and vivid.

And yet this 'sense of power', this nobility in labour, was betrayed and squandered by its careless treatment at the hands of a burgeoning capitalism. Voracious for wealth, the economic system that was beginning to dominate the twentieth century seemed utterly contemptuous of the men, women and children who were instrumentalized to its purposes. And as the passage from Cronin's novel makes clear, it was equally contemptuous of the natural world.

Bevan's father died in his arms in 1925, succumbing to the pneumoconiosis he had contracted in the mines. Black lung, as it was called, was the more or less inevitable result of breathing in coal dust and foul air. Assuming you avoided getting maimed or killed by a tunnel collapse or a methane explosion. And it was a grim death. It was a grim life.

A couple of years later a massive explosion killed fifty-two miners in a mine at Cwm Ebbw Vale. Bevan was a local councillor and a union rep at this point and led the fight for better working and living conditions. When he stood for Parliament in May 1929, at the age of only thirty-one, he was returned with a massive majority.

His reputation as an eloquent advocate of the rights of working miners preceded him. A reporter for the *Daily Herald* noted at the time: 'I do not think Mr Aneurin Bevan will be exactly lost in the crowd. He has a reputation for exceptional platform ability.' That ability was going to come in handy, nineteen years later, in the struggle to create the NHS.

Industrial homicide

I came here looking for the birthplace of a dream. At this point the dream sounds more like a nightmare. Maybe the nightmare seems long enough ago for us to dismiss it as irrelevant to the question of the care economy today. I'm going to get back to that. But before I do, it's worth pointing out briefly that none of the injustices that inspired Bevan have exactly gone away. Even in the most advanced economies in the world. Black lung is still killing ex-miners even in countries like the US and Australia. The WHO's joint report with the International Labour Organization (ILO) towards the end of the pandemic found that more than two million deaths each year are still caused by work-related disease or injury.

Just under a quarter of those are from chronic obstructive pulmonary diseases (COPDs) like black lung and asbestosis. Two-fifths of all work-related deaths are attributable to long working hours. It's the biggest killer of all. And these fatalities are just the tip of the iceberg. The 'burden of disease' from work is equivalent to ninety million disability-adjusted life years (DALYs) and typically costs a nation between 4 and 6 per cent of its national income.

Some progress has been made. In some places. In some respects. Over certain periods of time. Fatal injuries at work have declined massively since the mine explosion in Ebbw Vale. But most of that progress was made during the twentieth century and some of it has stalled and gone backwards in the twenty-first. Even in a country like the US, occupational injuries are now rising again. The rate of workplace fatalities has gone up by 16 per cent over the last decade.

And some of the damage is still falling on kids. Child labour rose by 5 per cent over the years preceding the pandemic and now stands at around 160 million children. That's equivalent to one in every ten kids worldwide. Of those kids, a million work in mines. And almost eighty million work under some kind of hazardous conditions. Routinely exposed to danger, poor air quality, toxic chemicals, long hours and injury. In poorer countries one in four kids – a quarter of the population between five and seventeen years old – are subject to some form of child labour. And these numbers too are on the rise. Another nine million children are at risk of being pushed into child labour in the coming years.

It hardly needs saying that these statistics represent a formidable challenge to the idea of prosperity as health. Atrocious and sometimes fatal working conditions have nothing to do with the care economy. The economy we have is killing people. And we can't just turn our backs on how and where and why that's happening. Nor can we really take our vision of prosperity for granted when it fails to account for this damage. If wealth is dependent on child labour and industrial homicide, can we even call it prosperity in the first place?

It's particularly problematic when the wealth is accumulated in one place and the DALYs are lost in another. Social justice must surely be a basic component of prosperity at the aggregate level – perhaps even at the personal level too. A nation that presides over deep inequality is prosperous only in a very narrow sense. What does it mean to call your personal wealth prosperity when it's acquired through death, disease and deprivation for others?

To ask such things is to query the dynamics of power and social organization. Empire. Colonialism. The hierarchies of domination. In some sense the questions themselves are timeless. All of those forces come into play as soon as we ask them. And we find ourselves moving closer to care's nemesis: violence and war.

For now, I'm just making a relatively simple point. Almost as an aside to the narrative in this chapter. That the story of dangerous and inhumane working conditions in Tredegar is not one we can simply dismiss as the weakness of a bygone age. Just like the folly in Llandod. It's part of a dynamic that persists. And yet the nightmare in Tredegar gave birth to the birth of a dream. As sometimes only a nightmare can.

'We are going to Tredegar-ise you'

Right around the corner from where we're having lunch is an unimposing two-storey building with the words 'Canolfan Dreftadaeth' written in elegant blue script above the door. Beneath those words, in gold lettering for foreigners like me, is the English translation: Heritage Centre. It was my first port of call when we arrived here a couple of hours ago. Outside is a plaque which reads:

> These were the offices of a mutual society (1890) formed by miners and ironworkers of the Tredegar Iron and Coal Co. Through modest weekly contributions, they were able to employ doctors, a surgeon and run a hospital.

The mutual society in question was the Tredegar Medical Aid Society. And this is the birthplace I'm looking for. In Bevan's own constituency he found the model that provided the inspiration for the NHS. Universal healthcare free at the point of use. For several decades before the NHS was formed, the Medical Aid Society had employed the same model. It was all that stood between injury, illness and death for the miners, the steelworkers and their families.

The Society started life in the 1870s as a health and education fund established by the Tredegar Iron and Coal Company. It wasn't unlike other similar initiatives. Private companies would employ a doctor to treat the victims of workplace injury and fight communicable diseases like cholera and tuberculosis. A healthy workforce was a good investment. Particularly when some of the costs could be deducted directly from employee salaries.

In 1890 the fund was merged with a variety of local initiatives which also serviced the local community and together they formed the mutual society. Management was transferred to an independent committee consisting mainly of workers. Doctors were paid a fixed salary rather than the entire proceeds of the compulsory contributions. And the destination for surplus funds was decided on by the committee.

In 1915 a former 'workhouse boy' named Walter Conway was appointed secretary and under his guidance the Tredegar Medical Aid Society really began to flourish. During the depression years it continued to offer services even when people couldn't pay. And by the mid-1940s, it was providing medical care to 95 per cent of the town's population.

The reputation of the Society definitely owes something to A.J. Cronin. *The Citadel* became enormously popular when it was first published in 1937. It hasn't been out of print since. Behind the compelling narrative of a young doctor finding his way in the world lay an excoriating attack on the damage caused inside his own profession by a healthcare system blind to science and driven by private gain.

The 'useless guinea-chasing treatments, the unnecessary operations, the crowds of worthless pseudo-scientific proprietary preparations we use – isn't it time some of these were eliminated?' his protagonist Andrew Manson asks in a court case that plays out towards the end of the novel. 'The whole profession is far too tolerant and far too smug.'

Cronin makes a passionate plea for a modern, local healthcare system built on a foundation of continual scientific research in which doctors themselves would participate. Its foundation would be a primary care system in which prevention and population health provide the guiding principles. In the final stages of the book Manson pioneers such a practice in a fictional community in middle England, partnering with a man he had first met in the Welsh Valleys.

The book is credited with popularizing the example of the Tredegar Medical Aid Society. In the years following its publication public sentiment began to call for a new health service. And in the aftermath of the war, the idea of universal healthcare free at the point of use began to gain traction across political divides. This was the dream I was talking about. This was the gift that Tredegar brought to the nation. Championed of course by the town's most famous son.

'All I am doing is extending to the entire population of Britain the benefits we had in Tredegar for a generation or more,' said Nye Bevan when he announced the formation of the NHS in 1948. 'We are going to Tredegar-ise you.'

Fast forward

From the perspective of the twenty-first century, it's fascinating to note that Cronin's proposals go beyond the idea of healthcare as a universal right. They remain innovative and potentially transformative even today. The relevance of preventative primary care and the focus on public health is something I'll come back to.

Relevant too is Cronin's passionate appeal for social justice. For decent working conditions and fair pay. Not only for the miners and the ironworkers. But also for those who undertook the task of caring for them. 'For years we've been bleating about the sweated conditions under which our nurses work, the wretched pittances we pay them,' says Manson. 'Well? They're still being sweated. Still paid pittances.'

Fast forward three-quarters of a century and these messages are still as relevant. Still as poignant. Still as unsettling. This winter, when I'm visiting Tredegar, hospital waiting lists are at an all-time high. Staff retention is at an all-time low. Health workers can't afford to live. Carers are resorting to food banks to survive.

A recent report from the King's Fund compares the NHS with healthcare systems in other similar countries. It presents a deeply uncomfortable picture. Some of what Bevan and Cronin fought for has been retained. Administrative costs are low by comparison with other OECD nations. And the UK has higher levels of universal health service coverage than many other countries.

But performance overall is poor. The UK healthcare system has less medical equipment, fewer beds, fewer nurses and fewer doctors than most of its peers. Diagnostic waiting times are higher. And most damningly of all, health outcomes are suffering. Avoidable mortality rates are the worst of any country in the OECD – with the notable exception of the US, where 'affordable health care' has been a political football for decades.

The foundation of the NHS has been described as 'the most far-reaching piece of social legislation in British history'. It was the first time a western country had introduced a universal healthcare system free at the point of use. And its influence across the world is widely recognized. Yet seventy-five years later, Bevan's stunning political success is being torn apart. And no one across the political spectrum seems to know what to do. The blame game is paralysing.

It's the cost of living. It's the aftermath of Covid-19. It's the worst flu season in a decade. It's too many years of 'sticking-plaster politics' from a party that was in power too long. It's all of the above. Some of that is undoubtedly true. Not since 1978's winter of discontent has the battle between keyworkers and government been so acrimonious – and so desperate – as it is during my visit to Tredegar.

And this desperation isn't an abstract phenomenon. It's a visceral reality. It's depicted in the appalling, trench-like conditions of the accident and emergency departments and the walk-in clinics. It's written in the stoicism of the nurses and doctors who endure those conditions day after day. It's engrained in the faces of those whose health and lives depend, not on Bevan's dream, but on the nightmare it has become in twenty-first century Britain. And the gift that Tredegar brought to the world seems tarnished beyond repair.

The causes of death

How did this happen? Where did it go wrong? Who is responsible for the death of the dream? It's not entirely trivial to unravel. But there are a few fairly obvious things to say. And it's worth a brief interlude to explore them.

To start with, some of what's happening here is political. For a long time the consensus around the vision held strong across the political parties. But healthcare is a significant budget line in central government's managed spending accounts. And whenever there's pressure on the public purse there's the potential for political consensus to waiver. Particularly when, as in this case, the budget line is rising in real and relative terms.

Healthcare spending in the UK has more than doubled as a share of the GDP since the early 1980s. Most of that increase came after the New Labour government came to power in the late 1990s. Spending rose from around 5 per cent to about 10 per cent of the GDP between 1997 and 2010. The increases stalled when Labour lost the election. But they rose again through the pandemic. And then fell back somewhat. In 2023 the share was 10.9 per cent. That figure represented around £292 billion.

As a share of the GDP, that's lower than some comparable countries such as Germany (12.7 per cent) and France (11.9 per cent) but higher than others such as Norway (8 per cent) and Ireland (6.1 per cent). In the US, the share of the GDP is almost twice what it is in the UK. But there are huge differences in the organization of health care between the two countries. In Britain more than 80 per cent of the spending comes from central government, with less than 20 per cent borne privately. In the US those numbers are more or less reversed.

That difference between two countries illuminates something vital about Bevan's dream. Whichever way you look at it, universal state provision of healthcare is going to be a big-ticket item for the public sector. Over the last decade, it represents around 25 per cent of the government budget. And that scale of spending relies on consistent political commitment. Broadly speaking, left-leaning governments tend to be more committed. Right-leaning tend to be less committed. And that leaves healthcare continually exposed to the ideological flavour of the moment. Buffeted by the winds of change, the NHS, like affordable care in the US, has become a political football.

But the pressure on financing healthcare has been felt by governments of all persuasions. Very early on, for example, prescription charges were introduced to combat a steep rise in the drugs bill. Progressively dentistry was defunded. And perhaps most influential of all, the introduction in the 1990s of public–

private partnerships (PPPs) and private finance initiatives (PFIs) dramatically changed both the culture and the economics of healthcare.

The result is a kind of ideological mission creep. Even as budgets increased, resources bled from the frontline of a nationalized healthcare system into the private sector. In the social care sector that problem has been even worse. The provision of social care has been underwritten by local government but delivered primarily by private providers. That model has attracted private equity firms into the sector. And that has turned into what one former health secretary described to me privately as a 'mistake of catastrophic' proportions.

My colleagues Christine Corlet Walker, Angela Druckman and I have explored the damage this 'catastrophic mistake' has wreaked on social care in the UK. Our analysis reveals huge property portfolios. Opaque management structures. Public money that ends up in offshore accounts. Low pay and poor working conditions. And social care that deteriorates dramatically. Those findings are not unique to the UK. Or to social care. The dramatic increase in private equity acquisition of hospitals in the US has been criticized for the same reasons.

One of the problems is obvious. Private equity doesn't just want its money back. It wants considerably more than its money back. Success means doubling or tripling the original stake. Sometimes even more. And investors are often prepared to cut corners, suppress wages and engage in unscrupulous financial practices to achieve that. But financing care doesn't need to be so costly. Governments can raise money at a fraction of the cost incurred by handing that task to equity finance. Under the right conditions, as the US economist Stephanie Kelton has pointed out, the state can finance the care economy directly through deficit spending and job guarantees. In other words the economic organization of care is critical. Both to the quality of care and to the costs involved.

But ideological mission creep is not the only thing that's going on here. The demand for healthcare has changed massively since the NHS was established in 1948. And that change points to something even more fundamental about the relationship between care and the economy.

The burden of disease

Back in 1890 when the Tredegar Medical Aid Society was founded, its principal tasks were to treat workplace injuries and fight infectious disease. Both those needs remain. Even before Covid-19 reared its ugly head, respiratory infections cost the world more than a hundred and fifty million years of healthy life. The upside is that those numbers were steadily falling. In the three decades before the pandemic, the combined burden of all infectious diseases fell by over a third. Nutritional deficiencies, neonatal disorders and unintentional injuries also declined. Global health should have been improving.

But here's the downside. Even as the battle against infectious disease was being won, another, wilier foe was advancing from shadows. The burden of chronic 'non-communicable' disease was rising slowly but inexorably for decades. Cardiovascular diseases are now the single largest contribution to the burden of disease worldwide. The burden of diabetes and kidney disease has more than doubled since 1990. Neurological disorders like Alzheimer's have increased by 70 per cent. The burden of cancer has risen by more than half. And substance abuse now destroys 55 per cent more years of healthy life than it did just over three decades ago.

One response to these statistics is to point out that we're living longer. In general. And that's due in no small part to our success in tackling infectious disease. As the population ages, the incidence of chronic disease is almost inevitably going to increase. The heart grows weaker with age. As most things do. Is the healthcare system just a victim of its own success?

There may be some truth in that. But it's not the whole story. Yes we are living longer. Yes we're better at treating and preventing infection. Yes we've done a good job reducing child mortality and (in some places) maternal morbidity (although in others it's rising again). But we've also been blindsided by a rising burden of disease from a completely different direction. Chronic disease now accounts for almost three-quarters of all global deaths. It affects rich and poor, young and old. And it's on the rise.

More worrying still is that the risk factors associated with these chronic diseases are rising too. One study found that a staggering 90 per cent of adults in the US now suffer from some form of metabolic dysfunction. That's a precursor to almost every chronic disease we know of. And it's driven, not by infection, but by lifestyle.

In October 2020 *The Lancet* journal published a massively insightful editorial devoted to this shift in the global burden of disease. Its conclusions are salutary. Public health is 'failing to address the increase in crucial risk factors' associated with chronic disease, the authors say. The standout culprits are: 'high systolic blood pressure, high fasting plasma glucose, high body-mass index (BMI), ambient particulate matter pollution, alcohol use, and drug use'. Rates of exposure to these risks are increasing 'by more than 0.5% per year'. And this steady rise is likely to pose 'a massive threat' to public health everywhere.

These findings are not just a worrying indictment of modern society. They are absolutely core to my inquiry into the relationship between care and the economy. Just to be clear, what the authors were saying is this. We're failing big time on the biggest public health challenge of the twenty-first century. And it's difficult to see how any healthcare system, let alone the NHS, is going to turn the ship around without some radical changes in thinking about how that could be achieved.

The heritage

The Heritage Centre was closed when we arrived earlier today. And from the sign on the door it looks like it won't be open before we have to leave. I should have phoned ahead, of course. Or checked online. But we only came by on the off chance. And just breathing in the atmosphere of the place has somehow been worthwhile.

This brief visit has illustrated how fragile care becomes when it rides the rollercoaster of economic history. That's not to deny the integrity of Bevan's dream. And the story Cronin tells in *The Citadel* is one of heroism and hope. But even in the birthplace of the NHS, it's evident things haven't worked as he or Bevan or Attlee might have wished they did.

I'm looking around wondering what to do when an elderly man dressed in what seem to be pyjamas approaches me. He's moving with a clear purpose. But his gait is slow and precarious. He's leaning heavily on a stick. A rolled-up newspaper under his arm. Rheumy eyes looking out at the world with a fierce gaze. Is it anger? Disillusionment? Or just pain. When he speaks, his voice has a rasping quality. Whether it's from exertion or from some kind of underlying pulmonary condition I couldn't say. It's almost a gasp. For air. For life. For meaning.

'Try the library,' he says, panting a little with the effort. With a hand that's visibly trembling, he points out an unprepossessing building just across the road from us. 'Museum,' he says. The effort seems to cost him dearly. I thank him.

'Croeso,' he mutters in Welsh. You're welcome. And he continues on his way.

Just opposite the Heritage Centre on the other side of The Circle stands the town library. And in a quiet corner at the very back of the building – you'd almost miss it entirely if you didn't know it was there – is the Tredegar Local History Museum.

Turns out it's a regular treasure trove. Crammed full of artefacts. From the mines. From the town. From the Medical Aid Society. From royal visits to celebrate the birthplace of the NHS. From the days when Tredegar was a thriving mining town. From the decade when unemployment ripped through the place and left almost three-quarters of the workforce out of work. From a past invisible in the well-dressed mothers in the Tredegar Arms. But blindingly obvious in the older male population, in particular. The man who pointed me to the museum. And the two who greet me when I enter. Delighted to have some customers.

The place is now run by ex-miners on a voluntary basis. I guess they're still miners. Today they mine the local history and excavate memorabilia. They're a wonderful source of information. On the Medical Aid Society. On life in the mines. On social justice. On politics. (No wonder Margaret Thatcher worked so hard to close the mines.) And of course on the dubious virtues of visitors like me. Men who've never been down a pit in their lives.

I think about telling them, actually, I have. A few years ago I took my then teenage daughter and her friend to a trampoline playground underneath a mountain in the heart of Snowdonia, not far from here. A former mine. Run by ex-miners. It was a surprisingly lucrative venture that brought much-needed employment to the former mining community. Even at the time, I remember feeling it was a little bit like the last satirical twist of some disrespectful knife from a decayed and exploitative capitalism. So in the end I don't mention it. I don't think they'd be particularly impressed.

But like the elderly gent I met on the street, these museum guides confirm my positive impression of miners as proud, decent human beings. Generous with their time. And – like the staff in the Memorial Hospital – just a little bit cheeky. Perhaps that's the Welsh.

I'm not complaining. For them I'm just a mild distraction on a quiet day and a potential source of revenue for the museum. And on that point I'm happy to oblige. The conversation was worth it. Since the proceeds are going to the upkeep of the museum, it seems like a pretty good cause. And anyway, I tell myself, it's all research. When you think about it, I suppose, what they're doing is itself a kind of care. Literally actually. The word curator comes from the same root *cura* in Latin as care.

They're obviously caring for the artefacts. But they're caring too for our sense of ourselves. Our place in history. They're helping us to balance the onward rush of modernity with a sense of perspective on the disappearing past. Returning humanity to the still point of a calm reflection on progress. And the lack of it. To the distinction between what matters and what glitters. They might not like the analogy. But what I've accidentally stumbled on is a little bit of the goddess in action. It seems she's everywhere when you start looking.

No good deed

It's getting late as we sip our tea in the Tredegar Arms. It would be tempting to stay the night here. We're told the rooms are comfortable and reasonably priced. But the demands of the 'real' world are pressing in on me now. It's time to get home.

I've just noticed a string of messages on my phone. Alerting me to things that need attention. Urgently. One of them, I will later find out, is an unexpected wake-up call that's going to place everything I've seen and thought about today in a completely new perspective. This real world. So insistent sometimes on its reality. So little respect for the slow assimilation of historical detail. Or even for thought itself, I sometimes think.

For a few brief moments, I'll enjoy my tea. Unwilling to move immediately. Unable to stay much longer. I find myself thinking about a maxim I once saw. No good deed goes unpunished. I remember thinking it makes no sense. Its logic is faulty. It's the wrong way round. What happened to the Golden Rule?

From Thomas Aquinas to John Bunyan, from the mouths of the apostles to the words of the Messiah, the message has always been pretty clear. Do unto others as you would have them do unto you. 'For as punishment is to the evil act, so is reward to a good act,' wrote Aquinas in his *Summa Theologica*. 'No evil deed is unpunished, by God the just judge. Therefore no good deed is unrewarded and so every good deed deserves some good.'

Good deeds are the bedrock of humanity. That's the point. It was drummed into me as a kid. They're the foundation of the civilized world. They carry that same sense of moral certainty that's embodied in concepts like care. This other maxim. It's just a mistake. Surely it must be. And yet here in Tredegar I'm suddenly less sure.

Fortune swept through the Welsh Valleys like a tornado. Leaving a path of destruction in its wake. The town grew rich from its mineral wealth. From the frenetic energy of industrial capitalism. From the insatiable needs of economic expansion and military conflict. For a while that process delivered success and status to the owners of capital. And perhaps even a certain kind of dignity to the working population. But it also ravaged the earth, devastated the natural environment, exploited the poor and wreaked havoc with the social infrastructure. It brought wealth to the few and took health from the many. In its wake it left a massive need for restoration.

I couldn't help feeling that Parc Bryn Bach had done a better job restoring nature than the town had done restoring its social fabric. The age of coal and steel was the foundation for the success of western civilization. Towns like

Tredegar were absolutely integral to that success. The people who lived here were used and used up by it. They laboured and sweated and toiled half-naked and lost their lives in horrific accidents. And were vilified for it all the same.

Yet somewhere in the middle of it all they found the resolve to formulate a coherent vision of something completely different. Something powerful enough to move political mountains and create unprecedented social change. Something that for a while at least inspired whole nations to give care a place inside the economy. Something which to this day provides inspiration. Something which allows us to understand that prosperity is first and foremost about health. And that care is worth fighting for.

When London hosted the Olympic Games in 2012, the centrepiece of the opening ceremony was a powerful tribute to the NHS. Created by the Oscar-Winning film-maker Danny Boyle, one short segment saw children and nurses briefly threatened by the enormous, towering, death-like figure of Lord Voldemort, Harry Potter's principal antagonist in the J.K. Rowling stories. They're soon rescued though. By a platoon of Mary Poppins figures descending under umbrellas to drive death from the stage.

Fanciful? Yes, for sure. But the implications couldn't be clearer. Even today it makes its point. Something valuable is under threat. More than a decade later that sense is heightened significantly. The future of the ideal is more uncertain now than it's ever been. And where the hell is Mary Poppins when you need her?

Tredegar's blessing is now its curse. The towns that built the industrial revolution. The towns whose men and women and children gave their lives in the name of progress. The people scarred with black lung and emphysema and crippling arthritis and chronic heart disease. The communities blighted by long-term unemployment. The visionaries who created the principle of universal healthcare, free at the point of need. The NHS that put those principles in practice. The doctors and nurses who live and breathe every single day the consequences of our failure to protect that vision. The patients who suffer as a result.

All punished.

And the punishment clearly isn't over. Nor will it be. Until we manage to reclaim something meaningful as a principle of care at the heart of our understanding of the economy. The path may still not be clear. The questions are still unanswered. But the goal itself has never seemed more vital.

No good deed goes unpunished.

I have no idea what to do about that Machiavellian logic. When I look up its source, I discover it's attributed to a man named Walter Map. Apparently he was a twelfth-century Latin author born in the Welsh Marches. On the border between England and Wales. Go figure. Of course he was.

It was written, I found out, a hundred years before Aquinas came along and turned it on its head to fit with Christian orthodoxy. I still don't want to believe in it. But in the case of Tredegar, I can't help but see the logic.

6

Passerelle

*'The real war is not between left and right,
but rather between expansionists and extinctionists.'*
Elon Musk, 2023

By a stroke of good fortune, the rain has stopped. It's been pouring for what seems like weeks. The kind of rain that drenches you in seconds. Getting soaked didn't seem that attractive after six hours in a conference. So I almost resigned myself to sitting out the afternoon in my Paris hotel room.

Now I'm glad I didn't. Unexpectedly the sky has cleared. And a low December sun is shedding its golden light from across the river and throwing a massive double rainbow above the roofs of the city. Picture postcard eat your heart out. Instagrammers are out in force. And the Jardin des Tuileries is suddenly looking its wintry best. There's another couple of hours before sunset. So I still have time.

I cross the river via the *passerelle* from the Quai des Tuileries to the 7th Arrondissement. There's been a crossing here since the middle of the nineteenth century. A cast iron bridge was first opened in 1861 by Napoleon III. It was built to commemorate the victory of the French and Sardinian armies against Austria at the Battle of Solferino. That battle has the dubious honour of being the last ever in which all the armies were under the personal command of the monarch. The losses on both sides were huge.

The original Pont de Solférino took a continual battering from the barges that kept crashing into it. So it was replaced a century later with a steel footbridge. That fared little better and was demolished after three decades. Not sure what that says about building standards over the years. But it was clearly a useful place to have a bridge. So the architect Marc Mimram was commissioned to design something worthy of a new millennium.

The new bridge was commissioned in 1999. Two huge metal arches span the entire width of the Seine, with no supporting pillars. Each arch carries a wide wood-panelled footpath. Pedestrians on the upper path are exposed to the elements the whole way across. But on the lower path you're sheltered by the upper path. Except for one section in the middle where the upper and lower paths magically meet before parting ways again.

The Passerelle Solférino won the Prix de l'Équerre d'argent (the Silver Square prize) for architecture. A few years later it was renamed to commemorate the centenary of the birth of the Senegalese poet and critical theorist Léopold Sédar Senghor.

So, to be accurate, I'm crossing the Passerelle Léopold Sédar Senghor. And I have a choice to make. I don't really want to miss out on the lightness of the upper bridge. But there's something magical about the way the sun is streaming through the gap between the two arches, so I choose the lower path.

Ahead of me, where the two paths meet momentarily, I see a couple silhouetted against the sun. They're stood side by side. And the light seems to bend magically and radiate around them. For the longest time neither of them moves. And as I walk towards them I wonder if they're caught up arguing. Or about to kiss. But as I get closer it becomes clearer. They're taking selfies. Of course they are.

None of my business. My concern is elsewhere. I'm keen to make it to the rue de Varenne with light to spare. Paris is a feast of museums. Elegance, grandeur and the extraordinary historicity of the old masters. But here in a quiet backstreet hidden away behind Les Invalides is my favourite. Please don't tell anyone. I prefer it when it's empty. Though even in the middle of winter that's hard to arrange.

My destination is the Musée Rodin. The former workshop of France's best known sculptor, Auguste Rodin. When I first came here years ago, there used to be a sense of unfinished chaos to the place. You had the feeling you'd meet the man himself in one of these high-ceilinged rooms. And still. When you walk in. There's a sense of comfortable familiarity to the place. It's definitely a good spot to sit quietly and reflect on the kind of day you've had.

Insult the guests

There are some pretty odd professions in the world. Pummelling clay, hammering stone and casting naked figures in bronze must be one of them. Mine isn't that odd. But it still flirts with the absurd sometimes.

Take today, for example.

I've spent most of the day at a conference on climate change organized by the French Ministry of Economics and Finance. I was there to provide a critical perspective on economic growth. That doesn't happen often, I assure you. I mean. The Ministry of Finance doesn't often want to hear a critique of economic growth. Particularly not in the opening plenary of a conference on climate change.

It's been one of those years though. A year of unexpected interest in what I call postgrowth economics. And to me that's a good thing. It seems clear enough that you can't always have your cake and eat it. You can't just grow your economy for ever and hope that growth will solve all the wicked problems like climate change for you. Problems which are made considerably worse by growth itself. That's a classic addiction scenario. The only thing you can think of to cure the hangover from your latest fix is more of the same. It's comforting to think that people are beginning to see the lunacy of that.

So I have high hopes for the day. Particularly because I'm to speak in the first panel session. Right after a welcome speech from the Minister and a moderated discussion between him and the world's most famous tech billionaire-turned-global climate philanthropist. When I arrive in the hall, I'm ushered to a seat in the front row. Right next to a phalanx of photographers crowded in the aisle and jammed up against the stage. They're not there for me of course. They're waiting for a glimpse of the Philanthropist.

Ten minutes later, he arrives. He's ushered into the auditorium by a suitably nervous Minister to the flash of a thousand cameras and takes his place a couple of seats down from mine. I'm looking forward to hearing what he has to say. But first. When the applause dies down. We're going to hear from the Minister.

He's graceful and hospitable. He speaks about ecology being not a political choice but a human obligation. He quotes Marcel Proust. And he talks about a 'new kind of growth' for the twenty-first century, something different from the growth we had in the twentieth century, and especially in the nineteenth century. Fair enough. Don't scare the horses just yet.

And then he starts to tell us why it's so important to articulate this new kind of growth. Because without it, he tells us, we'll pave the way for those who preach 'degrowth.' He's speaking in French.So it comes out as 'décroissance'. Which sounds a whole lot more appetizing of course. Something you might want for breakfast. But not for the Minister.

'I don't believe in this ideology of degrowth,' he says, 'and I will fight against it.' His demeanour has changed. Gone is the paternal politician. Gone is his hospitality. There's an animation to his delivery now that signals annoyance. Possibly even anger. And he's not finished yet.

'Degrowth is dangerous', he tells us. 'Because it leads to impoverishment. To inequality. To withdrawing into ourselves. To the loss of knowledge. Do you really believe that the United States will engage in degrowth? That developing countries will engage in degrowth?' It's false, he tells us. And France has proven that it's false.

He goes on to cite some statistics about the country's ability to decouple its carbon emissions from its economic output. To reduce its emissions while still delivering growth. Unfortunately the numbers don't really prove the case he's trying to make. The rate of decoupling achieved in France during the period he refers to is nowhere near what's needed to keep the world safe from dangerous climate change. But that's not quite the point.

The point is that degrowth is perilously close to what I've been invited here to talk about. It's a very weird moment. I'm sat in the first row. Directly in front of his podium on the stage. He looks up briefly and seems to look directly at me. Does he know what I'm doing here? Does he know that his own team invited me? And shouldn't he be a bit more polite to his visitors?

But then I remember that British ministers have made a habit of inviting French people to meetings and insulting them. Not that long ago 'insult the guests' was the *soupe du jour* at Brexit negotiations. So maybe it's fair enough. I take a deep breath and sit back in my seat as we all applaud. Rude not to. He is the Minister after all.

And now at least we can look forward to the discussion with the Philanthropist. His initial intervention is pretty clear. Don't you worry about climate change, he says, because technology will save us. And listen to this. It will also bring us growth. Ah. Now I'm confused. Did I really agree to this?

More specifically. It turns out. It's his technology that will save us. Technology which his foundation is seed funding will prevent climate change. And even if it doesn't, it will save us from the impacts of not preventing it. And all of that will sooner or later lead to profit. For people like him. So I suppose what he means is that climate change will bring *him* growth. Particularly if he can stay close enough to the ear of governments (who set the rules) by turning up at places like this and telling us all not to worry.

No. He didn't actually say all that. I'm interpolating. Or extrapolating. Or just reading the body language. Or the mood music. Which isn't difficult. It's turning into a religious ceremony now. A hymn to the never-ending possibilities for economic expansion. Growth begets innovation. Innovation begets growth. Growth will have climate change licked in no time. Whatever your problem, growth will fix it. This is the politics of addiction.

I realize my mind is wandering. But the discussion is coming to a close now. In another blaze of photo flashes the Philanthropist sweeps out of the room with the Minister at his elbow. Our panel is up next. And it turns out they won't even stick around to listen to the conversation I thought we were going to have. About growth.

You see what I mean about strange professions. They're all a bit odd. The Sculptor. The Philanthropist. The Minister. Even the paparazzi must occasionally wonder what it is they do for a living. But I suppose on this occasion I'm thinking about my own job as well.

I've been invited here to present a critical perspective on growth. To talk about postgrowth economics. Perhaps even about degrowth. Since *Prosperity without Growth* was first published, I've been to hundreds of events like this. Not always in finance ministries. But in so many situations where the conversation I thought we were going to have just doesn't happen. It's over before it really even began. In this case before the welcome speech is done. And the rest is just noise.

So what is the point exactly? Today I'm not sure. I make my arguments. I fulfil my role. And I come away feeling a bit like a court jester. A professional joker. A wild card wheeled out to mark the edge of consensus. Or to whip up cosmetic dissent. The voice of a view that everyone can agree to disagree with. The proponent of a heresy. The bearer of tidings that no one wants to hear.

It would be fair enough of course if the grit in the oyster would occasionally deliver a pearl. But the moment the discussion gets close to the core of the issue. The moment it threatens to question the unassailable shibboleths. Growth. Capitalism. Profit. Then suddenly no one's interested anymore.

Which wouldn't matter so much. I suppose. If it weren't for the opportunity costs. Pretending to have an open discussion about growth and climate change is almost worse than having no discussion at all. Particularly when it closes down the avenues for serious thought.

The Thinker

Even in winter this garden of the Musée Rodin possesses an other-worldly beauty. The lime trees cling to the last of their summer leaves. Their branches dance seductively in the lightest of breezes. A deepening sunlight burnishes the yellow stone façade of the Hôtel Biron in a golden blaze. Catching only the top half of Honoré de Balzac's cloaked figure, it picks out the green patina in his tarnished bronze robe.

I've always been intrigued by the *Monument to Balzac*. It's considered to be the first truly modern sculpture in art history. Commissioned by the Société des Gens de Lettres (roughly the Literary Society), Rodin was supposed to deliver it in just eighteen months. Instead he spent for ever researching his subject before finally unveiling a full-sized plaster model of the monument seven years later.

It was met with almost universal disdain. What kind of testament was this to France's most celebrated writer? To show the great man in his dressing gown! His features pitted and worn? His grin neither majestic nor noble? His face recognizable only as a caricature? It was tantamount to sacrilege. The Society received so much hate mail they revoked the commission.

Thirty years later, in his documentary series *Civilisation*, Kenneth Clark described Rodin's *Balzac* as 'the greatest piece of sculpture of the nineteenth century. Perhaps, indeed, the greatest since Michelangelo.' The robe is not a dressing gown. It's the monk's robe the writer habitually wore when he was writing. Yes it looks as ugly as sin. But that apparently was the point. 'Balzac, with his prodigious understanding of human motives, scorns conventional values, defies fashionable opinions,' says Clark. 'And should inspire us to defy all those forces that threaten to impair our humanity: lies, tanks, tear gas, ideologies, opinion polls, mechanization, planners, computers – the whole lot.'

Maybe you get a sense of why I'm intrigued by it. And how it might be relevant to the journey of this book. 'No society can legitimately call itself civilised,' said Nye Bevan in 1952, 'if a sick person is denied medical aid because of lack of means.' Or if we've forgotten where our humanity lies. Or if we've been caught up in appearances. Or if we're terrified of being on the wrong side of some moral consensus. So terrified that we've failed to think for ourselves. Or we've failed to think at all.

Brooding over all of this is the most famous Rodin sculpture of all. *The Thinker*. High on his pedestal. Silhouetted against the light. Right elbow resting on his left knee. The knuckles of his right hand supporting his chin. The sculpture is the archetypal monument to philosophy. To the idea of thinking. To the nature of thought. A testament to the human gift for contemplation. A gift that can easily get lost in the forward motion of a chaotic unthinking world.

It's a lesson taken seriously by the social philosopher Hannah Arendt. In her 1958 book *The Human Condition*, she establishes her task early on. Or. To be more accurate. She establishes the limitations of her task.

> To these preoccupations and perplexities, this book does not offer an answer. Such answers are given every day, and they are matters of practical politics, subject to the agreement of many; they can never lie in theoretical considerations, or the opinion of one person. . . . What I propose therefore is very simple: it is nothing more than to think what we are doing.

That sounds like a realistic aim to me. To think what we are doing. Though perhaps not as simple as it purports to be. Particularly in a world even hungrier for policy-ready proposals than the one in which Arendt was writing. I know that I will need to get to policy eventually. The care economy is desperately in need of it. But for now as I sit here in the pale December sun, feeling its unlikely warmth on my face, it occurs to me that my journey to Paris has not entirely been a detour.

There's a very specific sense in which the concept of the care economy emerges from these tangled questions about growth and degrowth. And a sense too in which this refusal to let go of our obsession with growth – so evident in this morning's session at the Ministry – is connected with our failure to protect the concept of care in the economy. Let me have a go at making those connections. And on the way perhaps, provide a little bit of an explainer on why the Minister finds degrowth so dangerous.

A degrowth explainer

If he's right. If degrowth really will lead to all those things he said it does – inequality, impoverishment, a descent into ignorance. Then maybe we would do well to steer clear of it. Just as he suggests. But whether that's the case or not depends partly on what exactly degrowth is. Or what it's taken to mean.

Part of the problem is the word itself. It's become quite popular over the last few years. But that may have been a double-edged sword. On the one hand, it means more people being prepared to ask questions about our obsession with growth. And on the other, it's sometimes sown the seeds of confusion. Because its meaning – at least as defined by those who think seriously about it – doesn't quite align with people's popular conception of it.

Degrowth seems to cast itself linguistically as the opposite of growth. But that's not quite what's meant by most of the people who use it. Early proponents of degrowth such as the philosopher André Gorz and the sociologist Serge Latouche (both French by the way) cast degrowth as an *opponent* of growth. A way of challenging growth. But to oppose something is not quite the same thing as proposing its opposite. Not everything is binary.

This unhelpful confrontation of opposites seems to suggest that there's a dial somewhere. It's probably located inside the Ministry of Finance, I suppose. Turn it one way and you get growth. Turn it the other and you get degrowth. Both directions are measured through the percentage change in the GDP. The Minister's job is to keep the dial turned up. As much as possible. Because that's where prosperity comes from. In his view. Naturally then, he's going to resist someone he believes is trying to turn it in the other direction. Because in his mind that would be the opposite of prosperity.

But the dial is a misconception. So is the idea that more GDP necessarily means more prosperity. So is the idea that degrowth is about turning the dial in the opposite direction from the one that politicians are aiming for. To oppose the obsession with growth doesn't just mean campaigning for its opposite. Degrowth proponents aren't asking for less prosperity. They're asking us to redefine prosperity. To work towards a prosperity that is equitable and sustainable. Fair – both to other people today and to other people tomorrow. Our kids most obviously. And their kids.

I should say here as an aside that there is a relatively marginal position known as 'collapsism' which does argue that we have no hope and no time left to reconfigure our societies and that the only alternative to save the planet is complete economic collapse. Perhaps that's an understandable response to the defiant 'growthism' that any questioning of growth is met with. But it's specifically not my position. Nor that of any degrowth scholar I know. Collapse would entail immense human suffering. It probably is the incarnation of the Minister's worst fears. But it's also the very opposite of care – in any meaningful sense of the word.

One of the reasons for thinking carefully about care is precisely this: to defend ourselves from false gods. Neither endless growth nor collapse is consistent with the concept of care I elaborated in Chapter 4. That principle of care as a restorative force returning us to health. That sense of seeking and maintaining the vital dynamic balance achieved by organic life. We may not yet know exactly what that entails in every case. Nor how precisely to achieve it in economic terms. But what we can clearly see is that neither relentless growth nor thoughtless collapse can come close to preserving it. Both things directly contravene the underlying principle of care.

But having such a principle to hand does draw our attention inevitably to the question of economic scale. Not just to the monetary size of the economy as measured by the GDP. But more importantly to the physical scale of its impacts on the planet. In fact this attention to scale has been at the heart of ecological critiques of growth since the work of such legendary pioneers as the ecological economist Herman Daly and the feminist economist Marilyn Waring.

It's also a key concern of those who have more recently proposed degrowth. My colleague Jason Hickel, for instance, has defined degrowth quite precisely as 'a planned reduction of energy and resource use designed to bring the economy *back into balance* with the living world in a way that reduces inequality and improves human well-being'.

Defined in this way, degrowth doesn't seek collapse at all. It doesn't even seek a reduction in the size of the GDP. But it does accept that we might need to think about a situation in which the GDP isn't growing for ever. Particularly for the advanced economies which have historically been responsible for pushing ecological systems so far out of balance.

Expansion vs extinction

All of this has been articulated extensively over the last couple of decades since and even before *Prosperity without Growth* was published. Much of it by people with whom I've worked very closely myself. So full disclosure. I've personally played a part in the degrowth debate. For better or for worse. But I still feel torn by what I've seen in the last year or so.

On the one hand, the terminology has brought a new generation of people into an important debate. Quite literally. In some cases. At another conference I attended, at the European Parliament, organized by the Green politician Philippe Lamberts, thousands of young people turned up to make themselves heard. To them degrowth offered a sense of hope that things might change. And to be able to express that hope inside the Parliament building was almost unheard of before it happened.

On the other hand, even their enthusiasm for change proves problematic when ministers who cling defiantly to old ideas fail to engage on the crucial issues that concern this younger generation. The debate becomes too easy to polarize. Jason and I and some other like-minded scholars recently published a commentary on degrowth in the journal *Nature*. It wasn't a polemic. It was a concise, informative exploration of the debate.

But of course most people only read the title. If that. And its reception on social media was, let's say, mixed. As it happens, this particular paper caught the attention of another tech billionaire. This one saw fit to describe our paper as: 'The extinctionists at work.' The real war is not between the left and right anymore, he went on to say, 'but rather between expansionists and extinctionists'.

Extinctionism sounds even worse than collapsism. And it's obviously meant to be pejorative. But how is concern for the only planet known definitively to support human life the same thing as advocating for extinction? It makes no sense.

Either it's a deliberate misunderstanding. Or it's a wilful failure to engage in serious debate. Or else it's an attempt to draw the battle lines in a way that demonizes the antagonist. And by the same token to paint the protagonist – in this case the tech bro expansionist – as the only brain in the room. On social media. In fact on X. Or more specifically X. Full stop.

There's an interesting feature of this particular expansionist. Elon Musk is a powerful advocate for space travel. He believes that our only hope of survival is to find some other habitable planet. As soon as possible. His version of expansionism is not just to appeal to a technology that will lead us to 'net zero': the point in time when no net carbon emissions are being emitted from human activity. It's an appeal to a technology that will lead us to the stars. Well. Mars at first. But ultimately. To infinity and beyond.

Isn't it strange? Just a decade or so ago the battle lines around growth could at least agree that planet Earth is our best bet for a comfortable home. And all the arguments were saved for debating whether that's possible if we expand the economy indefinitely. Those who believed that technology will always save us clung to the myth of eternal growth. Those who held a more sanguine view of technology's power suggested that there may still be some important limits to growth. Needless to say, I've always inclined towards the latter view.

But now come the self-confessed expansionists. Like the growth sceptics, they recognize that eternal growth on a finite planet probably isn't going to wash. But like the growth advocates, they can't let go of the idea of endless growth. So the only possible alternative, the only other place left to expand, is space. It's logical. But is it feasible? On a timescale anything like the one we'd have to achieve it in?

This house believes

I should say I'm not against the idea of space exploration in principle. That night in Pembrokeshire. When the stars came out. It seemed pretty attractive. I always have a couple of responses to the wonder of the night sky. One is how damn small you feel, when you think of us hurtling through the universe on the only inhabitable rock for millions of miles around. The other is how amazing it is that there's so much out there about which we know so little.

Mars ain't the kind of place to raise your kids, according to the 'Rocket Man' in Elton John's timeless classic. In fact it's cold as hell. But as lockdown projects go, NASA's landing of the *Perseverance* rover on the surface of the Red Planet back in February 2021 was a stunning feat of human ingenuity. Watching it reminded me that I once led a high-school debate defending the motion 'This house believes that humanity should go into space.'

I'm guessing this was around the time that Caspar Weinberger was trying to persuade President Nixon not to cancel the Apollo space programme. As kids, we'd seen with our own eyes the monochrome triumph of the Apollo 11 landing. We'd lived through the near disaster of Apollo 13 –immortalized in a 1995 Hollywood film – when Jim Lovell (played by Tom Hanks) and two rookie astronauts narrowly escaped with their lives by using the Lunar Module as an emergency life-raft. We knew it was exciting up there.

I remember later going to see *Apollo 13* (the film) with a friend who hadn't been born when the mission itself took place. 'What did you think?' I asked as we came out of the cinema. 'It was ok,' said my friend. 'Just not very believable.'

But we kids had been glued to our black-and-white TV sets the entire week of that mission. We watched in horror as carbon dioxide levels rose in the Lunar Module. We endured the endless blackout as the returning astronauts plunged perilously back to earth. We held our breath with the rest of the world as the expected four minutes stretched to five and hope began to fade. It was a full six minutes before the camera finally came into focus on the Command Module's parachutes – safely deployed above the Pacific Ocean. We felt the endorphin rush. We knew it was believable.

That was 1970. This was a full half-century later. And there I was again on the edge of another sofa. In the lingering uncertainty of the pandemic. Waiting for signs of life from another re-entry blackout on another barren rock, devoid of breathable atmosphere, three hundred million miles away. And when it came. That same excitement. That same endorphin rush. Quite difficult even for the most fanatical technophobe to witness the jubilation behind the surgical masks at mission control that day without feeling a glimmer of vicarious elation. Hope, even.

I'm not saying that's wrong. 'Going to Mars *would* be kind of cool,' my daughter insisted, as she and I and the cat recovered our breath on the sofa. It would. Especially when you'd just spent your entire first year at university in total isolation, as she had. With most of us still reeling from what the WHO has called a shadow pandemic in mental health, any kind of escape plan at all looked remarkably like paradise. Particularly at that point in our lives. And emigrating to Mars is one hell of an escape plan.

But something has definitely changed. Perhaps it's me. Maybe I'm no longer the kid from the debating society. This house believes that humanity should grow the fuck up. Before we spend trillions of dollars littering our techno-junk around the solar system, perhaps we should pay more attention to what's happening right here and now. On this planet. Pay attention. Care. Think what we're doing. Just like Arendt asked us to.

The good life

The sky is darker now. The air is colder. Pink clouds hover above the golden roof of Les Invalides, just visible beyond the walls of the museum. I won't see many stars in this sky. Too much city light. I walk briskly one last time around the ornamental lake to stretch my legs. There's still an hour before the museum closes and there's something else I want to see before I leave.

It's always a little dangerous to delve too deeply into other people's misconceptions and misdirections. But if the process lends some clarity to my journey, then maybe it's worth it. And I think there's something to be taken from this expansionist–extinctionist divide. Musk is wrong about the desire for collapse. But he's maybe not wrong that there's a kind of ideological conflict. A clash of ideals. A clash of values, even.

I've seen it before. On numerous occasions. I remember a speech at the World Economic Forum (WEF) in Davos that US President Donald Trump gave. It was shortly before the pandemic hit us. And not long after the extraordinary rise of the climate activist Greta Thunberg – still a high-school student at the time. That year she and her colleagues had turned up in force at Davos. They may just have been kids. But they'd already blocked the road and held up the President's limousine. It was time to put a stop to it.

'To embrace the possibilities of tomorrow,' Trump announced, 'we must reject the perennial prophets of doom and their predictions of the apocalypse. They are the heirs of yesterday's foolish fortune tellers.' Expansion or extinction. It was the same message. The same frontier mentality rejecting the same perspective of caution. Rejecting care. Ultimately. Isn't that what it is? As simple as that. Growth versus care?

There's a kind of blindness that growth has towards care. In its continual search for more, growth rushes forwards. Its role is functional when there is too little. When more is needed. When health relies on more, then growth is aligned with care. But health is never continually aligned with more. In fact its entire ethos lies in balance. In the vanishing space between more and less. In the importance of the still point.

And when we're lost in the relentless search for growth, we can never reliably find that point of balance. Because we're always searching for more. And even if we could recognize the point of balance, we'd always fail to stop for exactly the same reason. Because we're busy rushing past it. The search for more is insatiable. But it's also structural. It locks us into more of the same. It has its hold on our institutions. On our politicians. On our social norms. On our own expectations. And on our values.

It reminds me of Aristotle's search for the good life. His starting point was something he called *eudaimonia*. It's a word derived from the same word *eu* (well or good) that we already encountered in *eu*phoria and from the word *daimon*, or spirit. Being of good spirit, well in spirit, was for Aristotle the highest human good. It wasn't simply the presence of pleasure or the absence of pain. Rather it had something do with 'activity of the soul in accordance with virtue' (*aretē* in the Greek).

That may sound a bit sanctimonious to the modern ear. In the same way that care sometimes can. Virtue. Care. Empathy. Kindness. All that rose-tinted, noble, do-gooding nonsense. Save it for the flowers. Once we've solved all the real problems of the world, then we can worry about that stuff.

But it's worth pointing out that in Aristotle's day the word *aretē* had a different meaning. To be virtuous, in his sense, was to be good at something. To be capable of functioning well. To act to the very highest potential. To the very best of your ability. In accordance with the demands of the moment. A fitness, if you like, in the sense of evolutionary fitness. A fittedness to the needs of the task.

This sense of virtue applies of course to people. Rodin was a virtuous sculptor. Not because he was morally good. In point of fact he was a serial womanizer and cheated on Rose Beuret, his life-long companion and the mother of his son, over and over again. We may well want to judge that adversely. But that's not the same thing as judging his skill as a sculptor or being able to appreciate the outcome of his labours. He may have been flawed as a lover. But he was still a genius when it came to sculpture.

Virtue in this Aristotelian sense isn't only applicable to people. It's also applicable to objects. To things. Like bridges, let's say. The Pont de Solférino was a virtuous bridge. It did a great job for almost a century connecting the left to the right bank of Paris. It even withstood the assault of the barges whose helmsmen apparently were far less virtuous. The Passerelle de Solférino was a piece of 1960s crap. It fell apart within a few decades. And the Passerelle Léopold Sédar Senghor? Well, I suppose only time will tell. But from what I've seen it's an elegant, functional passageway that connects two of my favourite parts of Paris. And it's a fantastic place for selfies. So, yes. Let's call it a virtuous bridge.

Aristotle's concept of virtue is similar to what we mean by virtuosity. A perfectly honed skill. An extraordinary ability. A performance of exceptional beauty. Standout fitness. Faultless precision. Not in the abstract. But rather in the sense of being perfectly adapted to the environment – and to the task at hand. I suppose it carries something of the evolutionary sense of the word *fitness*. Adaptive fitness.

There's something else that's vital though. Each virtue, said Aristotle, is flanked by two vices. Deficiency on the one side. And excess on the other. Just as it's possible to have too little of something, it's also possible to have too much. And of course that's why I'm drawn to it. Isn't this exactly what's going on in the wisdom of the body? In the never-ending not-too-hot, not-too-cold Goldilocks regulation of homeostasis. In the constant attention to the balance of blood oxygen, water, salt, protein, acidity, calcium and cholesterol. Not to mention sugar. Blood glucose.

Yes. Strange to find myself writing about blood glucose. Remember that string of messages on my phone in Tredegar? I'm going to have to get back to them eventually. They're relevant too. Not just for personal reasons. But for the story I'm trying to tell. Which is after all a story about health.

Perhaps it's not surprising to learn that Aristotle wrote about virtue in a book called *The Nicomachean Ethics*, named for his father, Nicomachus, who just happened to be a physician. An entire philosophy devoted to the idea of prosperity as health. A vital clue that I'm not too wide of the mark here. And a clearer insight into what's wrong with prosperity as wealth. With a strategy that consistently prioritizes growth.

It's not that it's entirely wrong-headed as a model of prosperity. It's more that it's just half a model. The half that works when the problem is deficiency. Growth may sometimes fix the vice of deficiency. It's much less suited to fixing the vice of excess. And it has a tendency to lead you inexorably towards it. The philosophy of more is hostile to the philosophy of enough.

A Samurai sword is sharp as fuck. But it's not much good at cutting carrots. The long span of a bridge is a good way of avoiding drunk barge pilots. But it stops being useful when the bridge ends up in the garden of the Musée Rodin. And if you go on endlessly loading refined carbs and sugar into the human body, you end up with an epidemic of obesity and the uncontrollable rise of chronic disease. The thing about getting it right – about balance, about virtue as balance – is how easily it can get wrecked.

Postgrowth thinking

Aristotelian virtue gives us a bit more of an insight into what's wrong with the growth versus degrowth debate. It bogs itself down in simple dichotomy. Whether from linguistic misinterpretation. Or from genuine confusion. Or from deliberate misdirection. Or from a failure to 'think what we are doing'.

The modern degrowth movement has tried to shed itself of these misunderstandings. It's tried to present itself as 'agnostic' in relation to what happens to the GDP. But the subtlety of that point too often gets lost. Particularly in the furore of social media storms. And even. As I found out today. In the corridors of ministerial power.

Strangely, when it comes to my panel session, the facilitator takes a great deal of trouble to steer me away from the word *degrowth* and towards the terminology of 'postgrowth'. In light of the Minister's opening speech, that certainly seems like a kindness on her part. I am being offered the opportunity to side-step his warm welcome with a simple linguistic shuffle.

As it happens, I prefer this terminology anyway. Postgrowth has a less confrontational feel. It offers a more conciliatory framing. It doesn't set itself up as an opposite. Nor even really as an opponent to growth. But it still captures the idea that something different is needed. That we should think more carefully about our assumption that growth can go on for ever. It gently suggests that that might not always be the case.

In fact the growth that was forged by industrial capitalism, entrenched during two world wars and cemented by western consumerism has been slowing down for decades. In some places it's effectively over. Even where it's not, it's been running out of steam for a while now. Its failure to solve problems like climate change and the loss of biodiversity and the erosion of soils and the pollution of the seas is deeply worrying. And its hunger for mineral resources and cheap labour is already unsustainable.

Postgrowth thinking is different to this. It starts by asking what kind of economy we need so that people can live well as well as possible – virtuously in Aristotle's sense – within the limits of a finite planet. And this Aristotelian view brings us right back to the two central propositions of this book. It casts prosperity as health. It casts economy as care. It suggests that economic activities should supply our deficiencies. But they should not feed our excesses. They should test our resilience. But they shouldn't condemn us to chronic stress. They should be concerned with balance. Not obsessed by growth. They should focus on the return to health. Not the returns from wealth.

At its simplest, the postgrowth case is pretty straightforward. It doesn't deny technological solutions to the challenges we face. But it offers additional avenues for change. Structural change. Social change. System change – as the young climate activists at the European Parliament would call it. By letting go of growth-at-all-costs, the postgrowth case offers more degrees of freedom. More possibilities for living well.

The Cinderella economy

If we take these considerations seriously, a couple of implications follow. The first is that no sector has an absolute right to the moral high ground in the care economy. The second is that no sector has an absolute right to growth in the care economy. And a business or sector that has such rights at one point in time doesn't necessarily keep them for ever.

Special pleading. Virtue signalling. Historical incumbency. Investment return. Market share. Even financial success. None of these things prove desirability in the care economy if the business in question detracts from health. And whether a business is bringing us closer to or further away from health can change over time. According to underlying conditions which go beyond individual company performance. Conditions that are path dependent. Conditions that cannot simply be conveyed by market prices.

To think seriously about the care economy is to think about the *economy as care*. To apply the principle of care to economic activities. Throughout the economy. Even within the most basic sectors. The ones we can't possibly do without.

Take food and agriculture, for instance. We can't in any meaningful sense thrive without decent nutrition. But that doesn't give each and every food company a free pass to the care economy. It depends what's on offer. It depends how it operates. It depends how the food system itself works. Pumping fast food, rich in saturated fats, sugar and refined carbs into the food chain won't wash. However cheaply it's produced it cannot legitimately qualify as care. Particularly in a society where metabolic dysfunction is rising. And where obesity and chronic disease inevitably follow.

The traditional 'care sectors' are obviously key. But they don't necessarily get a free pass into the care economy either. We've already seen how medicine can lead us not towards but away from health. We've seen how commercialized care structures can depress healthcare outcomes. How pharmaceutical products can lead to dependency and addiction. How profiteering from people's aversion to pain – or their addiction to pleasure – can lead to tragic outcomes. Taking the principle of care seriously means paying attention to *how* as well as *how much* health and social care are delivered.

Beyond these more obvious sectors there are some other less obvious candidates that merit our attention. Tasks such as cleaning and restoration, maintenance and renovation. Often overlooked. Systematically undervalued. Frequently forgotten. They are vital to the conditions of health. Physiological health, self-evidently in the case of cleanliness. But also to the material health of our living environment. To its continuity. To its longevity. To its durability.

Durability relies on skill and on craft. The ability to design and make things that last. Not just in the sense of physical longevity. Or even reparability. But also in the sense of being socially durable. Products that are both functional and beautiful. Artefacts that persist. Objects whose social life can extend not just for years but for generations sometimes. The antithesis of the mass-produced profit-driven obsolescence that has come to define consumerism.

And to achieve all this, it occurs to me here in the garden of the Musée Rodin in the middle of Paris, there's something else that's vital to the care economy. I'm surrounded by creativity. It's on show in the galleries and museums. But it lives too in the design of its bridges. It thrives in the art schools and the universities. It's embodied in the poetry of Léopold Sédar Senghor. It's all around me. Its contribution to our mental wellbeing. To our sense of identity. To our experience of the world. To our understanding of our place in it. To our hope for the future. All of that is immense.

Care, craft and creativity. These are the core activities in the care economy. None of them have a free pass. But taken together, they provide a blueprint for a different kind of economy. Not just because they seek to restore and maintain our health. Not just because they all contribute profoundly to human flourishing. But also because they all tread lightly on the planet.

And yet all of them, it turns out, get poorly treated under capitalism. They're generally seen as poor cousins of the high-tech, high-profit, high-productivity sectors that are supposed to drive economic progress forwards. They suffer from neglect, underinvestment, poor working conditions and low pay. A colleague who read my earlier account of these sectors in *Prosperity without Growth* coined a phrase to describe them. He called them collectively the Cinderella economy. That part of the economy left behind sweeping up the ashes while capitalism enjoys itself at the ball. Why and how that happens matters. And it's something I'll return to in later chapters of the book.

The light within

Inside the museum it's almost closing time. The place is pretty much empty now. And it's even easier to imagine the artist at work. By the time I find what I'm looking for it's almost dark outside. The huge wood-panelled windows frame the falling night with deepening blues and a strange sense of loss. They make her seem even smaller than she is. The slender marble figure of the *Danaïde* is less than a metre long. And her diminutive size is a clear indication she belongs to a different world. She's a mythical creature.

To be perfectly honest. The myth is kind of stupid. If you take it at face value. The Danaïdes were the daughters of Danaus, a legendary king of Libya. There were fifty of them, supposedly. And in order to settle – or perhaps start – some territorial dispute, they were betrothed in marriage to the sons of Aegyptus, Danaus' twin brother, who was a legendary king of Egypt. Conveniently the sons also numbered fifty. Isn't it great when arithmetic works out in your favour?

At some point, Danaus seems to have got cold feet about the whole deal. Because he suddenly orders his daughters to slay their husbands on their wedding night. Yup. That's right. He wants his daughters to murder all his nephews. For some reason they almost all comply. (There's the patriarchy again.) All but one of them. Only his eldest daughter, Hypermnestra, fails to carry out the deed. She spares her husband because he respects her wish to remain a virgin. The rest had no such scruples.

This Danaïde is not Hypermnestra. She's clearly one of the forty-nine others who, for the crime of following their father's orders, were condemned to carry water from a well with a leaky jug. A thankless, futile, endless task. Here is the broken jug. Here is the water flowing. Here is her exhausted figure. Crouched despairingly over the barren rock. Desolate. Devastated. Lost.

The thing about Rodin's work. (And I suppose it might well have been the strangeness of his profession. Locked up all day in a huge mansion making sculptures of naked people. That's definitely weirder than playing court jester in the finance ministry.) The sculptures are a kind of fusion of ancient myth. Of physical sensuality. Of mortal frailty. Of something profoundly human. Some kind of inner life. An interiority. A quality that is so nebulous it sometimes evades clear description.

In this case it's all bound up with the unfinished quality the piece has. The Danaïde's impossibly smooth figure is fused almost magically with the rough unhewn rock from which she was born. As though she's still emerging from it. Or melting back into it. Perhaps she's actually Barbie. Carved from the earth. Condemned to mortality. What was I made for?

Or perhaps she's Care. An unlikely incarnation of the goddess herself. Engaged in a thankless, endless, ultimately futile task. A task whose importance is systematically overlooked and endlessly underappreciated. A task whose value is difficult to measure. Because it defies productivity. Because it misses deadlines. Because it reveals itself only slowly. If at all. Over time. And because eventually it fails. Eventually it fades away completely.

Even this extraordinary marble will be gone one day. And yet, for as long as it's there, it shines with this inner light. That's obvious for us all to see. That's why it has to be protected from us. We want that light. We're desperate for it. But in grasping for it, we extinguish it. Because it exists only in passing.

I still can't quite imagine how this extraordinary, ephemeral promise could be any compensation for the endless punishment of good deeds. But momentarily at least, I'm grateful for Rodin's attempt to convince us that, in passing, it might.

7

Shoot the Messenger

'Public health does not improve as a result of caring for people who happen to have a disease. It improves from interventions that keep the healthy healthy.'
Annemarie Mol, 2008

The sun's last light is no more than a faint rose-coloured tinge across the darkening sky as I retrace my steps through Paris to the Passerelle Léopold. When I get there, the breeze that ripples the surface of the Seine has grown perceptibly colder. This time I cross on the upper pathway. And stand for a while at the centre, gazing down on the river.

The Battle of Solferino was bloody, violent and short. It began around 4 a.m. on 24 June 1859. By mid-afternoon the Austrian ranks had been broken and Emperor Franz Joseph I's army was in retreat. After eleven hours of fighting, forty thousand men were left dead, dying or wounded. Another ten thousand or more were missing or captured.

Napoleon III had always been a reluctant warrior. For the most part his reign was one of enlightenment. The expansion of agriculture. Permission for women to attend universities. Just a few years before, he'd famously declared that 'the French Empire is for peace'. A month after Solferino, he signed an armistice with Austria, effectively bringing the second war of independence to an end.

He wasn't the only one appalled by the battle. A Swiss businessman named Henri Dunant had travelled to Solferino to petition Napoleon about water rights for a huge financial project he was developing in Algeria. He arrived on the afternoon of 24 June, just in time to witness the end of the battle. He was shocked by the plight of the wounded and dying soldiers on the battlefield. There was little in the way of care or treatment. And no solace in their final hours.

Back home in Geneva, Dunant wrote about his experience in a book called *Un Souvenir de Solférino* (*A Memory of Solferino*). It's a curious, idiosyncratic book. The first part reads like a glorification of combat. A description of the heroism of the soldiers in their defence of flag and country. The second part describes the horrific aftermath of the battle. Dunant is full of praise for those who respond to that suffering with humanity. But he's also curiously unquestioning of the transition from jingoism to grief.

> The gracious and lovely young ladies of the aristocracy, made lovelier still by the exaltation of passionate enthusiasm, were no longer scattering rose-leaves from the beflagged balconies of sumptuous palaces to fall on glittering shoulder-straps, on silk and ribbons, and gold and enamel crosses; from their eyes now fell burning tears, born of painful emotion and of compassion, which quickly turned to Christian devotion, patient and self-sacrificing.

The final part of his book is an entirely pragmatic proposal. Out of sheer humanity, Dunant suggested that the nations of the world should form 'relief societies' to provide care to the wartime wounded. '[I]n an age when we hear so much of progress and civilization,' he wrote, 'is it not a matter of urgency, since unhappily we cannot always avoid wars, to press forward in a human and truly civilized spirit the attempt to prevent, or at least alleviate, the horrors of war?'

The book was published in 1862 to immediate acclaim. And in February the following year the Société genevoise d'utilité publique (the Geneva Society for Public Welfare) convened a committee to explore the practicalities of putting Dunant's proposals into action.

The committee established the foundation for the International Committee of the Red Cross and laid the groundwork for the first Geneva Convention, which was signed in August 1864 by twelve signatory nations. It agreed to 'guarantee neutrality to sanitary personnel' and 'to expedite supplies for their use'. It also approved the adoption of a clear and visible identifier for these neutral relief workers. Most often a red cross on white background. To this day it's the emblem of the Red Cross.

Wherever you go. Wherever you are. You're never very far from a reminder of war and violence. But you're also never that far from the sheer persistence of care. Violence is care's nemesis. But care is never far away from us either. Even in war.

I shiver involuntarily. It's been a long day and I need something to eat. You'd think that would be pretty straightforward. This is Paris after all. But paradoxically it's not, any longer, quite so straightforward for me.

The logic of care

It seems a long time ago, that string of messages on my phone in Tredegar. By then the pain that started with my broken toe had found its way up the entire right-hand side of my body. And as I had no visible injuries, my conscientious GP suggested doing some blood tests. I'd had them done before we left for Wales. Those messages were reminders to book a phone call to discuss the results.

'There are no obvious signs of infection,' he told me, when we finally spoke a few days later. 'Most of your blood readings are normal.'

Normal sounded good to me. 'So there's nothing wrong with me?'

'There was one result. Your HbA1c is a little high.'

'And that means – ?'

'It's a blood sugar measurement. Actually you're in the pre-diabetic range. Quite close to the boundary for type 2 diabetes.'

'Diabetes?'

'Has your diet changed recently?'

'Not really.'

'It could be a one-off. Let's do another test in a few months' time. Along with a full lipid count.'

'Which is – ?'

'To measure your cholesterol. If your blood sugar doesn't come down and your cholesterol is high, we might want to think about some medication.'

Might we? Really? Fantastic. Like all those people hooked on oxy, I was probably hoping for a quick fix. Something to take the pain away. Or something more obvious by way of explanation for why I had the pain in the first place. But that definitely wasn't my only disappointment.

I'm the kind of guy that prides himself on keeping fit and eating healthy. I don't smoke. I rarely drink. I'm not overweight. Ok. I've had a few injuries. Some allergies. A few problems with my digestion from time to time. But I'd never remotely associate myself with those WHO risk factors for chronic disease. I knew about that stuff. Of course I did. I'd even written about it.

During the pandemic, my colleague Shimaa Elkomy and I had analysed the relationship between risk factors for chronic disease and coronavirus mortality rates. We'd shown how increased risk factors predicted higher Covid-19 mortality. We'd shown that in countries with better risk reduction policies, Covid mortality rates were lower. In other words, those risk factors don't just drive chronic disease. They increase our susceptibility to infectious diseases like the virus as well.

So I knew they mattered. But what did that have to do with me? With my own health? I spent a week or so in denial. And then I remembered something I'd read in Annemarie Mol's book *The Logic of Care*. It had been sitting somewhere in one of those piles of books that were now beginning to remind me of the game of Jenga. The one where you have to remove a block without the whole pile falling down. And I'd taken to dipping in and out of it every now and then. The writing is so accessible. And her insights are always incisive. Early on she'd written this. 'To presume that you and I are healthy would go against the soul of what I seek to say. Within the logic of choice "disease" is a strange exception, it has nothing to do with "us", while the logic of care starts out from the fleshiness and fragility of life.'

What she'd been saying. If I'd been listening. Is that my own health ought to have been a part of the story from the start. I've no more right to think of myself as separate from my subject than anyone else. Especially when the subject is health.

Diabetes

I had another reason for picking up *The Logic of Care* again now. Mol's book is a philosophical inquiry. But she uses a very specific context to illustrate her arguments. Diabetes. I hadn't particularly taken it on board at the time. I must have remembered it though. Because I found myself picking up her book again. And now. Of course. It was personal.

Diabetes is a chronic disease of the metabolism. Its characteristic biomarker is the presence of high levels of glucose in the blood. That's what that HbA1c number was measuring. It's an indication that my metabolism is broken. And over time this metabolic dysfunction can lead to all sorts of problems. Inflammation. Chronic pain. Increased risk of cardiovascular disease. It can also damage the eyes, the kidneys, the nerves, the reproductive system and even the brain.

One of the problems is that metabolic dysfunction can set in long before you experience any symptoms at all. And to be honest, I still don't know if the pain I was experiencing had anything to do with my own high blood sugar or not. I just know that I'm storing up trouble by having it.

Blood glucose itself is essential. It's how we get the energy we need to live and breathe. To stay active. To maintain the body's regulatory metabolism. To digest the food that will keep the energy cycle going. To write books, I suppose. All of it. And it works something like this. When we eat, the digestive system breaks down carbohydrates in our food into sugar which enters the bloodstream through the gut wall. From there it's transported to the cells and tissues, where it's used for energy. The 'key' that lets glucose into the cells is a hormone called insulin.

As glucose enters the bloodstream, blood sugar levels rise. That rise signals the release of insulin from the pancreas. It also signals to the liver to absorb some of the sugar in case it's needed for later. The liver is a kind of glucose battery. Replenished when there's plenty around. Depleted when there's not so much to spare. When the blood sugar level drops again, the pancreas stops releasing insulin. When it drops further, the liver releases more glucose to keep the concentration in balance and allow for a consistent supply of energy.

In short, blood glucose is one of those elegant homeostatic mechanisms stumbled on by Claude Bernard (he of the interior environment) and identified by Cannon (in *The Wisdom of the Body*). But just as Peter Sterling and Joseph Eyer predicted in the 1980s, it's also one of those balances which can easily get out of whack. Diabetes is one of the things that happens when it does.

There are two main varieties of the disease. Type 1 diabetes occurs when the pancreas produces little or no insulin. No one knows the exact cause. There's some suggestion that it's an autoimmune condition. But no consensus. And there doesn't seem to be a cure. Before insulin was discovered and administered as a treatment in 1922, the diagnosis of diabetes was more or less a death sentence. Now, as we'll see, it can be treated quite successfully.

Type 2 diabetes also involves the relationship between blood glucose and insulin. But in this case it's not that your pancreas produces no insulin. It's just that for one reason or another it can't produce enough insulin to allow the glucose in your bloodstream into the cells. That often reveals itself through consistently high blood glucose levels – a condition known as hyperglycaemia. And although there are non-dietary risk factors, hyperglycaemia is more often than not diet related. It's a pre-diabetic condition and it's dangerous in its own right. Over time it's a risk factor for metabolic dysfunction and for almost every chronic disease we know.

Type 1 diabetes used to be called juvenile or early onset diabetes. That name tends not to be used anymore because, increasingly, type 2 diabetes also occurs in childhood. But the two diseases have different pathologies, different treatments and very different implications for health. The International Diabetes Federation estimates that 95 per cent of diabetes cases worldwide are of type 2. It's diagnosed through measuring a consistent hyperglycaemia at a given level. That's the import of my HbA1c reading.

I'm going to come back to the implications of all this in a moment. But the discovery of insulin is another of those madly fascinating stories from medical science. So I can't resist a slight detour. The story is such a mixture of fortune, creativity, ingenuity, hubris, territorial dispute and fickle reward. Plus it has an interesting lesson for what care is and what it's not.

Insulin wars

Diabetes itself has been known since antiquity. It was named by the Greek physician Aretaeus after the Greek word for a siphon. The disease was seen as siphoning off the body's fluid and depriving it of life.

The process of glucose regulation was first identified by Claude Bernard. And his insights also paved the way for the hypothesis that the pancreas had something to do with things. In 1889 Oskar Minkowski and Joseph von Mering confirmed the hypothesis by famously removing the pancreas from an unfortunate dog and watching it die. But at that point the precise mechanism for diabetes was still unknown. And nothing in the way of a cure was available.

And then in the early 1920s, along comes a young medic named Frederick Banting. Decorated for heroism during the First World War. Trying to set up general practice in the city of London, Ontario, in Canada. Things weren't going too well. So to supplement his meagre income and keep his interest in research alive he accepted a position as 'demonstrator'. Teaching physiology students at Western University.

Late one Sunday evening in October 1920, he was prepping for class. The next day he had to talk to his students about the metabolism of carbohydrates in the body. Flicking through the latest edition of a medical journal, he stumbled on an article discussing the Minkowski and von Mering experiment. It gave him an idea for a new experiment. What if it was possible to isolate whatever secretion the pancreas produced and see if it could relieve diabetes? It was already after midnight at this point. So he jotted down a quick memo:

> Diabetus. Ligate pancreatic ducts of dog. Keep dogs alive till acini degenerate leaving islets. Try to isolate the internal secretion of these to relieve glycosurea.

Over the next couple of years that cryptic note spawned a ground-breaking experiment. After a few false starts and some moments when he almost gave up in despair. With the help of a physiology prof named John Macleod, a student lab technician named Charles Best and a biochemist named James Collip, Banting managed to isolate the newly named 'insulin'. In the early months of 1922 they administered it to a fourteen-year-old diabetic called Leonard Thompson. His symptoms improved dramatically.

On 3 May that year, Macleod delivered a full summary of their work to the American Association of Physiology. It was met with a standing ovation. Eighteen months later, Banting and Macleod were awarded the Nobel Prize. Banting was just thirty-two years old. The youngest Nobel laureate in medicine to this day.

Banting and Macleod shared their prize money with Best and Collip. But somehow the four scientists argued furiously with each other over who received the credit. Early on, the young bucks (Banting and Best) were convinced that the old guard (Macleod and Collip) were trying to steal their glory. Later on, they pretty much all fell out. And went on fighting about it until the last of them (Best) died in 1978.

I don't know about you. I guess I take a few lessons from this. First off, always keep a notebook. That's obvious. Particularly if you want a Nobel Prize for something. I'm pretty sure I've had some shit-hot ideas in the middle of the night. I just forgot to write them down.

Second, there must be a better way to do research than throw scientists into a painful competition for resources the whole time. Banting was a brilliant and troubled man. No doubt he brought some of the conflict on himself. But society is notoriously unforgiving when it comes to understanding division and promoting harmony. Uncaring. You could almost say. Perhaps deliberately so.

And finally. Maybe. Just maybe. There shouldn't be prizes anymore. I'm not entirely sure they bring out the best in people. And so many good people get thrown to the wolves. Just so that we can clap the lucky few on the back through gritted teeth. And sully the rest of our life's work with envy and regret or (if we're the 'lucky' ones) overconfidence and triumphalism. What's the point of that?

Type 2

It might have been a detour. But it's not an irrelevant one. The discovery of insulin was essential to the prognosis for type 1 patients. But it's also relevant for type 2 diabetes. And for our understanding of the key differences between the two diseases. Mol points out a couple of those differences in *The Logic of Care*. Both of them matter for my inquiry.

The first is about the relationship between care and technology. It's pretty obvious from my detour that type 1 diabetes patients benefit massively from technology. The discovery, administration and control of insulin was a triumph of modern science. It's the only thing that keeps people alive when the body's own mechanism has broken down.

Like me, Mol is wary of associating care with unequivocally 'good' qualities such as kindness. 'The point is not that kindness, dedication and generosity are irrelevant to daily life,' she writes. 'They are crucial. But as long as care is primarily associated with "tender love", it may be cast as something that is *opposed to technology*'. And that would be wrong, she insists. It casts care as a 'pre-modern remainder in a modern world'. Left over from the dark days. Old-fashioned. Something other than technology. But in reality care 'is not opposed to but includes technology', says Mol.

That conclusion would also follow from the principle of care that I sketched in Chapter 4. The technology of externally administered insulin allows the body to recalibrate the blood glucose balance that is absolutely essential for human survival. In particular circumstances, that's a form of care. It follows that there's no reason to exclude technology from the domain of care. And it's wrong to do so. It's false to position care and technology as being in some way opposed to each other. As fundamentally different approaches to the management of health.

That's a powerful lesson. Just as postgrowth thinking should not exclude or underestimate or discard the benefit of technology in addressing today's environmental or social challenges, so the care economy must have a place for technology in delivering prosperity as health. For the advancement of knowledge. For the application of science. Even if, as Mol points out, technology too should always be 'handled with care'.

The second point she makes is even more crucial for my inquiry. It's to do with the nature of disease. And the nature of care in the face of disease. In particular, it's about the challenge faced by the principle of universal healthcare in the face of the shifting burden of disease that I highlighted in Chapter 5.

More than one in ten adults worldwide now live with diabetes. Between 90 and 95 per cent of them have type 2 diabetes. The incidence of type 2 has increased more than five-fold since 1980 and is predicted to go on increasing rapidly. Almost the same number of people are believed to be pre-diabetic, though that's difficult to say for sure, since it often goes undiagnosed. But in the US, one in every three adults are pre-diabetic. Almost a third of the adult population has a disease that starts with hyperglycaemia. High concentrations of blood glucose.

The profile of the disease has also changed in the last four decades. It used to mainly affect older people in richer countries. But increasingly it's affecting younger adults and even children. And more than 80 per cent of cases now occur in low- and middle-income countries. The direct medical costs of all this are almost $1 trillion a year. And all the projections suggest that both the prevalence of the disease and the costs will go on rising.

With good reason, it's been called a 'pandemic of unprecedented magnitude'. But it's also a thoroughly preventable pandemic. It has nothing to do with autoimmunity. It's not transmitted by germs. It's not the result of an injury or accident. It's about the body's tolerance for glucose in an increasingly glucose-rich environment. The primary risk factors are to do with poor diet and lack of exercise. It is properly speaking a lifestyle disease.

And that brings me back to Mol's second point. The diseases are different. The burdens are different. The causes are different. The pathogenesis is different. Type 1 diabetes appears to be mainly about bad luck in the genetic lottery. But type 2 diabetes is about population health in the face of external conditions which are increasingly conducive to ill health. And, in consequence, as Mol points out in her analysis, it becomes very obvious that care in relation to type 2 diabetes must be construed very differently from care in relation to type 1 diabetes.

'Public health does not improve as a result of caring for people who happen to have a disease,' she writes. 'It improves from interventions that keep the healthy healthy.' And this process of prevention must also be regarded as care.

More than that. It is quite precisely care. In the sense in which I defined it in Chapter 4. Because it refers to a process of bringing glucose regulation back into balance. Not only at the level of the individual organism but at the level of society. Allostasis teaches us quite clearly that under certain kinds of circumstances the organism loses its ability to achieve a homeostatic balance through its own endeavours.

Its role as carer is thwarted by external conditions over which it has little control. In type 1 diabetes that can be treated at the individual level (up to a point) by the administration of insulin. In type 2 diabetes we are talking about external conditions that are forged at the cultural level.

Of course, you could argue that the individual does have some control over some of those external cultural conditions. After all, we all get to choose our own diet. At least in principle. And to the extent to which that's possible, as I was very much hoping to prove after that conversation with my GP, that 'choice' does allow us to play the role of (tertiary) carer. To facilitate the body's return to the homeostatic still point.

But at the population level, that would depend on billions of people having the knowledge, exercising the control and achieving the lifestyle changes necessary to shift those risk factors to any meaningful degree. And as I've been finding out for myself, that is an enormously difficult challenge. Particularly under cultural and social conditions that make it next to impossible.

Progress report

I think I left that medical conversation back in January with a slightly false sense of agency. I was still holding on to the illusion of being fit and healthy. Or perhaps I was just not giving due respect to the fragility of health.

But at least I tried. I watched what I ate. I cut down on sugary snacks. I walked more and stood on the scales a lot. I figured out what my Body Mass Index (BMI) was and felt a little bit vindicated when I found that I was well within the conveniently green-coloured healthy weight range. See? There's nothing wrong with me. Maybe not quite in the middle. But definitely not overweight. Come the summer it was time to get some more tests done. I was pretty sure I had it licked.

This time I was referred to the diabetes nurse to discuss my results. At that point I was still struggling with the meanings of the various numbers and ranges. She was very patient with me. No. The HbA1c level (blood glucose) had not improved. In fact, it had slightly worsened. Fantastic. Did I really give up sugar for nothing?

But now we also had some serum lipid results. My LDL cholesterol (the one they call bad cholesterol) was too high. Not massively. But high. My HDL (the good one) was too low. Not massively. But low. And since the main indicator of cholesterol health is the ratio between the high and the low, it didn't look brilliant. Triglycerides. Also high. But what does it all mean?

'It means you're not just pre-diabetic,' she said. 'In fact, because you've had two readings in a row around the threshold, we would probably classify you formally as having type 2 diabetes.'

That's not what I was expecting.

'And your risk of heart disease is higher than we'd like.'

She put all the stats into a cardiovascular risk algorithm and quoted a figure at me. It wasn't awful. But it didn't inspire hope.

'Have you thought about changing your diet?' she asked me.

I thought about it. I thought I had changed my diet. 'I've definitely cut out a few things,' I said, tentatively.

'I can talk to the doctor about medication.'

'What kind of medication?'

'Statins, initially.' I had a sudden unhappy image of compartmentalized plastic pill containers for the rest of my life. Nothing against them. I know from my mother's lengthy care regime they can be incredibly useful. But not what I was ready for.

'I could also send you some leaflets about diet if you'd like to try that first.'

'I'd like to try that first.'

Deep learning

And this time round, I put a bit more effort in. It took me a while to realize that my body is cleverer than I am. It was incredibly good at tricking me. Pretty soon, I discovered I was in fact addicted to sugar. It's an addictive substance. Physiologists know that. Food manufacturers know that. That's why there's so much of it. Everywhere. In almost everything we eat. And my brain knew it too. It would do whatever it takes to get its sugar fix.

Yes, I'd cut down cookies. And I didn't add sugar to anything anymore. But I would surreptitiously add a little honey to my tea. Eat more fruit. An awful lot of grapes. Which as it turns out are a very accessible form of glucose. Looking back, I realized how much I had taken to snacking incessantly on things with a high glycaemic index (GI). Releasing glucose too quickly into the bloodstream.

I was caught in a sugar loop. And getting out of it was not fun. It felt like detox. It was detox. And as for reducing carbs. I felt like I'd been at the gym for three hours on an empty stomach. All the time. At first.

I also discovered it wasn't just about carbs and sugar. I drank more water. A lot more water. At the right times. Between meals. Not at them. I restricted caffeine to once a day. I ate more veg. A lot more veg. More seeds. Some nuts. I cut down on cheese. Another tough one that. I discovered that cheese contains a substance called casein which is an opioid. Yup. You guessed it. I was addicted to cheese as well. More detox required.

With more than a little help from my partner Linda, who enthusiastically took on our new dietary regime as a kind of joint mission, I ate virtually nothing that was highly processed or full of additives and preservatives. And eventually I cut out wheat and most other grains as well. In particular, highly engineered grains that appear in almost everything bread-like. Oat is a far less engineered carbohydrate. It has more protein and is better tolerated in the gut. Apparently.

I lost some weight. Quite a lot of weight. That was a bit worrying. Especially as losing weight without trying is a symptom of diabetes. But I guess I was trying. Or at least I had massively changed my diet. So my body had to relearn itself. At one point I had to take on a bit more protein to stabilize things. But my BMI was now bang in the middle of the green. It felt odd. It all felt very odd.

And then slowly. Very slowly. I began to feel things change. The cravings faded away. Cheese took longer than sugar to let me go. Weirdly. But eventually it did. I felt lighter. I moved more easily. I had less pain. I hadn't had this physique since my thirties. It made me realize how much we normalize ourselves around the mean. I'd never felt overweight. Because the mean kept going up around me. But I had been overweight. My body knew that. My joints knew that. My sleep knew that.

With the new regime my digestion improved. That was an unexpected win. On and off for years, I'd been taking an antacid called omeprazole or esomeprazole. I didn't much like taking it. But every time I tried to stop I immediately had stomach pain. Getting off it seemed worse somehow than before I started taking it. Turns out I was hooked on that too.

And what I discovered when I looked into that particular folly in more detail is that the entire concept of antacids is quite often plain wrong. Omeprazole is a 'proton pump inhibitor'. It works by stopping your stomach from producing acid.

Nobody tells you this. But that's tantamount to sacrilege. Because you need stomach acid to break down the food into a form that you can digest if it's to provide you with nutrition. Without enough acid, food ferments in the stomach. Fermentation means gas. Gas needs to get out. Ironically that's what causes the reflux. Quite often the problem isn't too much but too little stomach acid to start with. Preventing full digestion. That can happen for all sorts of reasons, mostly to do with the wrong diet. But also to do with something as simple as drinking too much water with a meal.

But hey. Who cares? Eat what you like. We have a pill for it. No matter that the pill does exactly the wrong thing. It's so much easier to shoot the messenger. And it's also incredibly profitable. The global proton pump inhibitor industry has a 'bright future' according to Pharmiweb.com, a global pharma news and resources website. The market is growing at more than 5 per cent a year and expected almost to double in value over the next decade.

Profit and loss

It all began to make me wonder exactly how much of what we call care is in fact the very opposite of care. How many of our responses are about shooting the messenger rather than listening to the message. Failing to listen to the signals the body is sending. Failing to nurture its own regulatory strengths. Failing to protect us from the profit-seeking mechanism of the market.

When food passes undigested into the intestine, it irritates the lining of the gut. Some kinds of food, particularly gluten, actually tear at the gut lining and create small holes in it. Through those holes pass partly digested food molecules that are not supposed to be there. The body thinks it's being invaded by aliens. It *is* being invaded by aliens. So it sends out its defence troops *en masse*, triggering an inflammatory response. Inflammation leads to pain. And is a precursor to almost every chronic disease as well.

Care would be to ensure people eat well. To provide nutritional advice when things go wrong. To protect them from exposure to relentless advertising for the wrong kind of foods. To insulate them from the instincts that were designed for an age when refined sugar and saturated fat were incredibly hard to come by. To regulate against the widespread use of pills that destroy the integrity of the body's own regulatory mechanisms. But don't worry. We have a pill for that too. And here's a surprise. The global pain management market is also growing at more than 5 per cent a year. By 2028 it will be worth almost $110 billion.

While we're at it, it's probably worth mentioning that the market for statins is expected to grow by just under 5 per cent a year over the same time. Market growth for the diabetes drug metformin is forecast at 6 per cent a year. And the market for anti-obesity drugs like Ozempic and Zepbound is expected to expand by a whopping 11 per cent each year over the next decade.

Meanwhile the global market for confectionery and snacks will continue to grow at almost 6 per cent a year, the market for oils and fats at 6.6 per cent, the market for ready meals at 6.9 per cent and the market for bread and cereal products at over 7.6 per cent. Year on year on year.

The global food industry is pump priming obesity. It's delivering unprecedented levels of metabolic dysfunction. And it's driving an epidemic of preventable chronic disease. But that's ok. Because it all feeds growth in the pharmaceutical industry. And typically it will be the nation state, taxpayers rather than shareholders, who pick up the cost.

I knew none of this stuff before. And it came as a shock to me. I plundered every resource I could to teach myself about it. About diet. About nutrition. About the medications we're sold to fix the problems driven by heavy-handed marketing of dietary products that systematically harm us. About the body I'd lived in so long and somehow never really understood.

There are some amazing resources out there now. Some of what I found was thoroughly peer-reviewed modern science. Some of it was old-fashioned nutritional understanding. Some of it was a brand-new and absolutely fascinating science of the gut biome. Some of it was downright flaky, for sure. But I also found people who said eminently sensible things, backed up by solid academic research, who got flamed, trolled and even cancelled for daring to say it.

One of the most authoritative, thoroughly researched and accessible sources of information for me was the work of the US endocrinologist Robert Lustig. He's spent his entire working life treating diabetes. And understanding its link to the food system. He's also had his unfair share of being trolled. But his 2021 *New York Times* bestseller *Metabolical* is a masterful synthesis of the underlying science. And a profoundly useful guide to liberate the reader from the tyranny of a healthcare system gone wrong.

Another extraordinary resource was Dr Casey Means' bestselling 2024 book *Good Energy: The Surprising Connection between Glucose, Metabolism and Limitless Health*. Thoroughly accessible. And firmly grounded in the science that people like Lustig worked for forty years to establish. *Good Energy* is an excoriating attack on her own medical training. The 'biggest lie in health care,' she says, 'is that the root cause of why we're getting sicker, heavier, more depressed, and more infertile is complicated'. On the contrary she insists, chronic disease is almost all the result of metabolic dysfunction brought on by modern lifestyles. Simple as that.

These resources didn't just transform my personal health. They helped me realize that the ideological battles being fought around nutrition and health simply could not be disentangled from the vested interests of the food lobby and the pharmaceutical industry. From the hierarchies of scientific medicine. From industry's role in medical research. From the economics of the healthcare system itself. From the addictive propensity of our own genetic makeup. And from the complete failure of government to regulate. Even when the health bill from not doing so is rapidly becoming unpayable.

Yes, some of the science is complex. I don't pretend to understand it all. And I'm not making any recommendations. None of this should be read in that vein. Do your own research. Work out what works for you. Don't be fooled by anyone's cure-all. Take as few pills as possible. Stop eating shit. When it comes to nutritional advice, that's about all I'm prepared to say.

But some of what's going on is blindingly simple. We eat too much of the wrong kind of stuff and it's creating an uncontrollable crisis in public health. We're encouraged into this by people whose interest does not in the least coincide with our own. Our own genetic make-up is being used against us to make things worse. We're being sold pills to fix the pills that fail to solve the problems caused by buying things we shouldn't have been sold in the first place.

And our economies are structured around this dysfunctional arrangement. We are supposed to believe that only by growing an economy that's harming us can we afford the healthcare that will save us. We're constantly urged to celebrate that growth. Our governments have given up on their most basic responsibility to protect people's health. And they appear almost pathologically unable to see that their own failure is directly responsible for rising healthcare costs which drain the public purse.

It also became clear to me that the battle we are fighting is one we are losing. That it's a battle is clear. It's playing itself out everywhere. In the press. In the media. On the internet. In the scientific literature even. And we are losing it. That's also clear. Our health is suffering. Prosperity in any meaningful sense is evaporating.

This seems suddenly worse to me than the debates about degrowth. In a sense it *is* the debate about growth and degrowth. All over again. In a different incarnation. A particular incarnation. A particularly bad incarnation. Because health is at stake. And because it's a battle that health is losing. Prosperity as health is losing out to prosperity as wealth.

Beyond humanitarianism

The light has faded now. I can barely see the water that flows beneath the bridge. Every now and then a *bateau mouche* comes through. Blazing light and blaring noise. Still haven't solved what to eat tonight. Won't do by freezing my ass off here. But there's something a little seductive about just standing on the Passerelle. Absorbing its history. Contemplating its relevance. To this intellectual journey. To my own health.

Don't get me wrong. I'm under no illusion that one man's health is anything more than an irrelevant anecdotal blip on the radar of an 'unprecedented' pandemic. None of this would matter at all if it was just about individual experience, individual choice and individual response.

But it's clearly not. It's part and parcel of the unsupportable burden on public health. And the impact of that on our healthcare systems. It's part of the impossible challenge facing the visionary ideal of universal healthcare. It's representative of one of the most striking changes in the burden of disease. A shift away from infectious diseases and towards chronic diseases that are now responsible for almost three-quarters of all deaths worldwide.

They're also a source of massive ill health. Of suffering. Of lost years of healthy life. Of escalating medical fees. And by 2030, if not before, they will cost the global economy upwards of $47 trillion. In the process, of course, they will carry away any chance of doing justice to the WHO's founding definition of positive health. Not just the absence of disease. The ability to thrive.

It seems to me we're getting closer to the dilemma I posed at the start of this book. If it's blindingly obvious that prosperity is about health. And if it's blindingly obvious that the economy should be about care. Why doesn't the blindingly obvious happen?

What's already clear is that it's not some random inability to take health seriously. It's not an arbitrary failure to operationalize care. We are living in and colluding with and giving credence to an economic system that is systematically operating against those very ideas. And it seems increasingly clear that tinkering at the edges of a system so broken and polluted that it's making us sick from the inside isn't going to fix that.

That's not to say there aren't obvious things that could be done. To prevent harm. To regulate malpractice and malfeasance. To invest in health. To value care. To reward carers. All of this still makes sense. It makes even more sense. But getting to the point of enacting those changes seems to demand something more. Something else. A different momentum. Something like the momentum that gave rise to the formation of the welfare state in the aftermath of the Second World War.

And the aftermath of the Battle of Solferino was also one of those moments. A shift in human sentiments. Or some confluence of the stars. A point where the soup of conflicting values in which we swim was stirred around a little. And out of the froth of violence and pain something new emerged. Compassion perhaps. Or at least a desire for something different. Something better.

Henri Dunant was an accidental witness to the horrors of battle. He'd arrived in Solferino with financial interests on his mind. But he left with a humanitarian mission. He pursued that mission with the zeal of a convert. He ploughed his time and money into the political process that established the Geneva Conventions. He achieved what he set out to achieve. But by 1867 he was bankrupt. The water rights for his Algerian project had never been granted. The company running that scheme had been mismanaged. His attention had been elsewhere for too long.

His friends deserted him. He lost pretty much everything. Within a few years he was living the life of an itinerant beggar. For the next two decades he lived in virtual obscurity. By 1892 he was being looked after in a nursing home in the town of Heiden in Switzerland. It was there that he was discovered in 1895 by a persistent Swiss journalist writing about the origins of the Red Cross. The article was reprinted in a German illustrated magazine and from there found a wide audience right across Europe. The world had rediscovered Henri Dunant.

In 1901 he was jointly awarded the very first Nobel Peace Prize. Fame barely touched him. He couldn't afford to spend the prize money during his lifetime for fear his creditors would get their hands on it. And he died a pauper in the nursing home in 1910. His last words were: 'Where has humanity gone?' Allegedly. I wonder what he might have said today. He would at least have known that the International Red Cross he helped found is still there. Still active. Still saving lives. Still reminding us that we are human. Maybe I was wrong after all about prizes.

8

The Lost Generation

'You are all a lost generation.'
Gertrude Stein, 1926

The sun is rising as I draw back the curtains. Its first rays reflect magnificently from something golden far away. Perhaps it's the dome of Les Invalides. The effect is dazzling. The light cascades precipitously across the landscape of roofs that tumble haphazardly towards my Parisian garret. Dancing as it goes.

Ok. It's not exactly a garret. It's a comfortable hotel room. But it happens to be up in the eaves. Six storeys up. So the view across the city is spectacular. The street below is barely awake. But here in the field of dreams I'm transported momentarily to another life. A distant memory. Something left over from teenage aspirations maybe. Romantic notions of the artistic life. Too much Hemingway probably.

If I'm up this early, it's obviously because I was out all night. Dining late. Drinking whisky. Listening to Cole Porter in smoke-filled bars. Playing chess maybe. Hanging out with Gertrude Stein's 'lost generation'.

It was a timely label. Not just for that brilliant community of writers, artists and musicians who gathered around Stein in Paris during the 1920s. But also for an entire generation who had come of age during or shortly after the First World War.

Hemingway had driven ambulances for Henri Dunant's International Red Cross. Wounded in action in Italy. Decorated for bravery. He'd thought about shooting himself as he lay there – tortured by fear that he'd be disabled for life. Instead he survived. Long enough to win the Nobel Prize in Literature in 1954 'for his mastery of the art of narrative ... and for the influence that he has exerted on contemporary style'.

Stein. Hemingway. F. Scott Fitzgerald. Djuna Barnes. Pablo Picasso. Henri Matisse. Ezra Pound. Edith Sitwell. Kay Boyle. They were the defining voices of modernism. A century ago now. An attempt to topple the old institutions in favour of something new and better. Or perhaps just to make sense of life in the aftermath of the Great War's abject nihilism. Its meaningless genocide.

'You are all a lost generation.' Hemingway cites Stein as saying this in one of two epigraphs to his 1926 novel *The Sun Also Rises*. In the other he quotes from the book of Ecclesiastes. 'One generation passeth away and another cometh; but the earth abideth forever.'

The old truths were gone. Gone or meaningless. Or treacherous as hell. Religion. Authority. Hierarchy. State. Class. Even decorum. It had all been used against them. It had cast young women as vassals of the patriarchy. It had turned young men into cannon fodder. Modernism was going to free them from all of that. Or at least it would consign the rules of the decrepit generals and their society wives to the bonfire of disrespect. And then we'd have a chance to see what was left. What if anything might abide.

Stein was at the centre of that rebellion. Orphaned at seventeen, she graduated *magna cum laude* from Harvard just a few years later. Her tutor there was the famous psychologist William James. He called her his 'most brilliant woman student'. By the time she graduated, she'd already published a paper in the *Psychological Review*. With James's encouragement, Stein enrolled at the Johns Hopkins School of Medicine.

Women had only recently been accepted as medical students there and overt sexism was still the order of the day. A professor of obstetrics named John Whitridge Williams delighted in giving ribald lectures on 'anecdotal midwifery' to a hall full of appreciative male students. The handful of women in attendance squirmed uncomfortably.

When Stein challenged him on it, the obstetrician told her he was free to teach as he wished. And by the way, anecdotal midwifery was a compulsory part of the curriculum. If she didn't like it, she could leave. She lost not only that particular battle but ultimately also her interest in medicine. The world would have to change fundamentally, she reasoned, before this misogynistic spectacle made any sense.

She fled to Paris and set up house with her brother Leo. Together they established themselves as art collectors. And their house on Rue de Fleurus – just round the corner from Rue de Varenne where I spent yesterday afternoon – became home away from home for the lost generation.

That's all very well. I shake myself out of my reverie. Another day of meetings ahead. And I need something in the way of breakfast to fortify myself.

You are what you eat

In the basement of the hotel the restaurant is still empty. I'm greeted warmly by the kitchen supervisor. Yesterday I was a curiosity. But today she's no longer offended that I've brought my own cereal. She's even found some almond milk for me. Without asking, she brings me a pot of hot water with a couple of slices of lemon in the side. But just in case I've come to my senses, she asks:

'Toujours pas de café?' Still no coffee?

'Non merci,' I smile. 'Merci quand même.' Thanks all the same.

Explaining breakfast without coffee is impossible in French. So I don't even try. After months of effort and with the best will in the world, it still feels like a Herculean task getting a handle on my dietary health. There's a mountain of good advice out there. Much more than there used to be. But social norms are powerful. The brain's neurochemistry evolved in a different environment. Access to healthy food is a relentless struggle. And getting nutrition right feels like swimming against an unruly tide.

Not so long ago the sheer abundance of bad food was a peculiarly Western problem. And in some places, of course, it's still an abominable luxury. More than three-quarters of a billion people still face chronic hunger. Not all of them in the global South. That number has been increasing in recent years. And nutritional deficiencies are rising even in so-called advanced western countries.

But alongside these harsh realities sits a much bigger and growing problem. Access to healthy food competes hopelessly, one-sidedly and endlessly with an overabundance of fast, fickle and ultra-processed foods. Sugar. Refined carbohydrates. Saturated fats. Trans fats. Empty calories. Dietary toxins. It's a nutritional disaster. But trying to counter it even at the individual level is almost impossible. Expecting an entire population to achieve that monumental task is wishful thinking.

During the early period of my own dietary revolution, I would wander through the supermarket aisles besieged and bedazzled by the ubiquitous and seductive lure to eat badly. The devious skill of the marketers who designed it all – the packaging, the product and the product placement – never ceased to amaze me. Impressive. If it wasn't so Machiavellian. And that's without the subtle and not so subtle messaging that rains down on you from every corner of life.

It's a minefield you're committed to navigating if you decide to take it on personally. But at the societal level it's a train crash playing out in slow motion. Getting a handle on chronic disease means getting a handle on diet. But we're still a million miles from doing that. And the backlash against it is still going strong.

One of the confounding arguments raised by the food lobby is that no individual is the same. It's not just that diets vary. It's that our physiology varies.

Our genetic make-up is different. So it's impossible to prescribe a healthy diet for everyone. And it's impossible to proscribe specific foods either. We're all different. So why intrude on people's freedom of choice? Interfering with individual food preferences is unscientific, oppressive and useless – according to this argument. It's a brilliant way of confusing the issue.

Doctor and media presenter Chris van Tulleken tried to cut through the obfuscation by conducting his own personal research experiment. On himself. In *Ultra-Processed People* he describes how he spent four weeks eating virtually nothing other than highly processed foods. The aim was to collect data to attract funding for a much bigger study. By the end of those four weeks he felt so sick, he says, that it worked as a kind of aversion therapy. Not a strategy I'm tempted to try. But telling all the same.

A case study of one person isn't scientific, of course. Probably van Tulleken was unlucky. Maybe he's just missing the gene that tolerates ultra-processed foods. You know, the one they haven't discovered yet? The argument that chronic disease is largely genetic is a hugely convenient one for a pharmaceutical industry that wants to sell you a cure. And a food industry intent on maximizing profit. But the evidence so far suggests that genes are directly responsible for less than 10 per cent of metabolic dysfunction. And that leaves a lot of the responsibility for damage at the door of diet and lifestyle.

Chronic overnutrition. Nutrient deficiency. A depleted gut microbiome. Chronic stress. Pharmaceutical drugs. Sleep deprivation. Environmental toxins. These are among the culprits that Means identifies in *Good Energy*. They all damage the mitochondria which convert food energy into cellular energy. At the very heart of the metabolic dysfunction which drives chronic disease lies the age-old adage: 'You are what you eat.'

Intrigued by this, I went searching for the roots of that idea. Predictably I found myself back with Hippocrates. In fact, he's credited with an even more radical idea. That the best way to health is through diet. 'Let food be thy medicine and let medicine be thy food.' And interestingly, it's still cited far and wide. Not only by advocates of holistic nutrition. But even by reputable medical journals.

Pure, white and deadly

A few years ago the *BMJ* dedicated an issue to the fallout from a WHO report which had dared to link diet to the upsurge of chronic disease worldwide. *Diet, Nutrition and the Prevention of Chronic Diseases* laid out the evidence and made a couple of blindingly obvious recommendations. Added sugar should comprise no more than 10 per cent of a healthy diet, said the WHO. And governments should limit our kids' exposure to junk-food ads.

The backlash was savage. The Sugar Association wrote to Dr Gro Harlem Brundtland, who was Director General of the WHO at the time. They threatened 'to exercise every avenue available to expose the dubious nature' of the organization's work. And it seems they weren't bluffing. Congressmen 'recruited by the food industry' lobbied the US government to withdraw America's annual contribution to the WHO budget.

They didn't succeed. But this particular issue of the *BMJ* reported a leaked letter from the US Department of Health putting pressure on the WHO to retract its dietary recommendations. The letter accused the agency of reaching 'unsubstantiated conclusions' that 'specific foods are linked to non-communicable diseases and obesity'.

And yet those conclusions had by then been known for many decades. *Pure, White and Deadly*, John Yudkin's brilliant exposé of the sugar industry, was first published in 1972. It too was subject to a ferocious backlash and claims that it was 'science fiction'. But as Robert Lustig points out in *The Hacking of the American Mind*, if we'd heeded those concerns at the time, we'd not now be facing an epidemic of childhood obesity.

I learned for myself that added sugar is tantamount to poison. It's simply too concentrated for the body to regulate effectively. It'll give you a short-term energy hit, for sure. But it will also scream at your pancreas to release as much insulin as possible to bring your blood sugar levels down again. If your pancreas is still working, that will throw you into a sugar low and you'll be craving sugar again. It's a classic addiction dynamic.

You can tolerate all this for a while. But eventually it will catch up with you. Like it did with me. And yet there is an entire industry attempting to bypass science, bully those who oppose it and bribe government to protect their interests.

In his editorial for the *BMJ* issue, which was titled 'Let food be thy medicine . . .', the editor at the time, Richard Smith, made an 'unadventurous prediction': that 'we will be hearing much more about the science, medicine and politics of food' in the next few years. 'Hippocrates would be pleased,' he concluded. In the intervening two decades we have heard a lot more. But it hasn't gone unopposed.

Even the Hippocrates quote itself has come under scrutiny. Did he ever say let food be thy medicine in the first place? Not according to a researcher at the Descartes University right here in Paris. She took the trouble to search through the entire Hippocratic Corpus – the body of collected writings of the father of medicine. Having done so, she declared that the phrase was categorically nowhere to be found.

Over the previous thirty years, though, she found, at least one reputable biomedical journal each year had perpetuated the 'myth'. This enthusiastic medical detective, perhaps angling for a career somewhere in Big Pharma or in Big Food, concluded that the misquotation was a 'fabrication' which had 'mistakenly helped scientists confirm the importance of food to health'.

Confused and bewildered, as no doubt I was supposed to be, I decided to go looking for myself. I discovered that actually Hippocrates did highlight the links between food and health. In numerous places. The link is even embedded in the original wording of the Hippocratic Oath that doctors take when they promise 'first, do no harm'.

The original text of the oath promises to 'apply dietetic measures to help the sick to my best ability and judgment'. The 'dietetic measures' here comes directly from the Greek word *dietimasi* (διαιτήμασί), which includes some notion of lifestyle as well as diet. In English it's often translated simply as 'treatments'. But applying treatments to help the sick is not the same thing at all as acknowledging that the dietary and lifestyle conditions in which people live affect their health. Massively. Hippocrates knew this.

Fighting over what Hippocrates may or may not have said two and a half thousand years ago all seems a bit academic. But I'm beginning to see that the real battle plays itself out – and has done for a very long time – behind the camouflage of these seemingly innocent 'intellectual' disputes. And that the disputes themselves are a thinly veiled cover for the economic interests that shape our diet, our health and our lives.

Cambridge professor Martin White and his colleagues have explored the relationship between commercial food systems and their impact on our health. What they find is eerily reminiscent of the debates around the economy and its impact on the planet in which I've been involved for decades.

Driven by the desire for short-term profit and shareholder value, the study finds, food companies have engaged in a range of clever strategies to promote continual growth in throughput. Some of them involve increasing agricultural productivity. Some of them involve an increase in processing. Some of them involve pandering to our epigenetic desire for sugar, salt and saturated fats. Some of them involve engaging in complex financial strategies that consolidate power and using that power to influence policy. And all of them have contributed to the huge external costs we now face from obesity and chronic disease.

What's clear is that this isn't simply a matter of volume growth. It's a shift in direction, deliberately driven by strategy, which has changed the shape of our diets in ways that are irreconcilable with good health. Ways (it's worth adding), which have contributed to climate change, biodiversity loss, soil degradation and the pollution of rivers and waterways.

My own story is a statistical irrelevance. I'm just a pawn in this intricate game. A minnow at the mercy of the pikes. But I'm beginning to get a sense of what my colleague Tim Lang and his collaborator Michael Heasman have called 'food wars'. The struggles for control and influence over our diet and nutrition. And to understand that behind them lies a desperate tussle between public health and the pursuit of profit.

I glance at the clock. Still a little while before I have to leave for my meeting. Time for a little light reading. I pick up the slim volume I brought with me to Paris. Nothing too heavy – physically or metaphorically. It's just a hundred pages long. But it's been on my desk for a while now. And this moment of quiet contemplation ahead of my day of meetings seems like a good opportunity to make a start on it.

Sisters of Mercy

Notes on Nursing was written in 1859, the same year as the Battle of Solferino. Its author was the founder of modern nursing. Florence Nightingale. The legendary 'lady with the lamp'. She was bequeathed an almost saintly reputation by the wounded soldiers she tended with unstinting compassion through the wee small hours of their darkest night in a military hospital in Scutari during the Crimean War. But the real Florence Nightingale was no lightweight sugar-coated angel. She was a force of nature.

Fifty years before Stein fled to Paris to escape a misogynistic medical profession, Nightingale also came here to escape the 'gilded cage' of Victorian society. And to pay a visit to the Sisters of Mercy – a community of Catholic women dedicated to the service of others.

She'd been brought up in relative luxury. Her father was the son of a Sheffield banker. The family moved between comfortable homes in England and travelled extensively abroad. Encouraged by her father, she'd read widely and was already well educated by the time she was sixteen. At that point, she experienced some kind of spiritual awakening. One of several 'calls from God'.

As she saw it, the call was very specific. She was to dedicate her life to the relief of human suffering. She decided to become a nurse. Unfortunately in those days nursing was seen as a totally inappropriate occupation for a woman of her class. Nurses and midwives were just one rung up the ladder from witches and whores. Which is not to demean either of those ancient professions. Except in the eyes of Victorian fathers.

This particular father hadn't reckoned with his daughter's persistence. For a decade or so the best she managed was to visit some sick relatives and do some voluntary work in local hospitals. But eventually she persuaded him to let her travel to Europe to study nursing. And that's when she visited the Sisters of Mercy here in Paris.

She also spent several months with a Lutherian community of deaconesses in the historic Kaiserswerth district of Düsseldorf in Germany. The community had been established in 1836 by a Pastor named Theodor Fliedner and his wife Friederike. Their aim was to train young women from middle- and lower-class backgrounds as nurses. In return for their bed and board the women would dedicate the rest of their lives to the service of others.

The concept sounds very worthy. Laudable even. I guess it isn't entirely above reproach. A host of vulnerable young women giving up certain freedoms, within a hierarchical system overseen by a powerful male authority figure. Possibly two if you count both Fliedner and God. Might there be an abuse of power going on here?

On the other hand, the deaconesses were granted a surprisingly high degree of autonomy. Perhaps more autonomy than they might have expected in wider society at that time. That's clearly something Nightingale could relate to. And maybe it's sufficient recompense for the exercise of patriarchal power. A lot hangs on the existence of a genuine reciprocity, I suppose.

For the moment, I'm steering clear of that one. Though I'll have to come back to the question of patriarchy later. But whichever way you see it, there's little doubt that the deaconesses played a fundamental role in the development of modern nursing. Together with the Sisters of Mercy they brought a kind of discipline that simply hadn't existed before. And Nightingale brought that discipline back to Britain with her.

There was still no obvious role for her to play when she got home. So, with the help of an annual stipend from her father, she took up a post as superintendent of the Institute for the Care of Sick Gentlewomen in London. There she spent a year honing her organizational skills, which proved to be as formidable as her ability to care. And then, out of almost nowhere (unless you believe in fate or divine intervention), things changed dramatically for her.

Death in Scutari

Seen from our perspective, the Crimean War has some pretty eerie resonances. It involved an unseemly dispute between Russia and the rest of Europe. And its immediate flashpoint was a dispute in Palestine. It's enough to make you think there's someone out there writing and rewriting the same old story. Very slightly varying the configuration of roles. With the same tragic ending.

In the middle of the nineteenth century, Palestine was part of the Ottoman Empire. Although it was an Islamic state, the Ottomans took a tolerant view of Christianity in their territory. Particularly in Jerusalem. For some time, they'd granted the Eastern Orthodox church authority to maintain religious sites and monuments there. One of those sites was the Church of the Holy Sepulchre. Believed to mark the place where Jesus of Nazareth was crucified.

And then. Somewhat unexpectedly. Egged on by France. The Roman Catholic church managed to persuade the Ottomans to pass those maintenance rights to them. The move angered Russia. Tsar Nicholas I saw it as an assault on Russia's agreed role as protector of the interests of Orthodox Christians in the Ottoman Empire. And to mark his displeasure he increased Russia's military presence in the Danubian principalities that formed the border between Russia and Turkey.

It's fair to say that behind all this there was more going on. As there often is. The Ottoman Empire had played a useful role in the balance of power in eastern Europe. It was now in decline. And France and Britain were becoming wary of the expanding influence of the 'Russian bear'. That wariness probably lay behind France's 'provocation' in Jerusalem. But it was substantially increased by Russia's military response in the principalities.

By this time, ironically, the two churches had managed to negotiate a compromise between themselves on the maintenance rights of the Holy Sepulchre. But territorial blood was now up on both sides of the dispute. And in September 1853 the die was cast. After seeking reassurances that France and Britain would support them, the Ottomans declared war on Russia.

For some time nothing much happened. But in 1854 British troops were drawn into a disastrously unsuccessful assault on the Russian naval base in Sevastapol on the Crimean Peninsula. The outcome was both tragic and avoidable. And when the wounded were evacuated to the military hospital in nearby Scutari the casualties mounted even higher. Conditions in the hospital were atrocious. And when news of this reached London there was outrage.

'Are there no devoted women among us, able and willing to go forth to minister to the sick and suffering soldiers of the East in the hospitals of Scutari?'

wrote the Irish war journalist William Russell in his despatches for *The Times*. 'Are none of the daughters of England, at this extreme hour of need, ready for such a work of mercy?'

In the ears of one woman this call was a sign from God. This was what her life had been waiting for. Nightingale offered her services to the War Office on 14 October 1854. And just a week later she and thirty-eight other nurses – some of them from the Sisters of Mercy – set sail for Crimea, arriving in Scutari on 7 November.

What they found was shocking. 'There were no vessels for water or utensils of any kind; no soap, towels, or clothes, no hospital clothes,' wrote Nightingale. 'The men lying in their uniforms, stiff with gore and covered with filth to a degree and of a kind no one could write about; their persons covered with vermin.' During that first winter more than four thousand men died in Scutari. More of them from preventable diseases like cholera and dysentery than from the wounds sustained in battle.

As soon as she saw what was happening, Nightingale sent word to the War Office demanding that the Sanitary Commission be sent to flush the sewers and improve ventilation. She also installed the same rigorous hygiene measures she had learned in Kaiserswerth and insisted that her nurses – and the doctors – did the same. It was immediately effective. The death rate in Scutari was more than 40 per cent before she got there. By the time she'd finished, it was 2 per cent.

Care as discipline

Nightingale returned home a national heroine. The war correspondents who precipitated her departure to Scutari now celebrated her return, amplifying her reputation. She became as well known in Britain as Queen Victoria. A fund was set up in her honour. And she used it to establish the first proper school of nursing at St Thomas' Hospital in London. She was in her element now. To all intents and purposes the Nightingale School established nursing as a profession for the first time. Similar schools were set up all around the world.

Her birthday on 12 May is still celebrated as International Nurses Day. When new NHS hospitals were built at lightning speed during the Covid pandemic, they were christened Nightingale hospitals. And each year the International Committee of the Red Cross recognizes the outstanding achievements of nurses from countries all round the world by awarding the Florence Nightingale Medal.

Of course there's still something deeply suspect about the gender politics of all this. Men get to fight about stuff. Women get to clean up the mess they make in the process. You wouldn't get away with that nowadays. Or would you?

We happily believe ourselves to be less prey to the gender division of labour than the Victorians were. The statistics say otherwise. Almost 90 per cent of nurses are still women. And more than 80 per cent of military personnel are still men. The implicit female 'duty to care' as proof of selfless devotion to men looms as problematically at the heart of today's division of labour as it did over Nightingale's mercy mission in Scutari.

But there's an irony in this story too. Nightingale's image as the meek and selfless lady with the lamp was not exactly a mirage. It wasn't entirely the opium-fuelled dreams of soldiers far from home. But it does her no justice. It does nursing no justice. It does care itself no justice.

One recipient of the Florence Nightingale Medal put it this way. 'As a student nurse, few things enraged me more than the thought of Florence Nightingale,' reflected Jane Salvage in the *BMJ* in 2001. What nursing needs 'is assertiveness and intellect, not sticky-sweet submissiveness and self-sacrifice', she said. But then she came to realize that Nightingale's reputation had little to do with the historical person. In fact, Nightingale herself hated the whole lady with the lamp mythology.

Compassion and altruism are clearly worth nurturing. Of course they are. Particularly in the domain of care. But to focus on these qualities to the exclusion of the task itself is a recipe for the devaluation of care. It's to render nursing a frail hostage to society's fickle affections. And it imposes unfair penalties on those who engage in care.

'When well educated, motivated, newly qualified nurses discover that health care decision makers see them merely as a slightly more skilled, slightly less starched version of the Victorian handmaiden,' said Salvage, they start dreaming of escape. 'We could do with a lot more of Miss Nightingale's savvy and singlemindedness,' she continued. 'Without it, nursing (and therefore health care) will remain in crisis.'

I'm inclined to agree with this. To value care in society is not about laying claim to the moral high ground. It's about recognizing the vital restorative function of care in the health of living organisms. To acknowledge its stabilizing and strengthening influence in society. To understand its position as a core organizing principle in life.

The story of the real Florence Nightingale matters. Its lessons cut to the heart of my inquiry in this book. They illuminate the exploration of care and its role in the economy. But that's not the only reason for telling it. There's something else here too. As I now discover. Something clear-sighted, prescient and entirely radical in Nightingale's own thinking.

Something I might have missed completely if I hadn't made the time to get hold of a copy of *Notes on Nursing*. If I hadn't decided to bring it with me to Paris. If I hadn't opened it this morning at breakfast. If I hadn't started reading.

> Shall we begin by taking it as a general principle that all disease, at some period or other of its course, is more or less a reparative process, not necessarily accompanied with suffering: an effort of nature to remedy a process of poisoning or of decay, which has taken place weeks, months, sometimes years beforehand, unnoticed, the termination of the disease being then, while the antecedent process was going on, determined?

Wow. I put the book down again. It may have arrived late on my Jenga pile. But that's probably a good thing. I now know enough to understand that its author is saying something revolutionary. She's taking up a very particular position in another of those scientific and intellectual debates that have been going on for centuries. For millennia. One I'm going to have to unravel if I want to make progress.

Disease as a reparative process. It has its roots in antiquity. It echoes the insights of naturopathy and natural hygiene. But it anticipates Claude Bernard's constancy of the 'internal environment' by almost twenty years. It hints at Walter Cannon's *Wisdom of the Body* eight decades before it was written. And it's beginning to re-enter the lexicon of our medical understanding more than a century after it was expunged decisively by modern 'scientific' medicine.

That frisson of surprise alerts me to a minor breakthrough in my own understanding. But wherever that's going to lead me is going to have to wait. Breakfast is over. It's time to get my skates on.

Conviviality

Upstairs in my garret, I pack up my belongings and prepare for the day ahead. My thoughts return to the lost generation. A part of me still lies captive there. I can still taste the whisky. I can still smell the cigarette smoke. The late-night conversations still echo in my mind.

And then it occurs to me. How much of any of that would be any good for me? How much of that would have contributed to my physiological health? Not much of it. Let's face it. Not the alcohol. Not the smoky ambience. Not the late dining or the sleepless nights. Not even the desperate search for meaning, come to that. Nor the lingering trauma of the Great War.

Maybe the chess. Elite chess players live fourteen years longer than the population average apparently. The Russian grandmaster Yuri Averbakh survived Covid when he was already well into his nineties and died at the ripe old age of one hundred. Not that last night's chess was elite by anyone's standards. Certainly not at my table. Enthusiastic at best. But chess players take their physical health pretty seriously these days. Some grandmasters bring their own nutritionists on tour with them. Apparently. So maybe chess is the exception.

But musicians, though. My goodness. That's another story. According to one study, the life expectancy of pop musicians has been twenty-five years shorter than the average life expectancy of US citizens during the last half a century or so. Edith Piaf died at the age of forty-seven. Pretty much bang on the statistical target. Amy Winehouse was just twenty-seven. Yet isn't music something we'd want to keep close in any meaningful vision of human prosperity? I know I would.

It's a timely reminder that physical health isn't everything. It matters, for sure. At the collective as well as the personal level. Who would not have wanted Edith Piaf to stay around a bit longer, for instance? Or Amy Winehouse? Or Jeff Buckley? Think what we missed out on as a result of their untimely deaths.

But our ability to thrive – the WHO's state of complete physical, mental and social wellbeing – is tangled up inseparably with our psychological health. With our sense of community. With our creativity. With our sense of ourselves as part of society. With our culture. For the human species at least, the task of living well can never be entirely physiological.

What was it that brought the lost generation together here in Paris? It wasn't only the desire for immortality. It was as much, if not more, a search for expression. It was to some extent the pursuit of meaning. It was a restless need to speak out against a society that could deliver a generation of young men and women to the horror of the First World War. A desire to bring down the repressive, hierarchical values that had led the West into madness and cruelty.

'Art is a cry of distress from those who live out within themselves the destiny of humanity,' said the composer Arnold Schoenberg. A cry from those who 'do not look away to preserve themselves from emotion, but instead throw their eyes wide open to encounter what must be encountered.'

The lost generation were searching for the foundations of humanity in the face of the destructive nihilism that had taken over society. They were in their own way trying to return society to health. To lead it away from violence and destruction. Their search was itself a search for balance. It was even in some sense an act of care in the sense I described in Chapter 4. An attempt to return to the still point. A point from which we could once again make sense of ourselves. And find our place in the world.

That there's a cost to this task seems perverse. And that the cost is sometimes measured in life years lost is tragic. But perhaps there is always a cost to care. Perhaps the forces of imbalance and chaos can only be tamed at some kind of price. Perhaps health itself is a costly endeavour. Can that be true?

As I shake these questions from my mind and prepare myself for the more mundane tasks of the day ahead, I'm sure of one thing. Whether or not there was a cost, there was also a reward. A sense of conviviality that still seems wonderful. A kind of elixir. The key to a romantic dream that's persisted for a century. Something both elusive and tangible.

Something as ethereal as the last notes of an accordion fading into the dawn sky. As pungent as the scent of Gauloises lingering in the morning air. As enticing as the laughter of those drawn together here in Paris a hundred years ago by tragedy and loss and disillusionment. Able to find in each other – and in art, in the act of care – a sense of communion with like-minded souls. A conviviality that must surely be as much a part of the state of wellbeing as the physiological health on which it depends.

Serious people

I'm feeling strangely refreshed as I walk the few blocks from my hotel to the grand old building that occupies most of the Rue Croix des Petits Champs. It's turning into a crisp winter's morning. My spirits are lifted by the warmth of the sun on my face. And my brief encounter with the lost generation has given me a new perspective on what I'm doing here.

Needless to say, I wasn't actually out in bars all night. You probably guessed that already. I spent a few hours working on my presentation for this morning's meeting. A seminar at the Banque de France. I suppose the charade at the Ministry unsettled me slightly. And I want to be well prepared for whatever comes at me today. The only real reason for engaging at all in what sometimes seems to be a massively counter-cultural conversation is that the conversation needs to be had. Even if we can't agree on things.

There's a striking scene in the last season of the HBO series *Succession* where Logan Roy (played by Brian Cox) confronts his kids as they vie with each other both for his love and for the right to take on his media empire. 'I love you,' he says. 'But you are not. Serious. People.' And he walks out of the room. Sometimes it would be great to channel my inner Logan Roy. A young man greets me warmly in the massive foyer of the old building.

'We're so pleased you could make it,' he says.

'I'm happy to be here,' I reply. And then, with a hint of a question, I add, 'It's an interesting place for a discussion on postgrowth economics.' He picks up the implication immediately.

'We had to whisper it in the corridors,' he smiles. 'We were very careful not to use the D-word. In case someone got wind of what we are doing.'

The 'D-word' is degrowth, of course. We're here in the Banque de France to (not) talk about degrowth.

'And what are you doing?' I ask innocently.

'We're doing our job,' he smiles at me. 'As I understand it.'

And that seems right to me. More than right. It seems essential that the institution responsible for the nation's financial and monetary stability should concern itself with the possibility that economic growth might not go on for ever. And that at some point a different kind of economy might just be necessary. Or even, in fact, that it's already upon us.

I've made that case already. I made it in the Ministry. And I'll make it here again today. But my welcome already suggests that today's conversations will be slightly more meaningful than it was possible to have yesterday. I already feel less like a court jester. We may not agree on everything. But I can tell that this will be a more serious discussion. With serious people.

9

Care in the Time of Cholera

> *'Shall we begin by taking it as a general principle that all disease, at some period or other of its course, is more or less a reparative process?'*
> Florence Nightingale, 1859

Like many natural harbours around the British coastline, Chichester Harbour is stunningly beautiful. It's home to a legion of geese, cormorants, egrets, a dozen or so seals and even the occasional dolphin. It was designated an Area of Outstanding Natural Beauty (AONB) sixty years ago.

On this particular day the harbour is wearing its Sunday best for us. The sky is a pristine blue and a light northwest wind is tripping across the water. Rippling the surface as it goes. It's perfect winter weather.

My brother and I have sailed together since we were kids. At first it was an imaginary affair of the heart. An old cardboard box in our landlocked back garden. Later we'd take a dinghy out on a lake. Or once, when I was studying in St Andrews, on the volatile and unpredictable North Sea.

On his thirtieth birthday we chartered a thirty-foot cruiser with some friends and sailed her far enough off the coast of Devon to witness the total eclipse of the sun. Our aim was to find the path of totality. The trajectory beneath which the sun is completely obscured by the moon. It was magical. This moon. This aloof satellite. This indifferent carer. She's nonetheless an awe-inspiring companion. On that day you could sense the sheer mass of her, passing between earth and sun. Nobody spoke for the whole four minutes.

Today we're in the tamer habitat of Chichester. We're not saying much now either. Content simply to drift along on the tide with the faintest of breezes at our back. Soaking in the tranquillity of it.

Up ahead of us is a small flotilla of excitable dinghies. It's not uncommon. Even in winter. Exiled to weekend sailing club by overstretched parents, their voices reach us long before they do. From a distance they seem to be bobbing about aimlessly on the water. Up close you'll see they're racing each other. Seriously competitive. Looking around for the next racing mark. Or sometimes, when the wind picks up, just trying to stay upright. Not always successfully.

But these young crews are, on the whole, pretty adept at their task. There's a reason Britain has won more Olympic sailing medals than any other country. We're an island nation. The sea is a vast and omnipresent companion. Surrounding us. Defining us. Insulating us against the rest of the world. But also luring us outwards. Into the world. And yes. It seems big enough to wash away all evil. But it's not. Today it looks idyllic. And it's not.

Sweare Deep

As we reach a point known as Sweare Deep, where the Northney channel meets the Emsworth channel, something sinister happens. The water that was a clear dark turquoise has turned a suspiciously foamy brown colour. I check the app on my phone, hoping not to confirm the obvious. But sure enough there's been an 'incident' at the combined sewer overflow in Emsworth. No swimming today then, bro. And let's hope those kids stay upright.

These overflows are designed to function automatically. Storm water and sewage are collected separately and transported together to the local treatment works. The sewer is designed in such a way that when there's been heavy rain and the combined volume is too much for the capacity of the treatment plant, the excess flows over a concrete barrier and escapes into the surrounding watercourse. It's all ingenious. Except for its impact on our rivers and seas.

But here's the thing. I'm looking at the data. There really wasn't that much rain during the last month. Barely half the days had any rain at all. Let alone enough rain to justify an overflow event. So most of those discharges would have been illegal. Including today, it seems.

Sadly, proving that illegality is not straightforward. It took an investigation by the BBC to reveal that just three UK water companies released sewage on dry days for a combined total of 3,572 hours in a single year, including some days on which a drought had been declared. All of it illegal. But less than a third of the breaches were picked up by the regulator and there were barely a handful of prosecutions. By comparison with the profits, the fines were minuscule.

And as for Chichester Harbour, despite its protected status, there are no fewer than thirteen sewage overflows which discharge directly into this catchment area. Last month alone, I learn, raw sewage has been released for no less than twelve hundred hours. Given that there's only seven hundred and forty-four hours in a month at most, that's quite a feat.

If you happened to be out there rowing, sailing, kayaking, swimming, fishing or even just paddling on the beach during that time, you were at risk of exposing yourself to potentially pathogenic micro-organisms (germs). So too were your precious offspring. If you happen to be one of those overstretched parents hoping for peace of mind on a Sunday morning, you might want to download this sewage alert app. Or one like it. It's cold comfort. But it's better than swimming in ignorance. Or shit. Come to that.

If you're minded to, the app will also let you report a scientific sample of the water quality – usually measured by the concentration of a little bug known as *E. coli*. Its full name is *Escherichia coli*. *Coli* because it's discovered *en masse* in the colon of most animals. *Escherichia* after a German paediatrician named Theodor Escherich who discovered it in 1885. He'd been trying to figure out the reason for an outbreak of diarrhoea in his young patients and managed to isolate this particular organism from their faeces.

Since then, *E. coli* has won more Nobel Prizes than any other organism. Twelve in all between 1958 and 2015. That's partly because it's so easy to study. And partly because it's what biologists call a 'model organism'. Its single cell shares many characteristics of the trillions of cells that make up the human body. 'What's true of *E. coli*,' said one of those Nobel Prize winners, 'is true of the elephant.' Which seems odd. Because I don't see many elephants swimming around in the Northney channel. But there's an awful lot of shit.

The point is that the presence of *E. coli* in water is a pretty solid indicator of contamination from sewage. And if you or your kids are unfortunate or careless enough to capsize in Chichester Harbour on a day when the combined sewer overflow has released its charge into the water, that's what you are exposing yourself to. And the chances are you won't feel too good if you swallow it.

Germs make you sick. That much I've always taken as gospel. But recently I've been delving more deeply into one of those Jenga piles on my overcrowded desk. It turns out things are a bit more complicated. In fact at this point in the proceedings, almost three years into my journey, I realize I've stumbled on a battle that has haunted medical science for a couple of centuries now and whose roots lie in the even more distant past. A battle which was supposed to have been won more than a century ago.

Disease as a restorative process

Let's back up a little. I want to return to that short passage from the introduction of Florence Nightingale's *Notes on Nursing*:

> Shall we begin by taking it as a general principle that all disease, at some period or other of its course, is more or less a reparative process?

Like most medical ideas, it can be traced back to Hippocrates. He's supposed to have said it very precisely. 'Natural forces within us are the true healers of disease.' You can find it cited all over the place. The most authoritative source I found pointed me towards another equally authoritative peer-reviewed paper – written in Chinese. Unfortunately my Mandarin wasn't up to tracing it any further. So given the debacle with the food as medicine quote and short of trawling through the entire Hippocratic corpus myself, I'm just going to declare ignorance of the origins of that particular phrase and go with what I do know.

In his book *On the Nature of Man*, Hippocrates' son-in-law Polybus describes the Hippocratic model of health as a balance between four bodily 'humours'. Each humour is associated with a different bodily fluid system: blood, phlegm, yellow bile and black bile. But they also hold associations with the four seasons. With different moods and temperaments. With different organs. With different external conditions. And with different ages in the life cycle.

A very similar idea can be traced to an even older system of medicine from Taoist philosophy. It dates back to the Shang Dynasty between 1600 and 1046 BCE. In the Chinese system the taxonomy involves five elements – wood, fire, earth, metal and water – rather than four. But aside from this dimensionality, the two systems are remarkably similar. In the Chinese system there are once more links between the elements and the seasons. And there are again associations between the five elements and different moods, temperaments, organs of the body and external conditions.

More importantly health is conceived as a state in which these different elements are in balance with each other. Disease is manifest as an imbalance between them. It's a slightly more complex representation of the Aristotelian metaphor of health as a balance between deficiency and excess. But in this case the excesses and deficiencies are relative to some ideal balance between different elements.

In other words both the Hippocratic and the Taoist tradition see healing as a process of restoring balance. The same is true in the ancient medical tradition of Ayurveda. All these models suggest that the body itself tends towards balance. And that what manifests as disease is the body's process of trying to come back into balance.

It's reminiscent – although I should really say prescient – of the ideas of Claude Bernard on the 'constancy of the internal environment' and of Walter Cannon on the 'wisdom of the body'. In effect what Bernard and Cannon were doing was providing the physiological detail of the regulatory systems through which the organism attempts to restore health. Through fever, for example.

Through the immune response to poison and infection. Through the attempt to regulate blood glucose.

Even the concept of allostasis and the allostatic load that we met in Chapter 3 holds echoes of the idea that the organism is continually attempting to return to the constancy of the internal environment. Not always successfully. But what we classify as disease is in fact this process of attempted restoration and repair.

The same broad idea has been incorporated into modern medicine's understanding of the immune system – that 'complex network of cells, tissues, organs, and the substances they make that helps the body fight infections and other diseases'. The immune system is a sophisticated expression of the organism's own attempt to restore health.

The mirage of health

There are two or three striking ramifications of this. The first is something I've hinted at already. When the external conditions are powerful enough, then disease is all we're left with. No matter what disturbed that balance in the first place, there are limits to the body's ability to restore it.

The greater the resilience of the body, the healthier it is to begin with, the more chance it has of restoring balance. But the stronger the external conditions, the more likely it is to be overcome. The maintenance of health is itself a tussle between the wisdom of the body and the strength of the external conditions that disrupt its balance. When conditions are too powerful or resilience is already compromised, then the maintenance of health becomes impossible. Eventually the battle is always lost. But the struggle remains important throughout the life cycle.

When a novel form of coronavirus swept through a population with no immunity to it, the external conditions – the attack of the virus – was particularly powerful and mortality rates were initially very high. But as Shimaa Elkomy and I showed in our studies, they were much higher in some places than in others. They were markedly lower in countries which had already made some effort to address the risk factors associated with chronic disease.

The epidemic nature of chronic disease is in itself indicative of powerful external conditions. What we witness is obesity, diabetes, inflammation, hypertension. And we know that these things lead to cardiovascular disease. They lower our immunity to respiratory infection. They compromise health. But the conditions themselves are not the pathogens. They're not the causes of disease. They're not even infections in the sense that we normally attribute to that word. They are the symptoms of the body's attempt to restore itself to health in the face of powerful – and ultimately violent – external conditions.

The second implication was drawn out by the Pulitzer Prize-winning French author (and medic) René Dubos in his 1959 book *Mirage of Health*. The individual organism is inevitably and continually faced with changing external conditions. It's continually trying to maintain the balance of its internal environment in the face of those changes. So disease – understood as the process of restoring balance – is also continual and inevitable. But it's even further complicated by the fact that everything we do changes that external environment. Including the adaptations we make when it changes.

In other words, says Dubos, 'complete freedom from disease and from struggle is almost incompatible with the process of living. Life is an adventure where nothing is static.' Of course. You don't need to tell that to the kids on those dinghies. Health – like sailing – is a continual process of trying to stay upright in a harbour filled with sewage.

That doesn't mean we should give up on the task. But it changes how we think about it. Since the struggle is constant, imbalance is inevitable. So restoration is always needed. Disease becomes a part of health. A part of care. A part of the body's attempt to return itself to health.

The French medical philosopher Georges Canguilhem made a remarkably similar point. In his 1943 book *The Normal and the Pathological*, he argued that medical science had adopted a far too binary approach to health and disease – to normalcy and pathology. In demonizing disease, we missed the point that it's part of the process of maintaining health. And in consequence we missed that disease is the functional response of the body to external conditions.

There's a further implication of all this. It defines more clearly the role of care. The role of the healer. The return to health – if it's possible at all – is being driven from the outset by the wisdom of the body. '[A]n effort of nature to remedy a process of poisoning or decay', as Nightingale calls it. An attempt by the internal processes of the organism to respond to external conditions that are no longer conducive to its internal stability.

When we look at disease, it's the body's response to those conditions that we are seeing. And from Nightingale's point of view – and to some extent Cannon and Canguilhem after her – it is to those conditions that we should look when we seek to exercise care.

The aim of care in this view is two-fold. On the one hand to aid and strengthen the body's own restorative forces. And on the other hand to reduce and diminish the conditions that are threatening the body's internal balance.

Care should improve resilience and it should reduce the need for it. It should teach its kids to sail. And it should stop filling the harbour with shit.

Natural hygiene

As I read on, I found more and more resonances between Nightingale's short pamphlet and those ideas. In particular in her insistence on the principles of hygiene. The restorative power of fresh air. The importance of thermal comfort. The attention to cleanliness in the environment. In the air. In the water. In the diet. The value of stillness and quiet for the process of recovery. These are the fundamentals of nursing. The things she learned in Kaiserswerth. And put into practice in the Crimea. And built into the profession of nursing.

At various points across this deeply pragmatic advice, we find clues to her underlying philosophy. Neither nurses nor doctors nor surgeons cure sickness, disease or injury. 'Nature alone cures,' she says. 'Surgery removes the bullet out of the limb, which is an obstruction to cure, but nature heals the wound.' The aim of the nurse, of the doctor, of the surgeon, is to remove obstructions. To address the external conditions. And to aid the body's own restorative process.

It may be out of kilter with the understandings of modern medicine. And you could argue that it's not entirely surprising to find these views expressed by a pre-modern practitioner with no real knowledge of that science. You could dismiss it as the ignorance of a bygone age. But the more I read, the more I realized that Nightingale's views were firmly rooted in traditions and practices that have persisted for millennia. For a lot longer than modern medicine has.

Two key principles emerge from those ancient systems of medicine. One is the principle of vitalism. The idea that the healing power resides in the organism itself. The other is the principle of holism. That we can't treat disease as an individual malfunction of an isolated organism. Both of them are present in Nightingale's philosophy.

The restorative force of nature – from the Latin *vis medicatrix naturae* – was a key concept in medical debates of the nineteenth century. It was a time when philosophers, doctors, and social reformers were all desperately trying to make sense of medicine in the face of massive changes to the conditions of society. The rise of industrialization. Mass movements of people from the country to the city. Poor housing. Appalling sanitary conditions. Poor nutrition. And the enormous stress of working conditions through the industrial revolution. All of these things were affecting health.

Medicine had earned itself a dubious and somewhat disreputable reputation. It was a process of peddling mostly useless and generally unscientific cures and remedies to those who could afford to buy them. At best those remedies obscured the symptoms of disease. Sometimes the interventions made things incomparably worse. Access to any of it depended on having sufficient income to pay whatever the medic demanded. Those who could did. Those who couldn't were sometimes better off without. Given the nature of some of the 'cures'.

We've seen already some of that process of peddling cures and remedies. It happened in Llandod. It happened with oxy. The corruption of healing in the pursuit of profit is key to the dysfunctionality of care under capitalism.

Strangely the water cure – the central proposition in Llandod's success – is something we may want to separate from that dysfunctionality. Its scientific value in cold water swimming is something we've already seen from Chapter 3. And the ability of water to aid the body's own healing process has roots that go back to Hippocrates and the Tao.

Hydropathy – and naturopathy more generally – was one of the fundamental principles from antiquity. It received a renewed interest in the medical debates of the nineteenth century. By the time Nightingale was practising, it had become a key foundation in the *Lebensreform* (life reform) movement in Germany and in the natural hygiene movement in the US.

One of the founders of natural hygiene was an American doctor named Russell Thacker Trall. Born in 1812, he was a close contemporary of Nightingale's. Like her he argued that diseases are 'in reality processes of cure – efforts on the part of nature to right a wrong'. He compared this process to the mechanism of the sneeze. An attempt of the body to expel 'morbid matter' from the body. And just as it's wrong to try and smother a sneeze, so it's counterproductive to suppress the symptoms of disease. Or as he put it in *The True Healing Art* in 1872:

> All morbid actions are evidence of the remedial efforts of nature to overcome morbid conditions or to expel morbid materials. All that any truly philosophical system of medication can do, or should attempt to do, is to place the organism under the best possible circumstances for the favorable operation of these efforts.

Trall founded the New York Hydropathic and Physiological School in 1844 and was influential in organizing the American Health Conference in 1850. The conference aimed to unify the various health reform efforts that were taking place particularly in the US. It's possible that Nightingale was aware of it at the time. Particularly given that she was such an avid reader and was passionately interested in healing.

It's also possible that she learned of these naturopathic principles from another close contemporary. Sebastian Kneipp was born in 1821 in Germany. When Nightingale was in Kaiserswerth, Kneipp was a Catholic priest in Bavaria. And around that time he was already developing what later became known as the Kneipp Cure. It aimed to restore health through five (now familiar) interventions: hydropathy, exercise, nutrition, herbal remedies and balance.

Natural hygiene was the foundation for much of the holistic and complementary medicine in the US. The Kneipp Cure became a central plank of the *Lebensreform* movement and retains a place in German cultural identity even today.

In other words it's clear that Nightingale's philosophy was built on principles which have been known from time immemorial. Those principles were alive and well in the middle of the nineteenth century. They provided the foundation for the profession of nursing. But all of them were about to come under fire as the foundations of medicine began to shift and change.

Sanitary reform was not the only widespread shift in medical understanding in the nineteenth century. In fact, it was about to be obscured and driven into the shadows. Very soon most of its principles would be derided as quackery and exiled from professional medicine. It would be another century and a half before they found their way back into the lexicon of healthcare. And then still only at the margin of what became known as modern 'scientific' medicine.

Nursing itself survived. It's doubtful healthcare as we know it would have been possible without its contribution. But it would be forced to play a minor, supporting role in the theatre of medical science. And that too would be the result of understandings – and misunderstandings – long since obscured by circumstance and the mists of time.

The Great Stink

In 1854, the same year that Florence Nightingale set sail for Crimea, London suffered a major outbreak of cholera. It was the third such outbreak in the space of as many decades and the death toll was already running into the tens of thousands.

At that point, the common belief was that diseases like cholera were caused by a miasma – a kind of foul-smelling fog associated with rotting organic matter. In an early colour lithograph the English illustrator Robert Seymour depicted cholera as a huge robed and hooded death-like figure hovering over London, surrounded by a dark noxious cloud. In fact the miasma theory was supposed to account not just for diseases like cholera but even for conditions such as obesity.

Of course, there was some logic to the belief. Because almost invariably cholera and the foul smell came together. But as every good statistician knows, association is not always causation. Sometimes the causal link goes in the opposite direction from the one you imagine. And sometimes there's some further factor which accounts for both the effect and the apparent cause. Sometimes the butcher isn't obese from the smell of the meat but from eating too much of it.

One man already had his doubts about the miasma theory. Maybe cholera wasn't some ghostly cloud wandering the land indiscriminately. For sure there was a god-awful stink from the sewage being pumped into the river. But that was also the river from which the city was drinking its water. So maybe, just maybe, the disease was being contracted by drinking water which had been contaminated with sewage.

John Snow had published the first edition of his book *On the Mode of Communication of Cholera* in 1849. Unfortunately his ideas held no truck with the crowd. Or even the government. The power of belief in the miasma theory was just too strong. So this time around, Snow was intent on proving his point.

He managed to trace the source of a particularly severe episode in August 1854 to a specific water pump on Broad Street near Soho. Those who drank from the pump water were getting sick. Those in the same area who had access to independent water supplies remained free of the disease. He persuaded the local council to remove the pump handle and the outbreak subsided almost immediately.

A month or so later there was another outbreak in an area of southeast London served by two overlapping water companies. Both drew their water from the nearby river Thames. But one of them, the Southwark and Vauxhall Company, drew from a place on the river just downstream from a sewage outlet. The other, the Lambeth Company, had shifted its intake upstream of the outlet. Snow managed to show that the death rate in families who were drinking the polluted water was more than eight times higher than in those who weren't.

Association is not causation. But this was a good indication that the disease wasn't caused by the ubiquitous stink of the sewage. It was being transmitted through water contaminated by it. He published the results in a second edition of his book. This too fell largely on deaf ears. And then by coincidence, the weather intervened. The summer of 1858 was an unusually hot one and the state of the river was attracting outrage.

The Illustrated London News ran an article demanding change. 'Let us then agitate for pure air and pure water and break through the monopolies of water and sewer companies, as we would break down the door of a house to rescue some fellow creature from the flames that raged within,' demanded the poet Thomas Miller. 'It rests with ourselves to get rid of these evils.'

I feel the same today about the companies tipping sewage into Chichester Harbour. It's not yet quite as bad as the 'Great Stink' that assaulted London in 1858. And I hope it doesn't have to get that bad before something is done to stop it. But that's what it took to turn back the tide of cholera in Britain. As the blisteringly hot summer wore on, the foul stench rising up from the river outside the Houses of Parliament was finally too much to bear, even for Westminster politicians.

A man named Joseph Bazalgette was commissioned to start work on a massive sewerage system for the city. He'd had the design ready to go for a while. But the work had been shelved several times. In 1858 it was finally given the go-ahead. A network of drains would collect both rainwater and effluent and transport them along massive tunnels running parallel to the Thames until they reached Barking, outside the city limits. At that point, it was believed, the sewage could be discharged safely into the tidal estuary. Far enough from the city to be washed out to sea. The sea absolves us of all our sins.

Sadly Snow would not live to see that triumph. In the middle of that long hot summer, he collapsed from a stroke. He died several days later at the tender age of forty-five with scant recognition for his work on cholera. Today, though, he's widely revered as one of the founders of epidemiology, the scientific study of the patterns of health and disease. And the incident of the Broad Street pump has passed into folklore.

A turn in the tide

Today's combined sewer overflows are more or less direct descendants of Bazalgette's design. They borrow the same philosophy. Often they borrow the same infrastructure. Sometimes they run through the very tunnels he designed and built. Legislation now insists that the effluent is treated before it can be discharged. But as my brother and I have seen today, that doesn't always happen.

We're past the sinister coloration now. And making our way through the gaggle of young sailors. Still searching for that elusive next mark. One of them calls out to us. Have we seen Sweare Deep? We look at each other. Try that way, I say. Pointing in the wrong direction. Their enthusiasm is contagious enough. Why send them into the path of danger?

The wind is picking up as we approach the harbour entrance. And it's also become more northerly. For a while it's right in our backs. But as we swing up into the Itchenor channel, we find ourselves increasingly hauling in the sheets. Close hauled on the starboard tack, the low sun is behind the sails and we're definitely feeling the winter's chill. Mercifully though, the water is a clear deep blue.

You would think that the lessons of the nineteenth century would have endured. But strangely they didn't. Not sufficiently at least to stop what happened today in Sweare Deep happening way too often.

I can't help wondering if that failure too was the result of a shift in medical perspective that was about to happen, even as Snow and his colleagues were unravelling the mechanisms of cholera transmission. The strange thing about cholera is that it gave birth to two distinct perspectives on medicine. At almost exactly the same time.

The sanitary revolution of the late nineteenth century massively improved the health of urban populations. Not just in Britain but across western Europe and North America. Within a decade or so, cholera was more or less a thing of the past in the affluent countries of the global North.

But it still rears its head whenever sanitation goes missing. Even today, 1.7 billion people use a drinking water source that is contaminated with faeces. And waterborne diseases kill over half a billion people each year. In times of war, when basic infrastructure is destroyed, it comes back with a vengeance. During the Israeli bombardment of Gaza, Oxfam reported that all five of the wastewater treatment plants in the strip had been forced to close and most of its sewage pumping stations were out of action. The WHO began to warn of a cholera epidemic that could kill more people than the bombs.

Basic principles of hygiene, like those that Nightingale set out in *Notes on Nursing* and Trall set out in *The True Healing Art* are as effective now as they always were at keeping most waterborne microbial diseases at bay. But the efficacy of their perspective on disease – and on health – was about to come under a sustained attack. Not from the miasma theory of the past. But from the medical science that swept it away. Ironically that science too had its origin in the urgency of tackling cholera.

10

Pathogenesis

*'When the tide is receding from the beach it is easy
to have the illusion that one can empty the ocean
by removing water with a pail.'*
René Dubos, 1959

Approaching the land from the sea is not the same as approaching the sea from the land. It generates a curious sense of achievement. Of homecoming. Even if it's just mooring up briefly on the Itchenor town jetty from the safe haven of Chichester Harbour. It feels like an accomplishment. A reward for the folly of leaving your natural habitat.

Despite our distant origins the ocean is a hostile environment to humans. Pay your respects. That's my motto. And while you're at it, pay your subscription to the Royal National Lifeboat Institution. The RNLI. Even if you never need them, somebody will.

Outside the tavern a couple of brave souls are huddled in the wind. Inside the place is buzzing with life. It's Sunday, of course. Families out with their kids. Locals complaining about the tourists. Staff on overdrive. My brother orders a half of some local brew. I sip my water. With so few daylight hours it's always a bit of a race against time. So half an hour later we're on our way again. Food in our stomachs. Beer in our belly. Well. In one belly out of two. But maybe I caught some miasma of beer just by walking in there. Damn, it's cold.

Down by the boat a crowd is waiting for the ferry. The wind has risen a notch or two while we were inside. And the bow resolutely hugs the pontoon. But that's another thing about the boundary between the land and the sea. A sense of conviviality survives there too. A couple of the waiting passengers step forward without being asked and give the bow a shove for us. We wave our thanks. And we're out on the river. Heading for home.

At this rate it will take us no time at all to reach the harbour entrance. Not long enough, sadly. When we turn north against the wind, things will be chilly, for sure. But for now we're on a broad reach under a brisk northerly. The sun is on our nose. The tide is in our favour. The blue water gurgles happily beneath the bow. And the wake that spreads behind us is clear and sparkling. No sign of the brown stuff.

There's another curious feature of leaving the land behind. The way that time behaves. As though it too has released its grip on reality. Something like the realm of care. *Kairos* and not *chronos*. A subtle loosening of linearity. The constant motion of the waves.

It's easier to think when you're not so grounded. To allow the mind to wander. Without any great pressure to arrive at anything. The ideas drift by. Arranging and rearranging themselves like the patterns of light on the water. And my thoughts drift, of course, to the world I left behind on my desk. And in particular to the puzzle – for that's what it's become now in my mind – the puzzle of pathogenesis.

Enter the germ, stage left

In the same year that Snow was mapping the epidemiology of cholera in London, an Italian doctor named Filippo Pacini was busy looking at the microbiology of the disease. During an outbreak in Florence he found millions of tiny comma-shaped organisms – he called them *vibrions* – in the gut and faeces of cholera victims.

Each one was an 'organic, living substance, of a parasitic nature, communicating, reproducing, and then producing a disease of special character', he wrote in his notebook in 1854. Their impact seemed to be to tear away at the *villi* that line the small intestine and leave the gut wall with the appearance of having been 'eaten by moths'. It was this damage to the gut, he concluded, that was responsible for the symptoms – the watery diarrhoea – of cholera. Pacini's discovery also went unrecognized at the time. It wasn't until thirty years later that the bacterium was rediscovered, this time by a German scientist named Robert Koch.

By that time, the phantasm of the miasma had given way to the microbiology of the germ. It was a transition that was to change medical science dramatically. Koch played a major role in that development. But he was not the originator of the idea that germs are the cause of disease. That honour belonged to the controversial figure of Louis Pasteur.

If you thought the spat between Banting and Macleod over the discovery of insulin was petty and unnecessary, it pales by comparison with the battle waged over the discovery – or to be more precise the explanation – of the process of fermentation. The breakdown of organic matter by microorganisms.

The process itself had been widely used for centuries. Wine and beer. Bread. Yoghurt. Cheese. Even some vegetables achieve their properties and their taste through carefully controlled processes of fermentation which have been handed down for generations. In the wrong place, though, fermentation is dangerous and poisons the human body.

If you studied chemistry – or if you know anything about milk – you'll have learned that it was the French chemist Louis Pasteur who discovered it. He also invented a method to stop it happening. By heating and then rapidly cooling liquids and foods you could kill harmful micro-organisms. And we could all remain healthy and safe. The process itself was given his name. Pasteurization. Pasteurized milk. It's pretty much everywhere.

Followers of another French chemist named Antoine Béchamp believe fervently that he was robbed. Béchamp discovered fermentation. Pasteur plagiarized his work. Pasteur simply claimed credit for ideas that had been in the public domain for some time and were first made known by Béchamp.

There's no doubt at all that Pasteur was a bit of a showman. He once insisted on repeating one of Béchamp's well-documented experiments pretty much identically. Nothing wrong with that. But to ensure it was attributed to him, he travelled all round France, carrying out the same basic experiment in a range of more and less exotic locations. Up mountains. Near oceans. In forests. Ostensibly to see if it made any difference. It didn't. But the publicity was amazing.

By all accounts, Pasteur also believed that attack is the best form of defence. As soon as there was even the slightest question about who got there first, he flung some pretty unpleasant accusations at Béchamp. And on top of all that, he enjoyed the more or less unrivalled patronage of the Emperor, Napoleon III. An honour he definitely made the most of. Pasteur is famous for discovering fermentation. A century after his death he's still a household name. Béchamp is barely remembered. History is written by the winners. But not always without contest.

None of this would be anything other than a footnote in the annals of chemistry if it weren't for the fact that the two men didn't only disagree on who got to fermentation first. They also had different understandings of the underlying mechanism. And from this they developed competing theories of disease. They were fighting, in other words, over pathogenesis.

Pasteur argued that disease is caused by small microbial organisms (germs) transmitted from one person to another by contagion or infection. Germs make you sick. It was the foundation for that 'gospel' I had taken for granted at the outset of my journey. But of course it was more sophisticated than that.

It was Robert Koch who formulated clear principles for what became known as the germ theory. It's not just that germs make you sick. Specific germs cause specific diseases. These specific germs could be isolated in people with that specific disease. The disease didn't appear in the absence of the germs. And the introduction of the germs into a healthy organism would reproduce the disease.

In 1876 he managed to demonstrate these principles through a series of experiments that isolated the anthrax germ. He discovered the tuberculosis germ in 1882. He (re)discovered the *Vibrio cholerae* in 1884. He won the Nobel Prize for these discoveries in 1905. Koch's principles revolutionized medical science and the great germ hunt was on. Escherich's discovery of *E. coli* in 1885 was just one step along the way.

Meanwhile Béchamp was busy licking his wounds and developing his alternative theory of disease. He didn't dispute the existence of germs. In fact, he argued, he had proposed a theory of germs himself. The world was full of micro-organisms. He called them microzymas. They're present everywhere. All around us. In the air. In the water. In the soil. In our bodies. Even in healthy bodies, he said.

Germs are present during disease, of course. But they aren't the cause of disease, Béchamp insisted. Association is not causation. Disease occurs when the internal environment (the terrain) of the body is disrupted or weakened. Germs already present emerge then as a symptom of decay.

To demonstrate this, Béchamp took the trouble to install a dead cat in a completely sealed container with no access to anything that might wander in from the environment. Four months later it was a pile of dust. This was the action of microzymas, he said. While we're alive, they're a part of our cellular life. And when we're ill or when we die, they emerge from the background to clean up the mess.

There was a fascinating sub-theme to the battle between germ theory and terrain theory. For germ theorists each germ has a single (*mono*) unchanging form (*morphus*). Germs are *monomorphic* – in the technical lingo. People fall sick with a specific disease when they're infected by a specific germ. For Béchamp the mycrozymas are *polymorphic*. They are able to change and take on many (*poly*) forms depending on specific disease conditions. That's why we see different germs.

And on the way from recently deceased cat to dust, these micro-organisms transform themselves from bacteria to yeast and fungi. And from yeast and fungi to mould. Each fulfils a different function in the cycle of organic life. Microbiologists called it pleomorphism. Bacteria feed on decaying flesh. Fungi exterminate the bacteria. Mould thrives on fungi. Leaving nothing but dust behind. Each has its own role to play. But their presence is a symptom not a cause of disease.

And so the lines were drawn. Or redrawn, perhaps we should say. In the wake of the dispute over who discovered fermentation emerged a new and even fiercer scientific battle. Miasma theory was long dead now. The new contest was between germ theory and what became known as terrain theory. The dispute was no longer a trivial altercation over intellectual property. It was about pathogenesis. About the causes of disease. And it was not a contest without consequence. Because believing you know the cause of disease has profound implications for what you consider to be the best and most effective way to treat it.

For germ theory, curing disease is all about identifying, isolating and eliminating germs. For terrain theory, it's all about changing those aspects of the environment (diet, lifestyle, toxins) which undermine the body's own ability to cure itself. Supporters of these two theories have been battling it out in medicine. In the history of science. In society. Ever since.

And the winner is ...

In the history of medicine the verdict is clear. Germ theory won the contest. Hands down. Within a decade or so Pasteur was the hero of the story. Béchamp was more or less forgotten. Germ theory became the dominant theory of disease. And it has remained so ever since.

The search for germs, the destruction of germs and inoculation against germs emerged as the foundations for a new 'scientific' medicine. Laboratory-based microbiology and pharmacology were the springboard for the pharmaceutical industry. They became the bedrock for modern healthcare. The key to a healthy society.

Antibiotics, antiseptics and vaccines were triumphs of modern biochemistry, definitive weapons against germs and the cornerstone of healthcare. The germ theorists claim as their own the retreat of typhoid, typhus, cholera and dysentery in the late nineteenth century and of polio, diphtheria, malaria and yellow fever in the twentieth. And of course victory over Covid-19 in the twenty-first.

On the back of its conquest of germs, scientific medicine set out to develop a panoply of other biochemical interventions. Analgesics. Anti-inflammatories. Antidepressants. Stimulants. Relaxants. Mood stabilizers. Anti-psychotics. Anti-emetics. Anti-pyretics. Statins. Semaglutides. Proton pump inhibitors. Some of them we've encountered already. The creativity of pharmacology appeared endless. It seemed as though there was no medical problem for which an effective remedial drug could not be found.

Terrain theory retreated. It remained the conceptual home for the earlier therapeutic traditions, which embraced holism and vitalism. Naturopathy. Natural hygiene. Herbalism. Acupuncture. Osteopathy. Complementary and alternative medicine continued to emphasize that health is a relationship between the organism and its environment. That disease is the body's own attempt to restore health and regain its balance. That nature cures. When given the chance to do so. And that the job of the physician is to facilitate this process.

But most of the traditions that sought refuge in this conceptual home found themselves swimming increasingly against the tide of modern medicine. More than that. They began to attract antipathy and ridicule. They were denounced as quackery and pseudoscience. Worse than useless. They were profiteering from people's misery and capitalizing on our endless desire for health.

In the early years of the twentieth century they found themselves more or less exiled from the realm of modern scientific medicine. Not 'more or less exiled'. In fact they were systematically expelled. Expelled and defunded.

In 1904 the American Medical Association established a Committee on Medical Education to streamline and systematize medicine. The Committee set up a rating system to determine which schools would receive funding and which wouldn't. And 'to hasten the elimination' of schools which failed to achieve their standard, they asked the Carnegie Foundation to commission a study of the state of American medical schools. The result was a three hundred and fifty-page report on *Medical Education in the United States and Canada*, written by a man named Abraham Flexner. It was enormously influential in the years following its publication in 1910.

Flexner became a minor celebrity and was invited to speak all over Europe. He contributed a similar study for the UK and even brought his ideas on professional medicine into the realm of social care. He had no medical training. But his report had a massive influence on medical education and on healthcare for many decades to come. It's no exaggeration to say that twenty-first-century healthcare is where it is today because of the Flexner report.

Some of Flexner's motivations may have been solid. He highlighted 'an enormous over-production of uneducated and ill trained medical practitioners ... in absolute disregard of the public welfare'. And he suggested that this was due in part to the 'the existence of a very large number of commercial schools, sustained in many cases by advertising methods through which a mass of unprepared youth is drawn out of industrial occupations into the study of medicine'.

To some extent, these concerns resonate with themes we've already visited. The commercial nature of medicine in the late nineteenth and early twentieth century was clearly problematic. And the Foundation's concern that ill-trained quacks were profiteering from health isn't in itself unsympathetic. But the devil in Flexner's recommendations was in the detail. In the criteria he proposed through which the number of medical schools should be culled. And in the directions he suggested under which the remaining schools should be funded.

There's a key chapter in the report where he rails against what he calls 'medical sects' – schools and training programmes that followed certain a priori principles about health and disease and rallied around specific concepts. Or sometimes the names of the people who coined them. That's wrong, he said. Medicine is a discipline in which

> the effort is made to use knowledge procured in various ways in order to effect certain practical ends. With abstract propositions it has nothing to do. It harbors no preconceptions as to diseases or their cures. . . . Modern medicine has therefore as little sympathy for allopathy as for homeopathy. It simply denies outright the relevancy or value of either doctrine. It wants not dogma, but facts. It countenances no presupposition that is not common to it with all the natural sciences, with all logical thinking. The sectarian, on the other hand, begins with his mind made up.

It sounds at face value eminently sensible. But then we get down to who exactly is a sectarian and who is not. And here Flexner is as dogmatic as they come. 'Sectarians, in the logical sense above,' he tells us explicitly, 'are (1) the homeopaths, (2) the eclectics, (3) the physiomedicals, (4) the osteopaths.'

Just to be clear about who's out and who's in, let me elucidate. Despite having 'as little sympathy for allopathy as for homeopathy', the former was in and the latter was out. Physiomedicalism was a movement very similar to the *Lebensreform* movement. It embraced vitalism, holism and a preventative approach. With an emphasis on diet, exercise and a healthy environment. Goodness knows what the osteopaths did to upset him. But the Eclectics simply wanted the best possible medical treatment available for whatever condition or disease you happened to be looking at. That's clearly an outrageous principle. They were obviously heretics.

In one simple stroke Flexner consigned most of naturopathy as it stood at the time to the dustbin. Without for a moment acknowledging that his own preference for laboratory-based bacteriology was as dependent on abstract propositions – 'germs cause disease', for example – as anything he rejected, Flexner had laid the ground for what seemed like a revolution. In hindsight it looks more like a cull. Vitalism and holism were out. Modern, lab-based, 'scientific' medicine was in. The allocation of funding for medical training enforced the new discipline.

The result was a rapid decline in the teaching of anything that smacked of naturopathy. Schools teaching complementary and alternative medicine were 'driven under by lack of funds and political harassment', according to two contemporary practitioners of Chinese medicine. The report also left fewer women in medicine than had been there at the turn of the century. The opening up that had brought Gertrude Stein to Johns Hopkins was reversed. Once again women found themselves 'shut down and shut out' of medicine.

Anything that smacked of terrain theory was consigned to the losing side in a historical spat between two French chemists. And anyone who questioned germ theory was deemed a quack.

And the truth is . . .

First glance, it looks like a slam dunk for Pasteur. Germ theory identified the cholera bacterium. The great germ hunt subsequently turned up a whole dictionary of pathogenic micro-organisms. Germ theory allowed us to develop antibiotics to kill them and targeted vaccines to inoculate against them. Germ theory kept our kids safer and extended our lives. The success and acceptance of germ theory accounts for my gut instinct. (Pardon the pun.) Germs make you sick. The question of pathogenesis has been answered.

No one has ever isolated microzymas. No one has ever proved the extreme pleomorphism that would be needed to transform them into the myriad of germs that science has now identified. Florence Nightingale believed she had seen diseases transforming themselves in her patients in front of her eyes. But we haven't observed it under the microscope. We've never reliably documented the transformation from bacteria to fungi, from fungi to moulds, from mould to dust, so beloved by the terrain theorists. The one that supposedly produced the magical decomposition of Béchamp's dead cat.

But there's always something a little troubling when sensible ideas with a very long pedigree – like the principle of holism, for example – are so soundly and roundly rejected as quackery. There's something suspicious about the demonization of anything outside the mainstream that happens even today. And something distasteful about the vigour with which those who espouse these views are condemned and even cancelled. It smacks of prejudice and it reeks of vested interest. As a process, it has nothing to do with the pursuit of truth.

Germ theory is after all a specifically western perspective on health and disease. Could it have been skewed by scientific reductionism? Could it have blinded itself to the wisdom of the past? Could some of the continuing ferocity of the battle be more about the protection of professional boundaries than the pursuit of health?

That sort of thing has only ever happened ... in the past. Right? We know so much better today than those bumbling idiots from the nineteenth century. Of course we do. But shouldn't we at least be a little concerned not to fall into that trap I identified way back in Chapter 2? To suppose ourselves cleverer than every previous generation just because they're dead and gone is a recipe for our own precipitous fall. After all, we'll also be dead and gone soon. And our ideas may seem as stupid then. Isn't a little humility in order?

I guess I'm always a little disturbed in the presence of hegemony. The dominance of one worldview over another can be ruthless and all-consuming. And it can also blind us to the truth. You could say I'm predisposed to recognize that blindness. I've stumbled on it so many times in a different field. In the economics of the growth debate.

When the mainstream is so ferocious in its condemnation of the margin, it raises some kind of red flag for me. I tend to suspect it's indicative of some weakness in the underlying arguments. Why would you be so terrified of an opposing theory unless you were scared your own doesn't stack up? Methinks thou doth protest too much. Could germ theory be hiding some skeletons in its closet?

Terrain matters

On closer inspection. As it happens. The slam dunk doesn't look so solid. Or at least. Let's put it like this. There is a strong case that terrain matters. The new science of the gut biome is making that clearer and clearer to us.

Take *E. coli*, for instance. Swimming around in its brackish soup in Chichester Harbour. Threatening our kids with all kinds of sickness. In the gut biome *E. coli* is essential. Plentiful. And beneficial. It was no surprise that Escherich found it in the faecal samples of his young patients. It's supposed to be there. One of its roles is to crowd out other bacteria – like *Vibrio cholerae*, for instance – which when they replicate promiscuously are nothing like so kind to us.

Just because it's meant to be in the gut doesn't mean, of course, that *E. coli* is supposed to be in the water supply. Or in our food. Or in our bloodstream. Or in our urinary tract. In all these places it can lead to bad outcomes. But without *E. coli* where it belongs, in the gut, our entire digestion would be stuffed.

Huh. Now that's a more complicated story. From germs make you sick we have shifted surreptitiously to some germs in the wrong places make you sick. If you don't have enough of the other germs in the right places to defend you. A healthy gut is all about having the right balance of the right microbes. Health is about maintaining that balance. Hang on a minute. That sounds familiar.

Where else might the sharp distinction between germ theory and terrain theory falter? Take pleomorphism, for instance – that ability for one kind of micro-organism to transform into another. Turns out that actually happens. Variation within species is common. Viruses constantly evolve. Covid-19 showed us that. So too do bacteria. That's still not pleomorphism in the guise proposed by terrain theory. But it's a clear indication that Koch's first postulate – specific germs equal specific diseases – isn't as straightforward as germ theory might like it to be.

Pleomorphism has also emerged as a key concept in understanding some cancers. It's responsible for some of the biggest challenges in modern medicine. The emergence of multi-resistant bacteria poses a huge health challenge for the way we approach our 'fight' against germs. We thought we had bacteria licked. All we had to do was throw antibiotics at the little fuckers. Now look what's happening. Soon, if we're not careful, the 'superbugs' may have *us* licked.

None of this proves the extreme pleomorphism that Béchamp called for. But it turns out you don't even need that assumption to make a modified version of the same theory work. All you need is a little population dynamics. Bacteria thrive under certain conditions – such as the presence of decaying matter. They clean up decay. Fungi thrive under different conditions – the prevalence of bacteria. Mould thrives in the presence of fungi. The science of the gut biome already suggests that the health of the gut is entirely dependent on those population dynamics.

Health is an adaptive struggle in the face of constant change. And even our struggle changes the terrain. That's the insight Dubos was trying to instil. Without an understanding of terrain theory, we can't hope for victory over disease. Health will evade us continually. Health is by its nature evasive. But only in understanding its evasion can we hope to approach it. What we call disease is in part at least the body's own attempt to restore itself to health.

Peering through ever stronger microscopes isn't going to help us here. Dividing up the microbial world with endless definitions and names and supplementary codes won't get us there either. The microscopic biome is as fickle as the four winds. It changes with the seasons. It changes with our moods. Almost literally. Our moods depend on its health. Our own happiness is coupled to the balance of microbes in our gut.

There's another reason to be wary of the germ theory prescription. Its default remedy is to kill. Germs make us sick. So let's get rid of them. The philosophy seems solid in the lab, where specific germs can be isolated and targeted for destruction. But in the body things are a lot more complicated. Because germs live in colonies. Picking one type of germ out of the cohort risks damage to the whole.

Anti-microbial resistance is not the only downside looming over the war on germs. Broad-spectrum antibiotics devastate the gut biome. And in doing so they make it susceptible to attack by other more virulent germs such as *Clostridioides difficile*, which causes diarrhoea, irritates the colon and is even implicated in colon cancer.

Germs matter. Perhaps that should have been Koch's first postulate. Without them we wouldn't even be here. And getting rid of them is tougher than we ever thought it would be. Maybe that's postulate number two. Largely because *in vitro* is not *in vivo*. What happens in the lab stays in the lab. In life things aren't so predictable. Terrain matters too. Modern medicine was led astray by Flexner's laboratory-based science. We demonize terrain theory at our own peril.

The limits of medicine

When it comes down to it, almost all pharmaceutical responses are based on poisons. They rarely come without some kinds of side-effects. Over the long term they inevitably contribute to the toxic burden our body tries to adapt to. Sometimes they hijack our own neurochemistry in disastrous ways. Trapping us in addiction. Contributing to the allostatic load. Holding us away from health rather than helping us return to it.

Perhaps most obviously of all, germ theory tells us nothing about how to deal with the pandemic of chronic, non-communicable diseases. It may even be undermining the conditions of health and contributing to that precipitous rise. That's a dangerous position from which to cling obstinately to a theoretical framework developed from a nineteenth-century perspective and imposed rigidly on our modern concepts of health and disease.

The burden of chronic disease is rising inexorably. It's a battle we're destined to lose if we cannot free our minds from the dogma of the past. To have any hope of tackling the pandemic of metabolic dysfunction we are left with no real choice. We have to import at least some of the wisdom of terrain theory. Chronic disease is invariably the result of the body's own response to external conditions. Its endless attempt to restore its own internal balance.

Lifestyle, diet, exercise. Our exposure to toxins. Our sugar intake. Our water intake. The way we breathe. The quality of our sleep. The patterns of stress. The organization of society. The culture we live in. Our access to technology. Our gut health. Our sense of self. Our sense of health and disease. Our relationship to each other. Our rapport with those we cast as healers. Our relationship to nature. All of this matters in the body's constant struggle to maintain its own internal balance. The terrain matters.

That's not to reject germ theory entirely. It's not to deny its occasionally stunning victories. Nor is it to diminish its deep insights into the relationship between us and the microbial world. Even if those victories are not so thorough as we were first led to believe. Even if the evidence in favour of the germ and against the terrain is not so one-sided as we were told it was. The science of the germ is still worth having. It made a major contribution to our understanding of pathogenesis.

But maybe it claimed its victories a little too easily. Maybe it forgot to give credit to the very philosophies it sought to expunge from the arena of scientific medicine. Could it be that the vitriolic denouncement of terrain theory is not just premature but disastrously ill considered?

In *Mirage of Health* Dubos comes to a remarkably similar conclusion. 'Clearly, modern medical science has helped us clean up the mess created by urban and industrial civilisation,' he writes. But by the time the germ theory came into the picture

> the job had been carried far towards completion by the humanitarian and social reformers of the nineteenth century. Their romantic doctrine that nature is holy and healthful was scientifically naïve but proved highly effective in dealing with the most important health problems of their age. When the tide is receding from the beach it is easy to have the illusion that one can empty the ocean by removing water with a pail.

When the tide is with you, things look easy. When it's against you, a whole army of helpers armed with the best buckets in the world will find themselves borne away in the flood. It's a compelling metaphor. Particularly for a sailor.

Low tide

The sun is setting behind us and the north wind has turned icy. The kids have all gone home. There's something almost surreal about the wetlands at this time of day. The light is dying from the sky. The silence is only broken by the sombre cry of a curlew. A cormorant perched on a channel marker escorts us from his territory with a watchful eye. An air of tranquillity descends on the harbour. But it's a fragile and deceptive one.

The news today has been full of outrage. And there's plenty to be outraged about. Three hundred people died in Gaza over the weekend. The death toll has reached eighteen thousand. It will more than double before I'm done writing. More than half of the casualties are women and children. Two days ago the US blocked a UN Security Council resolution calling for a cease-fire. Britain abstained.

Or perhaps some fury could be summoned against another kind of stain. The murky brown water still malingers around Sweare Deep as we make our way back up the Northney channel. Almost low tide now. And the dark grey mud gives off a pungent, noxious odour.

Wisdom surely requires some outrage against an antiquated sewerage infrastructure serving an area of outstanding natural beauty. It may have been functional a hundred and fifty years ago. It definitely isn't now. But today, as then, the water companies are driven by profit. And they've consistently preferred to enrich their shareholders at the expense of nature. And even human health.

Strangely, neither war nor sewage accounts for the outrage on the tip of the nation's tongue on this particular winter's day. It's reserved instead for a practising GP decorated for more than four decades of consistent service at the frontline of primary care. An honorary fellow of the Royal College of Physicians. A former chair of the NHS Alliance. A champion of the NHS Social Prescribing initiative. A man with impeccable credentials.

It's just emerged that King Charles III has appointed Dr Michael Dixon as Head of the Royal Medical Household. In fact Dr Dixon has 'quietly held that position' for a year. And no one even told us! That's scandalous, of course. But it's not the source of the outrage.

Dixon's crime is his support for complementary medicine. He's introduced faith healing and herbalism into his GP practice. He's written about the 'human effect' – the bond between patient and physician – in scientific journals. He believes in treating the whole person (holism). He accepts the restorative power of nature (vitalism). He promotes the idea that lifestyle and diet matter to our health (terrain theory). And worst of all. He's been known to wear a bowtie.

The newspapers are full of scorn. *The Sunday Times* broke the story, calling his appointment 'questionable' and his views 'unfashionable'. Experts cited in *The Guardian* are more forthright. The appointment is 'appalling', 'worrying' and 'irresponsible'. *The Daily Mail* condemns it outright. 'Alternative quackery' screams their headline.

Without a shadow of a doubt, society's antipathy to the wisdom of the ages is alive and well. Is it just my sensitivity to the intellectual violence imposed by the mainstream on the margin? Or is there something almost incomprehensibly stupid going on here? Is our era even blinder to scientific inquiry than previous ages, in spite of our belief that we are somehow cleverer than all of them? Or have I not made enough progress? Have I somehow misunderstood or misinterpreted the arguments around pathogenesis?

Looking back, I'm pretty sure I've been faithful to the history of those ideas. And yet there's still something that doesn't make sense. When and why did the scientific arguments around the question of pathogenesis become so toxic? How and where did the scientific disputes stop being scientific and turn into questions of prejudice? When did the question of pathogenesis itself become pathologized?

Germ theory established its dominance by dictate. Terrain theory was swept aside with little more than rhetoric. And yet anything other than the mainstream hegemony continues to be held in utter disdain. Despite the pedigree of those ancient ideas. Whatever the credentials of the messenger. And despite the fact that these ideas hold lessons that are absolutely vital to the dilemma in which we find ourselves.

Healthcare is struggling with rising costs, unbridled demand and an epidemic of chronic disease. Our indiscriminate use of the pharmaceutical model, as Dixon himself points out, 'has led to a nation that is over-medicalised and a generation of medicine-addicted patients'. It's unaffordable and it's ineffective. At the end of the day it's also unnecessary. Instead of contradicting nature's processes, says Dixon, 'we should be encouraging them and mobilising our patients as assets in their own healing'.

But instead of listening to the voices of reason and experience, we've fallen endlessly and easily into patterns of demonization that are reminiscent of the Dark Ages. We've reached a low tide in a journey through the land of the invisible heart. And the only advantage is that the stink has become apparent. We can no more wash it away than we can fill up the ocean again with a bucket.

The robber barons

We've been here before of course. At earlier points in the book. A couple of times at least. We've seen how vested interests have allowed profit to override care. How wealth has been allowed to trump health. It's a recurring theme by now.

It's clear that the pharmaceutical industry has an interest in selling as many drugs as possible. It's obvious that the food industry has an interest in selling as much food as possible. It's clear too that these two industries feed on each other's economic success and benefit from their own and each other's medical failures. The misery imposed on our health through poor diet is ripe territory for an endless succession of pharmaceutical interventions. And terrain theory, holism, vitalism, preventative public health – science itself in some sense – all represent a direct threat to the profitability of that venture.

But something else has emerged from this investigation now. Those financial interests were not innocent bystanders in the emergence of scientific theory. They played an active role in promoting the science they wanted and demolishing the wisdom that stood in their way.

It was not accidental that the rise of germ theory coincided with the rise of the pharmaceutical industry. Nor is it entirely true that the acceptance of germ theory was the reason for the rise of the pharmaceutical industry. Association is not causation. Sometimes the causation runs in the opposite direction. Sometimes there's a third independent factor in play. Something that gives rise to both the phenomena of interest. And that something, in this case, might well have been capitalism itself.

Germ theory won the support of the American corporate class, according to physician and public health advocate E. Richard Brown, because it offered 'an explanation of the causes, prevention and cure of disease that was strikingly similar to the world view of industrial capitalism'. It offered a view of healthcare in which there were profits to be made. Whole new sectors of the economy dedicated to the output of brand-new pharmaceutical products for which there would be unending demand. Which would create their own demand by failing to remedy the problems they were meant to solve. And sometimes even by causing new problems that would need more pharmaceuticals to solve.

Flexner's work – the *coup de grace* that ensured the victory of modern scientific medicine over holism and vitalism – was funded by the Carnegie and Rockefeller Foundations. The robber barons who had carved up industrial capitalism for profit in the late nineteenth and early twentieth century had their fingerprints all over the model of scientific medicine that still dominates our lives in the twenty-first.

And if that weren't enough, it transpires that an updated form of this dynamic survives and thrives to this day. Health expert Anne-Emmanuelle Birn has explored the role of what she calls philanthropocapitalism in the global health agenda. She puts the spotlight on the influence of big money 'donated' by philanthropic foundations on global health.

In particular she's documented the influence the Bill and Melinda Gates Foundation has had in the twenty-first century and compared it to the role of the Rockefeller Foundation at the beginning of the twentieth. She highlights the role of public–private partnerships (PPPs) – structured by the philanthropocapitalists – which have dominated the way government finances its social priorities. Health is rightfully one of those priorities. But there is a clear moral hazard involved when public health becomes dependent on private finance, not just for its funding but for its structure, its philosophy, its scientific basis and its integrity.

We should be particular wary of the financial implications of this alliance. It looks like a win for everyone if very rich people are prepared to 'pay' for huge healthcare programmes. But Birn has argued that the net financial flows have been in the opposite direction and that 'most PPPs channel public money into the private sector, not the other way around'. Philanthropocapitalism is not funding healthcare. Health – and, worse, ill health – is financing the accumulation of capital.

In other words the unholy alliance between big capital and public health is not a solution to a long-term problem. It is a huge and powerful problem standing in the way of a long-term solution. Not only in the sense that it sends resources in the wrong direction. But, perhaps even more perniciously, in that it distorts the underlying science of public health. In the presence of philanthropocapitalism, accountability, democracy and ultimately even scientific integrity have gone missing. Or as Birn puts it:

> The pivotal, even nefarious, role it has come to play in international/global health in different eras draws from a series of nested factors: gargantuan resources enabled by profiteering of titanic proportions – amidst relentless ideological assaults on democratically-driven redistributive approaches – all contextualized by a procorporate geopolitical climate within still dominant (if declining) US global capitalism.

The blue pill

Back on dry land, struck by these reflections and by the ferocity of the media's attack on Dixon, I found myself more and more intrigued by the demonization of complementary medicine. Strangely, Wikipedia has no entry on the term. A search for 'complementary and alternative medicine' points instead to alternative medicine. And here the entry is extraordinary. Clear evidence of cancellation:

> Alternative medicine is any practice that aims to achieve the healing effects of medicine despite lacking biological plausibility, testability, repeatability or evidence of effectiveness ... [it relies] on testimonials, anecdotes, religion, tradition, superstition, belief in supernatural 'energies', pseudoscience, errors in reasoning, propaganda, fraud, or other unscientific sources ... with little distinction from quackery.

Alternative medicine is unscientific, flaky and useless. Don't you worry your pretty little head about the wisdom of the ages. Here's a few pills. Take one each morning to wake you up. Take another at night to help you sleep. Take this one to kill some germs. Take that one if you have some pain. Take another one if the last one gave you stomach cramps. Take the blue pill if you want to stay in the matrix. Take the red one if you want to leave.

It would be hilarious if it wasn't so tragic. Just like the ongoing spat between Pasteur and Béchamp. Just like the demonization of a respectable, hard-working, well-rounded champion of primary care as a quack. Just like the unsavoury battle that's raged for a century and a half over the role of germs. Just like the painful hubris that leads us to suppose that none of the wisdom of the past is worth heeding. Only our own unbridled ingenuity counts.

But let's suppose for one moment that the pursuit of knowledge isn't a straight line from the past to the future. Let's imagine there is no inevitability about the progress from ignorance to wisdom. Suppose perhaps that wisdom is not a linear projection with a ruler from the wisdom of the past at all. Suppose instead it's more like a rough unfinished circle sketched freely by hand, something each generation must approximate for itself. A world of the spirit without beginning or end. A tapestry of opposites rather than a bitter contest between contradictory ideas. Suppose our fixation with competition is itself a kind of pathogen.

Maybe it's even the consequence of another deeper pathogen. Perhaps capitalism itself is the pathogen. Its axioms, its structures and its rules privilege wealth over health. Its incentives and values prioritize profit over care. Not accidentally. Or occasionally. But systematically. And necessarily. It's an uncomfortable thought. And it poses a serious challenge to the project of defining – and enacting – the care economy. But it needs to be faced.

11

Death and the Maiden

> *'Give me thy hand, oh soft and lovely maid.*
> *I am thy friend, I do not come to reap.*
> *Nor am I evil, be thou not afraid*
> *And softly shalt thou in my wide arms sleep.'*
> Matthias Claudius, 1774

The sky is dark and starless. A light rain is falling. A cold breeze shakes loose the last of last year's leaves. As they cascade down around me I reach out to catch them. They melt like snow in my hands. Leaving traces of white dust like ash on my fingers.

Where am I?

Somewhere familiar. Somewhere I've been before. Many times. Somewhere on a journey to or from a familiar destination. I recognize the structure of this feeling. A sense that I'm caught between two worlds. Uprooted and disoriented. Temporarily lost.

I shield my eyes against the wind, peering through the rain to find some identifiable landmark. A sign perhaps. A signal. A clue as to how I should proceed. Dimly at first I catch a glimpse of ancient stones. Grey and resolute against the inclement weather. Unmoved and unmoving. Inscrutable like some long-forgotten truth.

A little way from the road, I can make out an enormous arch constructed from two massive upright stones with a third laid as a lintel across the top. And then I see more of the same configuration. Arranged in a horseshoe in a fold of the rolling hills. I recognize them now. The sarsen stones and the unmistakeable 'trilithons' of Stonehenge. And this road leads ... Yes I know where it leads. But I'd rather not bring it to mind. The knowledge lies dormant inside me. Unwelcoming. Unwelcome.

Suddenly the heavens open and the rain begins to pelt down relentlessly. I make a run for cover. Within minutes I'm drenched to the bone. But strangely neither cold nor wet. And no sooner have I reached the horseshoe of stones than the downpour stops. As suddenly as it began.

The clouds have disappeared. A blood-red sun hangs just below the horizon.

Waiting for its moment. The dawn light reveals a well-worn path in the grass towards the massive altar stone, strewn sideways on the ground. I approach it curiously. Half expecting to be met by someone. Or something. But there's no one around. Even today. On the autumnal equinox. At the exact division of the day between light and dark.

Stonehenge

Every age gets the Stonehenge it deserves – or desires, said the archaeologist Jacquetta Hawkes, writing in the 1960s. At that time, by all accounts, we desired a Stonehenge aligned with our astronautical dreams. The space race had just begun in earnest. Our imagination was pointed at the stars. And we invented for Stonehenge a Neolithic civilization whose knowledge of astronomy was infinitely more sophisticated than ours. Ancestors who had themselves conversed with extra-terrestrial visitors who had taught them things that our own generation had long since forgotten.

Astronomical Stonehenge was nothing like so dark as previous versions of Stonehenge. Druid Stonehenge, for instance, was occupied with stories of blood sacrifice and ritual slaughter. Horror stories designed as much to shore up our own sense of civility as to populate the past with real people.

In truth the evidence for either hypothesis is scanty. All we do know is that people gathered here. That they were buried here. That four and a half thousand years ago they transported the stones themselves over inconceivable distances. The altar stone came from the north of Scotland, over four hundred miles away. The bluestones of the middle circle came from the Preseli hills. In Pembrokeshire. Not far from where I began the journey of this book. And before that of course from somewhere deep in the Southern Ocean.

Nothing is still. Everything is a journey. All we ever experience is a moment on a journey. The journey of the stones from Gondwana to here. From one world to another. From the waking world to the world of dreams.

As I reach the altar, the sun bursts violently over the horizon, flooding the purple plain with golden light. It spills out around and between the trilithons. Almost blinding in its intensity. For a moment I see nothing. And then as my eyes grow accustomed to the brilliance I find myself looking at a vaguely familiar scene. Beneath one of the arches in the centre of the outer horseshoe stand a couple. Silhouetted against the light.

They seem to be perfectly still. As though they are deep in conversation. Or arguing over something perhaps. Probably taking selfies, says a voice in my head. And for a moment I'm back in Paris on the lower walkway of the Passerelle Léopold Sédar Senghor.

That can't be right. I search around me for clues. The rough worn grass and the tall stones tell me I'm still at Stonehenge. And as I walk uncertainly towards them, it occurs to me that they're not real. Maybe they're just statues.

Two ancient gods. A man and a woman. Not as old as the sarsen stones. Perhaps Greek or Roman. Carved in white marble. Their flowing robes draped loosely over one shoulder. The other shoulder naked. They are both taller than I am. Larger than life. They clearly belong together. Though it's not immediately clear what their relationship is.

With his left hand the man supports a tall staff which stands on the ground beside him. Around it curls a snake or a serpent. The body of the serpent winds upwards around the staff in a spiral from the ground. Its head is tilted towards the man's face. Its mouth is open slightly. It seems to be trying to attract the man's attention. To remind him of its presence. But he takes no notice. His stare is cast forwards. Towards me. Or perhaps past me. Concentrated and serious. Maybe even a little stern.

Another serpent is curled horizontally around the bent forearm of the woman at his side. Its head is inclined towards a shallow bowl which she holds in her opposite hand. This second serpent's mouth is also slightly open. Not in supplication. But in anticipation of sustenance. It's about to drink from the shallow bowl the woman is offering. And she watches it almost tenderly. Encouraging it to drink.

Now I recognize them. I know who they are.

Asclepius and Hygeia

The unsavoury battle between modern scientific medicine and naturopathy might seem like a recent affair. Or at best a historical tussle peculiar to the social conditions a century and a half ago. But it turns out there are even deeper roots to those two competing perspectives. And they rest in a time when, for a while at least, the two approaches lived together in harmony. As father and daughter even.

Asclepius and Hygeia. These are the gods who stand before me now on the plains of Salisbury. Out of time. Out of place. But somehow fully in character. Quite what they're doing here, I have no idea. Their presence makes a kind of sense. But I can't pin it down. I can't decipher their intentions. Perhaps they have none.

In the ancient cosmology Asclepius was the son of Apollo (and hence the grandson of our old friend Jupiter). He was the Greek god of healing, responsible for surgical and therapeutical interventions to treat disease. As legend has it, he became so good at his job that Jupiter killed him with a thunderbolt, fearing he would end up making humans immortal. That sounds like Jupiter, right?

Hygeia, on the other hand, was the goddess of health and wholeness. She symbolized the idea of living well. Her gift to those who followed her wisdom was the state of wellbeing. She was usually portrayed as the daughter – occasionally the wife – of Asclepius. And though each had their own separate cult across the centuries, they were often revered together. Complementary gods, I guess you could call them.

It's from Hygeia, of course, that we derive the word *hygiene* and from whom the natural hygiene movement of the early twentieth century took its inspiration. The staff of Asclepius, meanwhile, with the serpent wound around it, became a near universal symbol of modern medicine. It's been adopted by the WHO and by many other medical organizations around the world for years.

Back in antiquity, both gods had their respective place. The cult of Hygeia thrived particularly strongly in Greece in the wake of two devastating plagues in Athens in 429 and 427 BCE. And among the Romans after an outbreak in 293 BCE. But in the later years of the pre-Christian era, the cult of the daughter gave way increasingly to the cult of the father. In part because by then the Roman Empire was expanding rapidly. The cult of Asclepius thrived where the Roman legions were stationed. The soldiers' need for vitality doubtless coincided with a greater willingness to pay homage to his therapeutic magic.

As I inspect the two statues more closely, I notice something I've missed before. The serpent of Asclepius is not rising to meet the hand of the god. He's not climbing the rod. He's being cowed and controlled by it. The second serpent, on the other hand, the one wound around the naked forearm of Hygeia, is eager for the sustenance being offered by the goddess. Expectant and compliant. He's at one with his mistress. It's a striking contrast.

What's the meaning of these two serpents? They appear routinely in representations of the two gods. But what's the symbolism they carry? There's no clear agreement in the literature. In some versions the venom of the serpent is the source of remedies that the physician can use to heal. In others it's the ability of the serpent to shed its skin – to renew itself – that's supposed to symbolize health.

But as I examine these two creatures another interpretation dawns on me. Suppose the serpent represents disease. For Asclepius, disease is an enemy to be defeated. Overcome. Controlled at last. Perhaps even vanquished for ever. But for Hygeia, the relationship is completely different. Disease is an integral part of health. At one with her. A friend to be nourished and cared for. Suddenly the resonances are obvious.

I see now how these two perspectives have twisted themselves into the history of medicine. Into our modern ideas about health and disease. 'The myths of Hygeia and Asclepius symbolise the never-ending oscillation between two different points of view in medicine,' wrote Dubos. 'In one form or another these two complementary aspects of medicine have always existed simultaneously in all civilisations.'

And I can see too how one interpretation, one point of view, one symbolism, began over time to dominate the other. I see in the history of pathogenesis how the sustenance implicit in the Hygeian bowl gave way to the subjugation symbolized by the Asclepian staff.

I can sense how the time and attention inherent in Hygeia's act of nourishment began to take second place to the technical authority of Asclepius' dominion. As father to daughter. As man to woman. As physician to nurse. I can see how sanitary reform gave way to modern scientific medicine. How terrain was swept aside in favour of the germ. How the values of vitalism and holism retreated behind the *realpolitik* of pharmacology.

I understand too, more clearly than ever, that both perspectives matter. There's no doubt about their inherent interdependence, one with the other. It's not in question whether one should be privileged over another. It's not about the individual validity of their different perspectives. Rather it's a profound recognition of the tension – the complementarity – between them. Even though, in today's unhealthy configuration, Hygeia is not just diminished but outmanoeuvred. Not exactly outclassed but outlawed. Outgunned by the technical dominion of an emboldened and authoritarian Asclepius.

The long and winding road

I remember suddenly what I'm doing here. And where this road inevitably leads. I've travelled this way so many times that Stonehenge has come to represent for me the boundary between two very different worlds. The road itself is a tunnel. A portal. From one world to the other.

Behind me is the world of output and productivity. The challenges and complexities of my working life. That world is a means to a livelihood, of course. But it also carries a sense of its own importance. Offering me its fickle promise of reward, recognition and social standing. Perhaps even meaning and purpose.

Ahead lies something far more visceral. An arena of infirmity and frustration. The domain of physical and emotional care. An ailing mother and an infirm stepfather in the sunset of their lives, struggling with an impossible combination of physical and mental deterioration. A fragmented world of disability, dependency and uncertainty.

It's now some years since my stepfather was diagnosed with a degenerative physical condition. Gradual at first, its progress has accelerated recently. I remember on one particular occasion watching him fall. Apparently out of nowhere. Almost in slow motion. Was it fanciful to imagine that moment as a decisive victory of the disease over his determination to overcome it? There have sometimes been reprieves. But it's now reached a point where he's clearly unable to cope without more or less full-time help at home.

By contrast, my mother is still physically healthy. Like me, she's always taken pride in her fitness. She took seriously the idea of a healthy diet long before any such thing became fashionable. She has slowed up a bit in the last few years. But I recently found her a local yoga teacher. She used to love it when she was younger. And picking it up again seems to have given her a new lease of life.

The only trouble is she can no longer remember from week to week what she learned the week before. If I don't remind her, she forgets to go to the class. Sometimes she forgets that she's ever been there at all. She doesn't yet forget our names. But that may be coming soon. And the worst thing is that she's increasingly thrown out of kilter by the needs of my stepfather.

Care has become a balancing act between his physical and her emotional needs. Between a struggling health system and a chaotic social care system. Neither speaking properly to the other. Managing that tension from a distance is messy. Being there enough is impossible. For sure, there's something rewarding when I can. Immersion in task is part of it. The ability to give something back to the woman who gave me life. That's another part. And then there's this extraordinary distance between the visceral immediacy of care and the demands of my working life.

Each world has its separate logic, its distinct rationale, its individual currency. And there is no clear mapping from one to another. There is no easy exchange. Nothing to transfer value from one to the other. Only this strange liminal space in which I find myself now. Poised between two realities. Interrupted on a familiar journey from one place to another. Disoriented and uprooted. Momentarily lost. Torn between two distinct and contradictory ways of being.

Fleetingly, here in Stonehenge, I inhabit neither world. And perhaps only from here can I see more clearly how far apart from each other they lie. Not just in physical terms. But in my mind. In my consciousness. In my attention. And perhaps even in the fabric of society.

The human condition

The German-born sociologist Hannah Arendt once captured something of this divide when she named a distinction between two kinds of human action: labour and work. Despite the interchangeability of those terms in modern usage, she said, it's useful to recognize that they have slightly different meanings. And she took the trouble to tease those meanings apart as separate concepts.

Labour was the gift my mother gave me during the first months of my life and in the early years of my existence. The gift she continued to give me. And somewhere along the way also taught me how to give. Perhaps reckoning at some epigenetic level that, one day, I might be capable of giving some of it back. Today for instance. If I ever arrive at my destination.

Labour, according to Arendt, is the visceral engagement in the essential task of staying alive. And of keeping others alive. Labour is pregnancy and childbirth and the care of those unable to care for themselves. It's the sleepless nights, the changing of diapers, the tending of wounds, the cleansing of forms. It's the blood, shit and piss of survival.

But it's also at times the milk and the honey of life. The breastfeeding of infants. The planting of crops. The feeding of bodies. The construction and restoration of shelter. The maintenance of the conditions of sanitation within which health will either flourish or fail. Labour 'assures not only individual survival, but the life of the species,' says Arendt. Labour is the endless 'cycle of prescribed exhaustion and pleasurable rejuvenation' in the daily struggle for physical survival.

And when we catch our breath from the struggle for existence, something frightening happens. Hoping perhaps to find the sunny uplands of a carefree relaxation, we are assaulted instead by a sense of our own mortality. The awful brevity of human existence. The shocking fragility of life. Work, said Arendt, is our response to this sudden painful recognition of our own mortality. In a frenzied attempt to deny or to resist the inevitability of death, we find ourselves driven endlessly to produce, to create and to build.

The outputs of work are intended to deliver a commodity that is absolutely essential for our peace of mind. A sense of durability. Products are meant to last. Buildings are meant to endure. Monuments are supposed to stand for centuries. Art is destined to live beyond us. Work 'and its product the human artifact' is our best stab at bestowing 'a measure of permanence and durability upon the futility of mortal life'. It's our attempt to find some semblance of order in the chaos that greets us, each time we lift our eyes from the daily grind. It's our struggle to find meaning and purpose in existence. Our constant craving for consolation, beyond the 'fleeting character of human time'.

Work is like graffiti scratched on the face of a dark, uncaring void. Humanity was here. Each human artefact is intended as a *memento mori* for a fragile species living on a small rock, hurtling at extraordinary speeds through a cold and frightening universe.

The frontline

There's clearly an overlap between what Arendt calls labour and what Fisher and Tronto call care. It includes all the things we do to 'maintain, continue and repair our world'. We've seen already how much of this labour goes unrewarded. Unrecognized and undervalued. Or taken for granted. Yet these are precisely the same activities on which physical survival – the very foundation for any kind of prosperity – depends.

Nothing could have made this plainer than the years of the pandemic. The nurses, the doctors, the caregivers, the teachers, the social workers, the food retailers, the cleaners. These were suddenly the essential workers. They populated the frontline of the battle between society and the virus. And for once they were recognized for the vital role they play in our lives. Strange how, almost overnight, humble cleaners took their place amongst the most valuable people in society. We stood on our doorsteps and applauded them all.

Cashing out that applause in monetary terms was more difficult. Paying nurses decent wages seemed like a small return for what they had gone through. The real wages of UK nurses had fallen by 20 per cent since 2010. Nurses were effectively working one day a week for free. Teachers in the US were taking home more than $2,000 less in real wages than they had a decade previously. And the wages of low-paid workers had risen by only 0.7 per cent in the half-century since 1973.

But the post-pandemic world was a forgetful and unforgiving place. Nurses in the UK were offered a paltry 1 per cent pay rise in March 2021. This was, according to a health minister, 'the most the government could afford'. For the first time in its seventy-five-year history, NHS nurses went on strike. The dispute rumbled on for two years. The matter was eventually settled in March 2023 with a pay rise of 5 per cent, still less than the rate of inflation at the time and less than half the rate of inflation in the previous year. Frontline nurses were worse off in real terms than they had been at the end of the pandemic.

Some of that was down to geopolitics. War had pushed oil and gas prices to an all-time high and the cost of living soared. Wages in low-paid sectors were not enough to live on and industrial action spread rapidly. Junior doctors, medical consultants, ambulance drivers, postal workers, fire-fighters, teachers, university lecturers, rail workers, lorry drivers and refuse collectors all joined calls for better pay and working conditions in the face of long-term stagnation or decline in real pay.

Millions of families were visiting food banks just to survive. As the cost of living rose, forty-nine million citizens in the US turned to hunger relief programmes for support. One in six people across the nation couldn't afford to eat without resorting to charity. In the UK there was a one hundred and twenty-fold increase in the use of food banks in the decade and a half since the financial crisis. The families of lower paid workers across the world were forced into impossible choices between heating and eating. The ILO was warning of a global 'deepening' of poverty, inequality and social unrest around the world as real wages continued to fall.

But the pain of it all wasn't equally shared. Even as the cost-of-living crisis deepened, the salaries of chief execs in FTSE 100 companies were rising at 12 per cent a year, above the rate of inflation, bringing the average CEO pay to almost four hundred times the pay of the average company worker. Some of the highest pay awards were reserved for the bosses of energy companies. While household energy prices in Europe were spiralling, the annual remuneration of BP's chief executive, for example, more than doubled from £4.5 million to just over £10 million a year.

To call these comparisons shocking would be an understatement. But that's not quite my point here. If Arendt is right, if labour is 'quintessential' to human flourishing, if it's the very foundation of our ability to survive at all as a species, then why is this happening? Why is it allowed to happen?

What does our failure to represent labour's worth mean for the vision of social progress that capitalism held out to us for over a century? What does it tell us about our aspirations for social justice? Where does it leave our dreams of an egalitarian, fair, humane health service? The kind of dream that motivated Nye Bevan to establish the NHS in Britain in the aftermath of the Second World War, for example.

Death of a dream

Paradoxically work doesn't fare much better than labour under this system – for slightly different reasons. The social value of work lies in the permanence of the human artefact. Its proper return to society is the sense of durability we crave as an antidote to our own fragility. But durability is an anathema to capitalism, which revolves instead around innovation and expansion. The throwing over of the old in favour of the new. The restless excitement of novelty. The continual arousal of new appetites and desires.

This isn't just a quirk of culture. It's the foundation for what we believe is economic progress. Durability is not just a distraction from that process. It's antithetical to it. It's crucial to our economy that we fail to maintain – or sometimes even to respect – the material artefacts of production. We're continually persuaded to care as little as possible about them.

Capitalism constantly encourages what the economist Joseph Schumpeter called 'creative destruction' as the route to future prosperity. These processes have become central to the accumulation of wealth, to our sense of progress and even to the stability of the modern economy. But in doing so, they undermine the role the artefacts of work were intended to deliver. Durability perishes.

None of it makes any sense. We're locked inside a form of economic and social organization that seems to denigrate both the value of labour and the output of work. The dream of progress as a future of endless possibility is torn asunder. Its promise is undermined – both in its conception and in its outcome – by the myopia of the market.

The investment that would support both the value of labour and the durability of work is consistently overshadowed by greedy speculation in the hope of a swift return. The interest of the investor constantly trumps the stability required to achieve a genuine social progress. And the best we have for government consistently fails to rectify the damage caused. The fallout becomes more and more inevitable. More and more evident. It's all around us.

It's true of course that those who profit from the collapse of the dream can often insulate themselves from the impacts of its demise. The rich can always afford to buy the services of the poor. Equally it's obvious that wealth has a disproportionate influence over power. And when that happens, government inevitably fails in its duty to defend the values society professes to hold dear. It becomes instead an institution for the protection of unequally distributed property rights. None of this is surprising. It's not by any means a new story.

Yet modernity claims something better for itself. Liberal democracy supposes itself to be motivated by some greater vision. Universal access to decent food, clothing, education, medical care and social services. Security in the event of unemployment, sickness, disability, bereavement and old age. These values have been enshrined as social aspirations since the Universal Declaration of Human Rights in 1948. Many of them were reiterated in the Sustainable

Development Goals in 2015. But all of them depend on the contribution of labour and work. And in particular on the labour of care.

So how has that labour fallen so low in our collective esteem? How is it that our society has failed so abjectly to protect those who care from the decline of working conditions and the precipitous fall in real pay? How and why have we allowed this to happen?

The economics of sculpture

Lost in thought, I haven't noticed that the scene is changing around me. The sun has now crossed the pale blue arc of the autumn sky and is on its way down again. How long have I been here? I sneak a look at my watch. Its figures dance and spin in front of me. Refusing to convey information. This fact itself conveys some information. But its significance remains for the moment just outside my field of comprehension.

The stone figures of Hygeia and Asclepius are now bathed in a warm golden light. They look almost alive. It's no huge leap to suppose that the distinction between labour and work carries something of the mythical division between Hygeia and Asclepius. It's certainly true that labour, in this division, gets the same short shrift that Hygeia does in the arena of health. The thankless drudgery of survival stands in constant contrast to the spectacular productivity sometimes achievable in the world of work. Labour is constantly eclipsed by work as the goddess is by the god.

Hygiene, like care, is a daily struggle. It involves a constant attention to detail. It demands physical exertion. It calls for cleanliness, sustenance, endless reparation. The art of living well is never ending. Often thankless. And ultimately futile. As Boris Groys points out in his *Philosophy of Care*, it remains 'forever unfinished, and thus, can only ever be unrewarding'.

Asclepius, on the other hand, is hell-bent on immortality. A little too successfully in the jealous eyes of Jupiter. His task is the elimination of disease. The subjugation of the serpent. The prolongation of life. He's come to embody a view of medicine which sees the human body itself as an artefact. A machine to be dissected and reconstructed at will. A legitimate object for Arendt's concept of work. Driven by a fear of its own mortality.

How and why are we condemned to undermine both of these tasks? Where is the glitch in the program? I search their stone-cold faces for answers. But I find none. Asclepius is intent on guarding the horizon. Hygeia is absorbed in nurturing the serpent. Sustenance and vigilance. Both of them matter. But neither of them survives the rigours of modernity. Both of them have been undone by something buried deep in the organizational structure of capitalism. I'm still puzzling over it when a slow American drawl snaps me out of my reverie:

'Why do computers get cheaper and healthcare doesn't?'

I turn to see an elderly man gazing at the statues with the same rapt attention I have. Lanky and almost completely bald, he reminds me of someone I know. Perhaps he's famous.

'That's your question. If I'm not mistaken,' he tells me.

'Is it?'

'It's all about the economics of art.'

'The economics of sculpture?'

'Exactly. And the economics of care as well, when it comes to it. It's so much more time consuming to befriend the serpent, to nourish it, to care for its body and soul than it is to beat it down with a stick. Especially if you can mass-produce the stick.'

He turns to the sculpture of Hygeia. Reaches out his hand towards her. Almost caressing the head of the serpent. Without ever quite touching it. I have a clue now who he is.

'Are you . . . Professor Baumol? Professor William Baumol?'

'Delighted to make your acquaintance.' He laughs.

'But I thought you were . . .'

'An economist?' That isn't what I was going to say. 'Yes, I'm an economist. That's true. But you know that I taught sculpture for twenty years at Princeton. Alongside economics?'

'I didn't know that.'

'That's where it all started.'

'It started with sculpture?'

'It started with the "arts crisis". In the 1960s. The Twentieth Century Fund decided that Americans had become philistines. They were determined to encourage a bit more interest in the arts. So they set up a panel of the great and the good to convey to the world that the arts aren't just a communist plot.'

'And they asked you to be on it?'

'Goodness, no. I was neither great nor good. But they wanted to commission a "serious study". An economic study to look at funding. They knew I was interested in painting and sculpture. So they called me in, and I told them how I would go about it. And then the next day they phoned me and said, "We'd like you to do it." And I said, "I'm terribly busy. I can't." But I guess not that many economists are interested in the arts, right?'

'More's the pity.'

'So they called again, and I said, "Well, I'll do it on one condition. There's a young assistant professor here. Bill Bowen. And if he's willing to do it and you're willing to pay him, then I'll do it." And so they agreed.'

He laughs delightedly at the memory. Like a young child. I don't say anything. For a moment neither of us does. I want him to go on. I know he holds some kind of clue to my strange interlude here. After a moment his hand moves away from the sculpture and he scratches the back of his head.

'So anyway. Bill and I started working on the problem. And we started to get all these statistics about budgets and rising costs. I mean. It was right there in the statistics. But I still wasn't seeing it. And then one night it came to me.'

What came to you?

'One moment I was fast asleep. And the next I was wide awake.' He laughs again. 'And I said, "I know why those costs are going up!" It was four in the morning. I got up, wrote down a few notes and went to sleep again. That's literally how it happened.'

'And what exactly did you write down?'

'You've just come back from Paris, right?'

'I have.'

'Romantic visions of the starving artist?'

'How did you guess?'

'It's a common stereotype. A cultural meme, I guess you'd call it. A misplaced belief that squalor and misery are somehow noble and inspiring. But it still hides more than a grain of truth in it. It's the fate of the arts in a nutshell. There's a continual downward pressure on the wages of artists. And a continual upwards trend in the costs of production. Actors will work for less and less. But the cost of a theatre ticket still keeps going up.'

'And is that what you wrote in the middle of the night?'

'I wrote down Death and the Maiden.'

'Death and the Maiden?'

'It's the title of Schubert's 14th String Quartet. It was written in 1824. Two hundred years ago. I wrote it down to remind myself, when I woke up, of the answer to the riddle. The dilemma of the performing arts.'

'Which is?'

'That the output per hour of the violinist playing a Schubert quartet in a standard concert hall hasn't changed in two hundred years.'

'You're saying that labour productivity in the performing arts is more or less stagnant.'

'Over long periods of time.' He warms to his theme. 'I'm saying that you can mass-produce cheap toot that's thrown away tomorrow until the cows come home. But something like these two. Something like this ...' He sweeps his hand in a wide arc to encompass the entire horseshoe of sarsen stones. 'This takes time.'

And I know now why he's here. And what he's saying. He's here to remind me how deeply the demolition of both labour and work is embedded in the nature and structure of capitalism itself. Within an economic system that prizes efficiency and profit above all else, activities like care and craft and creativity turn out to be the poorest of poor cousins. Precisely because they absorb so much of our time and attention, they turn out to be antithetical to the relentless pursuit of productivity.

The end of labour

Time is money. Labour is a cost. Maximizing profit means getting as much out of your workers as possible each hour of every day. The return on capital depends on it. The accumulation of wealth hangs on it. The pursuit of what economists call 'labour productivity' is the engine of capitalism. It's the driver of economic growth. The whole economy is geared towards increasing the productivity of people's time.

That task fills the waking hours of CEOs and asset managers and finance ministers all over the world. It haunts the restless dreams of inventors and entrepreneurs. It's the object of a fierce and continual competition, as Baumol himself pointed out. It's the subject of a stubborn and relentless innovation. It motivates our technical ingenuity and it defines our sense of progress.

A lot of the heavy lifting is done by clever technology of one kind and another. The use of hardware and (more recently) software to replace the labour and (more recently) the thinking power of people. There's no doubt our ability to do this has been phenomenal. Human ingenuity is vast. And the speed with which we've used it to change our social world is extraordinary. Impressive in many ways. Unprecedented in history.

Who now would prefer to mix concrete with a spade? Or wash the bedlinen by hand? Or write books with an ink quill on papyrus? Or even tap them out on a typewriter like the lost generation would do in their Paris garrets? Less than a century ago. The ability to generate more and more output with less and less work has lifted our lives out of drudgery and delivered forms of material affluence unimaginable just a handful of generations back.

We've already more or less done away with the need for humans in manufacturing and materials processing. We've almost done so in construction and mining. We're poised to do so in transportation and distribution and retail.

We're hoping to do so in professional services. In design. In education. Even our creative capacities are about to be usurped by machine learning.

Just in the last couple of years we've seen one of those periodic explosions of interest in technologies so clever they don't just mimic but offer to improve massively on human capabilities. It's probably the biggest spike of enthusiasm since Isaac Asimov wrote the *I, Robot* stories back in the 1940s. Enthusiasm tinged with not a little alarmism and some genuine reasons to be fearful.

This particular explosion was the result of a machine learning program called ChatGPT by a company called OpenAI. Not just science fiction. Not a utopian dream. But an actual online application that can compose pretty much seamless answers to almost any question you decide to ask it. And, by the way, it has cousins who can write computer code, design graphics and create movies for you on demand as well.

You didn't need to take anyone's word for it. You could try it out for yourself. Ideas like this spread through word of mouth. So OpenAI's 'suck it and see' strategy was massively successful in promoting the vision. And in identifying the threat it might pose. To our jobs. To our incomes. To our livelihoods. Possibly even eventually to our existence. If AI is that clever, won't it one day realize we're unnecessary? Wouldn't the robots – and the planet – be better off without us?

But for every Luddite fear, there's a techno-optimist's wet dream. For many the arrival of machine learning is the beginning of a new dawn. Here comes the technology which will propel us headlong into an era of unimaginable affluence. More than that. It's the answer to all our prayers.

You know all these wicked problems like climate change and the destruction of other species? Much too difficult for humans to figure out how to solve them. But AI is going to be so much cleverer than we are. It'll be a walk in the park for ChatGPT's offspring. That was one of the arguments my favourite philanthropocapitalist used in Chapter 6.

We no longer need to worry about reaching net zero. All we have to do is ensure there's enough energy to fire up enough servers to deliver the phenomenal processing power achievable by generative AI, and the solutions will pop out already formed. Faster than you can even think about them. And you won't need to lift a finger. Just step aside, humanity. AI's cohorts will implement everything. You won't feel a thing.

For all its outlandish sci-fi utopianism, there's a perverse – and familiar – logic to this argument. New technology as a defence against old technology. Clean technology as a solution to the damage caused by dirty technology. These drugs as an antidote to those drugs. Today's strategy as a way of clearing up the mess from yesterday's strategy. And the best thing of all is this. It means a rapidly expanding horizon for the pursuit of profit. Increasingly clever technologies will make tech companies shedloads of money.

But this whole obsession with productivity finds its logical conclusion in a social absurdity. The continual drive to reduce labour costs – if possible to nothing at all – lies at the heart of capitalism. The ultimate aim of the capitalist, to paraphrase something Fritz Schumacher, the author of *Small Is Beautiful*, once said, is to have income without work and output without workers.

Chasing productivity

Chasing productivity is central to capitalism. Its proponents would argue that this is what's delivered us modernity. I see nothing wrong with accepting that it's helped us along our way. That it's led to unimaginable advances in social progress. But it's also caught us in a kind of trap. Two traps, as it turns out. Closely related to each other. One of them is central to the dilemma of growth. Both of them are critical to the paradox of care.

Trap number one is more or less about arithmetic. Ever-increasing labour productivity means that fewer and fewer people are needed to produce any given level of economic output. So if we want to keep full employment, we're going to have to produce more output. In other words our economies must grow continually to soak up those put out of work by the ever-changing technologies aimed at reducing the cost of labour to producers. If they don't expand, but labour productivity does, then unemployment rises. Like it or not, we find ourselves hooked on growth.

In the conventional view this shouldn't be a problem. Because when labour productivity grows, it means producers can pay their workers higher wages. Higher wages means they have more to spend. More spending creates more demand for goods and services. More goods and services means economic growth. That's one of the bargains written into the social contract drawn up between employers and employees. Everyone gets to share in the returns to productivity.

But what happens if aggregate growth just isn't to be had anymore? Maybe it's a financial crisis. A slowdown in consumer confidence. A war. A pandemic. A decline in trade. Or rising prices for resources like oil. Or perhaps it's even the need to rein in growth for the damage it's inflicting on the planet. Climate change. Deforestation. Soil degradation. Water pollution. The huge loss of biodiversity. Maybe it's any one or all of the reasons growth can no longer be safely and easily assumed in any of today's economies.

What happens in a non-growing economy, when producers, investors and policymakers are still chasing relentlessly after labour productivity growth? Two things are possible. The first is that they just don't find it. But in searching for it, the economy becomes increasingly unstable. The search for productivity crowds out investment in the things that matter. The second is that they do find it, but the inability of the economy to grow means that the demand for labour across the economy declines. The result is the same. Increasing productivity threatens to undermine full employment and ultimately destabilizes both economy and society. We end up addicted to growth to solve the problems growth creates.

Slow down

One solution to this dilemma would be to accept the productivity increases, shorten the workweek and share the available work. Such proposals have been enjoying something of a revival in recent years. The New Economics Foundation, a British think tank, has proposed a twenty-one-hour workweek. It may not be the workaholic's choice. But it's certainly a strategy that might make sense. It might even free up our time for the more important things of life. The British economist John Maynard Keynes proposed something very similar back in the 1930s.

But there's another really interesting strategy for keeping people in work when economic demand stagnates. Perhaps in the long run it's an easier and a more compelling solution. To loosen our grip on the relentless pursuit of productivity. By easing up on the gas pedal of efficiency and creating jobs in what are traditionally seen as low-productivity sectors, we have within our grasp the means to benefit from productivity growth and achieve full employment even within a non-growing economy.

At first this all sounds mildly counterintuitive. If not crazy. We've become so conditioned by the language of economics to believe that productivity is everything. But on deeper reflection that doesn't quite stack up. Or at least. It makes sense in some places. But not in others. There are sectors of the economy where chasing productivity growth doesn't make sense at all. Certain kinds of tasks rely inherently on the allocation of people's time and attention. They manifest a natural resistance to productivity growth.

This was at the core of Baumol's insight that night. He found it first for the performing arts because that's where he'd been looking. It's the time spent practising, rehearsing and performing that gives music, for instance, its enduring appeal. The time spent learning, rehearsing and playing Schubert's

Death and the Maiden matters. The value of the performance depends on it.

But he quickly realized that there are other powerful examples where the same dynamic holds. Take craft, for instance. It's the accuracy and detail inherent in crafted goods that endow them with lasting value. It's the time and attention paid by the carpenter, the seamstress and the tailor that make this detail possible. And because they rely inherently on craft and skill and attention to detail, repair and maintenance also tend to resist the pressure of productivity growth. It's often cheaper to throw things away or knock them down than to maintain, continue and repair them. To care for them – in Tronto's sense of the word. Even if this only happens at the expense of the planet.

The most obvious example of all is the realm of those sectors traditionally denoted as care. The care and concern of one human being for another is a peculiar commodity. It can't be stockpiled. It's degraded through trade. It isn't easily delivered by machines. Its quality rests almost entirely on the attention paid by one person to another. And on skills that can generally only be gained through years of training and practice.

A few years ago a humanoid robot named Pepper which could 'read' human emotions was touted as a revolution in hospitality and social care. Care robots have been particularly popular in Japan, where a combination of expertise in robotics and an ageing population has led to an influx of government-funded research and innovation.

After several years of experience, doubts began to emerge about this strategy. Quite often it took more time and effort for care workers to integrate the robots into the lives of their patients than could ever be saved by employing them. On top of all that they are, at the end of the day, material machines. They use energy to run. They need maintenance to keep going. They have to be repaired when they break and replaced when they're no longer functional. It's not unusual, apparently, for the robots themselves to end up shut away in a cupboard somewhere. Not even used. Just another pile of techno-junk waiting for the landfill.

Even to speak of reducing the time involved in care is to misunderstand the nature and value of such activities. That's not to say there aren't ways of improving how care is delivered. And some of those might well benefit from technology. But not all of them add value to the simple act of one human being paying attention to another. Some of them are scarcely worth the time, energy – and money – spent on them.

Conversely the time spent by those professions directly improves the quality of our lives. Making them more and more efficient is not, after a certain point, actually desirable. What sense does it make to ask our teachers to teach ever bigger classes? Our doctors to treat more and more patients per hour? What – aside from meaningless noise – would be gained by asking that string quartet to play *Death and the Maiden* faster and faster each year?

There's a couple of other positive things to note about this strategy of shifting the economy towards those labour-intensive activities which naturally resist productivity growth. Quite aside from their advantage in terms of maintaining full employment or the advantages they bring to our quality of life. The first point is that people often achieve a greater sense of wellbeing and fulfilment, both as producers and as consumers of such activities, than they ever do in the time-poor, materialistic supermarket economy in which most of our lives are spent.

The second point is perhaps the most remarkable of all. Since these activities are dependent on the input of human time rather than the relentless throughput of material stuff, they offer a half-decent chance of making the economy more sustainable, less carbon-intensive, less resource-intensive. Less damaging to the planet.

A shift towards an economy of care, craft and creativity, as I suggested in Chapter 6, is not just about the quality of our public services or the possibility of creating decent employment. It's a direct answer to the search for a sustainable prosperity. To the quest for the good life. To the desire to live well – within the limits of a finite planet.

And yet. For all these advantages. This Cinderella economy still faces a deeper challenge. One equally embedded in the DNA of capitalism. This second trap is an even more pernicious one.

What Baumol appreciated in the middle of the night six decades ago was not just that the time taken for a string quartet to play *Death and the Maiden* hasn't changed in two hundred years. He also realized that the cost of employing those four musicians has.

The cost disease

The setting sun is now no more than a pink glow disappearing fast beneath the horizon. The sky is a deepening shade of blue. It occurs to me that I have been here now almost a full day. And I'm strangely unclear how to resume my journey. I'm sure I was expected long ago. And yet here we still are. Sitting together on the altar stone, gazing at the dying embers of the sunset, with our backs to Asclepius and Hygeia.

'Imagine we split the economy in two,' Baumol says. He speaks very quietly. Almost like a voice in my head. 'In one part of the economy, labour productivity growth is high –.'

'The fast sector.'

'And in the other sector it remains stubbornly low.'

'The slow sector.'

'So what happens to wages in the fast sector?'

'They'll rise with productivity.'

'Exactly. That's part of the bargain between capital and labour. And what about wages in the slow sector?'

'They'll have to rise as well,' I venture.

'And why is that?'

'Because eventually even the starving artist can't afford to paint anymore.'

'And there's the dilemma in a nutshell. It's not just that the low productivity growth of the slow sector is unattractive to capitalism. It's that eventually the slow sector can't afford to pay the wage increases generated by the fast sector. That was the whole point of our study.'

'If you want to save the arts, you have to save the wage rate of the artists.'

'Exactly,' says Baumol.

'And the cleaners,' I say.

'And the nurses,' he says.

'Especially the nurses,' I say.

'Cost increases are the nature of the healthcare beast.'

'Because care takes time.'

'And the biggest danger is that government will go on cutting care and render it inaccessible, except for the rich. Well-meaning reformers do the same in education. In law enforcement. In handicraft services. In the renovation and refurbishment of our buildings. Ignorance and economics will systematically undermine the care economy.'

'Baumol's cost disease.'

'That wasn't our name for it, you know.' But he's pleased I've named it all the same. There's a moment's pause. Neither of us speaks. And in the silence a thought pops into my head. What better person to answer this.

'Is the cost disease a restorative process?' I ask.

'Why should it be?' He seems surprised.

'Well there's a perspective on health which sees disease as a restorative process,' I say.

'Really? How interesting! I'm not sure.' He thinks for a moment. 'Perhaps it's trying to restore our attention to the activities that matter most in life.'

'Maybe it's drawing our attention to a fault in the code.'
'In which code?'
'In capitalism itself.'
'I've never been a particular advocate of capitalism, as you know.'
'Even though you spent more than half a century thinking about it?'
'I always felt it was a good system for encouraging innovation.'
'And a bad one for protecting the things that matter.'
'I'm not sure I went as far as that.'
'I think you wrote about it. Even in your nineties.'
'My son used to tell me I don't know the difference between work and play,' he says.
'Or life and death,' I say. 'Apparently.'
He looks at me for a moment. Puzzled at first. And then he smiles.
'Look who's talking,' he says.
'What do you mean?' I stare at him blankly.
'Where do you think you are today?'
'Stonehenge.'
'And where are you going?'
'I'm on my way . . .'
'Yes?'
'To visit my mother?'
'Really?'
'And my stepfather.'
'Are you?' he says.

And that's when it hits me. This whole journey. This strange day. The arc of the sun. Its illusive trajectory across Stonehenge. The statues of Hygeia and Asclepius. Baumol himself. None of it is real. It's all just a dream. If it happened at all, it all happened long ago.

I look around me. Already it's dissolving fast. Soon there'll be nothing left. The trilithons are crumbling. The stars are disappearing. Everything is fading away. Except for the man at my side, who puts a consoling arm around my shoulder.

'Come with me,' he says. 'There's one more thing I want to show you.'

And the spirit of my favourite economist leads me through the remains of the old stone circle to the place where the two statues once stood.

The Caduceus

There's virtually nothing of Hygeia now. Just rubble. And the occasional fragmented body part. Like the aftermath of a bombing raid. Asclepius is still just about standing. But the white marble of his smooth flesh is dissolving fast. Blown like dust around us. Soon he'll be gone as well.

Only the staff remains. Still planted firmly in the ground. Stout. Resolute. Unmoving and unmoved. With the serpent still wound around it. The one surviving totem at the end of time.

'Look,' says Baumol. 'What do you see?'

'The staff of Asclepius,' I reply.

'Look again,' he insists.

And then I see. It's not the same one. It's not the staff Asclepius was holding earlier. This staff has two serpents. Wound in opposite directions around the vertical. Their heads both pointing towards the top of the pole where two small wings protrude on either side of the upright. They weren't there before either. I'm sure of it.

'That's not the staff of Asclepius,' I say. 'It's not the same staff.'

'It's called the Caduceus.'

'It's not the symbol of medicine.'

'In fact it sometimes is,' he tells me. 'The US Army Medical Department adopted it in 1917. And after that you can find both staffs doing the rounds. The staff of Asclepius and the Caduceus. Not quite interchangeably. Both claiming to symbolize medicine.'

'That's confusing.'

'Professional organizations mainly use the staff of Asclepius. Commercial organizations tend to use the Caduceus.'

'I suppose it doesn't really matter. It's just a symbol after all.'

'You may be right. But here's the funny part.' Amusement twinkles in Baumol's eyes. 'In Greek mythology, as you know, Asclepius is the god of medicine. So his staff is a pretty good symbol of health.'

'The World Health Organization thought so,' I say.

'But this staff . . .' He begins to chuckle to himself. 'This staff belongs to the Greek god Hermes – or Mercury, as the Romans called him. You know who he was?'

'The messenger?'

'The god of communication, yes. And commerce. And innovation too, as it happens.'

'A god for capitalism then.'

'But also . . .' He's beginning to chuckle at the unfolding of a private joke. 'The god of thieving. Of theft!' A belly laugh explodes as he chokes out the punchline:

'The symbol of . . . of medicine . . . has been usurped by . . . by the god of theft!'

And now his mirth expands to fill the entire plain where once the ancient monument stood. It's picked up by the breeze. It reverberates across the dark and starless sky. And it's carried away like the last of last year's leaves. Torn from their branches by a mad, tempestuous wind. Until eventually. Eventually it fades away. Into the empty darkness. Into the endless night. And I am once again alone. Incomprehensibly tired. So tired that I settle down right there on the ground, where once Hygeia stood. And finally I fall asleep.

12

Fuck the Patriarchy

> *'The whole thrust of patriarchal societies is to
> guarantee powerful men certainty of paternity.'*
> Sarah Blaffer Hrdy, 1999

I'm awake almost immediately. Gone are the ruins. Gone is the Caduceus. Gone the dying laughter of a dead economist. I'm lying in my own bed. Grateful for its confines. Haunted by a strange melancholy. And with a single line of prose or poetry running through my mind.

'Last night I dreamt I went to Manderley again.'

At first it means nothing to me. The dream was vivid for sure. But I was definitely in Stonehenge. Not Manderley. 'Last night I dreamt I went to Stonehenge again.' Has nothing like the same ring to it. Just one syllable different. But it can't hold a candle to the original. The latter is just clunky prose. The former is a perfect alexandrine.

And that's how I remember where it comes from. It's the opening line of Daphne du Maurier's 1938 novel *Rebecca*. When she wrote the story, she was living in Alexandria in Egypt. The alexandrine is a form of verse made famous by a twelfth-century account of the life and accomplishments of Alexander the Great, after whom the city was named. All sixteen thousand verses of the ancient French *Roman d'Alexandre* had the same meter as the opening line of *Rebecca*.

Manderley is more than just a word that scans well in iambic hexameter. It's the name of a mythical house inspired by a place called Menabilly in Cornwall, on the south-west tip of the British Isles. Du Maurier had fallen in love with it as a young woman, walking in the area with her sister. Later in life she would live there as a tenant for twenty years. In *Rebecca* the house becomes a character in its own right. Places are more important than people to a novelist, she once said.

But why this meter? This perfect alexandrine. It became famous as a flawless opening line. Was it a conscious choice? A deliberate connection between Alexandria and the subject matter of her novel? She had come to hate the city at that point and was longing for Cornwall. So maybe it was simply a trick of her subconscious.

There's no doubt that the subconscious is a strange and wonderful thing. Take that dream, for example. Today we're leaving for what will be my third winter writing retreat on the book. This year we've taking a break from Wales. We've rented a place in Cornwall. We're going to Daphne du Maurier country.

To get there we'll be travelling along *that* road. The road of my dream. The one that leads past Stonehenge. The road I travelled so many times in the final years of my mother's life. This time I won't be visiting her. Not even in my dreams. She won't be there. She's been gone five years now. Incredibly.

On the other hand. Baumol's been gone even longer. And that didn't stop him turning up. So who knows? Dreams have their own reality. But they also carry their own internal logic. A logic that sometimes we should listen to.

Jamaica Inn

Looking for somewhere to charge *en route* to our destination, I'm guided by my trusty Electroverse app to an inconspicuous looking car park in a tiny village called Bolventor in the middle of Bodmin Moor. There's an almost gothic air to the place. The mist is swirling around the cluster of old buildings that stand nearby. An antique-looking sign is swinging on its hinges outside the pub. Groaning slightly for effect. It seems an incongruous place for an electric vehicle charging point.

Driving electric vehicles is supposed to be one of the things that will save us from climate change. But with barely a decade to make the transition, the infrastructure remains woefully lacking. Anyone who's tried it – even as an experiment – can attest to the difficulties. Range anxiety and cable rage are endemic. Stranding is a real possibility. But so too is the discovery of an occasional jewel.

This stop hasn't made its mind up yet. The car park is barely half full. No one is competing for the two sad-looking charging points. That's good. But any number of things can still go pear-shaped. A malfunctioning charger. The wrong cable. No means of payment. On this occasion the charging point won't accept my Electroverse card. Access denied. Fortunately a debit card does the job. And we have at least an hour before there's any meaningful improvement in our battery life. Time for lunch at least.

Quite by accident we've fetched up at a place called the Jamaica Inn. Built in 1750 as a coaching inn, a rest stop for those travelling across the inhospitable Bodmin moor, it gained a reputation for smuggling in the days when smuggling in Cornwall was rife. And to be honest, the pub looks like it probably hasn't changed that much since then. From the outside at least. On the inside, it's a slightly kitsch homage to its own smuggling history. And to its most celebrated guest.

In 1930 a young English writer stayed here. She'd been out riding on the moor with a friend when the mist came down and they got lost. It's easy enough to imagine on a day like today. Eventually the pair had to dismount and let the horses lead them home. Fortunately for English literature, that worked out well. The writer stayed on a few extra days to recover from the ordeal. In the process she imbibed enough of the atmosphere and history of the place to write a novel about it. *Jamaica Inn*, published in 1936, was Daphne du Maurier's first big commercial success.

Set in the 1820s, it tells the story of a young Cornish woman named Mary Yellen. When her mother dies, Mary moves from Helston to live at the Inn with her Aunt Patience and her uncle, the landlord Joss Merlyn. There she's thrown into a cut-throat and violently masculine world. Joss is the ruthless ringleader of a gang of unscrupulous 'wreckers', men who lure ships onto the rocks at night, murder their crew and plunder the ship's cargo for profit. Smuggling. Taken to another level. It's a dark, unnerving subject matter.

At one level the novel is a page-turning thriller. But smuggling itself is not really the theme of it. In fact du Maurier is writing about gender. As she is to some extent in all her books. She's intrigued by the relations between the sexes. Not as a romantic trope. But as a deep exploration of sexuality. Of the difference between women and men. She's constantly confronting the male with the female. Contrasting what's accepted as masculinity with what's expected of femininity.

Her fascination was rooted in a close relationship with her charismatic father, the actor Gerald du Maurier. But it also involved a deep questioning of her own gender. Unhappy with the roles defined for women in the early twentieth century, she invented an alter ego whom she used to refer to as 'the boy in the box'. (Today we'd probably call that gender dysphoria.) And from an early age she had intense relationships with both women and men.

Shortly after her first novel, *The Loving Spirit*, was published in 1931, she was courted by a career soldier named Tommy Browning. He and his mate sailed up and down the Fowey estuary posing on the deck until they caught the eye of the du Maurier sisters. Three months later Daphne and Tommy were married. They had three kids together. And stayed together – more or less – until he died. Though both of them had affairs. At one point Daphne had an intense relationship with an older actress named Gertrude Lawrence who, when she was younger, had been one of her father's mistresses. That's messed up, right?

But out of this 'dysphoria' emerged some of the most subversively feminist fiction of the twentieth century. And its subversiveness rests not in explicit scenes or didactic assaults on men, but on smuggling the themes of gender into immensely successful novels. In popular fiction she found a lens through which to interrogate core truths about human sexuality. And a vehicle through which to subvert the social mores of her time.

Jamaica Inn presents the relationship between the sexes as a dramatic confrontation between the outright aggression of masculinity and the inherent fragility of women. It's David and Goliath with a gender twist. Even the best behaved of the male characters in the book are thieves or weaklings. The worst are liars, bullies, abusers and murderers. Mostly they have no conscience whatsoever. The only moral compass is held by women. And it's women who, in the face of the constant upheaval triggered by male violence, attempt to 'maintain, continue and repair' the social world. It's women who care.

Battle of the sexes

At first, I'm not entirely sure why du Maurier has turned up here as my spirit guide. She's clearly reminding me that the question of gender and care is far from settled. And she also carries something of the point made by Kathleen Lynch in *Care and Capitalism*. We can't hope to understand the fate of care within capitalism without confronting its nemesis: war and violence. But where does du Maurier go with that question? On the surface at least, her novels are very different from each other.

Jamaica Inn conjures a historical period where women might sometimes use their moral compass – and their femininity – to confront male violence. But they could never expect to win the contest. And that's in part because of the inevitable disparity between the sexes in a world where social power is negotiated through physical strength. It's also because of women's sexuality. Their fascination for masculine strength. To survive at all they must avoid falling prey to that fascination. But in doing so they risk losing a part of themselves.

The world of *Rebecca* is a very different place. The action is roughly contemporaneous with the author's own life. Which means that by the time we get to Manderley, we've moved on by at least a century. Du Maurier was born into a society where women had no vote. She turned twenty-one in 1928, just a few months before the Equal Franchise Act was passed. For the first time in history, women had the same voting rights as men. And du Maurier was one of that first generation of twenty-one- to twenty-nine-year-old women eligible to vote in the

1929 election. The same election, as it happens, which returned Nye Bevan as an MP for the first time.

But universal suffrage was by no means the extent of the social changes that distinguished the 1930s from the 1820s. An active police force and a coordinated coastguard service had put an end to the outright lawlessness that prevails in *Jamaica Inn*. They may have been intended mainly to protect the rights of property owners. But they created lasting changes in the relationships between the sexes. In particular they offered something more in the way of physical security for women.

Social norms no longer condoned male violence. The carnage of the First World War had made society weary, temporarily at least, of the maxim 'might is right'. The morality forged by the lost generation had percolated into society. And there were even early signs of a new and more open sexuality. If only in the upper echelons of society. The older Victorian ideal of the obedient and subservient wife hadn't disappeared by any means. But in Rebecca we already find the new sexual freedom proclaimed, for instance, by the Bloomsbury Group. And the novel's narrator, the second Mrs de Winter, is clearly fascinated by what she sees of it.

In fact it's this fascination which holds the novel together. The narrative thread in *Rebecca* is wound from these two contrasting colours. The dying sexual politics of the Victorian era and the emerging sexual mores of the twentieth century. The main protagonists offer us two distinct visions of what it means to be a woman in a society that has evolved in just over a century so quickly that it's almost unrecognizable from the world of *Jamaica Inn*.

Of particular interest is the way in which the dichotomy between violence and care has been weakened or softened in this new society. The physical violence of men against women still plays a critical role in the novel. But women may sometimes be more careless. And men may sometimes engage in something that could be called care. The husbandry of the Manderley estate is the core task of the principal male character in the book.

And yet, as du Maurier makes clear, women are still held captive in one way or another by men. The social legitimation of male brutality may have diminished. But the institutional and financial power that men hold over women remains. This is still a world in which women are the property of men. A world in which male authority is exercised through patrilineal control over physical and financial property. In du Maurier's hands Manderley itself is more than just a house. It's a symbol of that control.

The two female protagonists in *Rebecca* react very differently to that control. One is meek and subservient. The other brings the full force of her femininity to bear in challenging it. Both end up getting punished. But the author never allows the reader to acquiesce in that punishment. We may applaud the gripping nature of the ride. But we aren't being invited to accept the destination.

My Cousin Rachel

Yes. Perhaps it's clear why du Maurier is here. Especially at this point. What fascinates me most is the long sweep of her understanding of sex and sexuality. She's painfully aware and deeply critical of the social conventions that impose themselves on the sexes. But her writing is also rooted in brute nature. She's uncompromising about the innate differences between men and women.

Towards the climax of *Jamaica Inn*, Mary Yellen appears to have taken her battle against her uncle as far as she can. She's physically weakened and emotionally exhausted to the point where she feels she has 'no will of her own'. And there she is forced to accept the solicitude of a man she cannot ultimately trust because 'once more she knew the humility of being born a woman, when the breaking down of strength and spirit was taken as natural and unquestioned'.

This is a world where women are broken like horses and bent to the will of men. A world in which their own instincts leave them prey to that fate. That sense of latent violence – the violence of men towards women – may go underground at times, but it never entirely disappears from du Maurier's writing. It's there in *Rebecca*. And in *My Cousin Rachel*, written more than a decade after *Rebecca*, it appears again with something like the force it had in *Jamaica Inn*.

We're never told precisely when *My Cousin Rachel* is set. But it's clearly premodern. And here the author disrupts our expectations by casting the narrator as a man. Philip Ashley and his older cousin (and mentor) Ambrose inhabit an uncompromisingly masculine world, set once more on an estate inspired by Menabilly. Though still only in his forties, Ambrose's health is precarious. So he periodically travels to Italy to escape the Cornish winter, leaving the estate in the hands of his presumed heir. But one winter in Florence he meets their distant cousin Rachel and falls hopelessly in love with her. Within a few months they are married. To the dismay of the young Philip.

Shortly afterwards, Ambrose's letters home to Philip change in tone. From infatuation he has turned to distrust. His health is going downhill now and his letters hint at being poisoned by their cousin Rachel. Fearing for his mentor's life – and perhaps also for his own inheritance – Philip travels to Florence to save his cousin. But when he gets there, it's too late. Ambrose is dead. Rachel has disappeared. And Philip returns to Cornwall distraught and uncertain of his future.

As it turns out, Ambrose's last will and testament leaves everything to Philip and nothing to his wife. And for a while Philip revels in his victory over cousin Rachel. He's convinced that she's evil. That she plotted Ambrose's death. That she had her eyes only on their wealth. He swears that if he ever finds her he will wreak revenge on her. And then she turns up in Cornwall.

She is nothing like the image he has created of her in his mind. She is charming, erudite, thoughtful, darkly attractive. Before long, without at first admitting as much, Philip is falling in love with her. Just like Ambrose did before him. Therein lies the conceit of the novel. Is Rachel an innocent widow grieving her husband or a murderous gold-digger out to gain control of the estate? Du Maurier skilfully offers us two separate narratives on the same question woven in such a way as to keep the narrative tension high.

One is provided by the narrator's own vacillating view of his cousin Rachel from suspicion to love and back again. The other is built from a mix of deliberate uncertainty and heightened prejudice. Du Maurier holds a light to the sexual prejudice – the sexism basically – of a male-oriented society in the presence of a charming and sophisticated woman.

Beneath the plot twists and the ambiguities. Beneath the passion momentarily sparked in the two men. Beneath the aura of charm and sophistication of the central character. Beneath all the contrivances of a clever popular novel. The real subject matter is hiding in plain sight. Once again its focus is the relations between the sexes.

As in *Rebecca*, the question of male property rights is crucial. Ownership of real estate. Ownership of women. We are forced to acknowledge the prevalence of both in the course of the novel. But we're also confronted again with men's violence towards women, as we were in *Jamaica Inn*. As the action moves towards its climax, Philip Ashley ponders the different natures of men and women, in almost the same terms as those presented by Mary in the earlier novel. 'So we had come to battle,' he says. 'Her words were a challenge I could not meet. Her woman's brain worked differently from mine. All arguments were fair, all blows were foul. Physical strength alone disarmed a woman.'

This brings the reader dangerously close to the 'look what you made me do' of the physical abuser. The unacceptable apologia of the violent male. But in putting these words in her narrator's mouth, du Maurier is not asking us to accept them. She's asking us to question them. And to question the society and the social conventions that lie behind them.

Published in 1951, the novel was already prescient of the 'second wave' of feminism. It prefigured and perhaps even helped to encourage the 'resist' of the women's liberation movement in the 1960s and 1970s. It echoed the resounding 'j'accuse' of women against the suppression and violence enacted against them by men. And legitimized by a profoundly patriarchal culture.

My Cousin Rachel has been called the 'most overtly feminist' of du Maurier's novels. And yet the double bluff of the narrative structure also carries something else, even more subversive. The subtext of Philip's reflection on the 'battle lines' that define the confrontation of the sexes reveals the inherent insecurity of the male. Men's awareness of their own susceptibility to being outmanoeuvred by women. In part because of women's intellectual and emotional strengths. And in part because of their own attraction to the opposite sex. It's a tantalizing mirror image of the vulnerability of women to men portrayed by Mary in *Jamaica Inn*.

Both images are rooted in a view of human nature that would soon be rejected by some elements in second-wave (and third-wave) feminism. The idea that there are any 'natural' differences between men and women at all. That anything men can do women can do better. That differences between men and women are for the most part socialized differences. That they're the constructions of nurture not the rules of nature. The vicissitudes of culture not the necessities of evolution.

Du Maurier doesn't take that position at all. In fact she's remarkably forthright in her writing that the differences between men and women are profound. Nor is she particularly judgemental about them. Perhaps that was a consequence of her sympathy for the 'boy in the box'. Perhaps she too was a prisoner of the social expectations she was trying to cast off. But the endings of several of her novels hint at the possibility that, with sufficient will, those strictures can be evaded. And sometimes even (in *Rebecca* most notably) that a time will come when they will be gone for good.

Women and healing

There's another reason for du Maurier's presence on this stage of my journey, I realize now. One particular narrative draws my attention to it. A direct connection between women and healing. Admittedly it's portrayed in the book as a deeply ambivalent connection. But that ambivalence reflects a reality. And that's surely part of what the author is getting at.

We're introduced to cousin Rachel's role as a healer obliquely. In fact by its inverse – the fear that she's used her knowledge of herbs to poison Ambrose Ashley. But when she arrives in Cornwall it becomes a part of what draws people to her. She employs her skills to attend to the ailments of those who work on the estate and live in the neighbourhood. She even begins to cultivate the herbs she needs in the garden.

It speaks to a time when women's role as lay healers was widely acknowledged in society. To periods of history when what we now call primary care was entrusted mainly to the hands of women. In Florence, at the time of the novel, that wisdom was alive and well. In England it had already been partially lost. And so woman as healer must prove her worth. The doubt that hangs over Rachel's skill with herbs is central to the plot. The woman who can heal with plants could also use that knowledge for ill. And this ambivalence becomes a more precise version of men's anxiety towards women. Do they mean us well or do they mean us harm?

Of course, variations on the same fear present themselves in male medicine too. Is it in our best interests that the sellers of cures have at heart or only the profit margins they can reap from us? Can we ever really trust those in whose hands we place our health? The alleviation of that fear is what motivates the Hippocratic oath. First, do no harm. And the same concern over quackery and extortion was central to Flexner's reforms in 1910. It was the pretext for the professionalization of medicine.

Those reforms set women's role in medicine back by decades. If that was an accidental consequence of professionalization, it was clearly an unfortunate one. But there's a pretty solid body of evidence to suggest that it wasn't. It was a deliberate attempt to sabotage the role of women as healers in society. To professionalize tasks that women had carried out in the community for centuries. And in the process to enable men to take control of them – quite often in pursuit of financial gain. That at least is the case made forcefully by the 'women's health movement' that emerged in the 1960s and 1970s.

Along with the sexual revolution had come a rising indignation that women had been kept in ignorance of their own bodies for too long. In the early 1970s the Boston Women's Health Book Collective published a pamphlet designed to help women take back control of their own health. *Our Bodies, Ourselves* was intended as an educational tool. It soon became a rallying cry. More than four million copies were sold worldwide and it was translated into over thirty different languages.

Two people involved in that effort began to wonder how on earth it had happened. How had women become so disempowered in relation to their own bodies? Barbara Ehrenreich and Deirdre English were teachers at the State University of New York when they decided to create a course on the history of women's health and medicine. The task was something of a forensic challenge, as they described it several decades later.

Sometimes, in conventional histories of American medicine, we found tantalizing references to a time when women predominated as healers – but only as an indication of how 'primitive' American medicine had been before the rise of the modern medical profession.

A couple of years into the search, they were invited to a conference in rural Pennsylvania. They decided to use the opportunity to test out their emerging hypothesis. That modern scientific medicine had explicitly 'driven out' older traditions of female lay healing, including even midwifery. The response to their presentation was immediate and enthusiastic. So the two teachers sat down to write up their findings in what was initially a self-published pamphlet. Almost as soon as it was published, *Witches, Midwives and Nurses* became another classic text from the women's health movement.

Witches, midwives and nurses

There's something familiar about Ehrenreich and English's story of the popular health movement. It reached its height in the US in the 1830s and 1840s. It was clearly a precursor to the natural hygiene movement, which we've already encountered. And it captured many of the same ideas. Health could best be ensured by managing lifestyle, diet and exercise according to some clear principles and correcting imbalances through some simple herbal remedies.

But the two teachers also made something else clear. It was women who formed the backbone of the movement. It was women who found themselves increasingly in opposition to the largely male cohort of 'regular' physicians who had begun to emerge around the same time. It was women who come up against the power of the American Medical Association (AMA), founded in 1848 to defend the interests of the 'regulars'. From mid-century onwards the AMA waged an increasingly vicious war against lay healers. And against women practitioners in particular. The Flexner report was little more than the final culmination of this unseemly battle. The premeditated nature of the assault is shocking to read.

Even more shocking is the earlier expulsion of women from professional health in Europe. Lay healers were routinely condemned as witches, irrespective of whether their cures were successful or not. Their authority 'represented a political, religious and sexual threat to the Protestant and Catholic church alike', write Ehrenreich and English. Hundreds of thousands of people were executed during the pre-modern witch hunts. Eighty-five per cent of them were women.

Three main types of charge were laid against these women. First, they were indicted for every conceivable sexual crime. 'Quite simply,' say Ehrenreich and English, 'they are "accused" of female sexuality.' Next, they were attacked for 'being organized'. For forming groups and societies that shared knowledge with each other. Third, they were accused of having 'magical powers' affecting health.

It was not even that their powers were used for harm. In fact the ability of women healers to cure their patients was itself taken as evidence of witchcraft. But women's worst crime was not in curing people. Or even in failing to cure them. It was in being women – and daring to think. 'When a woman thinks alone, she thinks evil,' declared the *Malleus Maleficarum*, the Catholic church's witch-hunting handbook.

Flexner was drafted in to 'clean up' medicine on the pretext that it was riven with pseudoscientific practices whose sole aim was profiteering. And that's a laudable enough aim in its own right. But this is where Ehrenreich and English's research is most shocking.

Women's health in the pre-modern era was highly empirical, they argue. Lay remedies had been tested over centuries. Many of them even went on to form the base for modern pharmaceutical drugs. This was not pseudoscience. It was science. And it wasn't profiteering. Most of it was social exchange. Much of the practice of lay healing occurred in the context of the gift economy. The economy of reciprocal altruism that thrived within small, local communities.

The argument from scientific purity was a smokescreen. It wasn't the absence of science that bothered the church. It was its presence. The woman healer constituted a threat to the authority of the church *because* 'she was an empiricist; she relied on her senses rather than on faith or doctrine, she believed in trial and error, cause and effect ... empiricism and sexuality both represent a surrender to the senses, a betrayal of faith.'

In other words we can't remotely justify the suppression of lay healing and the execution of witches on the grounds of eliminating quackery. It was the very opposite. Flexner was not cleaning the stables of fake cures and purifying medicine. He was relegating women to the role of servants in the healing process and anointing in their place an elite hierarchy of white men as the high priests of a new church.

This church created an unholy division between Asclepius and Hygeia. Between curing and caring. Healing in its fullest sense consists of both. And the lay healers of the pre-modern era had embodied both. But with the development of modern scientific medicine 'the two functions were split irrevocably', argue Ehrenreich and English. 'Curing became the exclusive property of the doctor; caring was relegated to the nurse.'

This separation was born not from reason but from prejudice. It had nothing to do with the protection of science. The degree of demonization alone makes it clear that it was a deliberate power grab. Or as Ehrenreich and English put it, modern medicine was 'an active takeover by male professionals'. The ambiguity surrounding cousin Rachel's role as a lay healer was not just a fictional device. It was a genuine historical phenomenon.

Something deeply uncomfortable emerges from all this. It's not just that three-quarters of unpaid care and two-thirds of paid care is done by women. It's not just that women's health has taken second place to men's health in research and in practice. It's not just that the wages of those who care are systematically suppressed by the structural imperatives of capitalism.

It is all of these things. Of course. But even deeper injustices lie in the persecution of women as witches. In the organized suppression of lay healing by religious dogma. In the misuse of science. In the duplicitous exile of naturopathy from the canon of knowledge. In the unnecessary privileging of the germ theory over the terrain. In the suppression of the principles of holism and vitalism. In the victory of the Caduceus over the wisdom of Hygeia. Of thieving over care.

How can we ever find our way towards health? How can we begin to rebuild economy as care? How can we even hope for prosperity if we don't address these structural and cultural injustices? If we're not prepared to recognize that our structures and our cultures are gendered through and through? Or in other words. How can we approach the care economy without confronting the patriarchy itself?

From today's perspective that task ought to be pretty straightforward to address. Life was definitely tough for women when du Maurier was writing. But the world today is a very different place, isn't it? And as for the patriarchy. That's long gone, surely? An object of ridicule and derision. At least. If popular culture is to be believed.

Barbenheimer

On 21 July 2023 two blockbuster films were released in movie theatres around the world. One was a deceptively light-hearted fantasy directed by Greta Gerwig) about the toy doll Barbie (played by Margot Robbie). The other was a biopic directed by Christopher Nolan about the scientist Robert Oppenheimer (played by Cillian Murphy).

In case you missed it. Barbie started life as a racy German comic book character before morphing into a kid's toy designed by Ruth Handler and marketed since 1959 by Mattel Inc. Robert Oppenheimer was the man who led the Manhattan Project. The US-led race to develop the first atom bomb in time to drop it on Hiroshima and 'put an end to' the Second World War.

The two films were very different in style and energy. But together they became a kind of cultural sensation. In a limited sense, of course. They didn't solve world hunger or cure cancer. Or anything like that. But financially, at least, they were both successful. Both films have grossed almost ten times what it cost to produce them. And people liked them. It was the first time since the pandemic when cinemas finally felt they might not go bust.

Some bright spark came up with the word *Barbenheimer* to describe the same-day release and somehow it stuck. It became the basis for an opening night fever in which people turned up to both movies dressed for the part. It also sparked an ongoing 'friendly' competition between them. When it came to money, *Barbie* won out initially, grossing almost twice as much in the US and significantly more worldwide than *Oppenheimer*. Reflecting on the birth pangs of Armageddon isn't to everyone's taste I guess. Come award season, things were a bit different.

At any rate, the Barbenheimer phenomenon initiated a slew of clever comparisons between the two films. One critic decided that both movies were talking about the dangers of the Anthropocene. Consumerism on the one hand and nuclear power on the other. Another argued that both films were concerned with the convoluted relationship between imagination and reality. Probably the most insightful piece was by the *Washington Post*'s film critic Sonia Rao, who saw through the differences of style and story to declare that both films were talking about 'the corruptibility of men'.

In *Oppenheimer* Nolan explores how 'ambition and arrogance play into the creation and legacy of the atomic bomb'. In *Barbie* 'Gerwig considers how male fragility can wreck the infrastructure of a society'. That theme is heavily disguised in *Oppenheimer* behind the tortured justifications for war and the scientist's own pangs of conscience. In *Barbie* it's couched in humorous terms but far more explicitly embedded in the fantastical plot.

When Barbie suffers a crisis of meaning, she and her genitally challenged side-kick Ken have to leave Barbieland and visit the human world in order to try and fix the glitch in the matrix that connects fantasy to reality. That plan goes awry when Ken falls in love with the power that men exert in the 'real world'. He's particularly taken by seeing (male) police officers riding powerful horses. And so he decides to import the patriarchy back into Barbieland.

Needless to say, the director's own political leanings were never going to let that devious manoeuvre succeed. So 'the Kens' must eventually content themselves with a lesson in humility and a journey of self-discovery. But I can't help wondering if it must have been very slightly galling for Gerwig how things went down at the Oscars. In the biggest film awards of the year *Oppenheimer* swept up most of the honours.

Barbie's only Oscar was for Billie Eilish and Finneas O'Connell's haunting theme song 'What Was I Made For?' But it was side-kick Ken who pretty much stole the entire ceremony, thanks to Ryan Gosling's high-octane performance of 'Just Ken', the film's most memorable dance number. There's now talk, of course, of a spin-off sequel, with Ken back in the driving seat.

Admittedly most of the plot had been driven by Ken and his 'corruptibility'. And for some reason he was also given most of the best one-liners. Villains often are, I guess. For me the standout line is the one that accompanies Ken's eventual decision to abandon the patriarchal revolution. 'To be honest,' he says, 'when I found out the patriarchy wasn't just about horses, I lost interest.'

Taylor's version

Around the same time that Barbenheimer was interrogating the corruptibility of men, another seismic move was being made against the patriarchy. To be fair, this particular attack had been in progress for a while. But July 2023 definitely marked a key moment in its advance. That date coincided with the US release of Taylor Swift's re-recorded version of her own 2010 album *Speak Now*.

The album rose rapidly to the top spot in the US album charts. And this particular release marked Swift as having more number one albums than any other woman in history. By the end of the year, she had all three of the three best-selling albums in the US and was halfway through her (sell-out) 'Eras' tour. It seemed like an opportune moment for *Time* magazine to nominate her as their person of the year. She was only the sixth individual woman to have been nominated since awards began in 1927.

Since the award is supposed to celebrate 'the individual who most shaped the headlines over the previous 12 months, for better *or for worse*', and since the list of awardees also contains Adolf Hitler (1938) and Joseph Stalin (1939 and 1942), it perhaps shouldn't always be taken as an indication of approval. But in this case the nomination was unequivocal.

By this time, the 'Taylor Swift effect' could lift the flagging fortunes of the National Football League, turn the tide of electoral history and boost the GDP of any country she visited. She'd become a cultural icon. Successful.

Outspoken. And massively important to the 'Swifties' who found hope in her music and inspiration in her success. In a year full of darkness, said *Time*, Swift had 'found a way to transcend borders and be a source of light. No one else on the planet today can move so many people so well,' they declared.

If you're wondering what any of this has to do with the patriarchy, I guess it's just possible you had other things on your mind during the early 2020s. In spite of her enormous fanbase, Swift is still an outrider in a profession still dominated by men. A recent study from over a thousand top 100 songs from the last decade reveals an uncomfortable truth. Only 22 per cent of the artists were women. Just under 13 per cent of songs were written by women. And less than 3 per cent of songs were produced by women.

But this power imbalance proved no match for Swift. It was during the pandemic years that her long-running dispute with the industry came to a head. That's when the rights to the recordings of her first six albums were sold from under her and she was (allegedly) refused permission to play her own songs at the American Music Awards in November 2020. Taylor promised her fans she would re-record all six of the albums she had 'lost' to the 'incessant manipulative bullying' of the industry. By the end of 2023, she'd re-released four of those lost albums. She'd taken on the patriarchy, in other words, and won hands down.

This too was a source of inspiration for her young fans. A sign that things were changing. And just in case it wasn't obvious what she was doing, she incorporated a pretty clear message into another of her re-recorded songs. The ten-minute version of her anthem to lost love 'All Too Well', released in November 2021, included the immortal line which I've used as the title for this chapter.

Over the last few years it's become a rallying cry for an angry variant of 'fourth-wave' feminism that had simply had enough of rational arguments and peaceful protests. It's over a century since women achieved the vote. It's sixty years since the sexual revolution. It's already most of a decade since the #MeToo movement highlighted the continuing sexual harassment of women by powerful men. Maybe it's time to get a bit more direct. Which part of fuck the patriarchy is difficult to understand?

The drop to the top

Of course, no one could argue that Taylor Swift is living in the same world as Daphne du Maurier. Or Gertrude Stein. Or Florence Nightingale. Young women today face far fewer barriers than women did a hundred or even fifty years ago. In education. In politics. In employment. In society. In part because of the example of people like Swift. And du Maurier. And Stein.

In a BBC documentary aired in the early 1970s, du Maurier recalls the delight she experienced when she received the advance for her debut novel, *The Loving Spirit*. It wasn't a huge amount of money. Just sixty-seven pounds. But it was a massive moment for the young author. It signalled the beginnings of her own financial independence. Something that was enormously difficult for women to achieve in 1930. And still isn't straightforward today.

Du Maurier too was an outrider in a profession – and a society – dominated by men. The labour participation rate for women in Britain during the interwar years was just 38 per cent. It wasn't much different in any western economy. And almost all of the available jobs were in low-paid professions such as domestic cleaning, secretarial services and nursing.

By the early 2020s, that rate had almost doubled. And for a short time, during the pandemic, the employment rate for women rose higher than it was for men. That's not surprising, of course, since society relied so much on the services of women in the frontline of health and social care and retail and education. But parity (or near parity) in workforce participation doesn't necessarily equate to gender equality.

The Global Gender Gap Index has been compiled every year by the World Economic Forum (WEF) for almost two decades. It measures progress towards gender parity across four domains: educational attainment, health and survival, economic participation and political empowerment. Since 2006, the overall index has improved by a mere four percentage points. It now stands at 68 per cent – where 100 per cent would represent complete parity. And the pace of change has slowed in recent years. At the current rate of improvement it would take, on average, a hundred and thirty-one years to reach global gender parity.

There are striking differences across countries and also between the four dimensions of the index. It might come as a surprise to find that the Latin American countries are expected to reach gender parity soonest, in just over half a century. Considerably faster than Europe. And twice as fast as the US. And that's in spite of the enormous advances made in educational attainment in most western countries.

In the US, for instance, women now surpass men in educational attainment. Twice as many women graduate as men. And more than four times as many women gain doctoral degrees. That's an extraordinary turnaround from the days when Gertrude Stein fled from the misogyny of Johns Hopkins School of Medicine.

But strangely these educational attainments haven't translated into income parity. Or empowerment. And that's in part because even the so-called developed economies suffer from what the World Economic Forum calls the 'drop to the top': a sharp decline in gender parity as you move from the lowest to the highest rungs of the employment ladder.

That decline is particularly steep in sectors such as the finance sector, where almost half of the entry-level workforce is female, but less than a quarter of those in the C-suite (where the big guns live) are women. In fact only 10 per cent of CEOs in Fortune 500 companies are women. But the drop to the top is present even in sectors like healthcare. More than 70 per cent of those employed at entry level but only 40 per cent of those who reach the C-suite are women.

The high-income jobs are still disproportionately taken by men. Even in a sector predominantly staffed by women. And this continuing dominance is having an effect on how the healthcare sector is run. It's definitely not the only structural force that undermines the pay and working conditions of those on the frontline of care. That much we've learned from Baumol. But it's likely to be contributing to it. And it's clearly part of what reinforces the gendered nature of modern medicine.

Perhaps the most striking finding from the WEF report is that the gender gap in political empowerment remains massive. Even in a country like the US. Educational attainment is more or less at parity. Health is not far from parity. The gap in economic opportunity is closing slowly. But one hundred years after universal suffrage, political empowerment is still only a third of the way towards parity.

If women have fewer economic opportunities and very little political power, even in advanced western economies, is it any surprise to find that we're still facing a deeply gendered world, in which violence towards women and girls remains so problematic and in which care is consistently undervalued?

Is there any chance at all of rescuing the care economy when the underlying structures that we've inherited remain so profoundly gendered and the political power to change things rests mainly with men?

Bad men

There's something raw in du Maurier's writing about men. Something that betrays an affinity for the rawness in masculinity itself. It's reflected in the images and slogans that bedeck the walls of the Jamaica Inn, even today. Pirates, smugglers, villains. They wreak of sweat and testosterone. Their strength seems continually to be on the verge of exploding into violence.

There's something uncomfortable in this. There's something troubling in the way du Maurier teases the reader with Mary's conflicted response – almost attraction – to the brute strength of her uncle. And more obviously of his younger brother. It reminds me of something else. Something deeply disturbing. Something we've seen already in the pages of this book.

I'm reminded of it again by an old photograph I find here on the wall of the Jamaica Inn. Men in uniform. And women waving them off. Du Maurier was married to a career soldier. She knew what that was about. The perfect alexandrine with which *Rebecca* opens is a homage to the most violent patriarch in the history of 'civilized' society.

But it's not that either. It's something I've written about. Something from earlier in the story. Some echo of the societal division of labour between care and war. Nightingale in the Crimea? The patch girls in the coal mines of South Wales? And then I have it. Dunant's memoir. Part 1.

It's the women of Solferino. The ones we met in Chapter 7. 'Scattering rose-leaves from the beflagged balconies of sumptuous palaces to fall on glittering shoulder-straps, on silk and ribbons, on gold and enamel crosses.' Women's triumphant farewell to their menfolk as they set out on their way to slaughter. Or be slaughtered. The uniform effect. The effect of men in uniform on women. The GIs in London after the Second World War. The firefighters in the wake of the Twin Towers in New York.

A twenty-five-year-old Israeli soldier posts pictures of himself in uniform on a dating app. 'I feel that girls are throwing themselves at me since I started my reserve duty,' he tells a couple of journalists writing about the 'uniform effect'. 'A friend of mine and I went to a café in Tel Aviv in our uniforms a few months ago. A group of girls came up to us and just told us directly that they wanted to sleep with us because we were soldiers.'

Late on in the first season of the HBO series *True Detective*, two officers investigating the ritual murder of a young woman find themselves on the verge of crossing some line between order and chaos, between restraint and violence. One of the detectives, Marty Hart (played by Woody Harrelson), turns to his partner, Rust Cohle (Matthew McConaughey), and asks him if he thinks of himself as a bad man. After a moment's pause, Cohle looks at Marty.

'The world needs bad men,' he growls. 'We keep the other bad men from the door.'

It's a thoroughly uncomfortable premise. But it haunts our nightmares. It populates entire genres of literature and art. It lurks uncomfortably in the subconscious fabric of the patriarchal society. It legitimizes the existence of military force. It provides some kind of deeply worrying 'explanation' for the uniform effect. Society needs bad boys. And that's why girls love them. It all hangs on the dark premise that women find male violence attractive?.

In recent years there's been 'an alarming rise' in 'consensual' sexual violence even among quite young adults and kids. One study in the US found that 58 per cent of female college students have 'participated in' choking during sex. A high-school teacher in the UK reported to the BBC that children as young as fourteen were asking her advice on choking and being choked during sex.

The novelist Mary Gaitskill has speculated that young women are drawn to such destructive practices for a reason. The 'increased feminisation of society' leaves women 'so hungry to feel masculine strength that they will respond to it in this physically extreme form', she suggests.

That's definitely not a view that's shared by everyone. The US study reports a 'statistically significant' link between aggressive sexual behaviour and exposure to pornography. And in her best-selling book *The Case against the Sexual Revolution*, Louise Perry argues that the sexual freedoms which liberated women in the 1960s have created a more dangerous world for women.

'All in all,' she says, 'the evidence demonstrates that the acts that have become much more socially acceptable over the last sixty years are acts that men are much more likely to enjoy.' What started out as an attack on the patriarchy became absorbed in its terrifying fabric. And the beneficiaries have not been women.

The British journalist Mary Harrington goes even further. The social changes ushered in by the sexual revolution have failed for everyone, she says. And that's partly because of a fundamental division that haunts feminism itself. A division with profound consequences for the paradox of care.

'From the earliest days of feminist debate,' writes Harrington in *Feminism Against Progress*, 'a clear tension is visible between the efforts to *escape* the domain of care, for an equal share of autonomy – Team Freedom, if you will – and the efforts to *defend and valorise* that domain of care – Team Interdependence.'

Over the course of the next few decades, and in particular during the third and fourth waves of feminism, Team Interdependence lost out to Team Freedom. Efforts to defend and valorize care were abandoned in favour of a form of feminism that attempted to secure for women the presumed freedoms of men, all the while remaining within a grand vision of perfect relationships which Harrington calls Big Romance. But the attempt failed, she says:

> Rather than grant [us] all a marvellous new world of polymorphous sexual freedom, the surface sheen of Big Romance has served to obscure a collapse

of human intimacy into the 'marketplace'. And this hasn't delivered freedom, or happiness, or even equality. . . . For women, this dynamic tends towards variously exploiting youthful beauty and enduring 'zipless fucks' with only a 10 percent chance of orgasm. For men, it offers either a superabundance of 'human spittoons' or embittered celibacy and sometimes misogynistic violence.

According to the anthropologist Alice Evans, these new and tortured sexual politics are creating a global gender divide. It's tearing apart the ideological worldviews of young women and young men. Women are becoming more progressive. Men are becoming more reactionary. The two sexes no longer even want to hang out with each other.

And there's evidence that this trend is so strong that it's driving fertility well below the replacement rate, even in countries like South Korea and Romania – where the British-born 'influencer' Andrew Tate and his brother have headquartered their aggressive backlash to feminism – let alone in the sexually confused dystopias of the West.

Tate's dangerous appeal for young men seems to reside in challenging what he deems to be a lie and they already suspect is one. That men should give up their masculinity and then everything will be ok. He preaches a violent defence of the raw strength that du Maurier's female characters flirt with, feminism mostly rejects and society pretends to outlaw.

Reactionary feminism

Fuck the patriarchy is a great one-liner. It expresses something of the outrage that's conjured up by realizing how much damage our prevailing social structure has inflicted. On women. On men. On children. On medicine. On care. On society itself. But there remains something unsettling in the ambivalence – verging on self-deception – with which both sexes simultaneously reject and celebrate the 'good girls love bad boys' narrative. And in the face of an enduring gender divide which is undermining care, amplifying violence and destabilizing society, it seems to me we need to do better than this.

Paradoxically one suggestion might be to take the division of labour between the sexes seriously again. That's close to Harrington's proposal of a 'reactionary feminism'. Before capitalism lured us towards the cities and the centres of mass production, she argues, the household was a relatively equal place. Women worked mainly in the home. Men laboured mainly in the fields. Both were involved in the market.

The division of labour was clearly there. But it didn't engender the same moral suspicion it does today. There was less 'othering' of unpaid care. Its contribution to social life was more obvious. And there was less preferential treatment for paid labour. It was all labour. And to some extent it was all care. In a world where care was more broadly defined. Less subject to moral scrutiny. And where, as a result, both social power and moral worth were more equally distributed.

It's a tantalizing vision. One that Harrington proposes as part of her solution space to heal a broken society. But when I hold it up against the lawlessness depicted in du Maurier's *Jamaica Inn*, I can't help wondering if it's up to the task. To some extent both Harrington and du Maurier romanticize their visions of the past. One in favour of harmony between the sexes. The other in favour of strife. But even in Harrington's version, we're still left having to account for the persistent violence of the male.

And that persistence seems to have a much longer pedigree than the emergence of industrial capitalism. 'Superior physical strength has been a lynchpin of masculine social dominance for most of human history,' insists Gaitskill. 'It was vital for the survival of families and communities.'

We're back where we started. The world needs bad men to keep the other bad men from the door. It's not a comforting view. But it takes us deeper into the nature of the beast. It's a thread we should follow. If we want to confront the roots of the patriarchy.

The roots of the patriarchy

In her classic text *Mother Nature*, the anthropologist and primatologist Sarah Blaffer Hrdy comes close to doing just that. She accepts that men and women face very different biological imperatives. Particularly when it comes to ensuring their own genetic success. It's from these differences, she says, that fundamental features of social organization such as the patriarchy find their motivation.

Though ultimately they separate us, those imperatives derive from a common cause. We've seen it already. We are born into care. We arrive in the world only partially formed. Less developed than most other species. We're inherently dependent on the kindness of strangers. And the flipside of this dependency is an enormous parental commitment from those strangers. It has to last for the first decade or so of our lives. At least.

That commitment is justified, for the strangers, by a genetic drive for continuance. That's not to deny parental love, of course. But at the biological level this is all about investment. And like any investment, parental investment comes at a price.

For a female the price is straightforward. Her window of fertility is short. The period of gestation is long. And her offspring are vulnerable to attack or disease or starvation for even longer. The mother is faced, says Hrdy, with a 'perpetual, existential angst about who would help provide for her children. Would her mate survive, stick around, and if he did, how committed would he be.' Would he defend her and her offspring against the dangers that lurk within and beyond the boundary of hearth and home? In that context the physical strength of the male is an obvious asset to her. And to society. To protect and defend.

For the male it's different. His genetic interests coincide with his mate in the desire to leave behind healthy progeny. But his fertile window is longer. His immediate investment is briefer. His recovery period is shorter. His options for succession are limited only by the supply of available females. Yes, he has an interest in ensuring that his progeny survive. But once his job as an inseminator is done, the male has a genetic choice. To protect and defend. Or to hit the highway. And spread his seed more widely.

Both strategies have high risks. The risk of not sticking around is that none of his progeny survive. The risk of sticking around is the opportunity cost of not procreating elsewhere. That might not matter if he's successful in his role as a protector. But that role is time-consuming and dangerous. It involves hunting and scavenging. Defending against intruders. Confronting the 'other bad men'. Going off to fight. And these inevitable absences from his mate, short though they may be, provoke the most existential of all his anxieties: 'just who did sire his child?'

This is a world in which he can trust no one. He knows instinctively that other males can inseminate as easily as he can. He knows instinctively that his genetic imperatives don't entirely align with those of his mate. How can he convince himself that the time spent in parental investment – if that's the strategy he chooses – is protecting and defending his own kid and not the progeny of some other dude?

It's to cope with existential problems like this at the individual level that power structures emerge at the societal level, according to Hrdy. All species organize around power. From the perspective of evolutionary biology it's a given. Some are more egalitarian than others. But when paternity becomes a problematic question for males, then power structures tend to take a particular shape. 'The whole thrust of patriarchal societies is to guarantee powerful men certainty of paternity,' says Hrdy.

Patriarchy, in other words, is a defence against the existential insecurity of the male. It's built in its turn on a deep distrust. 'Few have zeroed in on the key issue quite so pointedly,' writes Hrdy, 'as the brilliant, troubled, and utterly misogynistic Swedish playwright August Strindberg', who in his 1887 play *The Father* finds himself tormented by his wife over the possibility that her child is not his child. When he eventually explodes in rage, it's to cry despairingly: 'If it's true we are descended from the apes, it must have been from two different species. There is no likeness between us, is there?'

It's the same male rage that haunts du Maurier's novels. It rears its head throughout *Jamaica Inn*. It provides the narrative drive in *Rebecca*. It generates Philip's despair in *My Cousin Rachel* at the impossibility of any genuine relationships between the sexes. Towards the climax of the book he laments that two people can never really 'share a dream. Except in darkness. As in make-believe.'

The same fury – and the same insecurity – fuelled the witch hunts which eliminated women healers and fundamentally distorted medicine. First and foremost amongst the accusations against witches was the crime of sexuality. 'All witchcraft comes from carnal lust,' rages the *Malleus Maleficarum*, 'which in women is insatiable.'

Can it really be true? Can this be where we stand? Beneath the violence and suppression of the patriarchy simmer the fires of a deep sexual insecurity?

In an attempt to solve a problem in genetic biology, humanity stumbled on a form of social organization that created nothing much better than hell on earth. And we still haven't found our way out of it. What's clear is this. Care, violence and gender define us to the core. And we have emerged as desperately insecure genetic beings. And as a broken civilization.

The chalice and the blade

For the most part, feminism has tended to reject arguments from nature as unsavoury forms of biological determinism. At best they risk falling into what the English philosopher G.E. Moore called the 'naturalistic fallacy'. Equating the 'natural' with the 'good'. At worst they encourage spurious sophisms that legitimize violence, criminality and anti-social behaviour. As a result, there's often a deep suspicion of the kind of evolutionary psychology that Hrdy is proposing.

And yet she declares herself a feminist. In her 1981 book *The Woman That Never Evolved* she makes that argument plain. Far from embracing biological determinism, she sets out specifically to demolish gender stereotypes about male violence and female passivity. She documents a wide variety of sexual and social behaviours across many species of primates. And the evidence is clear. Patriarchy is not the only evolutionary choice. It's one response to the underlying challenge. But not the only one.

The cultural historian Riane Eisler makes a similar point. In her 1987 classic *The Chalice and the Blade* she argues that any species with two sexes faces a simple (more or less binary) choice about the organization of society. Either one sex dominates the other – leading to what Eisler calls a dominator society. Or else the relationship between the sexes is based on mutuality and respect – in what she describes as a partnership society.

Patriarchy is clearly a dominator society. Much of what we've known is based on the dominator model. But Eisler argues that partnership societies were common in antiquity. Much more common than has ever been recognized by (male-dominated) archaeology. They endured as the norm until at least the collapse of the Minoan civilization. 'Even as late as the classical age of Greece the partnership society tradition of seeking divine revelation and prophetic wisdom through women had not yet been forgotten,' Eisler writes.

Those societies were often matrilineal. Descent was recognized through the maternal line and society was organized 'matrilocally'. Around the mutual support group of mothers. But this form of social organization isn't a simple inversion of patriarchy. It's not a matriarchy, in which women dominate men (and presumably each other too) as men dominate women (and each other) in a patriarchy.

In fact Hrdy is doubtful that matriarchal societies have ever existed. There is 'general agreement among anthropologists,' she says, 'that women living matrilocally among their kin tend to have more autonomy than when they do not'. But this arrangement has the characteristics of partnership in Eisler's sense. Not domination. Something about the way that women self-organize, it seems, when they have the social authority to do so, leads to less violent, more egalitarian, more cooperative societies. It's a clear argument for gender parity. Particularly in political power.

There's even evidence for the existence of such societies in isolated places in the world in modernity. As recently as the mid-twentieth century, according to Hrdy, some 15 per cent of the world's cultures were matrilineal. The problem is, she warns, 'such matrilineal arrangements are fragile, and they quickly disappear after contact with patrilineal herders, agriculturalists or wage economies'. After they come into contact with dominator societies, in other words. And that, concedes Eisler, may also be what happened to the Minoans.

None of this suggests an easy escape from patriarchy. But it's clearly enough to reject an essentialist view. According to Hrdy and Eisler, that essentialism is itself the result of gendered science. The anthropological evidence has been contaminated. Much as our views of medicine have. That's not to reject the wisdom that can be found there. It's simply to point out that when we're looking at science through a male lens, we're seeing only half the picture.

In a human voice

That same point has been made in a different way by the philosopher Carol Gilligan. In the mid-1970s she unearthed something that now seems both blindingly obvious and obviously bad. She found that theories of moral development had emerged primarily by listening to the voices of men and boys. There were virtually no developmental studies, she found, that listened to the voices of women and girls.

This meant that philosophy had missed something fundamental about how moral choices are made. Men tend to favour abstract frameworks of justice or utility which favour rational calculation. By listening to the accounts of women and girls, Gilligan found that women tend to privilege relationships and responsibilities to others. But in a world defined by a masculine framing of moral development, women ended up misunderstood and missing out. She coined the concept of an 'ethic of care' to complement the 'ethic of justice' framed largely through listening to men and boys.

In 1975 she wrote a paper setting out her findings. She called it 'In a Different Voice'. It was circulated first to her students. But they sent it to friends who sent it to friends. And before Gilligan knew it, the paper had become a kind of 'underground' sensation. One of those students happened to sit on the editorial board of the *Harvard Educational Review*. He suggested submitting it there for publication. It was rejected with one line of explanation. 'We don't know what this is.'

She added a few explanatory headings to make it look more like something they might recognize and re-submitted it. This time it came back with another one liner. 'This is not social science.' She was asked to rewrite the paper 'in an impersonal voice and from an objective standpoint'. She replied. 'It's called "In a Different Voice."' At that point, perhaps just to shut her up, they accepted the paper and published it. Five years after that it was reprinted in a longer form as a book. It became another seminal text in second-wave feminism.

Gilligan later realized she had missed something profound. The different voice that she had identified as female was in fact a quintessentially human voice. Because care is a quintessentially human quality. It is care that gives us our humanity. But this capacity is undermined in us, in both sexes paradoxically, early in life, because we are forced early on into gender binaries.

Neither men nor women are free to find their authentic voice. From very early in life, women are conditioned into care. Men are conditioned out of it. And both forms of conditioning are dangerous. To silence the voice of care leaves only the voice of self which feeds the violence of the patriarchy. To impose the voice of care is to silence the voice of self which might oppose the violence of the patriarchy.

'What this gives us,' says Gilligan in her follow-up book, called simply *In a Human Voice*, 'is a place to begin.' Or as Eisler puts it:

> Under [this] view of cultural evolution, male dominance, male violence and authoritarianism are not inevitable, eternal givens. And rather than being just a 'utopian dream', a more peaceful and egalitarian world is a real possibility for our future.

Of women and horses

Outside the mist is finally clearing. I feel refreshed. Recharged. I hope our EV does as well. The moors rise enticingly around us. They're dappled with patchy sunshine as it breaks through the cloud.

I feel released from something that's been haunting me. Perhaps from the moment that I found myself wandering without a passport in the land of the invisible heart. Long ago. Right at the beginning. I can still sense that earlier apprehension. But today at last I feel as though it's been redefined. Recalibrated. With the help of Taylor Swift. Daphne du Maurier. And Barbie. A weird lunchtime ensemble.

Two young women on horseback make their way leisurely across the yard. They're heading out for a trek across the sunny uplands. Iron horseshoes echo on the rough cobblestones. A man shouts after them from the door of the old coaching inn.

'Be careful out there on the moors!'

One of the women turns and waves at him. A little too dismissively, he feels.

'It's easy enough to leave,' he mutters. 'It's harder to find your way home.' He calls out to them again.

'You want me to come with you?'

The two women shake their heads and call back. 'We'll be fine.' 'Thank you!'

I imagine them laughing quietly to each other. Fuck the patriarchy.

Fuck its arrogance and its boundaries. Fuck its sense of entitlement. Fuck how it's distorted society. Undermined care. Destroyed health. Polluted science. Fuck the way it's fucked us all. Women and men alike. Fuck the patriarchy.

And then I see the mists come down again. The slow realization that we're lost. As lost as two young women on Bodmin Moor in the winter of 1930. One of them is our guide for this chapter. As the night falls, a storm breaks. To their horror, rain and darkness descend upon them:

> And there we were, exposed to the violence of night with scarcely a hope of returning. Struck what we thought was a farm but it was only a derelict barn. I was for staying, but Foy said we would catch our death. Blindly, helplessly, we let the reins lie loosely on the necks of the horses, and they led us back in the direction from which we had come, and by a miracle we saw in the distance the light from Jamaica Inn.

Ken would have known immediately, of course. You can do without the patriarchy. But you can't do without horses. Strong, dependable beasts who know their way home.

13

Land's End

*'By all outward appearances our life is a spark of
light between one eternal darkness and another.'*
Alan Watts, 1951

Storm Henk made landfall on the southwest tip of Cornwall sometime in the early hours of 2 January 2024. From the depths of sleep I'm woken by a sudden loud crash. A dustbin somewhere along the village street goes clattering over and a dog barks briefly at the din.

Outside, the trees are thrashing in the wind. The first drops of rain begin to batter the windowpanes. And from half a mile away I hear the persistent thunder of the waves breaking heavily against the shore. There's another sound too. Dark and menacing. Is it the undertow hissing savagely as it retreats over gravelly sand? Or is it the rain falling steadily now on the dark foliage and grey slate roofs along the street?

I roll onto my back and stare at the ceiling. And for a few moments I let the sounds wash over me. There's something vaguely comforting about listening to a gale. Especially when it's outside the window. Perhaps it's a false sense of security. The momentary security of a safe haven. A shelter from the storm. It's a lot better than being out there on the ocean at this point. That's for sure.

With sleep now evading me, I swing my legs out of bed and make my way quietly downstairs. This chapter in the book has been eluding me for too long now. And there's something about the dark hours of a stormy night that's luring me again towards its rocky subject matter: immortality. Or rather. I suppose. Mortality. The inevitability of death and our desire to transcend it. The pursuit of immortality.

Ultimately I guess it's all about security. Our craving for it. And its elusive nature. Especially on a night like tonight, when Alan Watt's 'eternal darkness' in the epigraph I've chosen for this chapter seems more real than the 'spark of light' that interrupts it. 'Nor is the interval between these two nights an unclouded day,' continues Watts in *The Wisdom of Insecurity*. 'For the more we are able to feel pleasure, the more vulnerable we are to pain.'

The treacherous coastline less than a mile from where we're staying is ample proof of this. The Lizard peninsula lies on the southern-most tip of the British Isles. Its shores have claimed literally hundreds of ships. Thousands of lives. Particularly dangerous are the Manacles. A reef of igneous rocks lying mostly submerged to the east of Godrevy Cove. A rich seam of 'greenstone' thrown up during another of those Precambrian tectonic shifts that gave the west coast of Wales its distinctive character.

At low tide the reef is clearly visible. If the sea is calm, the green-grey peaks rise prominently above the level of the ocean. As often as not they're colonized by gulls and terns and streaked with guano. An occasional seal is to be seen basking in the light. If the sea is rough, the stones are marked unmissably by an endless tapestry of white water and rising spray.

At high tide, though, you can barely see the rocks at all. And their treachery lies not in what's visible, but in what hides beneath the deceptive surface of the water. It doesn't even need to be a night of gale-force winds and driving rain like tonight for things to go badly wrong.

The Mohegan

On the afternoon of Friday, 14 October 1898, the SS *Mohegan* was sailing west through the English Channel, bound for New York. Visibility was good. There was a bit of breeze. But nothing like Storm Henk. The sea state was moderate. A far cry from the wild white horses out in the bay tonight.

She'd left London a day earlier under the command of Commodore Richard Griffiths, the most experienced captain in the Atlantic Transport Line, who owned the ship. There were ninety-seven crew on board. Along with seven cattlemen who were there to look after the cows and horses returning with them from New York. At lunchtime that day they'd stopped in Gravesend to pick up fifty-three passengers also bound for New York.

One of those was a certain Mrs Compton-Swift, travelling for health reasons with her personal physician, Dr Fallows. As you do. Another was a twenty-two-year-old opera singer. Maud Roudez had been training in Paris and was on her way home in the company of her mother, Lizzie Small Grandin. The young soprano was about to make her debut in a series of supporting roles for the Metropolitan Opera House. This was her big break. The two women were excited about what lay ahead.

When the gong sounded for dinner at six-thirty that evening, they made their way with the rest of the passengers to the sleekly furnished dining saloon. The atmosphere was relaxed. Almost jovial. They'd had a few squalls coming through the Channel. But as twilight fell, the sky had cleared and the waves were subsiding now. It seemed as though it would be a fine night ahead.

Twenty minutes later there was a loud metallic grinding sound. The ship took a sudden list to starboard, sending plates and cutlery flying from the tables. Some of the officers in the saloon made their way on deck to see what was going on. Others remained behind to calm any nervous passengers. Not all of them needed calming. Mrs Compton-Swift and Dr Fallows rose from the table when the shock was first felt. But hearing the reassurances of the crew and looking at the crowd on the stairs, Mrs Compton-Swift suggested they should sit back down and finish their dinner. Who knew when they might eat next. Composure at all times was something she prided herself on.

A couple of minutes later the lights went out. The *Mohegan* had run full tilt onto the Manacles reef and was holed on the starboard bow. Water was flooding rapidly into the engine room. It had already taken out the electrical circuits. Passengers and crew were plunged into a terrifying darkness.

By all accounts, the crew remained calm and organized. Iron discipline was a characteristic prized by the Commodore. And in any case, they were confident that a modern steel-hulled ship like the *Mohegan* could take a little knock from below. If she was aground already, then so much the better. She wouldn't be dragged or blown ashore. She wasn't going anywhere. The captain stood implacable on the bridge. Inspiring courage. Urging his crew to make haste with the lifeboats. Instructing them to get the women and children off first.

But soon things weren't so easy. The early starboard list had reversed itself. The vessel was down heavily on the port bow now. Two wooden boats released too quickly were smashed to pieces on the rocks. The boats on the starboard side were useless, so steep was the tilt to port. And to make matters worse, the *Mohegan* was already lying so low in the water that waves were breaking over the deck.

One of the quartermasters, a man named John Juddery, was barely able to stand and was struggling to hear the Commodore's orders. Crawling towards the bridge, he could just about make out instructions to get the remaining women and children into the rigging, the highest points on the vessel. But the *Mohegan* was listing too heavily for him to do anything. It was all he could do not to be swept away himself.

Meanwhile, Mrs Compton-Swift had managed to find a lifebelt and was sitting with as much dignity as she could muster in one of the steel lifeboats on the port side. There were twenty or so people with her. And the crew were struggling to get the lifeboat free of its davits. At the last moment, one of the lines jammed as they were lowering it. The boat fell lopsidedly into the ocean. Almost immediately it was caught by a wave and overturned, tipping its occupants into the sea.

Moments later, Quartermaster Juddery encountered the chief officer, a Welshman named Llewelyn Couch, who yelled goodbye to him. 'We've done all we can,' he said. 'Look out for yourself.' And then the vessel took her final plunge and Juddery watched helplessly as the chief officer was swept away before his eyes.

Just over fifteen minutes had elapsed between the initial collision and the moment the *Mohegan* sank beneath the waves leaving only the top of her masts, the mizzen rigging and the funnel showing above the water.

West by north

I've been intrigued by this story since we arrived here. You could call that morbid. I'll come to that point in a moment. But anyone who's sailed. Anyone who's been on the ocean. Anyone vaguely familiar with this stretch of shoreline might easily feel the same.

A couple of days ago we visited the local church. There in the graveyard is a grim memorial stone, now spotted with lichen, paid for by the local people. The single word 'Mohegan' is carved on the plinth. And inside the church, on a fine day, the morning light cascades in rainbow colours through the stained-glass windows which grace the east chancel wall behind the altar.

Here is St Christopher, the patron saint of travellers. Here is the Messiah calming the waves. And there on another pane St Paul is being greeted in Malta after he was shipwrecked in the Med. The implicit claim is clear. God is always present in the hour of our need. Beneath the images is a text which commemorates those who died that night a century and a quarter ago. Along with a crafty nod to the Atlantic Transport Line, who paid for the window. A bit of free advertising never goes amiss.

It's not so much morbidity. I think it's more about humility. A reminder of the frailty and finitude of life. The unpredictable forces of nature. That's easy enough to understand on a night like this as the rain lashes the windows. And maybe that's why my mind is now running in circles trying to understand what happened.

Here's the thing. The official explanation makes no sense to me. The Board of Trade held an inquiry within weeks of the tragedy. And their official verdict amounts to this. Around the time the ship passed the Eddystone light, just south of Plymouth, an experienced Commodore with thousands of hours at sea and a robust knowledge of the British coastline had set a compass course which put his vessel onto a direct collision course with one of the most well-known navigation hazards on the Lizard peninsula. This was human error. Pure and simple.

But this is what's puzzling me. The compass course the Commodore was supposed to have set – west by north, in case you're interested – would have brought the *Mohegan* ashore somewhere near Dodman Point. Some fifteen miles at least before she got to the Lizard. Possibly even earlier, with the wind in the southeast, as it evidently was that day. She'd never have reached the Manacles at all. It makes no sense to me.

And that's why, in the early hours of a raging storm, I go back to the inquiry report. I trawl through it one more time. I want to know where the evidence came from. Where 'west by north' came from. It's mentioned several times. But when I look more closely, I find that the whole verdict hinged on the evidence of just one man. There were no other survivors who could corroborate his testimony.

Admittedly this man was at the helm for two hours between 4 p.m. and 6 p.m. that day. So you'd think he'd know what course he was asked to steer, right? And yet he couldn't possibly be correct. Perhaps it was post-traumatic stress. Perhaps he was afraid his own helming had been at fault. Perhaps it was a confused attempt to avoid the finger of blame. I'm not saying he deliberately lied. But he can't have been telling the truth. That course steered over that time on that day would have wrecked the *Mohegan* for sure. But not on the Manacles.

The symbolic self

I sit back and sigh. What does it matter? What can it possibly matter now? At the time it might have mattered. But now it's all far too late. Even the survivors are long since gone. It's still a puzzle, of course. And puzzles persist in the public imagination. And in the local community. This one clearly does.

Rumours began to circulate within days of the tragedy. Some of them still do the rounds. At one point a story began to circulate that the captain had deliberately wrecked his ship over an altercation with the company. That he'd been picked up by a lifeboat and been ferried back to safety, incognito. Once ashore, he'd been seen sprinting up the hill out of the village and away from the scene.

Maybe it was to quash such rumours that the Board of Trade amassed so many witness statements confirming that Commodore Griffiths had gone down with his ship. And that he'd acted with impeccable calm and authority from the moment the *Mohegan* hit the rocks. But it's slightly confusing, to say the least, that in settling on a verdict that makes no navigational sense, the inquiry was quite happy to throw the Commodore's seamanship – and his reputation – under the bus.

Call no one happy until they're dead, said the Greek philosopher Solon. And perhaps not for a very long time after they're dead. If this story is anything to go by. Reputation matters. That's my point. And reputation lasts a long time. Longer than a lifetime. I think that's a part of why the story has a hold on me. That and its obvious reminder of our human frailty.

At any rate, it's a prompt, in case I needed it, that I still have to resolve a challenge that I identified early on in the journey of this book. Care is called into action not only in pursuit of the health of our physical bodies. But also in the creation and maintenance of our symbolic bodies. Our symbolic health, as I defined it in Chapter 4, matters as much as and sometimes more than our physical health.

Our sense of identity. Our status amongst our peers. Our anxieties and our fears. Our dreams and our aspirations. Our place in society. Our reputation. Our legacy. These are the essential elements of the symbolic self. They are inspired in part by the desire to protect and enhance and maybe even prolong that 'spark of light' that Watts was writing about in *The Wisdom of Insecurity*.

Knowing that we are going to die changes everything for us. It frames our existence. It affects our ambitions. It informs our decisions. What we aspire to. How we relate to each other. How we organize society. As Hannah Arendt pointed out, it motivates human work. It drives the pursuit of durability. The search for some semblance of permanence with which to counter the transience of human life.

It achieves all this, in part of course, because we care. In both the principal meanings of the word. The inevitability of death not only frames but also heightens the 'cares of the world'. Suffering. Loss. Grief. Anxiety. And this is part of what motivates our attention to needs. This is what provokes the care with which we respond to the cares of the world.

According to Martin Heidegger, this awareness of death is what makes care quintessentially human. Only humans truly care because we are uniquely aware of our own mortality. To be honest, I'm not so sure the evidence supports such a claim. Is it really true that no other species is aware of its own mortality? How would we even know this? It's not like we've paid much attention to the existential suffering of other creatures.

Elephants are known to grieve over the bones of dead relatives. Anyone who's seen or heard cattle being loaded into a truck bound for the abattoir might harbour suspicions that they too have some inkling of what's coming down the line at them.

A few years ago an orca named Tahlequah refused to leave her calf for seventeen days after it died. In fact she accompanied its corpse for sixteen hundred kilometres. Unable to abandon it. Unable to move on from the love of her child. Darwin certainly believed that animals could experience grief.

Does this mean they're aware of death? Maybe not. But it's clearly wrong to deny the existence – and the importance – of care in other species. I've made that point already. The ability to care isn't uniquely human. And suggesting that it is seems premature at best. It comes across as a kind of special pleading designed to cement human superiority in the moral universe. An attempt to 'other' and objectify those species who share the world with us.

So let's not get sidetracked by exceptionalism. The point is that care is never confined only to our physical health. In fact we're painfully aware that this particular battle is one we're destined ultimately to lose. And that's why we distribute our resources – our energy, our attention, our time – between caring for the physical body and caring for the symbolic body. Between staying healthy and being loved. Between staying alive and being remembered – and perhaps even celebrated – long after we've gone.

And this is in part, of course, why we find ourselves sitting late at night in smoke-filled bars drinking whisky with Gertrude Stein's lost generation in Paris. Yearning for conviviality. Struggling for artistic perfection. Striving for immortality. And often far too careless of our physical health in the process.

The denial of death

Knowing that we are going to die changes everything. That's very clear. It stimulates an existential anxiety in us. You might even call it terror. A terror brought on by the inevitability of death. And equally perhaps by our fears of inconsolable loss. Of being alone in the world. Of losing those we love.

How we respond to that anxiety, how we manage that terror, turns out to be pivotal in understanding our pursuit of symbolic health. In a Pulitzer-Prize-winning book first published in 1973, the cultural anthropologist Ernest Becker argued that Western society does its best most of the time to suppress the conscious awareness of death. Our culture tends to try and push mortality into the background. To deny death.

This denial turns out to be an extraordinary, time-consuming endeavour involving the allocation of enormous physical and mental resources. And I suppose that's not particularly surprising when you consider quite how many 'mortality reminders' surround us, day in and day out. You don't even have to spend your time in the small hours of a stormy night contemplating the shipwrecks that happened long ago to stumble on the intimations of mortality that haunt our daily lives.

They're in the graveyard memorials. They're in the stained-glass windows. They're in the street signs for a local hospital and the warnings of old people crossing the road. They're in the pension contributions subtracted from our paycheque. They're in the grey hairs we never used to have. They're in the lines in our forehead we can't see clearly anymore. They're in the boughs that break. The cradles that rock. The leaves that fall.

They're in the abattoirs and factory farms that support our flesh-hungry diet. They're in the health warnings on our packaging. They're in the proliferation of products designed to keep us looking young. They're in our dreams and our nightmares. They're in our subconscious fears of being left or abandoned. They're in the childhood trauma we buried long ago. They're in our family history. They're in the ordinary and extraordinary tragedies that dog our lives. And the lives of people we have never even met.

These are the subtle and not so subtle reminders that our time on earth is limited. That the time of those we love is limited. That before we know it, Watts' 'spark of light' will be gone. And the eternal darkness will be all that's left to us.

And it's precisely this feeling, this awareness, which spurs us to act in the world. This was Arendt's point. The social importance of the human artefact, the product of human work, lies in its promise to provide a semblance of durability. To create a sense of permanence. At the individual level, creative work becomes a part of the struggle to achieve significance. To find purpose and meaning in our existence. And perhaps even to transcend death. Our desire for immortality provides the motivation for enormous ingenuity. It's a never-ending source of creativity.

The pursuit of greatness. The founding of empires. The construction of durable memorials. Lasting works of art. The underlying force can take a variety of different forms. All of it is driven by insecurity. By a haunting fear of our own insignificance. By a restless desire for significance. And it drives us ever onwards in the search for what the philosopher Friedrich Nietzsche called 'great health . . . a new health that is stronger, craftier, tougher, bolder, and more cheerful than any previous health'.

The goal of great health has much in common with Groys' concept of care for the symbolic body and with what I've called the pursuit of symbolic health. And it leads, said Nietzsche, to a world so over-rich in what is beautiful, strange, questionable, terrible, and divine that our curiosity and our thirst to possess it have veered beyond control – alas, so that nothing will sate us anymore.

The point is well illustrated by Nietzsche's own life. His physical health was consistently bad. It was probably made worse by his relentless pursuit of great health. He had horrible migraines from childhood onwards. He had a severe mental breakdown at the age of forty-four. His final years were spent in a state of total physical dependency after he suffered a debilitating stroke. And he died in his mid-fifties. On the other hand, he's remembered still for his extraordinary philosophical ideas. For his creative genius. For his effervescent writing. Long after his physical demise.

Symbolic health, in this characterization, becomes the never-ending and sometimes febrile pursuit of symbolic immortality. The pursuit of great health becomes the driving force for social progress. Something central to culture. 'Earlier it was God who guaranteed the unity and continuity of times,' says Groys. 'But now it is the transhistorical fame of the creative few.' Or. To put it more bluntly. We live in a culture which has supplanted God with Fame.

Terror management

The US psychologists Sheldon Solomon, Jeff Greenberg and Tom Pyszczynski incorporated Becker's insights on the denial of death into a psychological understanding of what they call 'the worm at the core' of human existence. Awareness of our mortality eats away at our security. It undermines our sense of self. It torments our love for each other. It erodes our sense of meaning and purpose. It ruins our peace of mind.

It has the potential to deprive us not just of serenity, but also ironically of our physical health. It can tip us into that cortisol-fuelled state of fight or flight which brings death on even faster if it's allowed free rein. Or indeed, as I've already indicated, if it's deliberately stimulated through the external conditions of a profit-driven economy.

And yet that same anxiety is part of what drives us forwards. It motivates our constant search for significance. As individuals. As communities. As societies. As a culture. The worm at the core plays a dual role in society. Solomon and his colleagues developed a sophisticated psychological framework aimed at understanding the implications of this fact. They called it terror management theory.

The theory aims to understand what happens when mortality becomes 'salient' for us. When our awareness of death is activated. Either consciously or unconsciously. At times – right now, for instance – that awareness can be entirely conscious. At other times, it remains in the subconscious. It turns out that whether we react consciously or subconsciously to mortality reminders matters enormously. And how we react to them at each of those levels matters too. Let's look at conscious responses first.

Terror management theory predicts that our conscious reactions to mortality salience take two separate paths. In one we take active steps to avert the dangers which are posed by the threat of death. In the other we attempt to avoid, deny and suppress the awareness itself. To push it back down into the subconscious realm.

Here's a simple – and familiar – example. I'm alerted to the fact that my diet sucks. Too much added sugar is making me sick. Eventually it might even kill me. So I make a conscious decision to eliminate sugar from my diet. In doing so, I hope to have reduced the threat to my health – and to my life. In a sense you could say I've acted with care. Tertiary care, as I called it in Chapter 4. Helping my body bring its blood glucose back into balance. Restoring myself to health. And to the extent that I'm successful in that, I've also reduced my fear of an untimely death. For now.

But we've seen already how difficult a habit sugar is to kick. Our own neurophysiology works against us. In the clutches of capitalism we're easy pickings. The food industry has a whole box of tricks up its sleeve. To cajole. To persuade. To deceive. To mislead. Or even just to remind us how good it feels to eat something sweet. And feeling good is a wonderful antidote to feeling bad. The perfect way to banish those unpleasant thoughts of death. So what's not to like? For now.

Of course, that second path, if I'm tempted to follow it, carries echoes of addiction. It could have been alcohol. Or recreational drugs. Or prescription medicines. Or smoking. Or saturated fats. Or refined carbohydrates. Or the caseins in cheese. Or ultra-processed foods. We've already seen the harm in all these things. The way they can undermine our physical health.

But even if we become aware of the fact that they'll harm us. It's so much easier to deny and suppress than to break the addiction. Particularly in a culture which is deliberately manipulating our appetites and actively working against the better angels of our nature. So we push those unhelpful reminders away. Out of the focus of our attention. Back down into the subconscious.

The trouble is. Denial doesn't help us. And this is the other big lesson from terror management theory. We react to the stimuli anyway. This time subconsciously. And when this happens, our responses get particularly interesting. And potentially very powerful.

The subconscious response to mortality salience has two specific avenues. One is to bolster our self-esteem: to build up our sense of self and remind ourselves of our own importance. Psychologists call this 'self-esteem striving'. The other is to defend our cultural worldview: to build up and support the cultural values we espouse as a society. Psychologists call this 'worldview defence'.

What this means in practice depends very much on what self-esteem means for us as individuals and what sort of worldview our society clings to. And these things depend in their turn on the kind of culture we live in. As Becker pointed out, the culture of consumer capitalism is a very specific one. One in which self-esteem is often measured in terms of material wealth and our worldview is itself deeply materialistic.

The collapse of care

There's a classic example of this phenomenon. It happened in 2001. Shortly after the terrorist attack on the Twin Towers, President George W. Bush made his first public appearance. His aim of course was to calm the sense of panic and uncertainty following what had been an attack on life, on the economy and on US values. What he actually said was this: 'Mrs Bush and I would like to encourage Americans everywhere to go out shopping.'

It sounds banal. And somewhat out of place in the aftermath of tragedy. But beneath the banality are some intriguing implications. In the first place, of course, the comment illustrates the political importance attached to economic growth. The encouragement to shop is an invitation to spend. To keep the economy going. Particularly in the light of a sudden shock.

But terror management theory casts another fascinating light on Bush's suggestion. Consumerism isn't just about the economy. It's also a part of our worldview. It has a reputation for making us feel better about ourselves. In other words the US President was calling on people to defend their worldview and bolster their self-esteem by doing what they know and love best. Shopping. He was responding to death anxiety just as terror management theory predicts.

Soon afterwards, the US and its allies would resort to military violence in pursuit of the same existential goals. The War on Terror it was called. With no hint of irony. And no apparent insight into its underlying psychology. It was a war on terror. Of course. A subconscious war on the terror that lies first and foremost inside us.

The denial of death has driven us to places we no longer even understand. These subconscious responses to existential anxiety have left us in a very specific danger when it comes to defining and distinguishing the care economy. And this danger becomes particularly acute when moral claims and claims of human exceptionalism are brought together in defence of care.

I believe it's possible to confront – and avert – that danger. But before I get to that, let me try and define the dilemma as clearly as I can. It starts from a recognition that symbolic health matters. The care economy cannot escape from that reality. Care must include care of the symbolic body. That much is clear.

But in our consumer culture the pursuit of symbolic health has taken a particular form. Driven by our denial of death, we are drawn into very specific forms of self-esteem striving and worldview defence. Caring for symbolic health becomes virtually indistinguishable from the motivations of consumer capitalism. It becomes virtually synonymous with the pursuit of material affluence. The accumulation of wealth. And the desire for power, fame and glory.

Care for our symbolic immortality even begins to look like an essential prerequisite for a growth-based society. Its various incarnations provide the perfect fuel to drive the relentless process of economic expansion. And this sleight of hand is then used to legitimize the entire paraphernalia of accumulation, competition, conflict, aggrandizement, empire, celebrity, domination, aggression, narcissism, genocide and violence.

We start to justify all of this in the name of care. To define its moral worth by association with the assumed moral foundation of care. To legitimize it in terms of the pursuit of a 'great health' which now constitutes, as Groys points out, our supreme vision of social progress.

Needless to say, this case is not something I accept. It may well feel unfamiliar, almost bizarre, from the perspective of everyday language and our instinctive uses of the word *care*. But I've spent some time laying it out for a couple of reasons. In the first place because it emerges from an undeniable tension between symbolic and physical health. We've seen that tension throughout the book. And in the second because, perverse though it is, it makes some sense at last of the constant pendulum that swings between care and violence.

Violence is care's nemesis, wrote Kathleen Lynch in *Care and Capitalism*. I remarked on that relationship in Chapter 1 at the very outset of my journey. And we've seen the reality of it time and time again in the stories we've encountered along the way. And yet from this new perspective it's possible to see that care's nemesis (violence) emerges not as some arbitrary villain, or as an evolutionary distinction between women and men, but rather from being insufficiently careful with care itself. And in particular from being careless with what constitutes care for the symbolic body.

By accepting almost anything into the domain of care for the symbolic body and defending it all through the supposed moral worth of care itself, we are left with no distinction at all between the care economy and the dysfunctional growth-obsessed consumer capitalism we're trying to escape from.

The sacred canopy

Let me back up a little. Symbolic health matters. That's clear. And at the heart of symbolic health lies the need to come to terms with our own existential anxiety. That's also clear. Awareness of our own mortality presents us with a fundamental personal and cultural challenge. To make sense of our world. That challenge is perennial. It's the same challenge Watts addresses in *The Wisdom of Insecurity*. It's the challenge of creating and maintaining what the sociologist Peter Berger has called the 'sacred canopy'. A framework of cultural meaning within which to make sense of our lives.

This need is born from the never-ending desire to create meaning out of chaos. Its job is to offer us an overarching narrative. A myth. A set of myths. A framework for survival. A kind of a blueprint for the organization of society. A guide to what is valued and what is not. A chart to show us where meaning exists and where hope resides.

The principal task of the sacred canopy is to help us buffer the terror of mortality. To allow us to survive tragedy. To console us in the face of loss. To help us face the void. To make sense of Watts' 'spark of light'. To come to terms with the eternal darkness. And this need is neither trivial nor transient. It's constant and it's existential.

Not surprisingly, then, it matters massively how we approach the task. Not just at the personal level. Not just from some abstract concept of cultural stability. But because the sacred canopy governs our social world. Because it determines what we believe and how we act and who we favour. Because it has a profound impact on our health, our hopes and our wellbeing.

Each culture approaches the task anew. The creation and maintenance of the sacred canopy was once – and still is in many places – the principal task of religion. And in religious terms it quite often has a very specific structure. By rejecting Watts' two eternal darknesses, it allows us to reject the finality of death. And in doing so to face our own mortality. To bring our awareness into the open, if you like. And celebrate its role in our own spiritual progression.

I suppose you could argue that this is just a slightly more sophisticated form of denial. By positing a form of spiritual immortality, it attempts to make physical mortality irrelevant. Not always successfully. Our subconscious awareness is still activated by mortality reminders. And though a religious worldview creates a form of 'self-esteem striving' which revolves around spiritual rather than material progress, it also creates a very powerful form of 'worldview defence'. The conviction of being a chosen people. And there's no doubt that this conviction reinforces division. It can lead directly to violence. It's been the basis for war. It's legitimized genocide.

So I'm definitely not suggesting that old-school religion is the foundation for the care economy. In fact religion's sacred canopy is nowhere near as powerful today as it used to be. Especially in the affluent West. From the mid-nineteenth century on it began to fall apart. An increasingly secular society began to dream of escaping from the moral and spiritual boundaries imposed by religious elites.

We found that possibility, according to the playwright George Bernard Shaw, through a combination of intellectual materialism and Darwinian evolution. 'Between the two of them religion was knocked to pieces,' said Shaw:

> and where there had been a god, a cause, a faith that the universe was ordered however inexplicable by us its order might be, and therefore a sense of moral responsibility as part of that order, there was now an utter void. Chaos had come again. The first effect was exhilarating. We had the runaway child's sense of freedom before it gets hungry and lonely and frightened.

Unfortunately doing away with 'Old Nobodaddy', as Shaw called the nineteenth-century idea of God, didn't solve the underlying problem of coming to terms with our mortality. It simply demolished the sacred canopy which had tried and ultimately failed to do that job.

But here's my point. The sacred canopy isn't an optional extra. It's a fundamental sociological need for a functioning society. Not least because every society is faced with the same underlying problem. The inevitability of loss. Of suffering. And of death. Every society needs a sacred canopy. A framework of meaning within which to make sense of the world.

If one falls apart, then another must rise up to replace it. And that's one way of thinking about what happened next. It's one way of understanding consumer capitalism. The new religion of relentless growth became our sacred canopy. It substituted the idea of spiritual progress with the concept of material affluence. It swapped a self-esteem based on moral worth for a self-esteem based on wealth and power. And it replaced the promise of heaven with the pursuit of symbolic immortality.

What we've learned to our cost is this. That when we focus our attention on the relentless pursuit of symbolic immortality. On wealth. On social influence. On celebrity. On the extrinsic goals of the ego. And on power over others in pursuit of these goals. Then we end up with violence. Inequality. Alienation. Deaths of despair. Ecological destruction.

And the vessel we hoped would carry us to the brave new world ends up foundering on the sharp rocks of an eternal truth. Driven there by its own persistent denial of reality.

The Charlotte

When she managed to get her head above water, Mrs Compton-Swift's first thought was that she was trapped beneath the wreckage of the steamer. She had air to breathe. But there was no light to see by. And some kind of hard surface above her was constraining her movement. Maud Roudez and her mother Lizzie were there beside her. Between them the three women managed to figure out that they were trapped beneath the upturned hull of the steel lifeboat. There was little they could do but hang on and hope that help might come.

As it happens, the *Mohegan*'s fate was already clear to those on the shore. Puzzled observers had watched the ship's resolute progress across Falmouth Bay, unable to decide if she was trying to enter or leave the port. But as darkness fell and she approached the Manacles, it became clear that the vessel was heading into trouble.

James Hill, the coxswain of the Porthoustock lifeboat, was stabling his horse in the yard when he caught sight of the steamer's lights and realized she was either on or perilously close to the rocks. Firing off a signal to summon his crew, he galloped back down to the small hall that housed the RNLI lifeboat. And by 7.25 p.m. the crew had launched the *Charlotte* and were rowing as hard as they could towards the Manacles.

By this time it was almost completely dark and it was difficult to know where to steer. But after fifteen minutes at sea they heard the sound of a woman's voice, loud and clear above the noise of the waves. Pretty soon they came across an upturned boat and with some difficulty managed to right it.

That's when they found the three women. The opera singer – who had put her vocal skills to excellent use. Her mother – barely conscious after almost an hour in the water. And the unflappable Mrs Compton-Swift – now trapped beneath one of the wooden seats. One of the crew leaped into the steel boat. It was bobbing like a cork in the restless waves, at any moment likely to overturn again. But he managed to cut Mrs Compton-Swift free of the seat with a couple of blows from an axe. And the three women were transferred into the *Charlotte*.

A strong ebb tide was against them now, and after taking on another twenty-four survivors, it took them two hours to reach the safety of Porthoustock harbour. That's when it transpired that Maud's mother Lizzie had been accidentally wounded by one of the blows from the axe that freed Mrs Compton-Swift. They carried her from the boat as carefully as they could and laid her on some blankets on the beach. But she had lost too much blood on the long ride home. She was already losing consciousness. She died in Maud's arms that night.

They had survived the sinking of the steamer. They'd endured the overturning of the lifeboat. They'd kept themselves alive for an hour beneath the steel hull in the cold water waiting for help. They had reached the relative safety of the harbour. For all that to happen and yet for Lizzie to lose her life in this way seemed almost too cruel for words. Too arbitrary. Too tragic. Maud was inconsolable.

Of course, this story is just one tiny anecdote. Lizzie was a single statistic. One tragic casualty from that one night in that one place. One wreck among thousands along this one rocky shoreline. One death within a symphony of death being played out, in Becker's words, like 'a nightmare spectacular, taking place on a planet that has been soaked for hundreds of millions of years in the blood of all its creatures'.

And that's another reason their story grips me, I suppose. The challenge of terror management is at once profoundly cultural and deeply personal. The need for a sacred canopy is perennial and existential. It faces us anew each day. It faces each culture in turn. But religion has failed us. Capitalism has failed us. The patriarchy has failed us. Technology has failed us. Our own immense ingenuity has failed us. And the sacred canopy now stands in desperate need of renewal.

Capitalism as a disease

A long time ago now, it seems, I sat eating breakfast in a basement kitchen in Paris and opened a slim volume on nursing written by Florence Nightingale. It was the day I read these opening lines. 'Shall we begin by taking it as a general principle that all disease, at some period or other of its course, is more or less a reparative process?'

I recall how that simple suggestion drew my attention to a huge rift at the heart of our understanding of health and disease. A division that has its roots in antiquity. A widening chasm between the subjugating rod of Asclepius and the nourishing bowl of Hygeia. And the tragedy through which instead of working together the two gods of health had become embroiled in a battle for the soul of medicine. A battle lost on both sides when the Caduceus usurped them both and began to undermine the conditions for wellbeing.

It was a defining moment for me. Much of the journey from that point on was unforeseen at the outset. It led me back to pathogenesis. To the causes of disease. It reinforced in me that in searching for the causes of disease, we can never afford to ignore the terrain. It highlighted the conviction that for every living organism, the external conditions define and prescribe and circumscribe the possibilities for health.

I began to see how the pursuit of profit and the interests of capital had disfigured the history and progress of medical science. How they had distorted our model of health and deformed our understanding of disease. I began to understand more precisely how wealth is adversarial to health. How growth is inimical to care. And I began to formulate the uncomfortable idea that capitalism itself is the disease.

And now. Here. In the eye of Storm Henk. With the ocean pounding on the rocky peninsula and the ghosts of the past wandering the windswept shoreline. As the sky lightens almost imperceptibly towards the east. A curious question begins to form in my mind. If capitalism is the disease, then what is it trying to restore? What is the reparative process in which capitalism plays a role? What is it trying to cure?

I can immediately think of all kinds of things that capitalism might claim for itself in response to these questions. It's about the alleviation of poverty. It's about the democratization of government. It's the triumph of reason over religion. It's the culmination of human progress. Most of those legitimations are flawed at best. And some of them are a downright lie. But there's one that strikes me immediately as having a solid grain of truth in it.

Capitalism was part of an attempt to repair the dysfunctional sacred canopy of nineteenth-century religion. It was a bid to offer us a new and wonderful framework of meaning. Consumerism would deliver a world that was brighter and shinier than before. Growth would provide possibilities that go on for ever. Great health would light a spark that could never go out.

But this canopy too has failed us. Its vision was always problematic. Its concept of justice is flawed. Its distribution of rewards is unfair. Its impact on the climate, on the soil, on the water, on the air, is devastating. Its promise of material and physical comfort is deeply and perversely seductive. But it can only fulfil these promises by undermining our health, our happiness and our hope for the future. And far from creating a credible sense of security, it offers only a continual exercise in denial of our own mortality and of the widespread suffering in the world.

And yet. The disease of capitalism is also reparative. Its failure is also informative. Like those before it, this sacred canopy was an attempt to navigate the inevitability of suffering and loss. It was our response to existential anxiety. Our reaction to the 'cares of the world'. To see where its failure lies is to begin to understand how to rectify it.

Symbolic health still matters. Care of the symbolic body is paramount. That we are mortal beings aware of our own mortality won't change. That we're struggling for survival is obvious. That we're striving for security is part of our desperate desire for solid ground. But the relentless search for an elusive and ultimately futile form of immortality throws both individuals and society out of balance. It undermines our psychological, social and ecological health. It leads us towards conflict, destruction and chaos. And it does this by neglecting the most fundamental principle of all.

The untrammelled pursuit of symbolic immortality through material expansion and economic power *is not care*. It has no legitimacy as an act of care precisely because *it fails as a restorative force*. What claims to be care in capitalism's pursuit of symbolic health is outright carelessness.

And yet the disease of capitalism has illuminated our quest for the care economy. It has highlighted a vital task within that quest. It points to something invaluable. The care economy must return to the challenge that faces each and every society. A challenge that religion has failed to meet. A challenge that capitalism has done its best to deny. A challenge to face the intrinsic insecurity for which there is ultimately no cure. But which still demands our care.

West by south

You couldn't exactly call this daylight. Outside, dark clouds are scudding across the sky at an alarming speed and the wind is howling like a banshee. When I poke my nose briefly outside the front door, I find the gale's coming directly up the lane at me now. Warm, wet and vengeful. West by south. I would say. Give or take a compass degree or two.

West by south. The rain batters my face like an overenthusiastic paintballer. The wind pummels my brain. And my thoughts are scattered down the lane like so much debris. But something is trying to force itself on my attention. Some insight is hovering on the edge of my consciousness. I beat a hasty retreat from the storm and the front door closes with a bang.

On a sudden whim, I open up my navigation app and plot a path from the point where the *Mohegan* was supposed to have set her course to the tip of the Lizard peninsula. West by south. It's almost exactly west by south. On a fair day, with no wind, that course would have brought the ship to within clear sight of the lights on the Lizard peninsula. From there she could have charted a course safely.

What if this was the Commodore's intention?

The actual direction the ship travelled would depend on the force of the wind and tide. At that point the wind would have been the biggest influence. And we know it was a brisk southeasterly. It would have pushed her in a northwesterly direction. Maybe five degrees of leeway? Towards the Cornish coastline. With the perverse thrill of a sleuth on the heels of a villain, I add those five degrees of leeway to the west by south I plotted earlier. It takes the *Mohegan* directly onto the Manacles.

The course was west by south. It must have been. Or something like it. West by north could never explain how things turned out for the *Mohegan* that night. The Board of Trade was covering its tracks. Or trying to reassure the public. And it did a piss-poor job at both. Its inspectors didn't even check the nav.

Yes, it's still a tragedy. Yes, mistakes were still made. Perhaps the biggest one was not keeping a good enough look-out. Not checking the course you set is still the one you want to be on. That sounds like a very human error to me. And in the era before GPS? Before decent charts? Before proper channel markings? These would have been tragic but explicable miscalculations. Along with a massive dose of sheer bad luck.

Fate definitely had its sights on the *Mohegan* that night. And on Lizzie Small Grandin too. That goes without saying. Maud Roudez resumed her journey home. Alone this time. She arrived in New York on Saturday, 29 October and went straight into rehearsals. Just two weeks later she made her debut in the Met's touring production of Verdi's opera *La Traviata* in Chicago. A month or so after that she was on stage in New York as Mercédès in Georges Bizet's *Carmen*.

Mercédès' biggest number in *Carmen* is a dramatic trio with Carmen herself and their mutual friend Frasquita. The three women are shuffling and cutting a pack of cards to find out what fate has in store for each of them. Frasquita is destined for romance and adventure. Mercédès will marry a wealthy older man. But Carmen finds only death. No matter how many times she cuts the cards, the prediction doesn't change. 'Encore! Encore! Toujours la mort!' Again! Again! Always death!

It's a pivotal moment in Carmen's journey from restless free spirit to fatal victim of male violence. And the message from the cards is crystal clear. To paraphrase Oscar Hammerstein III's version of the same aria: it ain't no use to run from death if he is chasing you.

It must have been a phenomenal test of Maud's courage to go on stage each night with the loss of her mother still so raw and so recent in her memory. And yet somehow she did it. A few years later she married a wealthy older man named Willard Barling. And they spent two happy decades together. I like to think.

This year (as I write) is the two hundredth anniversary of the RNLI. Founded in 1824, the Institution has been crewed by volunteers and funded by private donations for its entire existence. And in that time it's saved a hundred and forty four thousand lives – an average of two people for every single day since its inception. Many of them were rescued from the wrecks that foundered on the treacherous coastline around the Lizard peninsula. Some of them were from the *Mohegan*.

Fifty-one people were saved that night in 1898. Thanks in large part to the *Charlotte* and her crew. And to an institution held together by goodwill and bravery. And by something that looks a lot like care. In one of its many incarnations.

14

Jenga

'Health is a state of complete physical, mental and social wellbeing and not merely the absence of disease or infirmity.'
The World Health Organization, 1948

The ocean is a wide expanse of shimmering glass. A sheet of pure silver against the pale grandeur of the winter sky. It's so still that from here you imagine you can see that the earth is round. There's a very slight curvature in the distant line between sea and sky. A gentle reminder that we're living on a finite planet.

It must be more or less high tide because the treacherous Manacles are barely visible. All you can see is a peak of dark rock rising above the surface of the water. It might almost be a small fishing boat moving infinitesimally slowly across the frame of a wide picture.

Otherwise. Only stillness. No gale to disturb the tranquillity of the deep. No whisper of shipwrecks from long ago. No intimation of tragedies yet to come. No painful reminder of our mortal frailty. It feels like a moment in which you could remain for ever. Even if, soon now, you must be on your way. It's almost time to pack up your books. Wrap up the arguments. And head for home.

The uninterrupted brightness reminds me suddenly of a blank sheet. *Tabula rasa*. Waiting to be written. The untouched vista of the empty page is as terrifying as any storm. It promises an infinite potential. But that promise is an illusion. The only book you can write is the one that will have been written by the time you get to the end of writing it. And as its concrete present obliterates its infinite potential, your only real option is to follow the words. Wherever they may lead.

And yet. The question always goes through your mind. At each turn. At each new blank page. At every opening of each new chapter. Where should I begin? How would I start if I could start all over again? What would I say if I was trying anew to set out my stall? How would I persuade you of my case?

Economy as care

My case is simple. Straightforward, let's say. Nothing is entirely simple. There are two central ideas. They are connected to each other in obvious ways. The first is that human prosperity, properly considered, is about health rather than wealth. The second is that, in consequence, the economy should concern itself primarily with care, in all its forms, rather than with growth.

The care economy, then, is a vision for an economy in which care – rather than restless expansion – is the central organizing principle. It's a blueprint for *economy as care*. Economy as a form of organization of society in which the guiding principle is to maintain and restore and improve our health. For as long as we all shall live.

Of course, we need to know what health is and what care means. And, fortunately, workable definitions of both are readily available. The WHO defines health as a state of complete physical, mental and social well-being. 'And not merely the absence of disease or infirmity.' Berenice Fisher and Joan Tronto define care as 'an activity that includes everything we do *to maintain, continue and repair* our "world" so that we can live in it as well as possible'.

With these definitions to hand, my thesis seems almost self-evident. If health is a complete state of wellbeing and care is everything we do to achieve that state of wellbeing, then isn't it clear that the economy should always and everywhere be a care economy? What else would it be doing?

And yet this vision seems a million miles from the desperate convulsions of modern capitalism. From the restless innovation of the entrepreneur. The cutthroat competition of the market. The disruptive speculation of the investor. The insatiable appetite of the consumer. The pursuit of wealth revolves around the continual promise of more. More money. More wealth. More goods and services. More everything – as the economic wheel keeps turning. Perpetually seeking growth. Perpetually accumulating wealth.

The pursuit of health has a very different dynamic. Of course it must pay attention to more when there is not enough. But it must also be able to pay attention to less when there is already too much. In other words it must be able to identify and arrive at the point of balance.

And this is why the dynamic of wealth is at odds with the dynamic of health. Because, in the first place, the endless quest for more obscures the point of balance. And because, even if we find it, the forward momentum of 'more' makes it difficult, if not impossible, to stop at 'enough'. We're on the rocks before we know it. With no reverse gear on the engine. This is how and why the care economy differs fundamentally from modern consumer capitalism.

The dangers of heaven

For all the clarity of these simple propositions, we're left with a profound puzzle. If the case for health is so clear, how did it become so derailed by wealth? If care is such an obvious foundation for our wellbeing, how did it find itself overpowered by growth? If the argument for the care economy is so blindingly obvious, why have we inherited an economy so careless even with care itself? The narrative of this book, in a nutshell, has been a journey in pursuit of answers to these questions.

That pursuit has meant questioning fundamental assumptions about care, about disease and even about health itself. There's nothing wrong with the WHO's definition. Its vision of complete wellbeing offers us a kind of aspiration. A desirable destination glimpsed briefly from a distance.

It's a bit like standing here on the hillside gazing out across this wide canvas of shimmering silver and imagining that now we understand the ocean. But today's perfect calm is illusory. It's the result of a high-pressure system, sitting above us for several days now. And a point in the tide where everything is still.

But the tide is already changing. It never stops changing. A low-pressure system is already building. It was always building. Building and collapsing and building again. In fact the high and the low exist only in intimate relationship to each other. The longer the high, the deeper the low that follows. The sweeter the semblance of calm, the more ferocious the storm. And if we're not prepared for it, schooled as we are in the expectation of heaven, we're in for a nasty surprise.

The danger of thinking about health as a state of wellbeing is that we become fixated on the illusion and overlook the dynamic processes of change. We centre our cravings on what we perceive to be the desirable characteristics of heaven. On the absence of pain, for instance. Or on the presence of pleasure. Attributes that are real enough, experienced in the moment. Traits that in some way belong to health. But none of them are entirely congruent with health. For the same reason that this shining mirage is not the ocean.

And this error is compounded by our own neurophysiology. We have a natural aversion to pain. We have a built-in attraction to pleasure. The mesolimbic reward system teaches us to avoid one and pursue the other. But this system was designed in the ancestral environment. The environment of evolutionary adaptation. It wasn't designed for capitalism.

The pursuit of profit has commandeered our neurophysiology and weaponized our desires. It's created an environment in which the avoidance of pain and the quest for pleasure yield enormous rewards for those who can monetize them and a living hell for those caught in the trap. This weaponization may deliver wealth. But let me be clear. This is not what I mean when I talk about prosperity as health. The monetization of our craving for euphoria is the antithesis of the care economy.

In casting prosperity as health, in seeking a model for the care economy, we must look elsewhere. To the lived experience of nature. To the dynamic forces that govern the animate and the inanimate world. To the wisdom of the body.

The mirage of health

A hundred and fifty years ago the French physiologist Claude Bernard laid down the basic principles of a revolutionary idea. The integrity and continuity of a living organism lies in its ability to regulate its internal environment in the face of continually changing external conditions. A process which has come to be known as homeostasis. The US physician Walter Cannon called it the 'wisdom of the body'.

Science suggests that our physiological health depends crucially on the values of certain physiological parameters such as body temperature, pulse, breathing rate and blood glucose. When the values of these 'vital signs' lie consistently within certain narrow ranges, then the prognosis for the organism is typically good. When they don't, the outlook is frequently bad.

And yet to align these values and ranges with health isn't quite correct either. The body itself will shift those parameters outside the normal ranges at times. To fight infection it raises the core temperature of the body. To cope with exertion the heart and lungs will work harder and faster. To deal with stress it will raise the level of certain hormones in the bloodstream. To cope with weightlessness it will gradually reduce the density of an astronaut's bones. To enable a Nepalese sherpa to exist at high altitudes it will increase the concentration of red cells and haemoglobin in the blood. A cold water swimmer will eventually develop greater deposits of brown adipose tissue to protect their vital organs.

There are clearly limits to this adaptability. Go to the top of Everest too fast and you're likely to be airlifted out of base camp with altitude sickness. Swim for too long in the ice-cold ocean and you'll end up in hospital with hypothermia. Live a life of unabated stress and the constant presence of cortisol in your bloodstream will place huge pressure on your heart and lungs. Health becomes impossible.

There's a tendency for the still point itself to shift in the presence of chronic changes in the external conditions. This tendency has been called allostasis.

And the impact this has on the organism is known as the allostatic load. At the societal level we can think of the allostatic load as the burden of disease that results from a continual process of trying to adapt to enduringly hostile external conditions.

Seen in this light, disease is a symptom of the body's efforts to adapt to those hostile conditions. And this insight complicates what we think we mean by health. Is health the endpoint – the state of wellbeing – elusive and ultimately futile? Or is it the process of adaptation? In *Mirage of Health* the French physician René Dubos argues for the latter view. It's the ability to adapt – and to learn how to adapt – which constitutes health.

That ability is governed by more or less autonomous mechanisms. To aid the body, we're configured with a complex neurophysiology that relates our basic functions to sensations of pleasure or pain. To ignore these is to hold the wisdom of the body in disdain. Something we do at our peril. But to confuse them with health is wrong and potentially dangerous.

Something quite profound follows from thinking of health in this way. 'Every manifestation of existence is a response to stimuli and challenges,' said Dubos, 'each of which constitutes a threat if not adequately dealt with.' Success in dealing with these threats bestows vitality on the organism. And this vitality provides the mechanism through which we are able to act in the world. But this action in the world further disturbs the external conditions to which we must continue to be able to adapt. The process of adaptation never stops. And its challenge increases in relation to its own success.

Complete freedom from disease, says Dubos, is 'almost incompatible' with the process of living. 'Life is an adventure in a world where nothing is static.' Salutary though this insight may be, it provides a frame in which we can see more clearly what care might mean. What the care economy might be. And how it might differ from what we have.

The myth of care

Every society clings to a myth by which it lives. Ours is the myth of growth. Growth is the answer to all our problems. The cure for all our disease. It's even supposed to cure the diseases growth itself has caused.

Myths are foundational stories. We cannot do without them. Their aim is to guide and frame our cultural world so that we may live better in the material world. But when you confuse the cure with the cause of the disease, you are likely to be trapped in a cycle of addiction. You know that the myth has failed.

When myths fail, we find ourselves wandering. We end up lost and disoriented in a cultural wasteland. Wracked by violence. Devoid of meaning. As Gertrude Stein's lost generation were in the aftermath of the First World War.

Our task in such times is not purely technical. Nor is it simply economic in a narrow sense of the word. It's not just about policies and measures. Though these clearly matter. It is also and perhaps primarily cultural. It is to restore and revitalize the mythical foundations for our social world. That task is essential for the continuance of the world.

The ancient Roman myth of care provides a starting point for such a project. The myth of the Goddess positions care as a restorative force that holds spirit and matter in the same plane of existence. It highlights the quintessential nature of care. It doesn't encourage us to claim the moral high ground. Nor does it assign an instant veneer of goodness to care. On the contrary, it calls on us to question the curious moral connotations of language itself.

Care has two distinct etymological roots in English. Both of them matter. One root runs from grief, suffering and loss. The cares of the world are common to all humanity. We share them with all creation. They remind us of the reasons to care. The other root points to the attention we must pay to the provisioning of needs. It reminds us to respect the principles of balance that define health.

Taken together these two meanings point towards our role as tertiary carers in a nested universe of care. They remind us that the restorative forces of nature and the extraordinary wisdom of the body are the primary and secondary foundations for health. They are the guide rails within which our own attempts at tertiary care must operate. Within which health may be retrieved. And within which society itself must function.

The terrain matters

The implications of these understandings of health and of care are profound. Health resides in the ability of the organism to adapt to external conditions. Disease itself is sometimes an agent of health. The success of the individual organism to adapt is circumscribed by the power of external conditions. Nutrition. Lifestyle. Circumstance. And 'care' itself in the conventional use of the term. All of them matter. The terrain matters.

Nowhere is this more obvious than in the pandemic of chronic disease that threatens to overwhelm healthcare systems worldwide. Metabolic dysfunction. Cardiovascular disease. Diabetes. Inflammation. Arthritis. Infertility. Dementia. And even cancer. These are some of the conditions which bear witness to the 'allostatic load' caused by ignoring the principles of care. They arise from the creation of external conditions which are largely inimical to the wisdom of the body. They are symptoms of an economy which profits from disease.

Some of the allostatic load has been imposed by a food industry which is out of control. By an agricultural sector that prioritizes quantity over quality. By diets overburdened with ultra-processed foods. By products masquerading as food which are devoid of nutritional quality and polluted by chemicals with long-term impacts on the immune system. By industrial strategies and business models which hijack our own neurophysiology to disrupt our physical health.

Some of the allostatic load has been imposed by patterns of living and working that pay no attention to the needs of the physical organism for movement, exercise and rejuvenation. Some of it has been imposed by inequalities that deplete the possibilities of dignity and purpose for whole swathes of the population. Some of it has been imposed by visions of the good life that are tenuous, unattainable and occasionally self-destructive. Some of it has been imposed by the systematic hierarchies of wealth which accord power to a few and leave the rest powerless. Without voice and without hope.

Some of the damage has been inflicted by science itself. By a pharmaceutical industry selling toxic ingredients to treat isolated symptoms. By medical practices that pay no attention to the care of the whole person or to the wisdom of the body. By a scientific dogma which has exiled both common sense and ancient wisdom in favour of its own hubris. And by a model of health that has itself been captured by the interests of industry and capital.

The careless economy

Medicine has achieved extraordinary miracles over the decades. But it has also become an accomplice in the hollow victory of wealth over wellbeing. Care has been corrupted by private interests. Health has been overturned by the pursuit of profit. And after two centuries of capitalism we are floundering helplessly in what can legitimately be called the careless economy.

The careless economy is characterized not simply by the absence of care, but by the systematic destruction of the grounds for care. The undermining of health. The monetization of disease. The denial of hope. Though some may turn a profit in the short term, this is ultimately a place where no one is free. None can be sure of health. No one can find solace. And any semblance of security is undermined by profound undercurrents of violence.

Violence is care's nemesis. But care is its only antidote. Care is by definition the force that holds us away from the abyss. Time and time again, we've witnessed the reality of that force. Even as we've also seen the countervailing forces that seek to undermine care and overthrow its wisdom. The ebb and flow between violence and care seems as inevitable as the movement of the planets. And to dream of an escape from violence into a paradise of care may seem naïve. But my point is this. A society which builds its civilization on the necessity for violence and on the systematic denigration of care is sowing the seeds of its own destruction.

The urgency of the care economy – an economy whose central organizing principle is the restorative power of care – has rarely been greater than it is in our conflict-ridden, profit-driven, power-crazed and desperately insecure world. But the transition to such an economy won't be achieved through wishful thinking. It demands an understanding of the structural, institutional, political and social barriers to change. It calls on us to diagnose what we might call the pathogenesis of the careless economy.

In a literal and fundamental sense the care economy is a casualty of the growth imperative which drives and governs the modern economy. This growth imperative is pathogenic in two specific senses.

On the one hand, the prioritization of wealth over health damages both health and wealth in the long run. On the other hand, the environment created by the continual pursuit of more overwhelms the wisdom of the body. Undermines its ability to regulate internal conditions. And results in an unmanageable allostatic load. That load takes the form of a rising burden of chronic disease and an increased susceptibility to infectious disease. The body's restorative capacity is phenomenal. But it cannot hold out against external conditions for which it was never adapted.

It's worth noting something slightly perverse here. In the early stages of development the dynamic of more and the dynamic of balance appear to coincide. Where there are deficiencies in nutrition or housing, clothing or education, reducing those deficiencies looks a lot like care and inevitably involves some growth. Statistical evidence supports the idea that, at low levels of development, prosperity is aligned with income growth as basic deficiencies in living standards are reduced.

The alignment diverges by degrees as those deficiencies are reduced or eliminated. But by this stage we find ourselves in the grip of path dependencies. The dynamic of growth is already in play. This dynamic creates an environment inimical to health. And it also locks us into institutional processes which hinder the investments needed to improve our health.

To transition from a system of growth, which approximates care in the presence of deficiencies, to a system of care, capable of regulating both deficiency and excess, is non-trivial precisely because of these path dependencies. It is to these path dependencies that we must turn if we want to understand the structural impediments to the care economy.

Baumol's lesson

Care demands attention. And attention takes time. The attention paid by one human being to another is the core value proposition of care. Time can only be squeezed from care activities to the detriment of the output. This quintessential feature of the care economy sets it against the central dynamic of the growth economy. The pursuit of labour productivity growth.

This pursuit lies at the heart of capitalism. It is the engine which drives the generation of profit and enables the accumulation of wealth. It greases the wheels of commerce. So long as labour productivity continues to rise, the producer can maintain a comfortable surplus. That surplus can be divided between workers and shareholders. Between the interests of the present and the investment needed to keep the dynamic going. Growth becomes a 'virtuous' circle.

The dynamic works best in the so-called fast economy, where production can easily be automated and where people can be substituted by machines. It's true that this tends to increase the material and energy intensity of production and suppress the need for labour. In other words it comes at the expense of both the environment and people's jobs. But at least the cycle continues. The system survives. For a while.

But the mechanism fails in the slow economy. In sectors like care, craft and creativity whose value depends intrinsically on the input of human time and attention. When labour productivity stagnates or declines, the inherent competition between workers and shareholders deepens. The trade-off between present and future intensifies.

The fast economy can insulate itself against the rising cost of labour induced by its own productivity increases. The slow economy cannot. The costs of care activities keep rising. Care can only survive in the market by suppressing wages. By imposing unrealistic productivity targets on overworked staff. Or by reducing the quality of care itself. This was the key lesson highlighted by the economist William Baumol.

In other words the core dynamic of the capitalist economy automatically 'selects in' the fast economy and 'selects out' the slow economy. Systematically favouring the former over the latter. The end result is clear – and perverse.

The care economy relies least on material and energy inputs. It creates less damage to the environment. It provides higher potential for employment. And it contributes most to the health of the nation and to our quality of life. But it is penalized for these very attributes. In short the care economy is a casualty of the deep structure of capitalism.

Structure and value

Knowing what to do about this is critical. Economic structure appears hard-wired to us. But structure always embodies value decisions. Nowhere is this more true than in the core dynamic of capitalism. The pursuit of productivity growth is coded into society. Through regulatory structures. Through legal frameworks. Through incentives and policies. And through the social norms that govern business practice. It appears both as an inevitable feature of economic life and as an objective and unassailable good.

But the pursuit of productivity embodies social value just as any feature of social structure does. Most obviously this happens by assigning value through market exchange. Economists have the strange conviction that markets represent some form of impartial representation of value. And that this value can be cashed out and measured in monetary terms. But markets are always and everywhere fallible, for numerous reasons.

They tend to prioritize short-term over long-term values. They depend on perfect information which is never available in practice. Asymmetries of knowledge and information are widespread. These asymmetries are exacerbated by power imbalances which allow for profiteering and extortion. Such imbalances are evident everywhere in the nexus of food, agriculture, pharmaceutical drugs, market and non-market care, and even the medical services on which our health depends.

Even if markets were perfect, we would be left with the problem of assigning value to goods and services which are not routinely exchanged in markets. Care is such a service. Some of it is unpaid. Much of it takes place outside the market. Its output consists in social goods such as health, longevity, resilience, enjoyment and quality of life.

To the extent that society values these outputs, it may designate levels of care to achieve them. Universal healthcare free at the point of need is an example of such a designation. The right to dignity in old age is another. So is the need to protect and nurture infants and children. These outcomes are assigned in society by society as part of the social contract between government and people. They can (with some effort) be reflected in monetary terms. But they have no 'objective' market value.

The core point here is this. Economic structure is neither immutable nor objective. Value decisions enter into structure at every stage. To allocate rights and responsibilities is a value decision. To prioritize healthcare or social services is a value decision. To assign value primarily through the concept of monetary exchange in supposedly free markets is in itself a value decision. To fail to regulate markets is also a value decision.

In short the denigration of care is ultimately the result of values enacted through structures. Which is to say that structure is the instrumental mechanism through which societal devaluation is enacted. Ultimately value is allocated by society not by markets. And so the denigration of care is not an unfortunate side-effect of an 'objective' economic structure. It occurs through a process of devaluation that happens at the societal level.

Value, culture and power

This might suggest that society gets the care economy that society wants. Or that we as consumers choose. Or that we as citizens value. But such an assumption neglects two factors which impact on the process of encoding value in structure. One is culture. The other is power.

The influence of power is to some extent the more obvious of these factors. A disproportionate influence over social decisions by a particular set of people will inevitably affect institutional structures. It's prone to distort the regulatory and legislative mechanisms that create these structures. It's likely to pervert the values coded in them.

The influence of culture is more complex. We can think of culture as a set of core values held by society which remain relatively stable over time. The sanctity of human life is such a value. The sanctity of marriage is another. These two are already sufficient to illustrate how culture changes (and remains the same) over time. The sanctity of human life has remained remarkably stable in western society for at least two millennia. The sanctity of marriage has not. And to the extent that it has not, the culture of the early twenty-first century can be considered different from the culture of the early twentieth century.

The point is that culture is in essence a historical record of values assigned by society over time and encoded in institutions. But the embedding (and disembedding) of cultural values within institutions is not always coincident with shifts in cultural value. For instance, the protections and economic advantages afforded to unmarried couples differ, even today, from those afforded to married couples. Despite the fact that the sanctity of marriage is held less strongly than it was a century ago.

Sometimes these lags in the embedded values of social institutions are an attempt by those in power to maintain a particular aspect of culture over time. Often for the purposes of maintaining power. But sometimes the lags are simply a function of the time it takes to change institutional structures. Institutions may encode values which are substantially at odds with contemporary societal values.

In short, institutional structures appear hard-wired. They seem to be shaped by supposedly immutable universal principles. They appear to be legitimized by natural phenomena. They claim allegiance to traditions that have persisted so long they go unquestioned. But they are really the fossilization of value allocations made at various points in time. Often in the distant past. And the values allocated at that time may not be remotely relevant to the values we believe we espouse today.

We live in a careless economy in part because our economic structure is polluted by power and in part because policy fails to keep up with changes in cultural values. These two mechanisms both disrupt the care economy. In combination they work to devalue care work and disrupt health. And both mechanisms are in evidence when it comes to the most striking reason for the denigration of care.

The patriarchy

The traditional division of labour between men and women casts care as women's work. This is particularly true in activities such as child-care, nursing, care for the elderly and care of the household. Even now more than three-quarters of these activities – paid and unpaid – are carried out by women. To this day, 90 per cent of nurses are women.

But the gendering of care runs far deeper than this well-documented division of labour. Women are more prone to chronic disease and they suffer for longer with disability. As Gabor Maté has pointed out, this is in part because of the discrepancies in power that continue to haunt society. And those discrepancies are both political and economic. Women are still underrepresented in governance. Their wages are still lower than for men. And gender pay gaps remain even within sectors where the workforce is predominantly female.

Perhaps most striking of all is that the model of health which dominates modern scientific medicine is itself gendered. Traditionally healing took the form of both cure and care. There was little distinction between these two goals until a fundamental schism emerged through the evolution of modern scientific medicine and the professionalization of medicine in the early twentieth century.

Cure began to dominate care. It became the reserve of the physician. And physicians were predominantly men. The tools of the physician were the knife and the potion. Surgery and modern pharmaceuticals emerged as the fundamental basis for modern medicine. Laboratory-based biochemistry and pharmacology became the arbiters of scientific quality.

Care was relegated to a secondary role. It was to be carried out primarily by nurses. And though nursing was professionalized, it was also circumscribed. The task was largely confined to maintaining personal hygiene for the patient and acting in the role of the physician's assistant in the monitoring of health and the administration of the cure. Most telling of all, care was delegated almost exclusively to women.

This highly gendered schism in the model of health has a colourful and violent pedigree. It involves the dominance of germ theory over terrain theory. It includes the persecution – and execution – of women healers as witches. It incorporates what looks like an organized power grab by men to professionalize medicine through institutions that systematically excluded women. It involves the use of corporate power masquerading as philanthropy to lay down the terms of health and the standards for modern medicine. It extends to the exclusion of anything which challenged the emerging wisdom. To this day the vilification of long-established principles of health such as vitalism and holism denigrates traditions that have long been held, practised and protected by women.

Much of this power grab has been legitimized by principles of scientific rationality, economic efficiency and quality control. But in reality these principles have become a fig leaf for far more devious motives which seem to stem from a profound mistrust of women by men.

No more sex war

To delve into this mistrust is a dangerous but necessary endeavour if the schism is to be healed. It too has some deep and surprising roots. At one level it arises from a longstanding division of labour between women and men. This division itself draws justification from the role of women in the gestation and nurturing of children. At another level the schism emerges through the social construction of gender roles during childhood and adolescence. Perhaps most surprising is the way in which women's sexuality is perceived by men both as a challenge to male authority and as a threat to genetic succession.

This legacy leaves the profoundly uncomfortable impression that the gendering of care – and its devaluation in society – is far from accidental. It is inseparable from patriarchal values which remain deeply embedded in society to this day. Such values are not exclusive to one particular culture or creed. They exist in capitalism. They exist in communism. They exist in Islam and Judaism and Hinduism and Christianity.

The anthropologist Sarah Blaffer Hrdy has suggested that patriarchy was a common evolutionary 'solution' to the problem of ensuring paternity for powerful males in close predecessors of human society. But she also points out that it is not the only possible solution to this challenge. Less hierarchical societies with greater weight given to cooperation – most often revolving around close cooperation between females – exist widely in nature.

Anthropologists identify the same diversity of solutions in human history. Riane Eisler highlights a fundamental distinction between what she calls dominator societies and partnership societies. In the former, one sex routinely dominates the other in power hierarchies. In the latter, the sexes work in partnership with no particular power accorded to one over the other. Patriarchy is self-evidently a system of social organization based on domination. It breeds hierarchy, oppression and violence. It systematically undermines the care economy.

Modern western societies believe themselves to have thrown off the more obvious shackles of a cultural patriarchy. Much has been made of the power of very successful women as icons of fundamental change. Enormous strides have been made in spheres such as access to tertiary education. In the US today more than twice as many women as men graduate from university.

Yet enormous political and economic disparities still persist. Patriarchal values remain encoded in social and institutional structures. The structures of capitalism are themselves a form of institutional patriarchy. Changing these structures demands political power. And it's in the realm of political power, even in the so-called advanced nations, that the gender imbalance remains solidly in favour of men.

Whether or not care itself is gendered – and there are good reasons to suppose that at some fundamental level it is not – the transition to the care economy almost certainly depends on tackling and reversing institutional patriarchy. Its persistent shadow may benefit an elite few. But it systematically damages ordinary women and men. Not least by undermining values and structures that would support the care economy.

Symbolic health

Health is a matter of wellbeing. Not only physiological but also social and psychological. The WHO definition of health makes that clear. Inevitably, then, the care economy must concern itself with social and psychological wellbeing. With identity. With self-esteem. With affiliation and social belonging. With a sense of meaning and purpose. Put another way, the care economy involves care of the symbolic as well as the physical body.

The importance of these psychological and social goals is heightened enormously by the awareness of mortality. Reminders of mortality are ubiquitous in life. When we're conscious of them, they may motivate us to care for our physical health. But they may also prompt us to suppress the awareness of death and to avoid the actions that might improve our health. This tendency offers some explanation for our failures to take physical health seriously. Both as individuals and as a society. According to the philosopher Ernest Becker, modern society is particularly prone to the denial of death.

But denial turns out to be dangerous. It leads to powerful subconscious expressions of existential anxiety. Mortality reminders trigger what psychologists call 'self-esteem striving' and 'worldview defence'. On the one hand we attempt to bolster and improve our perceived position in life and our importance in society. On the other hand we tend to defend and support the values and virtues of the culture within which we navigate our self-esteem and find collective meaning.

Much then depends on the kind of culture we live in. But our subconscious response to mortality salience has dramatic consequences. Particularly in a hierarchical, patriarchal, dominator society. At the individual level it motivates the search for fame and reputation – the desire to leave some permanent mark on the world through distinction from others. At the societal level it encourages power, domination and the legacy of empire. Together these traits constitute the pursuit of a kind of symbolic immortality – what the philosopher Friedrich Nietzsche once called 'great health'.

In such circumstances the pursuit of symbolic health – and in particular the pursuit of symbolic immortality – poses a deep challenge to the care economy. In a dominator society the extension of care to the symbolic body appears to legitimize many of the forces that are, on the face of it, inimical to the care of the physical body. To the care of society and planet. And even to the care of our symbolic health.

Competition. Material accumulation. The pursuit of affluence. Economic expansion. Social domination. Political power. Military might. Violence. They all seek justification through the pursuit of symbolic immortality. They all contribute significantly to the destructive social and ecological tendencies of capitalism. And yet they all lay claim to legitimacy through the supposed moral worth of care.

To accept this claim is to undermine the care economy as a vision distinct from the growth economy. But to reject the legitimacy of symbolic health as a domain of human care is clearly wrong. It runs the risk of marginalizing psychological wellbeing, suppressing human creativity and ignoring the perpetual challenge posed by awareness of our own mortality.

This is where the fundamental principle of care as a restorative force becomes crucially important. It's clear that health must include symbolic health. And it's clear that care must include care of the symbolic body. But the endless competitive pursuit of symbolic immortality is not restorative. It doesn't lead us towards balance. It undermines the conditions on which psychological and physiological stability depends. It is a kind of *anti*-care. It creates anxiety. It undermines our security. It subverts society.

This differentiation is vital for the care economy. It also reveals the need for a new and profoundly modern cultural project. Not only to care for physical and symbolic health. But to care too for what the sociologist Peter Berger once called the 'sacred canopy'. To restore, reimagine and rebuild a new framework of cultural meaning. To construct a new sacred canopy for a new age.

Something to replace the tarnished wisdom of outmoded religious beliefs and the fickle promises of a dysfunctional capitalism. Something to steer us away from the destructive denial of death and guide us towards an authentic vision of care. Somewhere to gain or regain a sense of hope. Somewhere to come to terms with insecurity and find a new place in the universe. Somewhere to build – or rebuild – the foundations for the care economy.

The state of wellbeing

Everything is packed up now. We're heading home today. The long journey is almost over. Its final stretch will have to take place in the quiet corners of my daily life. Between the demands of a university in crisis, everyday engagements with colleagues and friends and the continuing management of my own health and that of close family members.

I shall miss this rocky peninsula. I'll miss its unpredictable weather and its treacherous shoreline. I'll miss my temporary office here. It's served me well. It's been a place where my Jenga piles have had more space to grow and change – and occasionally collapse – than they have before.

The point of Jenga is to hone down structure to its bare minimum without precipitating collapse. That's what I've tried to do in this chapter. If I've been successful, it should stand as a coherent synthesis of the journey that's taken me from Wales to Mount Olympus. From ancient Greece to Paris. From London to Cornwall. A journey that's seen me tussle with the history of medicine, the philosophy of care, the meaning of work, the structure of capitalism and the evils of the patriarchy. Not to mention the intricate challenges of Daphne du Maurier's writing.

I'm glad we'll be passing by Jamaica Inn one more time. I'm grateful to all my spirit guides, alive and dead. The ones who brought me this far. And the ones I hope will help me in my one remaining task. To translate the insights from the journey into some signposts for the future. But before I tackle that one. Before we set out for home. Perhaps there's one last chance to immerse ourselves in the ocean.

Up close and personal, the silver mirage of that almost perfect plain has turned a glorious azure blue beneath the midday sun. The sense of unbelievable serenity we glimpsed from the hill is gone. It's clear now. The sea is in constant motion. And yet that motion still betrays itself as a restless return to an elusive still point. The still point is never entirely stationary. It progresses continuously as the moon drags the oceans from one side to the other of the planet. But it exists nonetheless.

From the vantage of a chilly winter swim you can almost eyeball it. It's not like the stillness you witnessed from afar, which seemed to be unitary and indivisible. This stillness is elusive and divisible. Its presence is felt mainly in its absence. In the continual ebb and flow of the water around the invisible equilibrium. In the myriad points of dancing light that mark its restless motion. In the way the water lifts you up and allows you to fall again. Until you become part of its rhythm. Until you're immersed in it.

And this rhythm is more than just a metaphor. It's a precise model for the way in which living organisms achieve and maintain health. And a profound insight into what it means to care.

15

The Red Pill

'May not the new insights into the devices for stabilizing the human organism, which we have been examining in the foregoing chapters, offer new insights into defects of social organization and into possible modes of dealing with them?'
Walter Cannon, 1932

'The question "What shall we do about it?" is only ever asked when we don't understand the problem,' wrote Alan Watts in *The Wisdom of Insecurity*. 'If a problem can be solved at all,' he said, 'then to understand it and to know what to do about it are the same thing.'

When I first stumbled on that quote, I laughed out loud. I've worked for a long time on the boundary between research and policy. Researchers are excellent at understanding things. But they're often very bad at distilling that understanding into precise recommendations for change. Policymakers, by contrast, have no time at all to understand anything. They're under constant pressure to decide what to do about it.

Bridging the gap between understanding and action is one of those challenges that somehow never seems to get any easier. There are times I would happily have thrown Watts' quote at some well-meaning adviser pressuring me to clarify how all my clever arguments could help their Minister to decide 'What shall we do?' If only I'd read *The Wisdom of Insecurity* earlier, I could have saved myself a heap of trouble. Or. Alternatively. I suppose. I might just have lost a few good colleagues.

What I'm trying to say is this. To end my journey with a definitive list of ready-made policy prescriptions would be delightful. But it's somehow a little beside the point. This is not a policy manifesto. If I've managed somehow to improve our understanding of the problem, then perhaps I should consider my work is done here.

And yet I have some sympathy with the impatience of the policymaker. With so much broken, isn't it imperative to find recommendations for the Minister? Which plans and policies should we put in place? What shall we do on Monday morning? After all. If no one thinks in terms of concrete change. Then how is anything ever going to change?

I suspect this means I haven't reached that level of enlightenment that Watts wishes for us all. But to be honest I think I'd be pretty pissed off myself if I got to this stage in this book and its author gave me no indication at all of what direction we might take.

And besides. As my epigraph at the top of this chapter indicates. The idea of teasing out some policy implications from an exploration of care and of health has a pretty solid pedigree. If it was good enough for Walter Cannon, it's good enough for me. So let me round off this journey by summarizing just a few of the things that we can 'do about it' and making a few fairly straightforward points about change.

Care as a legacy

I suppose the first thing to acknowledge is how much has already been said. From the International Wages for Housework movement in the 1970s to the WHO's *Health for All* initiative in the 2020s, it's not like we don't already know how to improve the treatment of care in society. We've known for decades. And that's thanks in no small part to the legacy bequeathed by more than half a century of detailed consideration on the role of care and the pursuit of health.

Madeleine Bunting in *Labours of Love*. The Care Collective in *The Care Manifesto*. Hilary Cottam in *Radical Help*. Nigel Crisp in *Health Is Made at Home, Hospitals Are for Repairs*. Sally Davies and Jonathan Pearson-Stuttard in *Whose Health Is It Anyway?* Emma Dowling in *The Care Crisis*. Riane Eisler in *The Real Wealth of Nations*. Nancy Folbre in *The Invisible Heart*. Ann Gallagher in *Slow Ethics and the Art of Care*. Ivan Illich in *Limits to Medicine*. Stephanie Kelton in *The Deficit Myth*. Kathleen Lynch in *Care and Capitalism*. Gabor Maté in *The Myth of Normal*. Annemarie Mol in *The Logic of Care*. Joan Tronto in *Caring Democracy*. Marilyn Waring in *If Women Counted*.

These are just a few of the many writers who have argued the case for care and proposed specific policies for a care economy. There are many more I've left out. The legacy of writing is an enormous resource for a government serious about the challenge. It won't in itself provide the leadership. That's going to have to come in part from political will. And societal pressure.

Care as a wishlist

In *The Real Wealth of Nations* the social reformer Riane Eisler set out comprehensive foundations for a caring economy. Drawing on the legacy of feminist economics and the philosophy of her own 1987 classic *The Chalice and the Blade*, she gathered together a wishlist for policy. It included the following items:

- Exposing the cultural devaluation of care.
- Measuring the things that matter.
- Rewarding and incentivizing care work.
- Treating care as an investment.
- Educating people in care.
- Campaigning for care and lobbying for change.
- Supporting a cultural shift to a partnership society.

A decade and a half later, my colleague Christine Corlet Walker and I interviewed a score of people (including Eisler) involved in understanding or working in the care economy. We talked to them about their experiences. About their conceptions of the care economy. About the obstacles that stand in the way of care. And of course. We also asked them. What should be done?

Thankfully none of them answered as Watts might have done. In fact with no effort at all they each came up with a numerous suggestions. Changes in values. Changes in structures. Changes in legislation. The obvious and the not so obvious. The costly and the not so costly. Not surprisingly these suggestions had considerable overlap with those that Eisler and others have proposed. Here is another wishlist. It's based on some of their proposals:

- Securing the right to universal healthcare.
- Protecting the wages and working conditions of care workers.
- Establishing a universal basic income to support unpaid care.
- Providing universal basic services (nutrition, water, housing, energy).
- Ensuring equitable access to childcare.
- Localizing the responsibility for care.
- Reversing the financialization of care.
- Socializing the provision of care.
- Eliminating gender inequalities.
- Removing perverse financial subsidies.
- Regulating financial markets in support of care.
- Redefining economics and retraining economists.

What was most striking about the exercise was how easy it was for people to come up with policy ideas. I've found the same thing with my students. In thirty years of teaching I've not yet had a class of students who couldn't come up with entirely reasonable prescriptions for change. Once they'd identified the problems and understood the challenges. Which I suppose supports the point that Watts was making.

Of course, our job is a bit more complicated than this. To paraphrase the economist John Maynard Keynes: the difficulty lies not in coming up with new ideas but in escaping the old ones. And that's where Watts' insight matters. It's not so much the lists that count. It's the understanding that lies behind them. And here I think there are few important conclusions. Some qualities of care, if you like, which are vital in understanding how change must happen. All of them flow from the arguments in this book. But they are also supported by the wealth of literature that's gone before.

Care as a principle

The first and most vital point to make is that care is not just a sector definition. It's a principle. Care is a restorative force that aids and abets the ability of the organism to maintain its internal balance in the face of changes in external conditions. It's an agent in the pursuit of physical and symbolic health. The care economy is an economy in which that principle is taken seriously. In which we prioritize *economy as care*.

Supporting the sectors traditionally seen as care is clearly critical to this vision. But it's not sufficient. To take care seriously is not simply to argue for ever greater healthcare budgets. In fact the healthcare bill for the careless economy is rapidly becoming unpayable. And this is happening because we have sacrificed health to wealth almost everywhere.

We're encouraged into poor diets. We're forced into sedentary lifestyles. We're seduced into addictive behaviours that damage our physical and mental health. We're exposed to chronic physiological and psychological stresses. We're persuaded to treat the resulting disease through endless pharmaceutical interventions. And we're persuaded into accepting these damages as part of the architecture of 'normal' life.

It follows that the role of policy for the care economy is all-encompassing. Policy to protect health and social care is vital. But it must also transform the food industry. It must revise dietary guidance. Reform the pharmaceutical industry. Decarbonize the energy sector. Restructure the water industry. Penalize companies who are profiting from tragedy and disease. Facilitate lifestyle change. Curtail extractive investments. And restore the restorative function of care. Not simply in the care sector. But across the economy as a whole.

Care as prevention

One of the most important findings to emerge from this book is that our model of care has itself been distorted by economic interests. Modern scientific medicine has brought with it extraordinary technological and pharmaceutical advances. But it's also exiled practices of lay healing and naturopathy which had operated for centuries. It's rejected well-established principles of holism and vitalism in favour of a mechanistic interventionist approach. And it's relegated simple principles of hygiene, nutrition and preventative care to the status of pseudoscience.

It's become clear that this over-medicalized model of health is failing to address the rising burden of chronic disease. That burden is being driven by poor diet, unhealthy lifestyles, chronic stress and the toxic side-effects of the very drugs that are supposed to cure disease. It is no longer credible to suppose that the same model can solve the problems it has inadvertently or deliberately created.

The principle of care as a restorative force suggests that the first response to disease should not be to medicate. Rather it should be to aid and strengthen the body's own ability to heal itself. To engage the principles of hygiene. To improve nutrition. To strengthen resilience through exercise. To reduce stress through non-pharmaceutical means. To enhance wellbeing through social prescribing. These measures are finally beginning to gain traction. But much more could be done to transform the structure of primary care and support the principle that prevention is better than cure.

Care as a postgrowth guide

Much of the damage caused by the careless economy is legitimized by the pursuit of growth. And by privileging the accumulation of wealth over the protection of health. From a conventional view, this triumph of wealth over health and growth over care is called success. But for society it's the source of a slowly unfolding calamity.

The growth-based economy is careless not only with physical health but also with the natural environment. With social justice. With financial stability. And even with our own symbolic health. Up to now, the proposed solution to the damage growth inflicts has been more growth. And yet increasingly that growth has been hard to come by. In some advanced economies we are to all intents and purposes already living in a postgrowth world. But we're trying to manage that world with a growth-based economics.

We need an economics with which to understand and address these postgrowth challenges. The care economy offers us a radical alternative. It presents us with a vision and a framework through which to reform the structures and institutions of an economy predicated on and designed around endless growth.

In practice this requires us to identify structural dependencies that tie us into growth. It calls on us to examine, sector by sector, the ways in which those growth dependencies operate. It demands that we design alternative institutions and structures which are growth independent. Institutions and structures capable of delivering good outcomes irrespective of the level of growth in the economy.

Above all, it demands that we approach the transition to a postgrowth economics with care. With an eye to the needs of different sectors of society. With attention to the distribution of rewards and the imposition of costs. With consideration to the design of ownership, business models, regulatory frameworks and legislative structures. It demands, in other words, that we impose the principle of care on the transition itself.

Care as an investment

One of the most valuable recommendations – it was suggested almost two decades ago by Riane Eisler and it was reiterated recently in the WHO's *Health for All* report – is very simple. Health is an asset. And like all assets it requires investment. Without investment it falls into disrepair and eventually fails. Care is that investment.

It follows that care expenditures should be treated as investment expenditures. That might seem a little abstract. But in financial terms it matters. As Eisler pointed out, investment expenditures are 'amortized'. Their costs are spread over the life of the investment. They're treated differently from current account spending not only in business accounts but also in government spending rules. That treatment recognizes both the timescale over which investments are made and the returns that flow from them.

This point is not just about accounting conventions. It's a recognition that there's something absolutely fundamental going on here. Health is the foundation on which vitality, labour, work, wellbeing, output, livelihood, commerce, politics, society and culture itself all depend. To invest in health is to invest in prosperity.

A society that fails to invest in its assets, a society that systematically devalues care, ends up fouling its own nest. Shooting itself in the foot. Cutting off the branch it's sitting on. Choose your own metaphor. Care is not an optional extra. It's the basis for everything. Care is the most fundamental investment of all. It's the foundation for the economy. For society. For life.

Care as an unpaid debt

What can it mean that we fail to invest in our most critical asset? That we undervalue care? That we fail to pay our carers? In practice it means that the careless economy gets to free-ride off the care economy. Unpaid and underpaid care constitutes a debt. A debt owed by the careless economy to the care economy. A loss incurred by the care economy so that the careless economy can reap a profit.

Capitalism plays a key role in the accumulation of this debt. It 'selects in' those economic activities where profit can be gleaned most easily. It 'selects out' those – like care, craft and creativity – where it can't. It sets up the rules for what counts as productivity. And in lionizing market values and externalizing social values, it systematically creates the debt owed by the careless economy to the care economy.

In the long run this dilemma may prove terminal. Either for capitalism itself. Or (if we fail to solve it) for society. But in the short run I suspect it's going to be tough to persuade politicians to dismantle capitalism. That means we need concrete financial or fiscal mechanisms specifically designed to reverse the syphoning of value out of the care economy and into the careless economy.

The precise nature of those mechanisms is a matter for detailed policy design. But several of the suggestions collected in the interview study I mentioned above – a universal basic income, a job guarantee, wage protections for carers, investments in the infrastructure of care, socialization of care provision, for instance – all speak to this immediate need to rebalance the accounts. To repay the unpaid debt to care.

Care as climate action

Earlier in the book I asked the question whether the smashing of windows in protest against the fossil fuel investments of HSBC bank could be thought of as an act of care. Whether the answer to that question is yes or no, there is clearly an argument that tackling climate change is an act of care.

At its most obvious that involves phasing out the use of fossil fuels. In doing so, we aim to restore the balance of carbon in the atmosphere and prevent runaway climate change. There are numerous ways of achieving that goal. Most attention has been given to improving the efficiency of the technologies that burn fossil fuels. Using renewable energy in place of fossil fuels. And changing our way of life so that it's less energy-intensive in the first place.

Achieving these things demands policy too, of course. And since energy is used always and everywhere across the economy, that means thinking deeply about how we organize the production of food, agriculture, transport, housing, chemicals and so on. It's not my intention to elaborate on that task here. There are numerous comprehensive treatments of the subject. Not least in the thirty-five-year literature of the Intergovernmental Panel on Climate Change.

But I do want to return to one key point here. The transition away from consumerism and towards the care economy is yet another avenue for tackling climate change. As we've seen in Chapter 6 – and again in Chapter 11 – the care economy is inherently less energy- and material-intensive and inherently more labour-intensive than the consumer economy. Policies to encourage and enable this shift – for instance to penalize pollution and incentivize labour – represent another vital avenue for change.

Care as freedom

The extraordinary ability of the body to regulate its internal environment in the face of changing external conditions has a somewhat surprising corollary. It's this ability which guarantees the organism freedom of movement. The lower the organism's regulatory ability, the more confined it is to a tightly controlled niche. The greater its adaptability, the more it has licence to wander.

Humanity has an extraordinary licence to wander. And this is precisely because of the power of homeostasis and its ability to regulate our internal conditions in the face of a wide range of external disturbances. (Up to a point – as we have seen.) Or to put it another way. Our relative freedom to wander is a direct corollary of our capacity for care.

In a fascinating epilogue to his classic book *The Wisdom of the Body* Walter Cannon introduces the idea of what he calls societal homeostasis. The potential for a dynamic regulation of the social organism analogous to the homeostatic regulation of the physical body. 'Might it not be useful,' he asks, 'to examine other forms of organization – industrial, domestic or social – in the light of the organization of the body?'

He draws an interesting sketch of what this societal homeostasis might look like. He points, for instance, to the need for balancing mechanisms. What we might call automatic stabilizers. He highlights the need for sophisticated avenues of communication to activate these stabilizers. And he emphasizes something both interesting and counterintuitive. Sometimes we need to 'squander' resources in order to achieve stability. Because in 'critical times, economy is secondary to stability'.

From the outset societal homeostasis would act to support biological homeostasis, in Cannon's view. Its function would be first and foremost to 'foster the stability, both physical and mental, of the members of the social organism'.

But this regulatory function, far from being punitive, would open up new horizons of possibility. It would 'help release the highest activities of the nervous system for adventure and achievement,' said Cannon.

In other words, Cannon was suggesting, the care economy would leave us 'free to enjoy beautiful things, to explore and understand the wonders of the world about us, to develop new ideas and interests, and to work and play untrammelled by anxieties about our bodily affairs'.

As a vision, this concept of care as freedom is as revolutionary as it gets. It offers us not only a blueprint but also an inspiration for change. And it reveals some additional demands for policy. Attention to the mechanisms of societal stability. Investment in the architecture of learning, personal exploration and enjoyment. And the protection of equitable access to those higher freedoms that make life worthwhile.

Care as the red pill

At one point in *The Matrix*, the classic 1999 movie from the Wachowski siblings, the film's hero Neo (played by Keanu Reeves) is about to discover his critical role in the narrative arc of the story. He's taken to meet the Oracle (Gloria Foster), who will make his destiny clear to him.

The waiting room outside the Oracle's kitchen is full of kids engaged in what look like esoteric magic tricks. One of them is a young boy dressed in the robes of a Buddhist monk. He's busy bending a spoon with the power of his mind. Neo watches in fascination.

Seeing his interest, the boy gives him an unbent spoon so he can try out the trick for himself. Neo takes the spoon. He's looking at it quizzically. Unsure what exactly he's supposed to do. 'Do not try and bend the spoon. That's impossible,' the boy tells him. Instead he should just try and realize the truth. 'What truth?' says Neo. And the boy says: 'There is no spoon.'

There is no spoon. In the film, of course, that's true by construction. Neo's world is an illusion. A simulation inside a computer program. Nothing is real. Including the spoon. And if we can understand this, the young boy tells Neo, we'll see that the task at hand is not to bend the spoon but to bend ourselves.

The Matrix was many things to many people. A sci-fi adventure to some. A spiritual allegory to others. And to some the inspiration for a whole 'new' cosmological perspective on the human predicament. The world is not real. We are living inside a simulation.

The computer scientist Rizwan Virk has probably gone further than most people in articulating this slightly outlandish hypothesis. His book *The Simulation Hypothesis* brings together AI, computer science, quantum physics and Eastern mysticism. It's an attempt to convince the reader that we're living inside a video game.

Seems to me there's something ironic in a culture which arrives at the conclusion that it's living inside a video game by learning to simulate reality in video games, assuming that someone out there must already have been clever enough to simulate reality in video games and then concluding that the reality in which it learned how to simulate reality is itself a video game. It's a long way round to reach an insight that's actually as old as the hills.

There's a reason the young boy in *The Matrix* is dressed as a Buddhist monk. The Buddha said it all thousands of years ago. Though not in quite the same way, of course. And this is also part of what Alan Watts is driving at in *The Wisdom of Insecurity*. It's through understanding what we call reality as a dream, he suggests, that we can learn to free ourselves from anxiety and live with insecurity. As the foundation for a new sacred canopy, the non-existence of the spoon might well be worth revisiting.

But my immediate point is this. However 'real' the physical world, our cultural reality is very much like that spoon. The institutions that shape and guide our social world possess the same curious duality. They seem to be solid and immutable. And yet they're composed of nothing but thin air and broken promises. Or lines of code. If you prefer. They're projections of the values – the ideas, fears, anxieties, wishes, aspirations and desires – that preoccupied our ancestors.

The appearance of solidity of our cultural institutions is deliberate. Their veneer of permanence is an essential element in our pursuit of durability. And the need for durability is a response to our existential anxiety. The fact that it's an illusion is all the more reason to make it seem like it's real. Security is part of its job. Because insecurity terrifies us.

Unfortunately the semblance of solidity has a downside. It's precisely this apparent immutability which makes change seem impossible. We believe we are locked into a dystopian world by cultural imperatives too strong to change. And yet, like the matrix, our prison is an illusion. We're held in it only through our own desire for security. And our refusal to recognize the truth. There is no spoon.

A careful attention to the dual structure of our cultural reality is all it would take for us to realize this. And to release ourselves from it. That would of course require us to turn and face our insecurity. And I'm not by any means suggesting that task is easy. What I am suggesting is that it now reveals itself as a vital cultural project of enormous societal importance. As a journey on which we have barely begun.

Acknowledgements

If prosperity is about health, then I should obviously begin by thanking those who helped me stay healthy during the writing of this book. For all its costs and shortcomings, I'm profoundly grateful for the dream of universal healthcare which has been kept alive for more than seventy-five years in my home country – even as the reality of that vision has been eroded by politics, ideology, economics, our own lifestyles and a massive shift in the burden of disease. We're all suffering the consequence of that erosion. None more so than the staff of our unfortunate NHS. Their task is now virtually impossible. But they continue to work with diligence, compassion and commitment. My thanks go in particular to those who helped me navigate my own diagnoses. I did eventually manage to bring those blood test results into a range where I'm now considered to be 'in remission' from diabetes and not currently at risk of being prescribed pharmaceuticals. I'm under no illusion that the responsibility for keeping it that way rests with me.

When it comes to the writing itself, I'm deeply indebted to my partner Linda. Her commitment has been unwavering from the outset. Even at the moments when mine faltered. And when the task itself seemed totally impossible, it was only her willingness to read, comment, advise and encourage which kept me going. I owe her my profound thanks for being not just a willing collaborator in our dietary revolution but also the principal architect of its success. And for sharing with me in the madness of cold water swimming.

At hand along the way were a number of other wise and generous individuals who helped me untangle some of the knots in which I tied myself. Steve Angus, Isabelle Cassiers, Hilary Cottam, Michael Dixon, Riane Eisler, Gaby Hock, Pete Jackson-Main, Robert Lustig, Roger Meecham and Jonathon Porritt were amongst those who shared their insights on issues as varied as diet, mental health, social care, terrain theory, gender and the wreck of the *Mohegan*.

The book rests in part on research in which I've been lucky enough to work with some excellent colleagues. Jasmine Coomber, Christine Corlet Walker, Angela Druckman, Shimaa Elkomy, Ben Gallant, Tara Garnett, Birgitta Gatersleben, Amy Isham, Andrew Jackson, Miriam Pepper and Peter Victor are amongst those whose collaboration has mattered enormously to this book. Some of that research was funded by the Laudes Foundation and I'm grateful to Megan McGill for her steady hand as our liaison officer during the last few years.

My arguments around care have been honed further during that time through various conversations with numerous others: Madeline Bunting, Mary Collins, Anna Coote, Laurie Don, Emma Dowling, Chris Foster, Ivana Gazibara, Jayati Ghosh, Christine Hine, Rob Johnson, Martin Jones, Tim Lang, Clive Lewis, Anastasia Loukianov, Caroline Lucas, Peter Michaelis, David Miller, Irena Moozova, Sarah Nottle, Gill Orrow, Maria Paez-Victor, Sylwia Spurek, Robert Sweeney, Jo Swinson, Matthew Taylor, Laeticia Thissen and Maria Walsh. I'm grateful to all of them for keeping me on track and occasionally leading me off it.

It's been fortuitous for me – although I suspect not always ideal for them – that the period of writing coincided with my term as a commissioner on the UK Food, Farming and Countryside Commission. I'm deeply grateful to Sue Pritchard and her team and to my fellow commissioners for all their wisdom and experience. Thanks are also due to Sarah Blaffer Hrdy and Annemarie Mol for granting me their kind permission to use extracts from their writing as epigraphs.

Inevitably a project like this depends on the symbolic as well as the physiological health of its author. I couldn't have maintained that equilibrium without the support of various extraordinary people. I'm grateful in particular to my brother John for being able to hold an accurate course and an interesting conversation with a sense of unwavering camaraderie; to my sister Rachel for her unique ability to span the intellectual, the emotional and the spiritual dimensions of life simultaneously; to my CUSP co-Director, Kate Burningham, for thirty years of collegiate solidarity and shared intellectual interest; to our Centre Coordinator, Catherine Hunt, for holding the fort so many times when we needed it; to my long-suffering executive assistant, Gemma Birkett, for keeping my diary manageable and my sanity intact for almost two decades now; to Alicia, Talitha and Zachary Jackson for providing both the inspiration to write at all and the most reliable distraction from doing so; and to my father Rich Jackson, whose belief in my ability to write this book was only surpassed by his impatience to see the final result.

I'm pretty sure the latter sentiment was shared by my commissioning editor, Louise Knight. From our naïve early conversations to the fraught latter stages, her support has been absolutely vital in bringing the work to fruition. I am grateful too for the support of all her wonderful colleagues at Polity: Neil de Cort, Sarah Dobson, Eve Hawksworth, Olivia Jackson, Emma Longstaff, Aoibheann O'Flynn and Anne Sullivan. Particular thanks are owed to my copy-editor, Justin Dyer, for his diligence and courtesy. And for becoming a willing co-conspirator in my disruptive punctuation.

The arc of a project like this is long. And it bends towards chaos. In such circumstances it's only to your partner, your best friends, your trusted colleagues, your close family, your commissioning editor and your spirit guides that you can really turn for help. To hold you to task. To keep you on track. And occasionally to distract you from the intensity of it all and help you forget about the chaos. I'm grateful to all of the above. Including those I've forgotten. It couldn't have happened without you.

As I think about it now, I realize that this book has its origins in the dim and distant past. I have in mind a picture of me at around six weeks old in the safety of my mother's arms. Not mewling and puking. But animated. Excitable. And hungry to comprehend the world. I think this is what passed for happiness for me in those days. *Plus ça change*. It had a lot to do with the person holding me. This book is dedicated to her. In loving memory.

Notes

Prologue

p. xiii   'What was I made for?': This is the title of Billie Eilish and Finneas O'Connell's single from the soundtrack of the 2023 movie *Barbie*.

p. xiii   The Myth of Care (a long time after) Gaius Julius Hyginus: This version of the Roman Myth of Care is adapted from the one first recorded by the historian Gaius Julius Hyginus around the second century CE (Scott Smith and Trzaskoma 2007, pp. 166–7). Evidently, I've taken some liberties. For example, there is no Roman equivalent of the Greek god Chaos. And so far as we know the first human being wasn't named after Barbie. Or vice versa.

Chapter 1 The Road to Hell

p. 1   'The road to hell': Attributed to various people, most definitively Samuel Johnson: Pell 1857, p. 89.

p. 1   The nature of human prosperity: This is the guiding question for the Centre for the Understanding of Sustainable Prosperity, which I've had the privilege to lead for almost a decade now: https://www.cusp.ac.uk.

p. 2   Definition of health: WHO 1948. Though its progressive nature is now taken as read, the definition has its roots in the socialized medicine of the Soviet Union and its adoption involved a careful process of negotiation in an era where the US was fearful of communist interests: Larsen 2021.

p. 3   Fisher and Tronto's definition of care: Tronto 1993, p. 103, emphasis added; see also Fisher and Tronto 1990.

p. 4   'invisible heart': Folbre 2001.

p. 6   Hilary Cottam on *chronos* and *kairos*: Cottam 2021, p. 26; see also: https://theapeiron.co.uk/understanding-how-the-ancient-greeks-viewed-time-will-make-your-life-richer-510e8b003ff.

p. 6   Annemarie Mol – time's twists and turns: Mol 2008, pp. 62–3.

Notes   261

p. 6   Build Back Better, $3.5 trillion: https://www.politico.com/news/2021/07/13/democrats-spending-plan-biden-agenda-499593; see also: https://www.whitehouse.gov/build-back-better/; and: https://www.commonwealthfund.org/blog/2022/history-balance-promise-build-back-better.

p. 7   Build Back Better stalled: https://www.forbes.com/advisor/personal-finance/build-back-better-plan-dead/. Manchin resistance: https://www.newyorker.com/news/our-columnists/joe-manchin-kills-the-build-back-better-bill.

p. 7   Casualties in Ukraine: https://www.nytimes.com/2023/08/18/us/politics/ukraine-russia-war-casualties.html.

p. 7   Western financial aid to Ukraine: This totalled $403 billion between January 2022 and April 2024: see: https://www.ifw-kiel.de/publications/ukraine-support-tracker-data-20758/.

p. 7   Costs to Russia: Shatz and Reach 2023.

p. 7   Stagflation: This is a combination of inflation and economic stagnation – the slowing down of economic growth: https://www.worldbank.org/en/news/press-release/2022/06/07/stagflation-risk-rises-amid-sharp-slowdown-in-growth-energy-markets.

p. 8   7 October casualties: https://web.archive.org/web/20231217222630/https://www.france24.com/en/live-news/20231215-israel-social-security-data-reveals-true-picture-of-oct-7-deaths. Some of these were from friendly fire: https://apnews.com/article/israel-hamas-hostages-investigation-friendly-fire-3b6fdd4592957340b32a8ee71505b8e9. Casualties in Gaza: https://en.wikipedia.org/wiki/Timeline_of_the_Israel%E2%80%93Hamas_war.

p. 8   One child dies every ten minutes: https://www.aa.com.tr/en/middle-east/who-says-1-child-killed-every-10-minutes-in-gaza/3073714.

p. 9   Broken promises: See, for example: https://www.jeffsachs.org/newspaper-articles/wgtgma5kj69pbpndjr4wf6aayhrszm; see also Sachs's evidence to the UN: https://www.youtube.com/watch?v=wm4qLWc_Co0.

p. 9   Mary Kaldor on toxic masculinity: PM, BBC Radio 4, 24 February 2022.

p. 9   'To ignore violence': Lynch 2022, p. 9; see also pp. 173ff.

p. 10   Conflict-related sexual violence: https://georgetownsecuritystudiesreview.org/2023/11/15/the-burden-women-bear-israel-hamas-war-sheds-light-on-conflict-related-sexual-violence-experienced-by-israeli-palestinian-women/; see also: https://news.un.org/en/story/2023/09/1141417.

p. 10   Kahlil Gibran: Gibran 1923, p. 21: 'On Children'.

Chapter 2 Euphoria

p. 13   'Life reveals itself in pain': Groys 2022, p. 87.

p. 13   Rosefeldt film installation: *https://www.theguardian.com/artanddesign/2023/feb/14/hopefully-some-people-hate-it-the-immersive-film-about-capitalism-coming-to-melbourne*.

p. 13   The HBO show *Euphoria*: *https://www.hbo.com/euphoria*. For a commentary on the show, see: *https://time.com/6152502/euphoria-hbo-teenage-drug-use/*.

p. 14   Definition of euphoria: *https://www.merriam-webster.com/dictionary/euphoria*. For a psychological definition, see: *https://dictionary.apa.org/euphoria*. For a medical definition, see also: *https://openmd.com/define/euphoria*.

p. 15   Llandrindod Wells: *https://www.storipowys.org.uk/news-1/dr-linden-and-the-miracle-waters-of-llandrindod-wells?locale=en*.

p. 15   Treatise on three medicinal waters: Linden 1756.

p. 15   Cuba's medical exports: *https://business.cornell.edu/hub/2021/05/19/is-cubas-army-white-coats-medical-diplomacy-or-contemporary-slavery/*.

p. 15   Cleveland Clinic salaries: *https://www.ft.com/content/dd25a898-58f0-43cd-9433-bcd2852363b3*.

p. 15   Cuban salaries: *https://worldsalaries.com/average-doctor-salary-in-cuba/*.

p. 15   NHS consultant salaries: *https://www.nhsemployers.org/system/files/2023-08/Pay%20and%20Conditions%20Circular%20%28MD%29%204-2023%20FINAL_0.pdf*.

p. 16   'disorders of the fair sex': Linden 1756, p. 84. Blood-letting: Linden 1756, p. 208.

p. 17   '[e]verybody lives in the anticipation of pain': Groys 2022, p. 88.

p. 17   History of opium: *https://museum.dea.gov/exhibits/online-exhibits/cannabis-coca-and-poppy-natures-addictive-plants/opium-poppy*.

p. 18   'optimize the internal equilibrium of the human body': Robson 1999, p. 161.

p. 18   Opium wars: *https://www.theguardian.com/society/2023/may/23/out-of-our-minds-opium-imperial-history-opium-wars-china-britain*.

p. 18   '[A] war more unjust': *https://hansard.parliament.uk/Commons/1880-06-04/debates/b53a59e8-4235-47f9-beec-31da92fdfbf4/TheOpiumTrade—Observations*.

p. 19   Opium dens in San Francisco: *https://www.history.com/topics/crime/history-of-heroin-morphine-and-opiates*.

Notes 263

p. 19 Hip resurfacing: https://www.whitehouse-clinic.co.uk/articles-and-advice/what-is-hip-resurfacing-the-andy-murray-hip; https://www.edwinsu.com/andy-murray-and-hip-resurfacing.html.

p. 21 Mesolimbic reward system: Kosten and George 2022.

p. 22 Heroin as cough syrup: https://museum.dea.gov/museum-collection/collection-spotlight/artifact/heroin-bottle.

p. 22 Opioid death rates: https://nida.nih.gov/research-topics/trends-statistics/overdose-death-rates; see also: https://www.commonwealthfund.org/blog/2022/too-many-lives-lost-comparing-overdose-mortality-rates-policy-solutions.

p. 22 Opioid epidemic statistics: https://www.cdc.gov/overdose-prevention/about/understanding-the-opioid-overdose-epidemic.html.

p. 23 Purdue Pharma story: https://www.theguardian.com/us-news/2023/aug/10/purdue-pharma-oxycontin-supreme-court-sacklers-bankruptcy-deal; https://www.theguardian.com/society/2018/sep/30/theyre-drug-dealers-in-armani-suits-executives-draw-focus-amid-us-epidemic; https://www.theguardian.com/news/2018/nov/08/the-making-of-an-opioid-epidemic.

p. 23 US opioid prescription rates: https://www.cdc.gov/drugoverdose/rxrate-maps/index.html.

p. 23 *Dopesick*: https://www.theguardian.com/tv-and-radio/2021/oct/11/dopesick-michael-keaton-hulu-opioid-crisis-purdue-pharma.

p. 23 *Pain Killer*, see Meier 2020 and *PainKiller* Netflix drama: https://time.com/6303583/painkiller-netflix-true-story/.

p. 23 DEA on oxycodone: https://www.dea.gov/sites/default/files/2020-06/Oxycodone-2020_0.pdf.

p. 24 Opioid overdose, WHO: https://www.who.int/news-room/fact-sheets/detail/opioid-overdose.

p. 24 Fentanyl story: Stanley 2014; https://www.pharmaceutical-technology.com/features/fentanyl-go-wrong/?cf-view.

p. 24 Fentanyl disguised as oxy: https://www.cfr.org/backgrounder/fentanyl-and-us-opioid-epidemic.

p. 24 Supreme Court overrules settlement: https://www.ncsl.org/state-legislatures-news/details/supreme-court-overrules-purdue-pharma-opioid-settlement-rejects-immunity-for-sacklers.

p. 25 '[P]ain is an *opinion*': Ramachandran and Blakeslee 1998, p. 224, original emphasis.

p. 25 Pain is a 'protector': Lyman 2022, p. 22.

p. 25	First known use of euphoria, 1665: *https://www.merriam-webster.com/dictionary/euphoria*.
p. 26	Rosefeldt: see Rosefeldt film installation, p. 13 above.

Chapter 3 Vital Signs

p. 28	'All the vital mechanisms': Bernard 1878 as cited in Goldstein 2019, p. R301.
p. 28	The geology of Pembrokeshire: *https://www.pembrokeshirecoast.wales/about-the-national-park/geology/*; *http://www.discoveringfossils.co.uk/how_britain_formed.htm*.
p. 29	The Bluetits: *https://thebluetits.co/pages/our-core-values*.
p. 29	Thermoregulation during sleep: *https://sleepopolis.com/education/thermoregulation-sleep/*; Janott 2020.
p. 30	Heatwave in Arizona: *https://www.nbcnews.com/science/science-news/arizonas-maricopa-county-shatters-record-heat-deaths-rcna122478*; Mecca: *https://apnews.com/article/hajj-heat-deaths-mecca-saudi-arabia-pilgrimage-9f97aae1032b14ada29bbea7108195d3*; heat deaths in Europe: Ballester et al. 2023.
p. 31	*The Ministry for the Future*: Robinson 2020.
p. 31	Hypothermia: *https://my.clevelandclinic.org/health/diseases/21164-hypothermia-low-body-temperature*.
p. 31	The Ice Mile: *https://internationaliceswimming.com/wp-content/uploads/2021/08/Ice-mile-check-list.pdf*.
p. 31	Marine ancestors: *https://www.cam.ac.uk/research/news/bag-like-sea-creature-was-humans-oldest-known-ancestor*.
p. 31	Yearning for a watery home: US marine biologist Wallace Nichols (2015) elevates this idea to a scientific theory of the 'blue mind'.
p. 32	The physiology of cold water immersion: Tipton et al. 2017.
p. 33	Endorphins and their role in pain management: Sprouse-Blum et al. 2010.
p. 33	On the difference between natural and synthetic opioids, see: *https://www.ucsf.edu/news/2018/05/410376/bodys-natural-opioids-affect-brain-cells-much-differently-morphine*.
p. 33	Vagus nerve: *https://my.clevelandclinic.org/health/body/22279-vagus-nerve*.
p. 34	'the sea can wash away all evils': Patton 2006.
p. 34	Cold water swimming and depression: van Tulleken et al. 2018.

Notes

p. 34   Positive emotions in nature: Richardson et al. 2016.

p. 34   Skill and challenge: Isham and Jackson 2022.

p. 34   Green social prescribing: *https://collegeofmedicine.org.uk/beyond-pills-campaign-dr-william-bird-on-the-impact-green-social-prescribing-can-have/.*

p. 34   Health benefits of cold water swimming: Burlingham et al. 2022; Massey et al. 2022; Overbury et al. 2023; Yankouskaya et al. 2023; see also: *https://www.kindmindpsych.com/using-the-divers-reflex-to-regulate-emotional-intensity/.*

p. 35   *BMJ* neuralgia case study: Mole and Mackeith 2018; see also Nichols 2015.

p. 35   *Chill*: Harper 2022.

p. 35   Science of cold water cure: *https://www.outdoorswimmingsociety.com/science-cold-water/*; see also Goldstein 2019.

p. 35   Harper and stress response: Harper 2022, p. 208.

p. 37   Mike Tipton interview: *https://www.theguardian.com/lifeandstyle/2023/sep/30/cold-water-immersion-therapy-do-the-benefits-outweigh-the-risks*; see also Tipton et al. 2017 and 2022.

p. 37   Nature and logic of the accumulation of wealth: Heilbroner 1985.

p. 37   Claude Bernard: Gross 1998.

p. 38   *The Wisdom of the Body*: Cannon 1932.

p. 38   Vital signs: *https://www.healthline.com/health/what-are-vital-signs.*

p. 38   History of vital signs: Kellett and Sebat 2017.

p. 39   Pain as a vital sign: *https://www.theguardian.com/us-news/2018/mar/30/enduring-pain-how-a-1996-opioid-policy-change-had-long-lasting-effects.*

p. 39   APS story, see: *https://www.theguardian.com/news/2018/nov/08/the-making-of-an-opioid-epidemic*; see also Gourd 2019.

p. 39   Normal values of vital signs: *https://www.viosmedical.com/resources/vital-signs-now-and-then/.* It's worth mentioning here that normality in medicine has to be treated with extraordinary care. Individuals can have differing 'normal' parameters: see Lustig 2021, p. 136; see also Canguilhem 1943; Maté 2022.

p. 39   Longitudinal study: Campbell 1996.

p. 41   *What Is Health?*: Sterling 2020.

p. 41   Sterling and Eyer on allostasis: Sterling and Eyer 1988.

p. 41   Allostasis in space: Williams et al. 2009.

p. 42   Allostatic load: *https://www.verywellmind.com/what-is-allostatic-load-5680283.*

p. 42	Normal response and allostatic load: https://www.researchgate.net/figure/Four-types-of-allostatic-states-The-top-panel-illustrates-normal-allostatic-responses_fig2_51492293.
p. 42	Deaths of despair: Case and Deaton 2020.
p. 42	Global suicide rate: https://iris.who.int/bitstream/handle/10665/31098 1/WHO-MSD-19.1-eng.pdf?sequence=1&isAllowed=y.

Chapter 4 The Myth of Care

p. 43	'Never looked for': From Act V of *Faust* Part 2 in David Luke's translation, Goethe 1832, p. 219.
p. 44	The 'demon-haunted world': Sagan 1995.
p. 44	The absence of care: Maté 2022.
p. 45	The maternal bond: Bohannon 2023; Hrdy 1999.
p. 45	The evolutionary basis for care: Eisler and Fry 2019.
p. 45	'If exploitation of others were all that matters': de Waal 2009, p. 43; see also Joyce 2007; Wright 1994.
p. 45	Romulus and Remus: https://www.britannica.com/biography/Romulus-and-Remus.
p. 45	Binti Jua: https://www.youtube.com/watch?v=puFCuMacoVk; see also: https://www.washingtonpost.com/news/animalia/wp/2016/06/01/when-a-toddler-fell-into-a-zoo-enclosure-20-years-ago-he-was-saved-by-a-gorilla/.
p. 46	Harambe: https://www.huffingtonpost.co.uk/entry/gorilla-killing-cincinnati-zoo-remember-jambo-binti-jua-saved-two-children-lives_uk_574bee90e4b0ebf6a329ce8c.
p. 46	Protecting gorillas: https://janegoodall.org/our-work/our-approach/.
p. 46	XR protest: https://extinctionrebellion.uk/2021/04/22/breaking-this-is-an-act-of-care-extinction-rebellion-women-break-windows-at-hsbc-canary-wharf-hq-in-latest-action-to-highlight-the-financing-of-climate-breakdown/.
p. 46	HSBC fossil fuel investment: https://www.ran.org/wp-content/uploads/2020/03/Banking_on_Climate_Change__2020_vF.pdf.
p. 46	Thermohaline circulation: https://www.britannica.com/science/thermohaline-circulation; https://en.wikipedia.org/wiki/Atlantic_meridional_overturning_circulation; https://www.washingtonpost.com/climate-environment/2021/08/05/change-ocean-collapse-atlantic-meridional/.
p. 47	Displaced children: https://www.unicef.org/reports/children-displaced-changing-climate.
p. 47	Sue Reid comment: See the link for the XR protest on p. 46 above.

p. 47	Suffragettes in March 1912: *https://bowstreetpolicemuseum.org.uk/shattering-suffrage/*.
p. 47	HSBC nine acquitted: *https://www.theguardian.com/environment/2023/nov/16/climate-protesters-cleared-of-causing-criminal-damage-to-hsbc-london-hq*.
p. 47	On civil disobedience, see Jackson 2021, Chapter 9.
p. 47	Clare Farrell and Sue Reid: See the link for the XR protest on p. 46 above.
p. 48	Caring for material things: Jackson 1996 and 2017.
p. 49	Boris Groys: Groys 2022.
p. 49	Global incidence of mental health disorders: *https://www.who.int/health-topics/mental-health#tab=tab_2* .
p. 49	Mental illness in the US: *https://mhanational.org/issues/state-mental-health-america*.
p. 49	On rising rates of depression: *https://news.gallup.com/poll/505745/depression-rates-reach-new-highs.aspx*.
p. 49	Economic costs of depression: *https://iris.who.int/bitstream/handle/10665/310981/WHO-MSD-19.1-eng.pdf?sequence=1&isAllowed=y*.
p. 49	Health inequalities: See, e.g., Marmot et al. 2010; for the US: Escarce 2019.
p. 49	*Gattaca*: *https://www.imdb.com/title/tt0119177/*.
p. 50	*Philosophy of Care*: Groys 2022.
p. 51	Language's blindness to its own cultural origins: Whorf 2012.
p. 51	Reich's 'History of the Notion of Care': Reich 1995.
p. 51	*In a Different Voice*: Gilligan 1982.
p. 52	*Kara* and *cura*: 'The primary sense [of the Germanic *kara*] is that of inward grief,' explains the Century Dictionary, 'and the word is not connected, either in sense or form with [the Latin] *cura* . . . of which the primary sense is pains or trouble bestowed upon something': *http://triggs.djvu.org/century-dictionary.com/djvu2jpgframes.php?volno=01&page=0821&query=care*.
p. 53	Hyginus' myth of care: Scott Smith and Trazskoma 2007, pp. 166–7.
p. 54	Reich, 'the primordial role of care': Reich 1995.
p. 54	Paul Simon, 'Everything Put Together Falls Apart': *https://www.youtube.com/watch?v=E1dMPwSfHmg*.
p. 55	*Faust*: Goethe 1994, pp. 219–21.
p. 55	Herder's poem: *http://www.zeno.org/Literatur/M/Herder,+Johann+Gottfried/Gedichte/Gedichte/Erstes+Buch/Das+Kind+der+Sorge*.
p. 55	Burdach's essay: Burdach 1923.

p. 55 Heidegger's book: Heidegger 1927, p. 184; 'permanently altered the course': https://www.britannica.com/topic/Being-and-Time: Groys (2022, p. 70) argues that this was the first time care was taken seriously in philosophy.

p. 56 Away from the upright as we orbit round the sun: 'Upright' here means perpendicular to the plane of our orbit round the sun; without the moon: https://www.youtube.com/watch?v=6MP92oxMCoQ.

Chapter 5 No Good Deed

p. 60 'No society can legitimately call itself civilised': Bevan 1952, p. 100.

p. 60 Parc Bryn Bach: https://www.parcbrynbach.co.uk/.

p. 61 Arrival of the NHS (5 July 1948): See the official National Theatre trailer for Tim Price's 2024 play *Nye* at: https://www.youtube.com/watch?v=VEWGqDqgt6Q.

p. 61 'Six months before the Appointed Day': Gregg 1967, p. 51.

p. 61 On the history of the NHS, see: https://history.blog.gov.uk/2023/07/13/the-founding-of-the-nhs-75-years-on/; see also Hardman 2023.

p. 62 Nye Bevan story: See, e.g., Foot 1962; Thomas-Symonds 2014; see also: https://www.nyebevan.org.uk/about-nye/.

p. 62 The patches and the patch girls: https://www.parcbrynbach.co.uk/our-history.

p. 62 On women and children in the mines, see also Bates 2012; Thompson 2014.

p. 63 Commission on conditions in the mines: https://www.ncm.org.uk/app/uploads/2023/02/1842-Commission.pdf.

p. 64 Central Labour College: http://www.unionhistory.info/timeline/Tl_Display.php?irn=3000017&QueryPage=../AdvSearch.php.

p. 64 'The mountain tops were hidden': Cronin 1937, p. 3.

p. 65 'I do not think Mr Aneurin Bevan will be exactly lost in the crowd': Cited in: https://nyebevan.org.uk/about-nye/.

p. 65 Black lung still killing ex-miners: Morgan 2018; Qi et al. 2021.

p. 65 WHO on work-related deaths: https://www.who.int/news/item/17-09-2021-who-ilo-almost-2-million-people-die-from-work-related-causes-each-year. Full report at: WHO/ILO 2021.

p. 66 DALYs: These measure the total burden of disease – both from years of life lost due to premature death and from years lived with a disability. One DALY equals one lost year of healthy life.

p. 66 Workplace fatalities in the US: https://www.bls.gov/news.release/pdf/cfoi

	.pdf; for the UK, see: https://www.statista.com/statistics/292272/fatal-injuries-at-work-great-britain-by-employment-y-on-y/.
p. 66	Child labour: UNICEF report on child labour: UNICEF/ILO 2021; see also: https://data.unicef.org/topic/child-protection/child-labour/.
p. 66	Children in mines today: ILO 2019.
p. 66	Social justice as prosperity: See, e.g., Hickel 2017; see also Jackson 2017a, Chapter 3.
p. 67	Tredegar Medical Aid Society Heritage Centre: http://tredegarmasheritagecentre.org.uk/.
p. 67	On the history of the Medical Aid Society, see: https://www.theguardian.com/healthcare-network/2018/may/22/south-wales-town-forged-nhs-points-future-tredegar; https://www.walesonline.co.uk/news/health/going-tredegar-ise-you-bevan-told-2187499; https://60yearsofnhsscotland.co.uk/history/birth-of-nhs-scotland/a-labour-delivery.html.
p. 68	'useless guinea-chasing treatments': Cronin 1937, p. 459.
p. 68	'We are going to Tredegar-ise you': Jones 2018; see also: https://www.aber.ac.uk/en/news/archive/2018/07/title-214582-en.html.
p. 68	'For years we've been bleating': Cronin 1937, p. 460.
p. 69	King's Fund report: Anandaciva 2023.
p. 69	UK vs US healthcare: https://www.theguardian.com/society/2017/jan/24/nhs-us-healthcare-austerity-politics-obamacare; see also: https://blogs.bmj.com/bmj/2020/02/17/comparative-twin-study-access-to-health care-services-in-the-nhs-and-the-american-private-insurance-system/.
p. 69	'the most far-reaching piece of social legislation in British history': https://sheendex.com/2017/06/03/the-aneurin-bevan-lecture-hay-festival-2017/.
p. 70	Healthcare spending in the UK: https://www.ons.gov.uk/peoplepopulationandcommunity/healthandsocialcare/healthcaresystem/bulletins/ukhealthaccounts/2022and2023; see also Jackson 2024.
p. 70	Healthcare spending in the US: https://www.cms.gov/data-research/statistics-trends-and-reports/national-health-expenditure-data/historical.
p. 70	Public spending as share of the GDP: https://www.statista.com/statistics/282778/uk-government-spending-as-gdp/.
p. 71	Private equity in social care in UK: Corlet Walker et al. 2022; see also Corlet Walker and Jackson 2021.
p. 71	Private equity in healthcare in the US: Kannan et al. 2023, p. 2368. The study found that: 'After private equity acquisition, Medicare beneficiaries admitted to private equity hospitals experienced a 25.4% increase in hospital-acquired conditions compared with those treated

at control hospitals.' See also: *https://hbr.org/2023/03/research-what-happens-when-private-equity-firms-buy-hospitals.*

p. 71   Stephanie Kelton on financing the care economy: Kelton 2020, p. 250.

pp. 71f.   Decline in pre-Covid burden of infectious disease: Statistics from the 2019 Global Burden of Disease study: *https://gbd2019.healthdata.org/gbd-results/.*

p. 72   The rise in chronic non-communicable disease: Statistics from *https://vizhub.healthdata.org/gbd-compare/.*

p. 72   Chronic disease as proportion of global deaths: *https://www.who.int/news-room/fact-sheets/detail/noncommunicable-diseases.*

p. 72   A staggering 90 per cent exhibit metabolic dysfunction: O'Hearn et al. 2022; see also Araújo et al. 2019; Lustig 2021, p. 149; Means 2024, p 21.

p. 72   *The Lancet* editorial on the shift in the burden of disease: GBD 2019 Viewpoint Collaborators 2020, p. 1137.

p. 75   Thomas Aquinas, *Summa Theologica*: *https://en.wikisource.org/wiki/Summa_Theologiae/Supplement_to_the_Third_Part/Question_14#Art._4_-_Whether_works_done_without_charity_merit_any,_at_least_temporal,_good.*

p. 76   London Olympics ceremony: *https://www.youtube.com/watch?v=4Asoe4de-rI.*

p. 76   Walter Map: Map 1923, p. 181.

Chapter 6   Passerelle

p. 78   'The real war': Elon Musk on X, 26 December 2023: *https://twitter.com/elonmusk/status/1739480643577196561.*

p. 78   Passerelle Solférino/Léopold Sédar Senghor: *https://soundlandscapes.wordpress.com/2014/04/13/the-passerelle-senghor-and-its-sounds/.*

p. 79   Musée Rodin: *https://www.musee-rodin.fr/en/museum/musee-rodin/sculpture-garden.*

p. 80   Finance Minister speech at climate conference: *https://presse.economie.gouv.fr/propos-dintroduction-de-bruno-le-maire-lors-des-rendez-vous-de-bercy-croissance-et-climat-le-mardi-5-decembre/.*

p. 81   Carbon emissions progress: *https://www.climate-transparency.org/wp-content/uploads/2021/10/CT2021France.pdf.*

p. 81   The Philanthropist, technology will save us: *https://www.youtube.com/watch?v=Aa8sYPZbdRA.*

p. 82	Hundreds of events like this: I describe some of these experiences in the Prologue to the second edition of *Prosperity without Growth* (Jackson 2017a).
pp. 82f	Rodin's *Monument to Balzac*: https://www.musee-rodin.fr/en/musee/collections/oeuvres/monument-balzac; see also: https://www.clarkart.edu/microsites/rodin/about-the-exhibition/monument-to-balzac.
p. 83	Kenneth Clark's *Civilisation*: https://www.youtube.com/watch?v=SsJkWkFMcwg.
p. 83	'No society can legitimately call itself civilised': Bevan 1952, p. 100.
p. 83	*The Human Condition*: Arendt 1958, p. 5.
p. 85	Collapsism: https://english.elpais.com/society/2022-08-10/the-discourse-of-collapse-divides-environmentalists.html.
p. 85	Herman Daly: Daly 1977. Marilyn Waring: Waring 1988.
p. 85	Jason Hickel: Hickel 2021, p. 1105, emphasis added.
p. 86	European Parliament conference: https://www.beyond-growth-2023.eu/.
p. 86	*Nature* article: Hickel et al. 2022.
p. 86	Musk on *Nature* article: See 'The real war', p. 78 above.
p. 89	'Trump and 'the perennial prophets of doom': https://www.youtube.com/watch?v=IBbBMVZHHSw.
p. 89	Ethos of health lies in the balance: see also Jackson 2021, Chapter 4.
p. 90	Aristotle and *aretē*: Aristotle 2004, Book 2, Chapter 6.
p. 91	*The Nicomachean Ethics*: Aristotle 2004.
p. 92	Preference for terminology of postgrowth: see Jackson 2021.
p. 92	Growth running out of steam: Jackson 2019; see also Jackson 2021, Chapter 2.
p. 92	Postgrowth thinking: see Jackson 2017a and b; 2019; 2021; see also: http://www.cusp.ac.uk.
p. 94	Care, craft and creativity tread lightly on the planet: Jackson 2017a, Chapter 8; see also Jackson et al. 2024.
p. 95	*Danaïde*: https://rodinmuseum.org/collection/object/96034; for the original mythology, see Scott Smith and Trzascoma 2007, p. 153.

Chapter 7 Shoot the Messenger

p. 97	'Public health does not improve': Mol 2008, p. 82.
p. 98	'The gracious and lovely young ladies of the aristocracy': Dunant 1862, pp. 108–9.

p. 98	'In an age when we hear so much of progress and civilization': Dunant 1862, p. 127.
p. 98	First Geneva Convention: *https://ihl-databases.icrc.org/en/ihl-treaties/gc-1864*.
p. 99	Pandemic preparedness: Elkomy and Jackson 2024.
p. 100	'To presume that you and I are healthy': Mol 2008, p. 13.
p. 100	Metabolic dysfunction and its effects: Lustig 2021; Means 2024; metabolic dysfunction is also known as metabolic syndrome (Lusis et al. 2008).
p. 101	Sterling and Eyer: Sterling and Eyer 1988.
p. 101	Diabetes: For useful background information, see the US Centers for Disease Control and Prevention (CDC): *https://www.cdc.gov/diabetes/index.html*.
p. 101	On type 2 diabetes specifically, see: *https://www.cdc.gov/diabetes/about/about-type-2-diabetes.html*.
p. 102	History of diabetes: Karamanou et al. 2016; see also Gemmill 1972.
p. 102	Diabetes before insulin: Barron 1920.
p. 102	Discovery of insulin: Bliss 1993a; Quianzon and Cheikh 2012.
p. 102	Extract from Banting's notebooks: Notebook: 1920–1. Fisher Rare Book Library, University of Toronto, Canada.
p. 102	Biography of Fred Banting: Bliss 1993b.
p. 104	Mol on care: Mol 2008, pp. 5–6, emphasis added.
p. 104	Diabetes prevalence and increase: Magliano and Boyko 2021; Means 2024; Zimmet 2017; see also Lustig 2021; Means 2024.
p. 105	'pandemic of unprecedented magnitude': IDF 2021; see also Singer et al. 2022; Tabish 2007.
p. 105	'Public health does not improve': See p. 97 above.
p. 107	Sugar as an addiction: Lustig 2017; Means 2024.
p. 107	High glycaemic index: it turns out that the glycaemic index is a flawed measure of the availability of glucose in the blood; a better measure (which takes account of the fibre in the food) is called the glycaemic load (GL) (Lustig 2021, p. 186).
p. 108	Proton pump inhibitor market: *https://www.pharmiweb.com/press-release/2023-10-16/global-proton-pump-inhibitors-industry-s-bright-future-anticipating-us-49-billion-revenue-with-a*.
p. 109	Inflammation as precursor to chronic disease: Lustig 2021, pp. 117–18; Means 2024, Chapters 2 and 3.

p. 109 Global pain management market: *https://www.bccresearch.com/market-research/healthcare/the-global-market-for-pain-management-drugs-and-devices.html.*

p. 109 Market for statins: *https://www.databridgemarketresearch.com/reports/global-statin-market.*

p. 109 Market for metformin: Market for metformin growing at 6 per cent: *https://www.databridgemarketresearch.com/reports/global-metformin-market.*

p. 109 Market for anti-obesity drugs: *https://tinyurl.com/3rf8wwb7.*

p. 109 Market for ready meals: *https://www.statista.com/outlook/cmo/food/convenience-food/ready-to-eat-meals/worldwide.*

p. 109 Market for bread and cereal products: *https://www.statista.com/outlook/cmo/food/bread-cereal-products/worldwide.*

p. 109 Market for oils and fats: *https://www.statista.com/outlook/cmo/food/oils-fats/worldwide.*

p. 109 Market for confectionery and snacks: *https://www.statista.com/outlook/cmo/food/confectionery-snacks/worldwide.*

p. 109 Resources for prevention: Means (2024) is a useful starting point for anyone wanting to take control of their own health. Valabhji and Kar (2023) offer a clear overview of the need. Lustig (2021) connects the neurobiological dots. Campbell-McBride (2020) offers a deep dive into the gut biome. The BBC's *Truth about Sugar* documentary is still worth a watch: *https://www.youtube.com/watch?v=9E9bnjwQG9s.* Chris van Tulleken's (2023) exposé of ultra-processed food is essential reading. Perhaps the most extraordinary resource I found is the work of the Australian health adviser Barbara O'Neill. Her 2014 book was an early attempt to bring some of the new (and old) understandings about the role of micro-organisms to a wider public and connect it to dietary health. Her online videos provide a wealth of advice if you can get past her undoubtedly eccentric presentation. I found very little that I could not verify somewhere in peer-reviewed papers in reputable journals. Extraordinarily, though, she was banned from working in Australia and appears to be the object of a concerted attempt at character assassination. Her Wikipedia entry (*https://en.wikipedia.org/wiki/Barbara_O%27Neill*) would make you think she should be avoided at all costs.

p. 110 'biggest lie in health care': Means 2024, p. xi.

p. 111 *Bateau mouche*: An open-topped excursion boat popular with tourists along the river Seine.

Notes

p. 111 Shifting burden of disease: https://www.who.int/news-room/fact-sheets/detail/noncommunicable-diseases; see also Lustig 2021; Means 2024.

p. 112 Dunant's story: Warner 2013; see also: https://www.nobelprize.org/prizes/peace/1901/dunant/biographical/.

Chapter 8 The Lost Generation

p. 114 'You are all a lost generation': Epigraph to Hemingway 1926, p. 4.

p. 114 The lost generation: https://en.wikipedia.org/wiki/Lost_Generation; see also: https://www.britannica.com/topic/Lost-Generation; https://www.bbc.com/culture/article/20210726-the-scandalous-memoir-of-the-lost-generation.

p. 114 Biographical details about Hemingway: Reynolds 1998. Nobel Prize: https://www.nobelprize.org/prizes/literature/1954/summary/. It's worth mentioning that critical opinion has moved decisively against the content of some of Hemingway's writing.

p. 114 Hemingway's epigraphs: See 'You are all a lost generation', p. 114 above.

p. 115 James's 'most brilliant woman student': https://tinyurl.com/45hacua8; see also: https://jwa.org/encyclopedia/article/stein-gertrude. The paper was a study of the human ability to carry out complex tasks with no conscious attention while simultaneously engaged consciously in others. The behavioural psychologist B.F. Skinner (1934) was later to link the paper to the 'stream of consciousness' writing beloved by the modernists.

p. 115 Stein at Johns Hopkins: https://tinyurl.com/2vpdm924.

p. 116 Three-quarters of a billion face hunger: https://www.un.org/en/global-issues/food.

p. 116 Nutritional disaster: See, e.g., John Yudkin's (1972) attack on the sugar industry; see also Marion Nestle's brilliant (2013) exposé of food politics and Tim Lang and Michael Heasman's (2015) exploration of 'food wars'.

p. 117 *Ultra-Processed People*: Van Tulleken 2023, pp. 10–11.

p. 117 Genetic responsibility for metabolic dysfunction: Lusis et al. 2008, Box 3, p. 823.

p. 117 WHO report: WHO/FAO 2003.

p. 118 Sugar Association pressure on the WHO: Dyer 2004.

p. 118 Leaked letter: https://www.nationalreviewofmedicine.com/issue/2004_02_15/features06.html.

Notes

p. 118   *Pure, White and Deadly*: Yudkin 1972, p. 168. *The Hacking of the American Mind*: Lustig 2017; see also Lustig 2014 and Lustig's lecture *Sugar – The Bitter Truth*, viewed twenty-four million times: *https://www.youtube.com/watch?v=dBnniua6-oM*.

p. 118   Richard Smith editorial: Smith 200.

p. 118   Misquotation of Hippocrates: Cardenas 2013: e260.

p. 119   The Hippocratic Oath: *https://en.wikipedia.org/wiki/Hippocratic_Oath*; see also: *https://www.nlm.nih.gov/hmd/topics/greek-medicine/index.html#case1*.

p. 119   Role of commercial food system on health: White et al. 2020.

p. 119   Huge external costs: see Jackson 2024.

p. 120   Food wars: Lang and Heasman 2015.

p. 120   Sisters of Mercy: Not to be confused with the 1980s rock band or the 1967 Leonard Cohen song. Despite a serious attempt to besmirch their reputation, these particular sisters are still going strong today: *https://www.sistersofmercy.org/*.

p. 120   Nightingale's visit to Paris: Porter 1996, p. 226.

p. 121   Kaiserswerth Institute: *https://www.vahs.org.uk/2013/05/feature-5/*. The term 'deaconess' refers to women who assisted in the ministry of the church, often through voluntary work in the community.

p. 121   The deaconesses and modern nursing: Susanne Kreutzer and Karen Nolte's excellent (2016) collection of essays covers pretty much every aspect of the history of the deaconesses. Interestingly, it sides with the idea that what God and the Fliedners asked of the deaconesses was not unfair. See their introduction here: *https://media.dav-medien.de/sample/400011355_p__v1.pdf*.

p. 122   Eerie resonances: *https://www.ceps.eu/ceps-publications/tsar-nicholas-is-crimean-war-and-putins-in-ukraine-plus-ca-change/*.

p. 122   History of the Crimean War: *https://www.nam.ac.uk/explore/crimean-war*; see also: *https://www.history.com/topics/european-history/crimean-war*; *https://www.encyclopedia.com/history/encyclopedias-almanacs-transcripts-and-maps/crimean-war-1853-1856*.

p. 122   Scutari is the English (and Italian) name for the town of Shkodër, which is now in Albania.

p. 123   William Russell in *The Times*: *https://microform.digital/boa/posts/category/contextual-essays/524/from-the-archive-william-howard-russell-and-the-crimean-wars-cultural-legacy*; see also: *https://www.thetimes.co.uk/article/how-the-times-went-to-war-with-a-government-over-crimea-8v5nx836cq6*.

p. 123 Conditions in Scutari: https://victorianweb.org/history/crimea/florrie.html.
p. 123 Death rate in Scutari: Porter 1996, p. 226.
p. 123 Nightingale School: https://editions.covecollective.org/chronologies/foundation-nightingale-training-school-nurses.
p. 124 Nightingale Medals: https://www.icrc.org/en/document/florence-nightingale-medal-2023-recipients.
p. 124 Proportion of women in nursing: https://www.who.int/news-room/events/detail/2022/10/11/default-calendar/the-best-of-both--creating-gender-equity-in-nursing-and-midwifery-leadership; see also RCN 2020, pp. 12–13, Figure 1.
p. 124 Proportion of men in the US military: https://www.cfr.org/backgrounder/demographics-us-military.
p. 124 Jane Salvage writing in the *BMJ*: Salvage 2001, p. 172.
p. 125 'Shall we begin by taking it as a general principle': Nightingale 1859, p. 7.
p. 126 Longevity of chess players: Tran-Duy et al. 2018; see also: https://www.chess.com/news/view/study-grandmasters-live-longer.
p. 126 Yuri Averbakh turns one hundred: https://www.chess.com/news/view/yuri-averbakh-100-years.
p. 126 Chess players' nutrition: https://www.psychologytoday.com/intl/blog/the-athletes-way/201305/checkmate-winning-life-strategies-chess-grandmaster.
p. 126 Life expectancy of musicians: https://theconversation.com/stairway-to-hell-life-and-death-in-the-pop-music-industry-32735.
p. 126 'Art is a cry of distress': Arnold Schoenberg (in 1910) as cited in translation by Alexander Sorenson 2022 in the *Los Angeles Review of Books*: https://lareviewofbooks.org/article/like-fences-in-a-flat-land-on-recent-returns-to-the-german-expressionist-lyric/#_edn1.
p. 128 Succession: https://www.youtube.com/watch?v=LZTaXjt2Ggk.

Chapter 9 Care in the Time of Cholera

p. 129 'Shall we begin by taking it as a general principle': Nightingale 1859, p. 7.
p. 130 Britain's Olympic sailing medals: https://www.teamgb.com/sport/sailing/3TRIDDMXbA5KBMQphAGuJr.
p. 130 Checking for sewage: https://www.sas.org.uk/water-quality/sewage-pollution-alerts/safer-seas-rivers-service/.

Notes

p. 130   BBC investigation: *https://www.bbc.co.uk/news/science-environment-66 670132*.

p. 130   Twelve hundred hours: *https://www.theguardian.com/environment/ 2023/nov/23/raw-sewage-discharged-chichester-harbour-over-1200-hours -month*.

p. 131   Nobel Prizes for *E. coli*: *https://microbeonline.com/e-coli-only-bacteria- that-wins-record-number-of-nobel-prizes/*.

p. 131   'What is true for *E. coli* is true for the elephant': ASM 2011.

p. 132   Authoritative source for Hippocrates quote: Fan 2021.

p. 132   On the Hippocratic humours: Jouanna 2012, Chapter 16.

p. 132   On the five elements: Beinfield and Korngold 1992; Ni 1995.

p. 133   Definition of the immune system: *https://www.cancer.gov/publications /dictionaries/cancer-terms/def/immune-system*.

p. 133   Covid mortality and health resilience: Elkomy and Jackson 2024.

p. 134   'complete freedom from disease and from struggle': Dubos 1959, p. 1.

p. 134   '[A]n effort of nature': Nightingale 1859, p. 7.

p. 135   'Nature alone cures': Nightingale 1859, p. 133.

p. 136   Trall quotes: Trall 1872, cited in Carrington and Shelton 1954, pp. 16–17.

p. 137   Kneipp Cure: Ko 2016.

p. 137   Kneipp Cure and German identity: *https://www.unesco.at/en/culture/in tangible-cultural-heritage/national-inventory/news-1/article/kneippen-als -traditionelles-wissen-und-praxis-nach-der-lehre-sebastian-kneipps*.

p. 137   History of cholera in Britain: Thomas 2015; see also: *https://www .theguardian.com/cities/2016/apr/04/story-cities-14-london-great-stink -river-thames-joseph-bazalgette-sewage-system*.

p. 137   Cholera epidemic 1854: Tulchinsky 2018, Chapter 5 (online at: *https:// www.ncbi.nlm.nih.gov/pmc/articles/PMC7150208/pdf/main.pdf*).

p. 137   Robert Seymour lithograph: *https://en.wikipedia.org/wiki/File:Cholera- nlm_nlmuid-101393375-imgAA.JPG#filehistory*.

p. 137   Miasma theory and obesity: Halliday 2001.

p. 138   Broad Street water pump: Tulchinsky 2018, pp. 79–82. There are several versions of the Broad Street story. In some it was Snow himself who removed the handle. Others have suggested the outbreak was already in decline before the handle was removed: Bynum 2013 McLeod 2000; Ruths 2009.

p. 138   Overlapping water companies: Tuchinsky 2018, p. 82.

p. 139   Thomas Miller quote: See history of cholera in Britain – *Guardian* link, p. 137 above.

p. 139 The Great Stink and the London sewerage system: Halliday 1999.

p. 139 Snow's early death: It's probable that this was the result of having experimented extensively on himself with chloroform. Snow was also a pioneer in anaesthesia.

p. 140 1.7 billion without safe drinking water: https://www.who.int/newsroom/fact-sheets/detail/drinking-water.

p. 140 Oxfam on wastewater treatment: https://www.oxfam.org/en/press-releases/gazans-face-threat-cholera-and-other-infectious-diseases-says-oxfam.

p.140 WHO on disease outbreaks: https://www.bbc.co.uk/news/world-middle-east-67554394.

Chapter 10 Pathogenesis

p. 141 'When the tide is receding from the beach': Dubos 1959, p. 24.

p. 142 Pacini and cholera: Carboni 2021.

p. 142 'organic, living substance': Lippi and Gotuzzo 2014, p. 193.

p. 143 Pasteur, plagiarism and Béchamp: Manchester 2007; see also Hume 1923.

p. 144 Robert Koch: https://www.nobelprize.org/prizes/medicine/1905/koch/biographical/; see also Segre 2013.

p. 144 On germs as symptoms, two slightly different explanations have been proposed. In one they were present in number because of the increased susceptibility of the diseased body. In another they were seen as functional cleansing agents whose role was specifically to help clean away decay: O'Neill 2014; Pearson 1942, p. 9.

p. 144 Béchamp's experiment with a cat: Hume 1923, p. 202.

p. 144 On pleomorphism: Wainwright 1997.

p. 145 Germ theory vs terrain theory: https://www.templeofthesoul.org/blog/germ-theory-vs-terrain-theory; https://salvatorebattaglia.com.au/blogs/news/terrain-or-germ-theory; see also Dubos 1955.

p. 146 Carnegie Foundation Flexner report: Flexner 1910.

p. 146 Flexner in Europe: Bonner 1989. Flexner on social care: Morris 2008. Flexner's influence a hundred years later: Duffy 2011.

p. 146 'an enormous over-production': Flexner 1910, p. x.

p. 147 'the effort is made to use knowledge': Flexner 1910, p. 156.

p. 147 'Sectarians', in the logical sense: Flexner 1910, p. 158.

p. 148 Impact of Flexner on complementary medicine: Stahnisch and Verhoef 2012.

Notes

p. 148   Driven under by lack of funds: Beinfield and Korngold 1992, p. 23.

p. 148   Impact of Flexner report on women: Moehling et al. 2019.

p. 148   Terrain theory as quackery: *https://sciencebasedmedicine.org/i-reject-your-reality/*; see also: *https://www.popsci.com/health/germ-theory-terrain-theory/*.

p. 149   On the science of the gut biome: Campbell-McBride 2020.

p. 151   Happiness is in the gut: Lyman 2024.

p. 151   Impact of antibiotics: Patangia et al 2022.

p. 151   Toxic burden of medicine: This point was made forcefully by Ivan Illich (1976).

p. 152   'Clearly, modern medical science has helped us': Dubos 1959, pp. 23–4.

p. 152   Dubos's second thoughts about germ theory: Dubos 1955; see also by way of riposte: Casanova 2023.

p. 152   Attacks on Dr Michael Dixon: *The Sunday Times*: *https://www.thetimes.co.uk/article/77fdb2f1-42d1-440b-901d-790479881c98*. *The Guardian*: *https://www.theguardian.com/uk-news/2023/dec/10/king-charles-criticised-appointing-homeopath-michael-dixon-head-royal-medical-household/*. *The Daily Mail*: *https://www.dailymail.co.uk/news/article-12977297/Who-Dr-Michael-Dixon-royal-doctor-King-Charles-Princess-Wales-operations.html*.

p. 154   'has led to a nation that is over-medicalised': Dixon 2023, pp. 235–6.

p. 155   Food/pharma conglomerates: *https://www.bayer.com/media/en-us/bayer-closes-monsanto-acquisition/*; *https://www.reuters.com/article/business/nestle-buys-us-firm-as-part-of-food-pharma-drive-idUSTRE74N1QM/*.

p. 155   'an explanation of the causes': Brown 1979, p. 10.

p. 156   Influence of Rockefeller: Fisher 1978.

p. 156   'most PPPs channel public money into the private sector': Birn 2014, p. 14. On the relationship between germ theory and the pharmaceutical industry, see also Wang 2009, Chapter 2.

p. 156   'The pivotal, even nefarious, role': Birn 2014, p. 19.

p. 157   Wiki definition as of August 2024: *https://en.wikipedia.org/wiki/Alternative_medicine*.

Chapter 11 Death and the Maiden

p. 159   'Give me thy hand': The poem 'Death and the Maiden' (originally in German as 'Der Tod und das Mädchen' and translated by the author here) was written by the German author Matthias Claudius in 1774 and provided the text for a song Franz Schubert composed in 1817. He used the same theme for his String Quartet No. 14 in D minor, written in 1824 at the age of twenty-seven when he knew already that he himself was dying.

p. 160 Every age gets the Stonehenge it deserves: Hawkes 1967, p. 174. Background on Stonehenge: https://www.nytimes.com/2022/02/17/arts/design/stonehenge-british-museum.html; https://www.britannica.com/topic/Stonehenge.

p. 160 Sources of the Stonehenge stones: Altar stone: https://www.bbc.co.uk/news/articles/c207lqdn7550#. Bluestones: https://www.discoveringbritain.org/activities/wales/viewpoints/preseli-mountains.html.

p. 161 Asclepius and Hygeia are their Greek names. In Roman mythology they are Aesculapius and Sanus. So my use of Jupiter below rather than Zeus claims some literary licence.

p. 162 Legend of Asclepius: Scott Smith and Trzaskoma 2007, p. 115.

p. 162 Asclepius and Hygeia as a symbolic division: Dubos 1959, pp. 129-34; see also: Dixon and Sweeney 2000, pp. 21-2; https://collection.sciencemuseumgroup.org.uk/people/cp97864/hygeia.

p. 162 Cult of Hygeia after plagues: https://pantheon.org/articles/h/hygieia.html. For a fascinating analysis, see Glomb 2021.

p. 163 'The myths of Hygeia and Asclepius symbolise the never-ending oscillation': Dubos 1959, p. 131.

p. 165 Arendt on labour and work: Arendt 1958, Chapter 3.

p. 165 Arendt labour quotes: Arendt 1958, pp. 108 and 133.

p. 165 Arendt work quotes: Arendt 1958, p. 8.

p. 166 'maintain, continue and repair our world': Tronto 1993, p. 103.

p. 166 Nurses' wages in the UK: https://www.rcn.org.uk/news-and-events/Press-Releases/nursing-staff-are-effectively-working-one-day-a-week-for-free-after-a-decade-of-real-terms-pay-cuts.

p. 166 Teachers' wages in the US: https://www.nea.org/nea-today/all-news-articles/average-teacher-salary-lower-today-ten-years-ago-nea-report-finds.

p. 166 Low-paid workers in the US since 1973: https://www.aei.org/articles/have-wages-stagnated-for-decades-in-the-us/.

p. 166 Nurses' 1 per cent pay offer, March 2021: https://news.sky.com/story/covid-19-1-pay-rise-for-nhs-staff-the-most-the-government-can-afford-says-minister-nadine-dorries-12236357.

p. 166 Nurses' 5 per cent pay settlement, March 2023: https://www.nursingtimes.net/news/workforce/breaking-new-pay-offer-for-nurses-in-england-announced-16-03-2023/.

p. 167	Energy prices at all-time high: https://www.consilium.europa.eu/en/infographics/energy-prices-2021/.
p. 167	One in six people in the US using food banks: https://www.prnewswire.com/news-releases/1-in-6-people-received-help-from-charitable-food-sector-in-2022-301865997.html.
p. 167	One hundred and twenty-fold increase in the UK: https://www.statista.com/statistics/382695/uk-foodbank-users/.
p. 167	ILO warns of global deepening: https://webapps.ilo.org/digitalguides/en-GB/story/globalwagereport2022-23#key-findings.
p. 167	FTSE 100 CEOs' pay: https://www.penningtonslaw.com/news-publications/latest-news/2023/negotiating-a-pay-rise-in-a-challenging-financial-climate.
p. 167	Highest pay rises for energy bosses: https://highpaycentre.org/wp-content/uploads/2023/08/Copy-of-CEO-pay-report-2023-1-1.pdf.
p. 168	Schumpeter and 'creative destruction': Schumpeter 1942, Chapter VII.
p. 168	UN Declaration of Human Rights: https://www.un.org/en/about-us/universal-declaration-of-human-rights.
p. 169	'forever unfinished': Groys 2022, p. 8.
p. 170	The Twentieth Century Fund: https://archives.nypl.org/mss/18811.
p. 170	Conversation with Baumol: Some of this section is adapted from an interview with William Baumol published as Krueger 2001, pp. 216–18. For more on Baumol's life and work, see: https://www.nytimes.com/2017/05/10/business/economy/william-baumol-dead-economist-coined-cost-disease.html.
p. 171	Baumol's note on Death and the Maiden: In fact, there's no record of what Baumol wrote down that night. But the examples are taken directly from Baumol and Bowen 1965. See also Baumol and Bowen 1966.
p. 172	Definition of labour productivity: typically labour productivity is defined as the output – measured in monetary terms – produced in each hour of work.
p. 173	Views on ChatGPT: Javaid et al. 2023; Ray 2023.
p. 173	The energy needs of AI: https://www.reuters.com/business/energy/us-power-tech-companies-lament-snags-meeting-ai-energy-needs-2024-04-18/.
p. 174	*Small Is Beautiful*: Schumacher 1974, Chapter 4.
p. 174	When aggregate growth isn't there: I've addressed the complexities of these arguments elsewhere: Jackson 2017a; Jackson 2019; Jackson 2021; Jackson et al. 2023.

p. 175   Twenty-one-hour week: https://neweconomics.org/2010/02/21-hours; see also: https://neweconomics.org/2018/11/five-reasons-why-nef-supports-the-4-day-week-campaign.

p. 175   Keynes' proposal on shorter working week: Keynes 1930.

p. 176   Experience with robots in social care in Japan: https://www.technologyreview.com/2023/01/09/1065135/japan-automating-eldercare-robots/; see also Persson et al. 2022. In spite of this the drive remains: https://www.telegraph.co.uk/global-health/science-and-disease/ai-robots-elderly-homes-social-care-health-secretary/.

p. 178   Fast and slow sectors: Baumol's original terminology for these two sectors was the 'progressive sector' and the 'stagnant sector'. My colleague Ben Gallant came up with this less pejorative alternative of 'fast' and 'slow'.

p. 178   'And the biggest danger': Adapted from Baumol's 1993 essay in the *New York Times*: https://www.nytimes.com/1993/09/05/business/l-health-care-and-high-cost-097293.html.

p. 179   'Even in your nineties': Baumol's last book, *The Cost Disease: Why Computers Get Cheaper and Healthcare Doesn't*, was published in 2012, five years before his death in May 2017 at the age of ninety-five.

p. 180   The staff of Asclepius vs the Caduceus: For a history of the confusion between the two, see Friedlander 1992. On commercial and professional uses, see Friedlander 1992, p. 153.

Chapter 12 Fuck the Patriarchy

p. 182   'The whole thrust of patriarchal societies': Hrdy 1999, p. 252.

p. 182   A perfect Alexandrine: https://www.britannica.com/art/alexandrine; *Le Roman d'Alexandre*: Zink 1994.

p. 182   Du Maurier in Alexandria: See Sally Beauman's Afterword in du Maurier 1938, p. 429.

p. 183   Electroverse: A network of electric vehicle chargers affiliated with the renewable energy company Octopus in the UK. According to the website, the 'Electroverse card and app give you one-tap access to hundreds of thousands of chargers across the UK & Europe'. The reality is not so simple. For more information, see: https://electroverse.octopus.energy/.

p. 185   Du Maurier's subversiveness: It's interesting to note that she did this without ever being sexually explicit. These are neither the erotic novellas nor the cheap romances of the period. They draw some of their

p. 186   Manderley as a symbol of male control: The clue may have been embedded in the names of the fictional house and its real-life inspiration, Menabilly, as Sally Beauman points out (du Maurier 1938, p. 438).

p. 187   We aren't being invited to accept the destination: The destination in *Rebecca* was deemed so unsavoury that the ending of the book was changed in Hitchcock's 1940 film.

p. 187   'once more she knew the humility of being born a woman': Du Maurier 1936, p. 257.

p. 188   'So we had come to battle': Du Maurier 1951, p. 308.

p. 188   The 'resist' of women's liberation: *https://psyche.co/ideas/the-origin-story-of-a-slogan-the-personal-is-political.*

p. 189   'most overtly feminist': Sally Beauman's Foreword to *My Cousin Rachel* (du Maurier 1951, p. x).

p. 190   *Our Bodies, Ourselves*: Boston Women's Health Book Collective 1973.

p. 191   'Sometimes, in conventional histories of American medicine': Ehrenreich and English 2010, pp. 10–11.

p. 191   Women lay healers as 'a political and religious threat': Ehrenreich and English 2010, p. 33.

p. 192   Three accusations: Ehrenreich and English 2010, p. 39.

p. 192   'When a woman thinks alone, she thinks evil': Cited in Ehrenreich and English 2010, pp. 41–2.

p. 192   The gift economy: see Hyde 1979; see also Kimmerer 2013.

p. 192   Woman healer as 'empiricists': Ehrenreich and English 2010, pp. 48–9.

p. 192   'two functions split irrevocably': Ehrenreich and English 2010, p. 96.

p. 193   'an active takeover': Ehrenreich and English 2010, p. 28; see also Brandt 2022; Furst 1997; Ring et al. 2024.

p. 193   Paid and unpaid care by gender: *https://www.oxfam.org/en/not-all-gaps-are-created-equal-true-value-care-work.*

p. 194   German origins of Barbie: *https://time.com/3731483/barbie-history/.*

p. 194   Barbenheimer: The term was allegedly first coined by Matt Neglia, editor of *Next Best Picture*: *https://twitter.com/NextBestPicture/status/1514997961566179329?lang=en-GB.*

p. 194   Sonia Rao: *https://www.washingtonpost.com/arts-entertainment/2023/07/26/barbenheimer-barbie-oppenheimer-patriarchy/.*

p. 195   Three best-selling albums of 2023: https://www.forbes.com/sites/hugh mcintyre/2023/11/05/taylor-swift-claims-the-three-bestselling-albums-in-america-in-2023/?sh=53e4a7e3175f.

p. 195   *Time* person of the year 2023: https://time.com/6342816/person-of-the-year-2023-taylor-swift-choice/, emphasis added.

p. 196   A profession still dominated by men: https://assets.uscannenberg.org/docs/aii-inclusion-recording-studio-jan2023.pdf; see also: https://publications.parliament.uk/pa/cm5804/cmselect/cmwomeq/129/report.html.

p. 197   BBC du Maurier documentary: https://www.youtube.com/watch?v=wmk8gjom1W0.

p. 197   Labour force participation in the interwar years: Hatton and Bailey 1988, p. 165.

p. 197   WEF's Global Gender Equality Index: https://www3.weforum.org/docs/WEF_GGGR_2023.pdf.

p. 198   The 'drop to the top': see: https://www.weforum.org/videos/global-gender-gap-report-csuite/; see also the Global Gender Index data explorer: https://www.weforum.org/publications/global-gender-gap-report-2022/in-full/data-explorer/.

p. 199   Israeli soldier and the uniform effect: https://archive.is/fc9Ai.

p. 199   *True Detective*: https://www.youtube.com/watch?v=DJXznk6cFko.

p. 200   Study on choking during sex: Herbenick et al. 2020.

p. 200   UK high-school teacher: https://www.bbc.co.uk/news/articles/cnkkqyek17z0.

p. 200   Mary Gaitskill: https://unherd.com/2024/03/on-choking-during-sex/.

p. 200   *The Case against the Sexual Revolution*: Perry 2022, p. 49.

p. 200   'From the earliest days of feminist debate': Harrington 2023, p. 16, emphasis added.

p. 200   'Rather than grant [us] all': Harrington 2023, p. 102.

p. 201   Alice Evans on global gender divide: https://www.ft.com/content/29fd9b5c-2f35-41bf-9d4c-994db4e12998.

p. 201   Andrew Tate's influence: https://www.theguardian.com/news/2024/jan/06/im-andrew-tates-audience-and-i-know-why-he-appeals-to-young-men.

p. 202   'Superior physical strength': See Mary Gaitskill, p. 200 above.

p. 203   'perpetual, existential angst': Hrdy 1999, p. 266; see also pp. 257ff.

p. 203   'just who did sire his child?': Hrdy 1999, p. 266.

p. 203   'The whole thrust of patriarchal societies': Hrdy 1999, p. 252.

p. 204   'Few have zeroed in' (and Strindberg citation): Hrdy 1999, p. 257.

p. 204   Never 'share a dream. Except in darkness': Du Maurier 1951, p. 298.

Notes

p. 204 'All witchcraft comes from carnal lust': Cited in Ehrenreich and English 2010, p. 42.

p. 204 Moore's naturalistic fallacy: *https://www.britannica.com/topic/ethics-philosophy/Moore-and-the-naturalistic-fallacy*.

p. 205 'Even as late as the classical age of Greece': Eisler 1987, p. 70.

p. 205 'general agreement among anthropologists': Hrdy 1999, p. 252.

p. 205 'such matrilineal arrangements are fragile': Hrdy 1999, p. 252.

p. 206 'In a Different Voice' and the *Harvard Educational Review*: Gilligan 2023, pp. 6–7. Reprinted in book form as Gilligan 1982.

p. 207 'What this gives us': Gilligan 2023, p. 23.

p. 207 'Under [this] view of cultural evolution': Eisler 1987, p. 73.

p. 208 'And there we were, exposed to the violence of night': This description is an extract from Daphne du Maurier's diary, as published in *Myself When Young* (du Maurier 1977, p. 185); see also de Rosnay 2018, p. 118.

Chapter 13 Land's End

p. 209 'By all outward appearances': Watts 1951, p. 13.

p. 209 'Nor is the interval': Watts 1951, p. 13.

p. 210 The SS *Mohegan*: The story is pieced together from various places, most notably the Board of Trade wreck report from 1898: *https://tinyurl.com/2rvv73rp*; and from contemporaneous newspaper reports: *https://newspapers.library.wales/view/3279996/3279999/36/wreck*; *https://timesmachine.nytimes.com/timesmachine/1898/10/15/105964788.pdf*. Some personal accounts were collected by the St Keverne Local History Society: *http://www.st-keverne.com/history/mohegan/mohegan.php*. Useful insights also came from a diver named Roger (Jan) Meecham who lived in Cornwall in the 1960s and interviewed locals in St Keverne who could still remember the disaster: *https://janmeecham.wordpress.com/2017/06/03/the-mystery-of-the-ss-mohegan/*.

p. 212 Board of Trade inquiry: See Board of Trade Wreck report – the SS *Mohegan*, p. 210 above.

p. 213 Rumours about the captain: See Roger Meecham's acoount, p. 210 above.

p. 214 Call no one happy until they're dead: O'Neill 2006, p. 166.

p. 214 Arendt on our knowledge of death: Arendt 1958 and see Chapter 11.

p. 214 What Heidegger says: See Chapter 4; see also Heidegger 1927.

p. 214	Elephants grieving: *https://www.youtube.com/watch?v=Ku_GUNzXoeQ*.
p. 215	Tahlequah the orca: *https://www.youtube.com/watch?v=9sNpMb4M7XM*. Darwin's beliefs: Darwin 1871.
p. 215	Stein's lost generation: See Chapter 8.
p. 215	Becker on the denial of death: Becker 1973.
p. 216	Nietzsche on 'great health': Nietzsche 1882; see also Glenn 2001.
p. 216	Groys' concept of care for the symbolic body: Groys 2022, pp. 25–34. 'a world so over-rich': Nietzsche 1882.
p. 217	Nietzsche's life: *https://www.britannica.com/biography/Friedrich-Nietzsche*.
p. 217	'Earlier it was God': Groys 2022, p. 32.
p. 217	'the worm at the core': Solomon et al. 2015.
p. 217	Terror management theory: Greenberg et al. 1986; see also Greenberg et al. 2008; Solomon et al. 2015.
p. 218	Food industry manipulating our appetites: Lustig 2017; Lustig 2021; Nestle 2013; van Tulleken 2023.
p. 219	The subconscious response to mortality salience: For an overview of these two avenues – and their interactions with health management – see Arndt and Goldenberg 2017.
p. 220	The culture of consumer capitalism: Becker 1973; see also Jackson 2017b.
p. 220	'Mrs Bush and I': Cited in Pyszczinski et al. 2003, Chapter 5.
p. 221	The 'sacred canopy': Berger 1967.
p. 222	'Between the two of them religion was knocked to pieces': Shaw 1921, p. lxiii.
p. 222	Consumerism as sacred canopy: Jackson 2018; Jackson and Pepper 2010.
p. 223	Mrs Compton-Swift's account: See Board of Trade Wreck report – the SS *Mohegan*, p. 210 above; with additional details from interviews in local newspapers in Cornwall: *https://www.newspapers.com/image/395666504/?clipping_id=51488853*; in Wales: see contemporaneous newspaper reports – the SS *Mohegan*, p. 210 above; and the *Titusville Herald* in Pennsylvania: *https://www.findagrave.com/memorial/62100791/maud-barling*.
p. 223	The rescue by the *Charlotte*: See Board of Trade Wreck report – the SS *Mohegan*, p. 210 above.
p. 224	'a nightmare spectacular': Becker 1973, p. 283.
p. 227	Maud Roudez arrives in New York: See the *Titusville Herald* in Pennsylvania – Mrs Compton-Swift's account, p. 223 above.

p. 227 Flora in *La Traviata*: https://archives.metopera.org/MetOperaSearch/record.jsp?dockey=0358957. And as Mercédès in *Carmen*: https://archives.metopera.org/MetOperaSearch/record.jsp?dockey=0358990.
p. 227 'Encore! Encore! Toujours la mort!': http://www.aria-database.com/translations/carmen.txt.
p. 227 It ain't no use to run from death: 'Dat' Ol' Boy (Card Song)' from the 1954 film *Carmen Jones*: https://www.thepeaches.com/music/composers/hammerstein/DatOlBoyCardSong.htm.

Chapter 14 Jenga

p. 229 'Health is a state of complete physical, mental and social wellbeing': This is the definition of health enshrined in the WHO's (1948) foundational documents.
p. 230 Fisher and Tronto's definition of care: Tronto 1993, p. 103, emphasis added; see also Chapter 1.
p. 232 Homeostasis: Bernard 1878; see also Goldstein 2019. On the wisdom of the body: Cannon 1932; see also Chapters 3 and 4.
p. 232 Allostasis and allostatic load: https://www.verywellmind.com/what-is-allostatic-load-5680283; see also Chapter 3.
p. 233 Health as adaptation: Dubos 1959, p. 1; see also Chapters 9 and 10.
p. 235 Industrial strategies which hijack our neurophysiology: Lustig 2017; Lustig 2021; Nestle 2013; van Tulleken 2023; see also Chapters 7 and 8.
p. 235 Model of health captured by industry: Illich 1976, p. 3; see also Chapters 3 and 10.
p. 236 Prosperity aligns with growth at low incomes: Jackson 2017a, Chapter 4; see also Chapter 6.
p. 237 The economy of care, craft and creativity: Jackson 2017a, Chapters 8 and 9; see also Chapter 6.
p. 237 The lesson of Baumol: Baumol 2012; Baumol and Bowen 1965; Baumol and Bowen 1966; Jackson et al. 2023; see also Chapter 11.
p. 238 Asymmetries and imbalances of markets: Meager 2020; see also Chapter 6.
p. 240 Traditional division of labour: See Chapters 8 and 12.
p. 240 Women, chronic disease and power: Maté 2022, Chapter 23; see also Bohannon 2023; Ehrenreich and English 2010; Chapter 12.
p. 241 Highly gendered schism in health: The history of this schism is covered in Chapters 11 and 12.

p. 242 Biological roots of patriarchy: Hrdy 1999; see also Chapter 12.

p. 242 Dominator and partnership societies: see Eisler 1987; Eisler and Fry 2019; see also Chapter 12.

p. 242 Twice as many women as men graduate from US universities: The Global Gender Index data explorer: *https://www.weforum.org/publications/global-gender-gap-report-2022/in-full/data-explorer/*.

p. 243 Care of the symbolic body: see Groys 2022; see also Chapters 4 and 13.

p. 243 The denial of death: Becker 1973; see also Chapter 13.

p. 243 'Great health': Groys 2022, Chapter 4; see also Chapters 4 and 13.

p. 244 The sacred canopy: Berger 1967; see also Chapter 13.

Chapter 15 The Red Pill

p. 246 'May not the new insights': Cannon 1932, pp. 305–6.

p. 246 'The question "What shall we do about it?"': Watts 1951, p. 69.

p. 247 International Wages for Housework: Toupin 2018. WHO's *Health for All*: WHO 2023.

p. 248 Eisler's foundations for a caring economy: Eisler 2007, p. 23.

p. 248 A raft of policies: Eisler 2007, p. 43.

p. 248 Another wishlist: Jackson et al. 2024.

p. 249 Paraphrase of Keynes: Keynes 1936: Preface.

p. 249 Damage as part of 'normal' life: Maté 2022.

p. 250 Social prescribing: *https://socialprescribingacademy.org.uk/what-is-social-prescribing/*.

p. 250 Care as postgrowth guide: see Chapter 6; see also Jackson 2019; Jackson 2021, Chapter 2.

p. 251 Growth dependency: Corlet Walker et al. 2024; see also Corlet Walker and Jackson 2021; Jackson 2020.

p. 251 WHO's 'Health for All': see WHO 2023.

p. 251 Care investments amortized: Eisler 2007, p. 44. In the case of a government that issues its own currency, as Stephanie Kelton (2020) points out, the care economy could also be financed directly from deficit spending. See also Turner 2015.

p. 253 Thirty-five years of climate policy: IPCC 2023.

p. 253 'Might it not be useful': Cannon 1932, p. 305.

p. 254 'economy is secondary to stability': Cannon 1932, p. 317.

p. 254 The function of social homeostasis: Cannon 1932, p. 324.

p. 254 Higher freedoms: Cannon 1932, p. 323; see also Jackson 2021.

p. 254 *The Matrix*: *https://www.imdb.com/title/tt0133093/*; see also: *https://www.youtube.com/watch?v=uAXtO5dMqEI*.

p. 255 *The Simulation Hypothesis*: Virk (2019) draws heavily on the inspiration of the science fiction writer Philip K. Dick.

p. 255 An insight as old as the hills: see my comparison of Buddhism and capitalism in Jackson 2021, Chapter 9.

References

Anandaciva, S. 2023. *How Does the NHS Compare to Health Systems of Other Countries?* Online at: *https://assets.kingsfund.org.uk/f/256914/x/7cdf5ad1de /how_nhs_compares_other_countries_abpi_2023.pdf*.

Araújo, J., J. Cai and J. Stevens 2019. Prevalence of optimal metabolic health in American adults: national health and nutrition examination survey 2009–2016. *Metabolic Syndrome and Related Disorders* 17(1): 46–52.

Arendt, H. 1958. *The Human Condition*. Chicago: University of Chicago Press (reprinted 2018).

Aristotle 2004. *The Nicomachean Ethics* (trans. H. Tredennick and J.A.K. Thompson). London: Penguin.

Arndt, J. and J. Goldenberg 2017. Where health and death intersect: insights from a terror management health management model. *Current Directions in Psychological Science* 26(2): 121–6.

Asimov, I. 1950. *I, Robot*. New York: Gnome Press.

ASM 2011. *E. coli: Good, Bad & Deadly. 'What is true for E. coli is true for the elephant.'* Online at: *https://www.ncbi.nlm.nih.gov/books/NBK562895/pdf/ Bookshelf_NBK562895.pdf*.

Ballester, J., M. Quijal-Zamorano and R. Méndez Turrubiates. 2023. Heat-related mortality in Europe during the summer of 2022. *Nature Medicine* 29: 1857–66.

Barron, M. 1920. *Relation of the Islets of Langerhans to Diabetes with Special Reference to Cases of Pancreatic Lithiasis*. Chicago: Surgery, Gynecology and Obstetrics.

Bates, D. 2012. *Pit Lasses: Women and Girls in Coalmining c.1800–1914*. Barnsley: Wharncliffe Books.

Baumol, W. 2012. *The Cost Disease: Why Computers Get Cheaper and Healthcare Doesn't*. New Haven, CT: Yale University Press.

Baumol, W. and W. Bowen 1965. On the performing arts: the anatomy of their economic problems. *American Economic Review* 55(1/2): 495–502.

Baumol, W. and W. Bowen 1966. *Performing Arts – the Economic Dilemma: A Study of Problems Common to Theater, Opera, Music, and Dance*. New York: The Twentieth Century Fund.

Becker, E. 1973. *The Denial of Death.* New York: The Free Press.

Beinfield, H. and E. Korngold 1992. *Between Heaven and Earth: A Guide to Chinese Medicine.* New York: Ballantine.

Berger, P. 1967. *The Sacred Canopy: Elements of a Sociological Theory of Religion.* New York: Knopf Doubleday.

Bernard, C. 1878. *Lectures on the Phenomena Common to Animals and Plants* (trans. H. Hoff, R. Guillemin and L. Guillemin). Springfield, IL: Charles C. Thomas (reprinted 1974).

Bevan, A 1952. *In Place of Fear.* London: Monthly Review Press (reprinted 1964).

Birn, A.-E. 2014. Philanthrocapitalism, past and present: the Rockefeller Foundation, the Gates Foundation, and the setting(s) of the international/global health agenda. *Hypothesis* 12(1): e8.

Bliss, M. 1993a. The history of insulin. *Diabetes Care* 16(Supp. 3): 4–7.

Bliss, M 1993b. *Banting: A Biography.* Toronto: University of Toronto Press.

Bohannon, C. 2023. *Eve: How the Female Body Drove 200 Million Years of Human Evolution.* London: Hutchinson Heinemann.

Bonner, T.N. 1989. Abraham Flexner as critic of British and continental medical education. *Medical History* 33: 472–9.

Boston Women's Health Book Collective 1973. *Our Bodies, Ourselves.* New York: Touchstone.

Brandt, S. 2022. *Women Healers: Gender, Authority and Medicine in Early Philadelphia.* Philadelphia: University of Pennsylvania Press.

Brown, E.R. 1979. *Rockefeller Medicine Men: Medicine and Capitalism in America.* Berkeley: University of California Press.

Bunting, M. 2020. *Labours of Love: The Crisis of Care.* London: Granta.

Burdach, K. 1923. Faust und die Sorge. *Deutsche Vierteljahrsschrift für Literaturwissenschaft und Geistesgeschichte* 1(1): 1–60.

Burlingham, A., H. Denton, H. Massey, N. Vides and C.M. Harper 2022. Sea swimming as a novel intervention for depression and anxiety: a feasibility study exploring engagement and acceptabilty. *Mental Health and Physical Activity* 23: 100472.

Bynum, W. 2013. In retrospect: *On the Mode of Communication of Cholera. Nature* 495: 169–70.

Campbell, J.N. 1996. APS 1995 Presidential Address. *Pain Forum* 5(1): 85–8.

Campbell-McBride, C. 2020. *Gut and Physiology Syndrome.* London: Chelsea Green.

Canguilhem, G. 1943. *The Normal and the Pathological* (trans. C.R. Fawcett). New York: Zone (reprinted 1991).

Cannon, W 1932. *The Wisdom of the Body: How the Body Reacts to Disturbance and Danger and Maintains the Stability Essential to Life.* New York: W.W. Norton.

Carboni, G.P. 2021. The enigma of Pacini's *Vibrio cholerae* discovery. *Journal of Medical Microbiology* 70(11): doi: 10.1099/jmm.0.001450.

Cardenas, D. 2013. Let not thy food be confused with thy medicine: the Hippocratic misquotation. *e-SPEN Journal* 8(6): e260–2.

Care Collective 2020. *The Care Manifesto: The Politics of Interdependence.* London: Verso.

Carrington, H. and H. *Jamaica Inn.* Shelton 1954. *The History of Natural Hygiene.* Mansfield Center, CT: Martino Publishing (reprinted 2010).

Casanova, J.L. 2023. From second thoughts on the germ theory to a full-blown host theory. *PNAS* 120(26): e2301186120.

Case, A. and A. Deaton 2020. *Deaths of Despair and the Future of Capitalism.* Princeton: Princeton University Press.

Corlet Walker, C. and T. Jackson 2021. *Tackling Growth Dependency in Adult Social Care.* An Economy That Works Briefing Paper Series No. 4. London: All-Party Parliamentary Group on Limits to Growth.

Corlet Walker, C., A. Druckman and T. Jackson 2022. A critique of the marketisation of long-term residential and nursing home care. *The Lancet: Healthy Longevity* 3(4): e298–306.

Corlet Walker, C., A. Druckman and T. Jackson 2024. Growth dependency in the welfare state – an analysis of drivers in the UK's adult social care sector and proposals for change. *Ecological Economics* 220: 108159.

Cottam, H. 2018. *Radical Help: How We Can Remake Relationships between Us and Revolutionise the State.* London: Virago Press.

Cottam, H. 2021. *REAL Centre: A Radical New Vision for Social Care.* REAL Challenge Annual Lecture, November. Online at: https://www.health.org.uk/sites/default/files/upload/publications/2021/ARadicalNewVisionForSocialCare_WEB.pdf.

Crisp, N. 2020. *Health Is Made at Home, Hospitals Are for Repairs: Building a Healthy and Health-Creating Society.* Billericay: SALUS Global Knowledge Exchange.

Cronin, A.J. 1937. *The Citadel.* London: Picador (reprinted 2019).

Daly, H. 1977. *Steady State Economics.* Washington, DC: Island Press.

Darwin, C. 1871. *The Descent of Man, and Selection in Relation to Sex.* London: Penguin Classics (reprinted 2004).

Davies, S.C. and J. Pearson-Stuttard 2020. *Whose Health Is It Anyway?* Oxford: Oxford University Press.

de Rosnay, T. 2018. *Manderley Forever: The Life of Daphne du Maurier*. New York: Allen & Unwin.

de Waal, F. 2009. *The Age of Empathy*. New York: Harmony.

Dixon, M. 2023. *Time to Heal: Tales of a Country Doctor*. Lewes: Unicorn.

Dixon, M. and K. Sweeney 2000. *The Human Effect in Medicine: Theory, Research and Practice*. Abingdon: Radcliffe Medical Press.

Dowling, E. 2021. *The Care Crisis: What Caused It and How to End It*. London: Verso.

du Maurier, D. 1936. *Jamaica Inn*. London: Virago Modern Classics (reprinted 2015).

du Maurier, D. 1938. *Rebecca*. London: Virago Modern Classics (reprinted 2015).

du Maurier, D. 1951. *My Cousin Rachel*. London: Virago Modern Classics (reprinted 2015).

du Maurier, D. 1977. *Myself When Young: The Shaping of a Writer*. London: Virago (first published as *Growing Pains: The Shaping of a Writer*; reprinted 2004).

Dubos, R. 1955. Second thoughts on the germ theory. *Scientific American* 192(5): 31–5.

Dubos, R. 1959. *Mirage of Health: Utopias, Progress and Biological Change*. New Brunswick, NJ: Rutgers University Press (reprinted 1996).

Duffy, T.P. 2011. The Flexner report – 100 years later. *Yale Journal of Biology and Medicine* 84(3): 269–76.

Dunant, H. 1862. *A Memory of Solferino*. Geneva: International Committee of the Red Cross (reprinted 1959).

Dyer, O. 2004. US government rejects WHO's attempts to improve diet. *BMJ* 328: 185.

Ehrenreich, B. and D. English 2010. *Witches, Midwives and Nurses: A History of Women Healers* (2nd edition). New York: The Feminist Press.

Eisler, R. 1987. *The Chalice and the Blade: Our History, Our Future*. New York: HarperCollins.

Eisler, R. 2007. *The Real Wealth of Nations: Creating a Caring Economics*. San Francisco: Berret Koehler.

Eisler, R. and D. Fry 2019. *Nurturing Our Humanity: How Domination and Partnership Shape Our Brains, Lives and Future*. Oxford: Oxford University Press.

Elkomy, S. and T. Jackson 2024. Health resilience and the global pandemic: the effect of social conditions on the COVID-19 mortality rate. *Journal of International Development* 36(5): 2342–71.

Escarce, J.J. 2019. *Health Inequity in the United States: A Primer*. Leonard Davis Institute of Health Economics. Online at: *https://ldi.upenn.edu/wp-content/uploads/2021/06/Penn-LDI-Health-Inequity-in-the-United-States-Report_5.pdf*.

Fan, D. 2021. Appropriate medical practice: natural forces and medical intervention. *Journal of Holistic Integrative Pharmacy* 2(1): 1–10.

Fisher, D. 1978. The Rockefeller Foundation and the development of scientific medicine in Great Britain. *Minerva* 16(1): 20–41.

Fisher, B. and J. Tronto 1990. Towards a feminist theory of caring. In E. Abel and M. Nelson (eds), *Circles of Care: Work and Identity in Women's Lives*. New York: University of New York Press.

Flexner, A. 1910. *Medical Education in the United States and Canada*. New York: Carnegie Foundation (reprinted 1972).

Folbre, N. 2001. *The Invisible Heart: Economics and Family Values*. New York: The New Press.

Foot, M. 1962. *Aneurin Bevan: A Biography*. London: Faber & Faber.

Friedlander, W. 1992. *The Golden Wand of Medicine: A History of the Caduceus Symbol in Medicine*. Westport, CT: Greenwood Press.

Furst, L. (ed.) 1997. *Women Healers and Physicians: Climbing the Long Hill*. Lexington: University of Kentucky Press.

Gallagher, A. 2020. *Slow Ethics and the Art of Care*. Bingley: Emerald Publishing.

GBD 2019 Viewpoint Collaborators 2020. Five viewpoints from the Global Burden of Disease study 2019. *The Lancet* 396(10258): 1135–59.

Gemmill, C.L. 1972. The Greek concept of diabetes. *Bulletin of the New York Academy of Medicine* 48(8): 1033–6.

Gibran, K. 1923. *The Prophet*. New York: Alfred A. Knopf.

Gilligan, C. 2023. *In a Human Voice*. Cambridge: Polity.

Gilligan, C. 1982. *In a Different Voice: Psychological Theory and Women's Development*. Cambridge, MA: Harvard University Press.

Glenn, P.F. 2001. The great health: spiritual disease and the task of the higher man. *Philosophy & Social Criticism* 27(2): 100–17.

Glomb, T. 2021. The spread of the cult of Asclepius in the context of the Roman army benefited from the presence of physicians: a spatial proximity analysis. *PLoS One* 16(8): e0256356.

Goethe, J.W. von 1832. *Faust Part Two* (trans. D. Lukes). Oxford: Oxford University Press (reprinted 1994).

Goldstein, D. 2019. How does homeostasis happen? Integrative physiological, systems biological, and evolutionary perspectives. *American Journal of Physiology* 316(4): R301–416.

Gourd, E. 2019. American Pain Society forced to close due to opioid scandal. *The Lancet: Oncology* 20(7): e350.

Greenberg, J., T. Pyszczynski and S. Solomon 1986. The causes and consequences of a need for self-esteem: a terror management theory. In R. Baumeister (ed.), *Public Self and Private Self*. New York: Springer.

Greenberg, J., T. Pyszczynski and S. Solomon 2008. Terror management theory of self-esteem and cultural worldviews: empirical assessments and conceptual refinements. *Advances in Experimental Social Psychology* 29: 61–139.

Gregg, P. 1967. *The Welfare State*. London: George G. Harrap & Co.

Gross, C.G. 1998. Claude Bernard and the constancy of the internal environment. *Neuroscientist* 4(5): 380–5.

Groys, B. 2022. *Philosophy of Care*. London: Verso.

Halliday, S. 1999. *The Great Stink: Sir Joseph Bazalgette and the Cleansing of the Victorian Metropolis*. Cheltenham: The History Press (reprinted 2009).

Halliday, S. 2001. Death and miasma in Victorian London: an obstinate belief. *BMJ* 323: 1469.

Hardman, I. 2023. *Fighting for Life: The Twelve Battles That Made Our NHS and the Struggle for Its Future*. London: Penguin.

Harper, M. 2022. *Chill: The Cold Water Swim Cure*. San Francisco: Chronicle.

Harrington, M. 2023. *Feminism Against Progress*. London: Forum.

Hatton, T. and R. Bailey 1988. Female labour force participation in interwar Britain. *Oxford Economic Papers* 40(4): 695–718.

Hawkes, J. 1967. God in the machine. *Antiquity* 41(163): 174–80.

Herbenick, D., T.-C. Fu, P. Wright et al. 2020. Diverse sexual behaviours and pornography use: findings from a nationally representative probability study of Americans aged 18 to 60 years. *Journal of Sexual Medicine* 17(4): 623–33.

Heidegger, M. 1927. *Being and Time* (trans. J. Stambaugh). Albany: State University of New York Press (reprinted 1996).

Heilbroner, R. 1985. *The Nature and Logic of Capitalism*. New York: W.W. Norton.

Hemingway, E. 1926. *The Sun Also Rises*. New York: Scribner (reprinted 1996).

Hickel, J. 2017. *The Divide: A Brief Guide to Global Inequality and Its Solutions*. London: Heinemann.

Hickel, J. 2021. What does degrowth mean? A few points of clarification. *Globalizations* 18(7): 1105–11.

Hickel, J., G. Kallis, T. Jackson et al. 2022. Degrowth can work – here's how science can help. *Nature* 612: 400–3.

Hrdy, S.B. 1981. *The Woman That Never Evolved*. Cambridge, MA: Harvard University Press.

Hrdy, S.B. 1999. *Mother Nature: A History of Mothers, Infants and Natural Selection*. New York: Pantheon.

Hume, E. 1923. *Béchamp or Pasteur? A Lost Chapter in the History of Biology*. Bendigo, Victoria: A Distant Mirror (reprinted 2006).

Hyde, L. 1979. *The Gift: Creativity and the Artist in the Modern World*. New York: Vintage Books (reprinted 2007).

IDF 2021. Diabetes is a 'pandemic of unprecedented magnitude' now affecting one in 10 adults worldwide. *Diabetes Research and Clinical Practice* 18: 109133.

Illich, I. 1976. *Limits to Medicine – Medical Nemesis: The Expropriation of Health*. London: Marion Boyars.

ILO 2019. *Child Labour in Mining and Global Supply Chains*. Online at: https://www.ilo.org/wcmsp5/groups/public/---asia/---ro-bangkok/---ilo-manila/documents/publication/wcms_720743.pdf.

IPCC 2023. *AR6 Synthesis Report: Climate Change 2023*. Online at: https://www.ipcc.ch/report/sixth-assessment-report-cycle/.

Isham, A. and T. Jackson 2022. Finding flow: exploring the potential for sustainable fulfilment. *The Lancet Planetary Health* 6(1): e66–74.

Jackson, T. 1996. *Material Concerns: Pollution, Profit and Quality of Life*. London: Routledge.

Jackson, T. 2017a. *Prosperity without Growth: Foundations for the Economy of Tomorrow*. London: Routledge.

Jackson, T. 2017b. Beyond consumer capitalism: foundations for a sustainable prosperity. In P. Victor and B. Dolter (eds), *Handbook on Growth and Sustainability*. Cheltenham: Edward Elgar.

Jackson, T. 2018. *Paradise Lost? The Iron Cage of Consumerism*. Guildford: Centre for the Understanding of Sustainable Prosperity. Online at: https://cusp.ac.uk/themes/aetw/blog_tj_consumerism_as_theodicy/.

Jackson, T. 2019. The post-growth challenge: secular stagnation, inequality and the limits to growth. *Ecological Economics* 156: 236–46.

Jackson, T. 2020. *Wellbeing Matters – Tackling Growth Dependency*. An Economy That Works Briefing Paper Series No. 3. London: All-Party Parliamentary Group on Limits to Growth.

Jackson, T. 2021. *Post Growth: Life after Capitalism*. Cambridge: Polity.

Jackson, T. 2024. *The False Economy of Big Food: The Case for a New Food Economy*. London: Food, Farming and Countryside Commission. Online at: https://ffcc.co.uk/publications/the-false-economy-of-big-food.

Jackson, T. and M. Pepper 2010. Consumerism as theodicy: an exploration of secular and religious meaning functions. In T. Lyn (ed.), *Consuming Paradise*. Oxford: Palgrave-Macmillan.

Jackson, T., B. Gallant and S. Mair 2023. *Towards a Model of Baumol's Cost Disease in a Postgrowth Economy – Developments of the FALSTAFF Stock-Flow Consistent (SFC) model*. CUSP Working Paper No. 37. Guildford: Centre for the Understanding of Sustainable Prosperity. Online at: *https://cusp.ac.uk/themes/aetw/tj_baumol_wp37/*.

Jackson, T., C. Corlet Walker and B. Gallant 2024. *The Case for the Care Economy*. CUSP Working Paper No. 40. Guildford: Centre for the Understanding of Sustainable Prosperity. Online at: *https://cusp.ac.uk/case-for-care-economy*.

Janott, C. 2020. Analysis and management of sleep data. In W. Zgallai (ed.), *Biomedical Signal Processing and Artificial Intelligence in Healthcare*. London: Academic Press.

Javaid, M., A. Hallem and R.P. Singh 2023. A study on ChatGPT for Industry 4.0: background, potentials, challenges, and eventualities. *Journal of Economy and Technology* 1: 127–43.

Jones, R. 2018. Happy birthday NHS. *British Journal of General Practice* 68(672): 307.

Jouanna, J. (ed.) 2012. *Greek Medicine from Hippocrates to Galen: Selected Papers*. Leiden: Brill.

Joyce, R. 2007. *The Evolution of Morality*. Cambridge, MA: MIT Press.

Kannan, S., J.D. Bruch and Z. Song 2023. Changes in hospital adverse events and patient outcomes associated with private equity acquisition. *JAMA* 330(24): 2365–75.

Karamanou, M., A. Protogerou, G. Tsoucalas, G. Androutsos and E. Poulakou-Rebelakou 2016. Milestones in the history of diabetes mellitus: the main contributors. *World Journal of Diabetes* 7(1): 1–7.

Kellett, J. and F. Sebat 2017. Make vital signs great again – a call for action. *European Journal of Internal Medicine* 45: 13–19.

Kelton, S. 2020. *The Deficit Myth: Modern Monetary Theory and How to Build a Better Economy*. London: John Murray.

Keynes, J.M. 1930. Economic possibilities for our grandchildren. In *Essays in Persuasion*. New York: W.W. Norton & Co., 1931.

Keynes, J.M. 1936. *The General Theory of Employment, Interest and Money*. London: Macmillan.

Kimmerer, R. 2013. *Braiding Sweetgrass: Indigenous Wisdom, Scientific Knowledge, and the Teachings of Plants*. Minneapolis: Milkweed.

Ko, Y. 2016. Sebastian Kneipp and the Natural Cure Movement of Germany: between naturalism and modern medicine. *Uisahak* 25(3): 557–90.

Kosten, T.R. and T.P. George 2022. The neurobiology of opioid dependence: implications for treatment. *Science & Practice Perspectives* 1(1): 13–20.

Kreutzer, S. and K. Nolte 2016. *Deaconesses in Nursing Care: International Transfer of a Female Model of Life and Work in the 19th and 20th Century.* Cambridge: Cambridge University Press.

Krueger, A. 2001. An interview with William Baumol. *Journal of Economic Perspectives* 15(3): 211–31.

Lang, T. and M. Heasman 2015. *Food Wars: The Global Battle for Mouths, Minds and Markets.* Cambridge: Polity.

Larsen, L.T. 2021. Not merely the absence of disease: a genealogy of the WHO's positive health definition. *History of the Human Sciences* 35(1): 111–31.

Linden, D.W. 1756. *A Treatise on the Three Medicinal Mineral Waters at Llandrindod, in Radnorshire, South Wales.* London: J. Everingham and T. Reynolds.

Lippi, D. and E. Gotuzzo 2014. The greatest steps towards the discovery of *Vibrio cholerae*. *Clinical Microbiology and Infection* 20(3): 191–5.

Lusis, A., A. Attie & K. Reue 2008. Metabolic syndrome: from epidemiology to systems biology. *Nature Reviews: Genetics* 9, 819–30.

Lustig, R. 2014. *Fat Chance: The Hidden Truth about Sugar, Obesity and Disease.* London: Fourth Estate.

Lustig, R. 2017. *The Hacking of the American Mind: The Science behind the Corporate Takeover of Our Bodies and Brains.* New York: Penguin Random House.

Lustig, R. 2021. *Metabolical: The Truth about Processed Food and How It Poisons People and the Planet.* New York: HarperCollins.

Lyman, M. 2022. *The Painful Truth: The New Science of Why We Hurt and How We Can Heal.* London: Penguin Random House.

Lyman, M. 2024. *The Immune Mind: The New Science of Health.* London: Penguin Random House.

Lynch, K. 2022. *Care and Capitalism.* Cambridge: Polity.

Magliano, D.J. and E.J. Boyko (eds) 2021. *IDF Diabetes Atlas* (10th edition). Brussels: International Diabetes Federation.

Manchester, K.L. 2007. Louis Pasteur, fermentation, and a rival. *South African Journal of Science* 103: 377–80.

Map, W. 1923. Of the Lad Eudo, who was deceived by the Devil. In E. Hartland (ed.), *De Nugis Curialium [Of the Trifles of Courtiers]* (trans. M. James). Cymmrodorion Record Series No. IX. London: Honourable Society of Cymmrodorion.

Marmot, M., J. Allen, P. Goldblatt et al. 2010. *Fair Society, Healthy Lives: The*

Marmot Review. Online at: https://www.instituteofhealthequity.org/resources-reports/fair-society-healthy-lives-the-marmot-review.

Massey, H., P. Gorczynski, C.M. Harper et al. 2022. Perceived impact of outdoor swimming on health: web-based survey. *Interactive Journal of Medical Research* 11(1): e25589.

Maté, G 2022. *The Myth of Normal: Trauma, Illness and Healing in a Toxic Culture.* London: Penguin Random House.

McLeod, K.S. 2000. Our sense of Snow: the myth of John Snow in medical geography. *Social Science & Medicine* 50(7–8): 923–35.

McNeill, J. 1951. *A History of the Cure of Souls.* New York: Harper.

Meager, M. 2020. *Competition Is Killing Us: How Big Business Is Harming Our Society and Planet – and What to Do about It.* London: Penguin.

Means, C. 2024. *Good Energy: The Surprising Connection between Glucose, Metabolism and Limitless Health.* London: HarperCollins.

Meier, B. 2020. *Pain Killer.* New York: Hodder & Stoughton.

Moehling, C.M., G.T. Niemesh and M.A. Thomasson 2019. Shut down and shut out: women physicians in the era of medical education reform. Ostrom Workshop, April. Online at: https://ostromworkshop.indiana.edu/pdf/piep2019/moehling-niemesh-thomasson.pdf.

Mol, A. 2008. *The Logic of Care: Health and the Problem of Patient Choice.* London: Routledge.

Mole, T.B. and P. Mackeith 2018. Cold forced open-water swimming: a natural intervention to improve postoperative pain and mobilisation outcomes? *BMJ Case Reports*: bcr-2017-222236.

Morgan, J. 2018. Black lung is still a threat. *The Lancet: Respiratory Medicine* 6(10): 745–6.

Morris, P.M. 2008. Reinterpreting Abraham Flexner's speech 'Is social work a profession?': its meaning and influence on the field's early professional development. *Social Service Review* 82(1): 29–60.

Nestle, M. 2013. *Food Politics: How the Food Industry Influences Nutrition and Health.* Berkeley: University of California Press.

Ni, M. 1995. *The Yellow Emperor's Classic of Medicine: A New Translation of the Neijing Suwen with Commentary.* Boston: Shambhala Publications.

Nichols, W.J. 2015. *Blue Mind: The Surprising Science That Shows How Being Near, In, On, or Under Water Can Make You Healthier, More Connected, and Better at What You Do.* New York: Back Bay Books.

Nietzsche, F. 1882. *The Gay Science.* Online at: https://www.anthologialitt.com/post/nietzsche-on-the-great-health.

Nightingale, F. 1859. *Notes on Nursing: What It Is and What It Is Not.* New York: D. Appleton and Company (reprinted 1860).

O'Hearn, M., B. Lauren, J. Wong, D. Kim and D. Mozaffarian 2022. Trends and disparities in cardiometabolic health among US adults, 1999–2018. *Journal of the College of American Cardiology* 80(2): 138–51.

O'Neill, J. 2006. Citizenship, wellbeing and sustainability: Epicurus or Aristotle? *Analyse & Kritik* 28(2): 158–72.

O'Neill, B. 2014. *Self-heal by Design: The Role of Micro-organisms for Health.* Minnesota: Sheridan.

Overbury, K., B.W. Conroy and E. Marks 2023. Swimming in nature: a scoping review of the mental health and wellbeing benefits of open water swimming. *Journal of Environmental Psychology* 90: 102073.

Patangia, D., C. Ryan, E. Dempsey, R. Ross and C. Stanton 2022. Impact of antibiotics on the human microbiome and consequences for host health. *MicrobiologyOpen* 11: e1260.

Patton, K. 2006. *The Sea Can Wash Away All Evils: Modern Marine Pollution and the Ancient Cathartic Ocean.* New York: Columbia University Press.

Pearson, R. 1942. *Pasteur: Plagiarist, Imposter. The Germ Theory Exploded.* Bendigo, Victoria: A Distant Mirror (reprinted 2006 as Book One of Pearson 1923).

Pell, R.C. 1857. *Millelulcia: A Thousand Pleasant Things Selected from Notes and Queries*, New York: D. Appleton & Company.

Perry, L. 2022. *The Case against the Sexual Revolution: A New Guide to Sex in the 21st Century.* Cambridge: Polity.

Persson, M., D. Redmalm and C. Iversen 2022. Caregivers' use of robots and their effect on work environment – a scoping review. *Journal of Technology in Human Services* 40: 251–77.

Popper, K. 1963. *Conjectures and Refutations: The Growth of Scientific Knowledge.* London: Routledge (reprinted 2002).

Porter, R. (ed.) 1996. *The Cambridge Illustrated History of Medicine.* New York: Cambridge University Press.

Pyszczynski, T., S. Solomon and J. Greenberg 2003. *In the Wake of 9/11: The Psychology of Terror.* Washington, DC: American Psychological Association.

Qi, X.-M., Y. Luo, M.-Y. Song et al. 2021. Pneumoconiosis: current status and future prospects. *Chinese Medical Journal* 134(8): 898–907.

Quianzon, C.C. and I. Cheikh 2012. History of insulin. *Journal of Community Hospital Internal Medicine Perspectives* 2(2): doi: 10.3402/jchimp.v2i2.18701.

Ramachandran, V.S. and S. Blakeslee 1998. *The Phantom Brain: Probing the Mysteries of the Human Mind.* New York: William Morrow.

Ray, P.P. 2023. ChatGPT: a comprehensive review on background, applications, key challenges, bias, ethics, limitations and future scope. *Internet of Things and Cyber-Physical Systems* 3: 121–54.

RCN 2020. *Gender and Nursing as a Profession: Valuing Nurses and Paying Them Their Worth.* London: Royal College of Nursing. Online at: https://www.rcn.org.uk/Professional-Development/publications/pub-007954.

Reich, W.T. 1995. History of the notion of care. Online at: https://care.georgetown.edu/Classic%20Article.html/.

Reynolds, M. 1998. *The Young Hemingway.* New York: Norton.

Richardson, M., K. McEwan, F. Maaratos and D. Sheffield 2016. Joy and calm: how an evolutionary functional model of affect regulation informs positive emotions in nature. *Evolutionary Psychological Science* 2: 308–20.

Ring, N., N.M. McHugh, B.B. Reed, R. Davidson-Welch and L.S. Dodd 2024. Healers and midwives accused of witchcraft: what secondary analysis of the Scottish Survey of Witchcraft can contribute to the teaching of nursing and midwifery history. *Nurse Education Today* 133: 106026.

Robson, P. 1999. *Forbidden Drugs: Understanding Drugs and Why People Take Them.* Oxford: Oxford University Press.

Ruths, M.B. 2009. The lesson of John Snow and the Broad Street pump. *Virtual Mentor* 11(6): 470–2.

Sagan, C. 1995. *The Demon-Haunted World: Science as a Candle in the Dark.* New York: Random House.

Salvage, J. 2001. Reputations: Florence Nightingale – iron maiden. *BMJ* 323(7305): 172.

Schumacher, E. 1974. *Small Is Beautiful: Economics as if People Mattered.* New York: Harper & Row.

Schumpeter, J.A. 1942. *Capitalism, Socialism, and Democracy.* New York: Harper.

Scott Smith, R. and S. Trzaskoma 2007. *Apollodorus' Library and Hyginus' Fabulae: Two Handbooks of Greek Mythology.* Indianapolis: Hackett Publishing.

Segre, J.A. 2013. What does it take to satisfy Koch's postulates two centuries later? Microbial genomics and *Proprionibacteria acnes. Journal of Investigative Dermatology* 133(9): 2141–2.

Shatz, H.J. and C. Reach 2023. *The Cost of the Ukraine War for Russia.* RAND Corporation. Online at: https://www.rand.org/content/dam/rand/pubs/research_reports/RRA2400/RRA2421-1/RAND_RRA2421-1.pdf.

Shaw, G.B. 1878. *Back to Methuselah*. London: Penguin (reprinted 1921).
Singer, M.E., K.A. Dorrance, M.M. Oxenreiter, K.R. Yan and K.L. Close 2022. The type 2 diabetes 'modern preventable pandemic' and replicable lessons from the COVID-19 crisis. *Preventive Medicine Reports* 25: 101636.
Skinner, B.F. 1934. Has Gertrude Stein a secret? *The Atlantic*, January: 50–7.
Smith, R. 2004. 'Let food be thy medicine...' *BMJ* 328(7433): 0.
Snow, J. 1849. *On the Mode of Communication of Cholera*. London: John Churchill.
Solomon, S., J. Greenberg and T. Pyszczynski 2015. *The Worm at the Core: On the Role of Death in Life*. New York: Allen Lane.
Sprouse-Blum, A.S., G. Smith, D. Sugai and F.D. Parsa 2010. Understanding endorphins and their importance in pain management. *Hawai'i Medical Journal* 69(3): 70–1.
Stahnisch, F.W. and M. Verhoef 2012. The Flexner report of 1910 and its impact on complementary and alternative medicine and psychiatry in North America in the twentieth century. *Evidence-Based Complementary and Alternative Medicine*: 647896.
Stanley, T.H. 2014. The fentanyl story. *The Journal of Pain* 15(12): 1215–26.
Sterling, P. 2020. *What Is Health? Allostasis and the Evolution of Human Design*. Cambridge, MA: MIT Press.
Sterling, P. and J. Eyer 1988. Allostasis: a new paradigm to explain arousal pathology. In S. Fisher and J. Reason (eds), *Handbook of Life Stress, Cognition and Health*. New York: John Wiley & Sons.
Tabish, S.A. 2007. Is diabetes becoming the biggest epidemic of the twenty-first century? *International Journal of Health Sciences* 1(2): v–viii.
Thomas, A. 2015. *Cholera: The Victorian Plague*. Barnsley: Pen and Sword.
Thomas-Symonds, N. 2014. *The Political Life of Nye Bevan*. London: I.B. Tauris.
Thompson, C. 2014. *From the Cradle to the Coalmine: The Story of Children in Welsh Mines*. Bangor: University of Wales Press.
Tipton, M., N. Collier, H. Massey, J. Corbett and M. Harper 2017. Cold water immersion: kill or cure? *Experimental Physiology* 102(11): 1335–55.
Tipton, M., H. Massey, A. Mayhew and P. Morgan 2022. Cold water therapies: minimising risks. *British Journal of Sports Medicine* 56: 1332–4.
Toupin, L. 2018. *Wages for Housework: A History of an International Feminist Movement, 1972–77*. London: Pluto Press.
Trall, R.T. 1872. *The True Healing Art: Or, Hygienic vs Drug Medication*. New York: S.R. Wells.

Tran-Duy, A., D. Smerdon and P. Clarke 2018. Longevity of outstanding sporting achievers: mind versus muscle. *PLoS ONE* 13(5): e0196938.
Tronto, J. 1993. *Moral Boundaries: A Political Argument for an Ethic of Care*. New York: Routledge.
Tronto, J. 2013. *Caring Democracy: Markets, Equality and Justice*. New York: NYU Press.
Tulchinsky, T. 2018. *Case Studies in Public Health*. London: Elsevier.
Turner, A. 2015. *The Case for Monetary Finance*. Paper presented at the 16th Jacques Polak Annual Research Conference. International Monetary Fund. Online at: *https://www.imf.org/external/np/res/seminars/2015/arc/pdf/adair.pdf*.
UNICEF/ILO 2021. *Child Labour: Global Estimates 2020, Trends and the Way Forward*. Online at: *https://data.unicef.org/resources/child-labour-2020-global-estimates-trends-and-the-road-forward/*.
Valabhji, J. and P. Kar 2023. Rise in type 2 diabetes shows that prevention is more important than ever. *BMJ* 381: p910.
van Tulleken, C. 2023. *Ultra-processed People: Why Do We All Eat Stuff That Isn't Food and Why Can't We Stop?* London: Penguin Random House.
van Tulleken, C., M. Tipton, H. Massey & C.M. Harper 2018. Open water swimming as a treatment for major depressive disorder. *BMJ Case Reports*: bcr-2018-225007.
Virk, R. 2019. *The Simulation Hypothesis: An MIT Computer Scientist Shows Why AI, Quantum Physics and Eastern Mystics All Agree We Are in a Video Game*. San Francisco: Bayview Books.
Wainwright, M. 1997. Extreme pleomorphism and the bacterial life cycle: a forgotten controversy. *Perspectives in Biology and Medicine* 40: 407–14.
Wang, M.-L. 2009. *Global Health Partnerships: The Pharmaceutical Industry and BRICA*. Houndmills: Palgrave Macmillan.
Waring, M. 1988. *If Women Counted: A New Feminist Economics*. New York: HarperCollins.
Warner, D. 2013. Henry Dunant's imagined community: humanitarianism and the tragic. *Alternatives: Global, Local, Political* 38(1): 3–28.
Watts, A. 1951. *The Wisdom of Insecurity: A Message for an Age of Anxiety*. London: Penguin.
White, M., E. Aguirre, D. Finegood, C. Holmes, G. Sacks and R. Smith 2020. What role should the commercial food system play in promoting health through better diet? *BMJ* 368: m545.
WHO 1948. *Official Records of the World Health Organization No. 2: Summary*

Report on Proceedings, Minutes and Final Acts of the International Health Conference Held in New York from 19 June to 22 July 1946. Geneva: World Health Organization.

WHO 2023. *Health for All: Transforming Economies to Deliver What Matters*. Final report of the WHO Council on the Economics of Health for All. *https://iris.who.int/bitstream/handle/10665/373122/9789240080973-eng.pdf*.

WHO/FAO 2003. *Diet, Nutrition and the Prevention of Chronic Diseases*. Online at: *https://www.who.int/publications/i/item/924120916X*.

WHO/ILO 2021. *WHO/ILO Joint Estimates of the Work-Related Burden of Disease and Injury*. Online at: *https://iris.who.int/bitstream/handle/10665/345242/9789240034945-eng.pdf?sequence=1*.

Whorf, B.L. 2012. *Language, Thought and Reality: Selected Writings of Benjamin Lee Whorf* (2nd edition). Cambridge, MA: MIT Press.

Williams, D., A. Kuipers, C. Mukai and R. Thirsk 2009. Acclimation during space flight: effects on human physiology. *Canadian Medical Association Journal* 180(13): 1317–23.

Wright, R. 1994. *The Moral Animal: The New Science of Evolutionary Psychology*. London: Abacus.

Yankouskaya, A., R. Williamson, C. Stacey, J.J. Totman and H. Massey 2023. Short-term head-out whole-body cold-water immersion facilitates positive affect and increases interaction between large-scale brain networks. *Biology* 12(2): 211.

Yudkin, J. 1972. *Pure, White and Deadly: How Sugar Is Killing Us and What We Can Do to Stop It*. London: Penguin.

Zimmet, P.Z. 2017. Diabetes and its drivers: the largest epidemic in human history? *Clinical Diabetes and Endocrinology* 3: 1.

Zink, M. (ed.) 1994. *Le Roman d'Alexandre*. Paris: Livre de Poche.

Index

accumulation of wealth 26, 42, 220
act of care 48, 55–6, 127, 252
acupuncture 146
addiction 18–19, 42, 81, 93, 107, 110, 118, 151, 218, 233
adrenaline 32
Age of Empathy, The (book) 45
aggression 185, 220
alcohol 72, 218
Alexander the Great 182, 199
allopathy 147
allostasis 41–2, 63, 105, 133, 232
allostatic load 42, 133, 151, 233–6
alternative medicine *see* complementary and alternative medicine
altruism 124, 192
American Medical Association (AMA) 22, 146, 191
American Pain Society (APS) 39
amortization, of care investments 251, 288n
antibiotics 145, 148, 150–1
anxiety 34–5, 49
Aquinas, Thomas 75
Arendt, Hannah 83–4, 88, 165–6, 214, 216
areté (virtue) 90
Aristotle 90, 92
art(s) 126, 165, 170–1, 175, 178, 215–16
arthritis 23, 35, 76

artificial intelligence (AI) 46, 173, 255
Asclepius 161–3, 169, 177–81, 192, 225
Attlee, Clement 61
autoimmune disease 101, 105
Ayurveda 132

bacteria 144, 148, 150
balance 29, 58–9, 127, 134, 137, 226, 244, 253
 in blood glucose *see* blood glucose
 vs growth 42, 85–6, 89, 92, 236
 in gut biome 150–1
 health as 37–40, 89–92, 132–3, 152, 218, 230, 234
 virtue as balance 91
Banque de France 127–8
Banting, Frederick 102–3, 142
Barbenheimer 193–5, 283n
Barbie xv, 54, 95, 193–5, 207
battle of the sexes 185–7, 189, 241–2
Baumol, William 170–2, 177–81, 183, 198, 237, 281n
Baumol's cost disease 237
Bazalgette, Joseph 139
Béchamp, Antoine 143–5, 148, 150, 157
Becker, Ernest 215, 217, 219, 224, 243
Being and Time (*Sein und Zeit*) (book) 55

Index

Berger, Peter 221, 244
Bernard, Claude 28, 37–8, 101–2, 125, 132, 232
Best, Charles 102–3
Bevan, Aneurin (Nye) 60–5, 68, 73, 83, 167, 186
Binti Jua (gorilla) 45
biodiversity loss 120, 174
Bird, William 34
black lung 65, 76
blood glucose 38, 42, 72, 91, 100–1, 104, 106, 218, 232
blood metabolism 38
blood pressure 35, 38–9
Bluetits (cold water swimmers) 29, 31
BMJ (*British Medical Journal*) 34–5, 117
Board of Trade, inquiry 212–13, 227
body mass index (BMI) 72, 106, 108
body temperature 29–30, 38–9, 232
Boston Women's Health Book Collective 190
breath xii–xiii, 32, 38–9, 40, 152, 232
British Medical Association (BMA) 61
Broad Street pump 138–9, 277n
brown adipose tissue 30–1, 232
Brown, E. Richard 155
Brundtland, Gro Harlem 118
Buddhism 254–5, 289n
Build Back Better 6–7, 261n
Burdach, Konrad 55
burden of disease 11, 65, 71, 73, 111, 233
Bush, President George W. 219
business models 251

Caduceus 180, 182, 193, 225
calories 30, 41, 116

cancer 35, 72
Canguilhem, Georges 134, 265n
Cannon, Walter 38, 132, 232, 246–7, 253–4
capitalism 12–13, 60–5, 82, 94, 172, 174, 218, 230
   and balance 41
   as creator of unpaid debt 252
   as a disease 157, 224–6
   relationship to germ theory 155–6
   structural imperatives of 193
   and the undoing of care 169–70
cara (Saxon) 52
carbohydrates 100, 102, 107, 116, 218
cardiovascular disease 72, 133–4, 234
care
   defined 2, 43, 166
   as freedom 253–4
   and gender 52, 240–1
   see also gender
   as investment 203, 248, 251–2, 254
   see also investment
   as prevention 105, 117, 250
   as quintessential 55, 207, 214, 252
   as restorative force 11, 58, 85, 234, 236, 244, 249–50
   of the symbolic body 220
   see also symbolic health
   as an unpaid debt 252
   and violence 10, 12, 66, 98, 235
   see also violence
Care (goddess) xi, xiii, 53–4, 56, 95
Care and Capitalism (book) 9, 185, 220
Care Collective, the 247

Index

care robots 176
care sector(s) 58, 93, 176
care's nemesis 9–10, 66, 98
care, craft and creativity, economy of 94, 177, 237
careless economy 235, 240, 250
cares of the world 52, 214, 226, 234
caritas 53
Carnegie Foundation 146–7, 155
Case, Anne 42*Case against the Sexual Revolution, The* (book) 200
casein(s) 107, 218
Catholic church 191–2
celebrity 49, 220, 223
Chalice and the Blade, The (book) 205, 248
Charlotte (lifeboat) 223–4, 228
child labour 62–3, 66
childcare 238, 248
cholera 67, 123, 129, 137–40, 142, 145, 148
cholesterol 91, 99, 106
Chill: The Cold Water Swim Cure (book) 35
Christianity xiv, 122, 242
chronic disease 35, 76, 93, 116, 133
   epidemic of 154
   pandemic of 151, 234
   prevention of 273n
   rising burden of 72, 91, 111, 151–2, 236, 250
   risk factors for 72, 99
chronic obstructive pulmonary diseases (COPDs) 65
chronos time 6, 142
Church of the Holy Sepulchre 122
Cinderella economy 93, 177
Citadel, The (novel) 64, 68, 73
Claudius, Matthias 159, 279n

Cleveland Clinic 15
climate change 3, 28–31, 47, 56, 79, 120, 173–4, 225
Clostridioides difficile 151
collapsism 85–6
Collin, James 102–3
combined sewer overflow 34, 130–1, 139
compassion 50, 98, 112, 120, 124
complementary and alternative medicine 137, 146, 148, 153–4, 157
consumerism 194, 219–220, 225, 230
conviviality 125–7, 141, 215
cooperation 242
cortisol 32, 35, 42, 217, 232
cost disease (Baumol's) 177–9
Cottam, Hilary 247
Couch, Llewelyn 212
Covid-19 1, 6, 8, 13, 65, 71, 126, 133, 150, 166
craft 94, 172, 176–7, 237, 252
creative destruction 168
creativity 94, 102, 126, 145, 172, 177, 216, 237
Crimean War 120, 122–3, 135
Cronin, A. J. 64–5, 68, 73
culture 36, 42, 193, 239, 256
cura (Latin) 52–3, 267n

Daly, Herman 85
DALYs *see* disability-adjusted life years)
Danaïde 94
Darwin, Charles 215, 222
Davos 89
de Waal, Frans 45
deaconesses of Kaiserswerth 121

death(s) xv, 214, 221
  awareness of 217–18
  denial of 215, 217–20, 226, 243–4
  of despair 42, 49, 223
  inevitability of 165, 214
Death and the Maiden 159, 171, 176–7
Deaton, Angus 42
degrowth 80, 84–6, 92, 111, 128
depression 34–5, 49, 110
diabetes 42, 72, 99–110, 133–4, 234
diet 62, 106–9, 116, 145–7, 152, 191, 218, 249
  see also food
Diet, Nutrition and the Prevention of Chronic Disease (report) 117
digestive system 100, 108, 150
dignity 64, 75, 235, 238
disability-adjusted life years (DALYs) 65, 268n
disease(s) 129–40, 146, 150, 178, 233–4
  chronic *see* chronic disease
  infectious 71, 111, 143, 236
  as reparative process 125, 129, 131, 224–6
division of labour *see* labour, division of)
Dixon, Dr Michael 153–4, 157
domination 66, 205, 220, 242–3
dominator societies 205, 242–3
dopamine 21–2, 25, 33, 42
Dopesick 23
Draper, William 38
drug(s) 13, 19, 21–4, 39, 72, 109, 145, 218
du Maurier, Daphne 182–208, 245
  sexuality 184, 189
  subversiveness in 185, 189, 282n

Dubos, René 141, 150
  mirage of health 134, 152, 233
  myths of Hygeia and Asclepius 163
Dunant, Henri 97, 112
durability 93–4, 165, 168, 214, 216, 255

E. coli (*Escherichia coli*) 131, 144, 149–150
Eastern Orthodox Church 122
Ecclesiastes, book of 115
economic growth *see* growth
economics 1–4, 170–173, 178–80
  feminist 4, 9, 85, 248
  of healthcare 67–73
  see also postgrowth economics
economy as care 2, 4, 10, 93, 112, 230, 249
Ehrenreich, Barbara 190–3
Eisler, Riane 205–7, 242, 247–8, 251
empathy 50, 90
empire 66, 73, 216, 220, 243
endorphins 33, 35, 88
energy prices 77, 167, 174
English, Deidre 190–3
epigenetics 119, 165
Escherich, Thomas 131, 144
ethic of care 51–2, 206
ethic of justice 51, 206
etymology of care 53–4
eudaimonia 90
euphoria 13–14, 17, 21–2, 25–7, 33, 41
evolution 44–5, 63, 202–4, 231
exceptionalism 215, 220
exercise 147, 152, 191
existential anxiety 203, 219, 226, 243
expansionism 78, 86–7, 89

Experimental Physiology (journal) 37
exploitation 17–18, 45
external conditions 57, 59, 132–5, 225, 253
   culture as 41, 105–6, 217, 233–6
   response to 30, 38, 134, 152, 232–4, 249
Extinction Rebellion (XR) 46–7, 50, 52
extinctionism 78, 86, 89
Eyer, Joseph 41, 101

fame 217, 220, 243
fast sector 178, 237
Faust (Goethe's) 55
feminism 4, 9, 52, 184–9, 200–2, 204
   fourth-wave 200
   in fiction 185, 189
   reactionary 201–2
   second-wave 188–9
   third-wave 189, 200
Feminism Against Progress (book) 200–1
fermentation 108, 142–3, 145
fertility 48, 201, 203
fight or flight 33, 217
finance 7, 71, 119, 174, 248, 252
First World War 64, 102, 114, 126, 186, 234
Fisher, Berenice 3, 43, 48, 166, 230, 247
five elements (Chinese) 132
Flexner, Abraham 146, 151, 155, 190, 192
Flexner report 146–8, 190–1
Folbre, Nancy 4, 247
food 61, 93, 119–120
   food banks 167

food industry 109, 119, 155, 218, 235, 249
   role in diabetes 109
fossil fuels 46, 253
fragility 165, 185, 194
freedom 7, 92, 134, 200–1, 222, 233
   care as 253–4
   sexual 186, 200
fungi 144, 148, 150

Gaia xiii, 57
Gaitskill, Mary 200, 202
Gates, Bill 81, 156, 173
gender 4–5, 197–8, 201–7, 240, 248
   and care 4, 52, 242
   dysphoria 184–185
   inequality 197–198, 248
   pay gap 240
   stereotypes 204–5
   and violence 9, 12
genetic(s) 19, 40, 45, 50, 105, 110, 117, 202–4
Geneva Convention(s) 98, 112
germ(s) 105, 130–1, 142–5, 148–152, 154–5, 278n
germ theory 144–5, 148–52, 154–5, 157, 193, 241
Gibran, Kahlil 10, 44
Gilligan, Carol 51–2, 206
Gladstone, William 18, 21
Global Gender Gap Index 197
glucose *see* blood glucose
glycaemic index (GI) 107, 272n
Goethe, Johann Wolfgang von 43, 55
Good Energy (book) 110, 117
good life 89, 91, 235
government 39, 61, 63, 69–71, 110, 118, 225
   failure of 110, 168, 178

government (*cont.*)
　finances 8, 70–71, 156, 166, 251, 288n
　lobbying 118
　policy 6, 247–8
　social contract 238–9
great health 216–7, 220, 225, 243
Great Stink 137, 139
green social prescribing 34, 250
Greenberg, Jeff 217
gross domestic product (GDP) 26, 70, 84, 86, 92, 195
growth 1, 7, 89, 110, 230–1, 236–7
　addiction to 84, 174–5
　vs care 225, 243
　critiques of 79–80, 82, 87
　dependencies 251
　as an indicator 84–5
　and innovation 81
　political importance of 219
　as religion 220–2
　secular stagnation 92
Groys, Boris 13, 17, 49–50, 169, 216–17, 220
gut biome 100, 109, 142, 149–52

Hacking of the American Mind, The (book) 118
Handler, Ruth 54, 194
Harper, Mark 35, 37
Harrington, Mary 200
Hawkes, Jacquetta 160
HbA1c (glucose reading) 100–1, 106
healing 51, 152, 162, 192, 240
　corruption of 136
　god of 162
　herbal 189–190
　restoring balance 132
　and women 189

health 2, 24, 132–5, 150, 180, 230
　as adaptation 11, 150, 233
　as an asset 251
　goddess of 162
　health workers 68–9
　monetization of 15, 17
　as restless dance 29, 40
　as state of wellbeing 2, 111, 229, 231, 260n
Health for All (WHO report) 247, 251
healthcare
　Affordable Healthcare 69
　economics of 11, 15, 70–1, 110, 249
　impact of private equity on 71
　role of philanthropy in 156
　spending 70, 251–2
　universal *see* universal healthcare
heart rate 38–9, 232
Heidegger, Martin 55–6, 214
Hemingway, Ernest 114
herbalism 146, 153
Herder, Johann Gottfried 55
heroin 22
Hickel, Jason 85
hierarchy 110, 115, 121, 126, 192, 235, 242–3
Hippocrates 18, 117–19, 132, 136
Hippocratic Oath 119, 190
holism 146–8, 153, 155, 163, 193, 235, 250
homeostasis 38–41, 91, 105, 232
　diminution with age 40
　licence to wander 253
　as secondary care 57
　societal homeostasis 253–4
hormones 35, 232
Hrdy, Sarah Blaffer 182, 202–4, 206, 242

Index

Human Condition, The (book) 83, 165
human nature 10, 26–7, 189
humanitarianism 111–12
hydropathy 136–7
Hygeia (goddess) 161–3, 169, 177–8, 181, 192–3, 225
hygiene 162, 250
Hyginus, Gaius Julius xv, 53–5, 260n
hyperglycaemia 101, 104
hypothermia 31, 40, 232

identity 49, 94, 214, 243
Illich, Ivan 247
immortality 126, 209, 215–17, 221
immune system 133, 235
In a Different Voice (book) 51, 206
In a Human Voice (book) 207
inequality 66, 80, 84–5, 167, 223, 235
inflammation 35, 42, 100, 109, 133–4
inflation 7–8, 166–7
insatiability 75, 89, 204, 230
insecurity 189, 216, 226, 255
institutions 89, 240, 255
insulin 101–2, 105, 142–3
Intergovernmental Panel on Climate Change (IPCC) 253
internal environment 18, 28, 37, 40, 144, 152, 249, 253
International Committee of the Red Cross 98
International Labour Organization (ILO) 65, 167
International Wages for Housework 247
investment 4, 168, 251–2, 254
  in health 251–252
  in infrastructure of care 252
  in learning 254
  return on 93
  as speculation 168
invisible hand (Adam Smith) 4
invisible heart (Nancy Folbre) 4, 154, 207

Jamaica Inn 183, 185–7, 198–9, 202, 204–5
Johns Hopkins School of Medicine 115, 148, 197
Jupiter (god) xiii, xv, 53, 162
Jupiter (planet) 57
just transition 251

Kaiserswerth, Düsseldorf 121, 123, 135, 137
Kaldor, Mary 9
kara (high German) 52, 267n
Kelton, Stephanie 247, 288n
Keynes, John Maynard 175, 249
Kneipp Cure 137
Koch, Robert 142, 144, 150–1

labour 4, 62, 64–5, 167, 174
  as care 202
  division of 4, 123, 199, 201–2, 240–1
  fate under capitalism 172
  participation rate 197
  vs work 165, 169, 172
labour productivity *see* productivity
laudanum 18, 25
lay healing 190–3, 250
Lebensreform (life reform) movement 136–7, 147
legitimization 26, 39, 186, 189, 204, 220–5, 243

lifestyle 72, 105, 117, 119, 145, 152–3, 191, 234, 250
Linden, Diederich Wessel 15, 17
Lizard peninsula 210, 213, 227–8
logic of care 6, 98, 100, 103, 164
Logic of Care, The (book) 100, 103
logic of choice 100
lost generation 114–15, 126–7, 186, 215
Loving Spirit, The (novel) 184, 197
Lustig, Robert 110, 118, 273n
Lyman, Monty 25
Lynch, Kathleen 9, 185, 220, 247

Macleod, John 102–3, 142
maintenance 57–8, 93, 133, 165, 176, 214, 221
Malleus Maleficarum 192, 204
Manacles, The 210–11, 213, 223, 227, 229
Manderley 182, 185–6, 283n
Map, Walter 76
market(s) 4, 93, 108–9, 168, 201, 230, 237–9, 252
Mars (god) 45
Mars (planet) 87–8
masculinity 9, 184–5, 198, 201
materialism 177, 219, 222
matriarchy 205
Maté, Gabor 44, 240, 247
Matrix, The (film) 157, 254–6
#MeToo movement 196
meaning 216–7, 221, 225, 234, 245
Means, Casey 110, 117
medicine 11–12, 93, 135, 190, 225, 235, 240–2
  complementary *see* complementary and alternative medicine

modern medicine *see* modern scientific medicine
men 185–9, 201–7
  and care 186, 207
  mistrust of women 241
  superior physical strength 202
  and violence *see* violence
mental health 49, 88, 217, 249
Mering, Joseph von 102
mesolimbic reward system 21–2, 33, 231
metabolic dysfunction 72, 100, 117, 152, 272n
Metabolical (book) 110
miasma theory 137–8, 140–2, 145
microzymas 144, 148
midwifery 58, 115, 120, 191
Miller, Thomas 139
mining 62–67, 73, 172
Ministry for the Future, The (novel) 31, 47
Ministry of Economics and Finance (French) 79, 128
Minkowski, Oscar 102
Mirage of Health (book) 133–4, 152, 232–3
misogynism 115, 204
modern scientific medicine 133–7, 146–8, 151, 162, 192
  as active takeover 193
  as gendered 193, 198, 240–1
  as power grab 241
Mohegan, SS 210, 214, 223, 227–8, 286n, 285n
Mol, Annemarie 6, 97, 100, 103, 247
monetization 17, 231, 235
Monument to Balzac 82–3
morality 51, 57, 124, 220

and gender 51
moral compass 185
moral hazard 156
moral responsibility 222
moral worth 202
morphine 19, 21–2, 25, 33
mortality 54, 95, 165, 209, 214–222, 229
mortality salience 217, 219, 243
Mother Nature (book) 202
mould 144, 148, 150
Mount Olympus xiii, 53–4, 245
Musk, Elon 78, 86
Musée Rodin (Rodin Museum) 79, 94
My Cousin Rachel (novel) 187–8, 204
myth(s) 26, 45, 94–5, 180–1, 221, 233
myth of care xiii, xv, 43, 53, 56, 59–60, 233–4

National Health Service (NHS) 15, 60, 65, 67, 123
  birthplace of 11, 72
  far-reaching social legislation 69
  plight of workers 166–167
  tribute in London Olympics 76
national income 7, 65, 70
natural hygiene 125, 135, 146, 162, 191
naturalistic fallacy 204
nature 135, 146, 189, 212
naturopathy 125, 136, 146–8, 193
nervous system xiii, 30, 32–3, 37, 254
net zero 87, 173
neurophysiology 27, 116, 151, 231, 233, 235

Nicomachean Ethics 91
Nietzsche, Friedrich 216–7, 243
Nightingale, Florence 120–5, 129, 131, 148, 199, 224
  lady with the lamp 120, 124
  and natural hygiene 134–7, 140
  Nightingale Medal 123–4
  Nightingale School 123
nihilism 114, 127
Normal and the Pathological, The (book) 134
normalcy 29, 35, 39–42, 99, 134, 249, 265n
North (global) 12
Notes on Nursing (book) 120, 125, 131, 140
nurses 58, 76, 124
  as essential workers 166
  as profession 120, 137
  wages of 68–9, 166, 178
nutrition 110, 116, 234, 250

obesity 91–3, 152
  childhood 118
  miasma theory of 138
  as risk factor 133
On the Mode of Communication of Cholera (book) 138
On the Nature of Man (book) 132
opioid(s) 19, 22–6, 107
  deaths from 24
  prescriptions for 23, 39
  receptors 25, 33
opium 17–9, 25
Oppenheimer (movie) 194–5
Oppenheimer, Robert 193–4
osteopathy 147
Our Bodies Ourselves (book) 190
oxycontin 22–3, 39, 136

Pacini, Filippo 142
pain 5, 22, 26, 100, 231–3
    as fifth vital sign 39
    management of 17, 19, 23, 108–9
    as an opinion 25
    pain-killers 19, 41, 109
    as protector not detector 25
PainKiller (documentary) 23
pandemic 1, 10, 111, 166
    aftermath 6, 194
    diabetes as 105
    economic impacts of 174
    shadow pandemic 88
Paracelsus 18, 25
parasympathetic nervous system xiii, 33, 36–7
parental care 44, 129, 202–3
Paris Agreement (on Climate Change) 46
partnership societies 205, 242, 248
Pasteur, Louis 142–3, 145, 148, 157
pasteurization 143
patches (patch-working) 62–4
pathogenesis 105, 130, 141–158, 163, 225
    arguments over 143–5
    of the careless economy 236
    culture and society as pathogenic 27, 36, 42
patriarchy xiv, 115, 121, 181–208, 224, 245
    as dominator society 205
    as evolutionary strategy 182, 202–5, 242
    and horses 195
    as object of derision 193
    patrilineal control 186
Patton, Kimberley 34
Pepper (the care robot) 176

Perry, Louise 200
pharmaceutical(s) 108, 145, 151, 154
pharmaceutical industry 24, 39, 109–10, 155, 235, 249
pharmacology 145, 163, 241
philanthropy 80, 156, 173, 241
philosophy of care 17, 50, 169, 245
Philosophy of Care (book) 50
physiology 102, 107
physiomedicals 147
pleasure 10, 22, 25, 33, 44, 90, 93, 209, 231, 233
pleomorphism 144, 148, 150
policy 6, 84, 139, 246, 249
pollution 72, 92, 120, 138, 178, 253
Polybus 132
polymorphism 144
popular health movement 191
population health 61, 68, 105
postgrowth economics 11, 80, 91–2, 104, 128, 175, 251
power 220, 238–9, 241
prevention 105, 147, 250
primary care 57, 68, 153, 157, 190, 250
private equity 71, 270n, 269n
private finance initiatives (PFIs) 71
productivity 171–5, 178, 237, 281n
profit 136, 217
    pursuit of 25–6, 41, 131, 174, 231
    as shibboleth 82
profiteering 25–6, 147, 192, 238
property rights 186, 188
prosperity 15–16, 24, 26–7, 85
    as health 2, 4, 10, 16, 27, 66, 91, 111, 230–2
    nature of 1, 85, 260n
    as wealth 27, 41–2, 91, 111

Prosperity without Growth (book) 82, 86, 94, 271n
proton pump inhibitor(s) 108, 145
pseudoscience 146, 192, 250
public health 97, 105
　crisis in 110–1
　distortion of 156
　preventative 155
　and pursuit of profit 120
public–private partnerships (PPPs) 70–1, 156
Purdue Pharma 23–5, 39, 263n
Pure, White and Deadly (book) 118
Pyszczynski, Tom 217

quackery 12, 24, 137, 146–8, 154, 157, 190, 192

Ramachandran, V.S. 25
Rao, Sonia 194
Rebecca (novel) 182, 185–7, 199, 204
reciprocity 121, 192
Red Cross 98, 112–14, 123
red pill 157, 246–56
regulation 23, 105, 109, 251
Reich, Warren 51–2, 54
religion 115, 193, 221–2, 224
resilience 59, 250
respiratory infection(s) 71, 133
respiratory rate *see* breath
restorative force *see* care, as restorative force
reward circuits 42
robber barons 155–6
Robinson, Kim Stanley 31, 47
robot(s) 173, 176
Rockefeller Foundation 155–6
Rodin, Auguste 79, 90, 95–6
Roudez, Maud 210, 223–4, 227–8

Royal National Lifeboat Institution (RNLI) 141, 223, 228
Russell, William 123

Sackler family 23–4
sacred canopy 221–5, 244, 255
sailing 129–30, 134, 210
Salvage, Jane 124
sanctity of life 239–40
Sanitary Commission 123
sanitary conditions 135, 140
sanitary reform 140, 163
saturated fat(s) 41, 93, 119
Saturn (god) xiii, xv, 53–4
Schoenberg, Arnold 126
Schubert, Franz 171
Schumacher, Fritz 174
Schumpeter, Joseph 168
scientific medicine *see* modern (scientific) medicine
Scutari 120, 122–4, 275n
sea 28, 34, 139, 141
sea-level rise 28
Second World War 61, 112, 167, 194, 199
Seguin, Edward 38
self-esteem 219–20, 222, 243
Senghor, Léopold Sédar 79, 94
Sertürner, Friedrich 19
sewerage system 130–1, 138–9, 153
sexism 16, 188, 196
sexual revolution 186, 190
sexuality 184–6, 190–2
Seymour, Robert 137
Shaftesbury, Earl of 63
Shaw, George Bernard 222
Simulation Hypothesis, The (book) 255
Sisters of Mercy 120–1, 123

slow sector 178, 237, 282n
Small Is Beautiful (book) 174
Smith, Adam 4
Smith, Richard 118
smuggler(s) 184, 198
Snow, John 138–40, 142, 278n
social care 71, 164, 166, 270n, 269n
social contract 174, 238
social justice 66, 68
social media 46, 86
social norms 89, 116, 186–7
social prescribing 34, 250
soil(s) 3, 48, 120, 174, 225
Solferino 78–9, 97, 112, 199
Solomon, Sheldon 217
South (global) 12
Souvenir de Solférino, Un (book) 97
staff of Asclepius 162, 180
stagflation 7, 261n
state of wellbeing 2–3, 49, 127, 162, 230–1, 233, 244–5
statins 106, 109, 145
Stein, Gertrude 114–15, 120, 148, 196–7, 215, 234, 274n
Sterling, Peter 41, 101
still point 41, 56, 59, 74, 105, 127, 232, 245
Stonehenge 159–61, 163, 178, 182–3
stress 32–6, 41–2, 93, 232, 152, 249–50
Strindberg, August 204
structural change 92, 248
struggle for existence 165, 226
Succession (HBO TV series) 128
suffragettes 47
sugar 41–2, 93, 107, 116, 119, 152, 218
suicide 42
Summa Theologica 75

Sun Also Rises, The (novel) 115
Swift, Taylor 195–7, 207
swimming 16, 29, 31–7, 40, 60, 116, 130–1, 136, 146, 149
symbolic body 49, 213–16, 220, 226, 243
symbolic health 49–50, 214, 216–17, 242–4
  in consumer capitalism 220
  as domain of care 49–50, 244
  importance of 220, 226
  in tension with physical health 220
symbolic immortality 219, 222, 226, 243–4
sympathetic nervous system 32–3, 37
system change 92

Taoism 132
teachers 58, 166
tech billionaire(s) 80, 86
Terra (goddess) xiii, xv, 53
terrain theory 144–6, 148–9, 150–5, 225, 234, 241
terror management theory 217–19, 224
tertiary care 59, 218, 234
Thinker, The (sculpture) 82, 84
Thompson, Leonard 102–3
Tipton, Mike 37
toxic masculinity *see* masculinity
toxins 116, 145, 152
Trall, Russell Thacker 136
Treatise on the Three Medicinal Waters (book) 15–16
Tredegar Iron and Coal Co 67
Tredegar Local History Museum 73
Tredegar Medical Aid Society 67, 71, 73–4
triglycerides 106

Tronto, Joan 3, 43, 48, 166, 230, 247
True Detective (HBO series) 199
True Healing Art, The (book) 136
Trump, Donald 89
tuberculosis 67, 144
Type 2 diabetes 99, 101, 103–6
　see also diabetes

ultra-processed food(s) 116–7, 218, 235
Ultra-Processed People (book) 117
UN Declaration of Human Rights 168
UN Security Council 153
UN Sustainable Development Goals (SDGs) 168–9
unemployment 64, 73, 77, 174
UNICEF 47
uniform effect 199–200
universal basic income 252
universal basic services 168, 248
universal healthcare 67–71, 104, 111, 238, 248
US Army Medical Department 180, 182

vaccines 145, 148
vagus nerve 33
van Tulleken, Chris 117
Vibrio cholerae 144, 149
vibrions 142
vice (Aristotelian sense) 91
Victorian(s) 121, 124, 186
violence 8–10, 12, 188, 223, 234
　as care's nemesis 8, 66, 98, 185, 220, 235
　legitimization of 220, 243
　of men 9–10, 185, 198, 201
Virk, Rizwan 255

virtue (Aristotelian sense) 90–1
vis medicatrix naturae 135
vital signs 28, 38–9, 42, 232
vitalism 146–8, 153, 155, 163, 193, 250

wage(s) 64, 71, 205, 252
　of artists 171
　of care workers 166–7, 193, 237, 248
　and productivity 174, 178
　of women 197, 240, 247
Wales 3, 6, 11, 28, 31, 41, 77, 245
　Ebbw Vale 65
　Llandrindod Wells 13–16, 20, 25, 34, 136
　Tredegar 60–77
　Welsh Valleys 61–2
west coast of 210
war 8, 61, 64, 114, 120, 219
Waring, Marilyn 85, 247
water cure 16–17, 24–5, 136
water industry 130, 138–9, 152–3, 225, 249
Watts, Alan 209, 214, 216, 221, 246–9
wealth
　accumulation of 27, 41, 230
　vs health 16, 225
　hierarchies 235
　influence on power 168
welfare state 61, 112
wellbeing 2–3, 94, 126–7, 162, 231–3, 243–4
　see also health
West, 7, 9, 12, 126, 201, 222
What Is Health? (book) 41
White, Martin 119
Williams, John Whitridge 115

Wisdom of Insecurity, The (book) 209, 214, 221, 246, 255
wisdom of the body 38, 41–2, 91, 125, 132, 232–3, 235–6
Wisdom of the Body, The (book) 101, 253
witch(es) 120, 191–3, 204
Witches, Midwives and Nurses (book) 191
Woman That Never Evolved, The (book) 204
women 4, 189–92, 207
    autonomy in matrilocal societies 205
    as healers 190, 192
    as progressive 201
    sexuality 241
women's health movement 190–1
work 235
    conditions of 64, 66, 69, 135, 248
    hours 65, 175
work sharing 165
workplace injuries 63, 65–6, 71
World Economic Forum (WEF) 89, 197–8
World Health Organization (WHO) 24, 65, 111, 117–18, 140, 162, 180
    definition of health 2, 49, 126, 229–30, 243, 260n
    Health for All 247
    US withdrawal of budget 118
worldview defence 219–20, 222, 243
Worm at the Core, The (book) 217
wreckers 184

yeast 144
yoga 36, 164
Yudkin, John 118